The American Constitution and the Debate over Originalism

Located at the intersection of law, political science, philosophy, and literary theory, this work of constitutional theory explores the nature of American constitutional interpretation through a reconsideration of the long-standing debate between the interpretive theories of originalism and nonoriginalism. It traces that debate to a particular set of premises about the nature of language, interpretation, and objectivity, premises that raise the specter of unconstrained, unstructured constitutional interpretation that has haunted contemporary constitutional theory. The book presents the novel argument that a critique of the underlying premises of originalism dissolves not just originalism but nonoriginalism as well, which leads to the recognition that constitutional interpretation is already and always structured. It makes this argument in terms of the first principle of the American political system: By their fidelity to the Constitution, Americans are a textual people in that they live in and through the terms of a fundamental text. On the basis of this central idea, the book presents both a new understanding of constitutional interpretation and an innovative account of the democratic legitimacy and binding capacity of the Constitution.

Dennis J. Goldford is an associate professor of politics and Director of the Program in Law, Politics, and Society at Drake University, where he has been teaching since 1985. He received his A.B. in political science from the University of Michigan, an M. Litt. in philosophy from Oxford University, and an M.A. and a Ph.D. in political science from the University of Chicago. He teaches in the areas of political theory, American politics, and constitutional law.

The American Constitution and the Debate over Originalism

DENNIS J. GOLDFORD

Drake University

CAMBRIDGE
UNIVERSITY PRESS

CAMBRIDGE UNIVERSITY PRESS
Cambridge, New York, Melbourne, Madrid, Cape Town, Singapore, São Paulo

Cambridge University Press
40 West 20th Street, New York, NY 10011-4211, USA

www.cambridge.org
Information on this title: www.cambridge.org/9780521845588

© Dennis J. Goldford 2005

First published 2005

Printed in the United States of America

A catalog record for this publication is available from the British Library.

Library of Congress Cataloging in Publication Data

Goldford, Dennis J., 1948–
The American Constitution and the debate over originalism / Dennis J. Goldford.
  p. cm.
Includes bibliographical references and index.
ISBN 0-521-84558-0 (hardback) – ISBN 0-521-60779-5 (pbk.)
1. Constitutional law – United States – Philosophy. I. Title.
KF4550.G645 2005
342.73'01–dc22   2004062890

ISBN-13 978-0-521-84558-8 hardback
ISBN-10 0-521-84558-0 hardback

ISBN-13 978-0-521-60779-7 paperback
ISBN-10 0-521-60779-5 paperback

To Sharon, whose love is truly a gift.

Contents

Preface

This book originated serendipitously in the course of exploring what at first appeared to be two distinct and independent topics: the originalism debate in contemporary American constitutional theory and the question of how we properly understand the nature of law and constitutionalism. Writing separate papers on each topic, I began after a while to discover that I was developing the same argument implicitly in papers on both topics. While identifying and untangling that argument has been a difficult and time-consuming task, it has been nevertheless an exciting process as I learned that the two apparently independent topics are in fact related. Exploring the originalism debate in depth leads to important insights into the nature of law and constitutionalism, and those insights in turn illuminate – and, I believe, alter – the contours and premises of the originalism debate.

I offer this book, therefore, in the belief that it is indeed possible to say something original about the originalism debate. This project in one sense is a long way from my focus on the philosophy of Hegel during the early stages of my academic career, but in another sense it reflects two fundamental methodological perspectives I derived from that earlier work. First, what appears to be familiar to us usually stands most in need of careful reconsideration and analysis. As Hegel famously stated, "What is 'familiarly known' is not properly known, just for the reason that it is 'familiar.'"[1] Scholars of American constitutional theory are sufficiently familiar with the various dimensions of the originalism debate that it is perhaps time to be wary of the familiarity.

---

[1] G. W. F. Hegel, *The Phenomenology of Mind*, trans. J. B. Baillie (New York: Harper Torchbooks, 1967), 92. The German text reads: "Das Bekannte überhaupt is darum, weil es *bekannt* ist, nicht erkannt." *Phänomenologie des Geistes* (Hamburg: Felix Meiner Verlag, 1952), 28. Less formally, I would say that it's not what we don't know that gets us into trouble; it's what we think we know but don't.

The second methodological perspective I learned from studying Hegel is that when caught unproductively in the conundrum of two opposing arguments or intellectual positions, we should take an analytical step back and explore whether such an opposition actually stems from a shared structure of premises. In other words, rather than hit Position A over the head with the arguments of Position B or hit Position B over the head with the arguments of Position A, we should look to see what common assumptions might be responsible for generating their opposition in the first place. To do so results not in a victory of one position over the other, but leads rather to the possibility of transcending the shared structure of premises and thus getting beyond what becomes a less and less fruitful repetition of standard arguments from the opposing positions.

That is the goal I have set for myself in this book. I agree with originalism that the purpose of a constitution is to bind the future to the principles embodied in the text, but I present what I believe is the novel argument that the originalist approach to constitutional interpretation cannot accomplish that goal. At the same time, I do not offer a brief for what is inelegantly known as "nonoriginalism." Rather, I attempt to identify the structure of premises about constitutional interpretation that generates the debate between originalism and nonoriginalism precisely in order to move beyond that debate. And at the root of all of my analysis here is the attempt to understand the remarkable phenomenon of a people living in terms of a written text.

I wish to express my gratitude to the National Endowment for the Humanities Summer Stipend Program for supporting this work in the early days when I was just beginning to consider it as a book project. The Department of Politics and International Relations at Drake University provided a harmonious intellectual environment, and my colleague Arthur Sanders commented insightfully on key portions of the manuscript at various stages of its development. I am grateful to the University Press of Kansas for permission to quote extensively (3–7, 11, 14–15, 35–6, 40, 42, 47, 49–50, 53–62, 64, 68, 75–6, 84, 92, 94–9, 102, 104–5, 110–11, 162, 164, 176–7, 179, 181, 203, 210, 215–16, 218, and 236) from Keith Whittington's *Constitutional Interpretation: Textual Meaning, Original Intent, and Judicial Review* (Lawrence, KS: University Press of Kansas, 1999) in my detailed analysis of his argument for originalism. I also thank *Polity* for permission to reprint the following portions of an article of mine entitled "The Political Character of Constitutional Interpretation," *Polity*, Volume XXIII, No. 2 (Winter 1990): 262–6 in Chapter 3, 272–3 in Chapter 9, and 255–7, 259–60, and 277–9 in Chapter 10.

I am especially grateful to Lewis Bateman, my editor at Cambridge University Press, for his interest in this project during a long review process, and to the two anonymous reviewers for their support and constructive criticism of the manuscript. Reviewer B, in particular, twice wrote lengthy and detailed critical comments and suggestions that contributed immensely to improving the complex structure of argument I present. Last, but not least, Helen Wheeler and Helen Greenberg provided welcome guidance in preparing the manuscript for publication. Any persisting errors remain, of course, my own responsibility.

Finally, I want to acknowledge my debt to my father, who taught me that some things are worth arguing about; to my mother, who taught me that some things are not; and, above all, to my wife, Sharon, who teaches me every day how to tell the difference.

Introduction

Despite its apparent remoteness from everyday politics and its often esoteric character, constitutional theory in the United States is never a matter of
purely abstract, disinterested speculation. As the legal expression of essentially political conflict, controversies in American constitutional theory are,
rather, the theoretical and principled expression of intensely partisan, practical concerns. Stimulated by the Warren Court and its jurisprudential legacy,
the dominant controversy in contemporary American constitutional theory
for some fifty years has been the conflict over the merits of the interpretive
paradigm known as "originalism," "the theory that in constitutional adjudication judges should be guided by the intent of the Framers."[1] As a work
of constitutional theory, this book seeks to explore the nature of American
constitutionalism through an analysis of the nature of constitutional interpretation. Specifically, its guiding premise is that a reconsideration of the
originalism debate will illuminate the essentially constitutive character of
the Constitution, and, in turn, that an understanding of that constitutive
character will cast a fresh light on the familiar originalism debate.

Although the originalism debate brewed quietly in academic and intellectual circles throughout the 1970s, the general public's awareness of it was
stimulated by the determined and single-minded jurisprudential agenda of
the Reagan administration during the 1980s. "The most basic issue facing
constitutional scholars and jurists today," stated a 1987 report of the Office
of Legal Policy in the Reagan Justice Department, "is whether federal courts
should interpret and apply the Constitution in accordance with its original
meaning."[2] With the passing of the Reagan years and, in particular, the failed

---

[1] Earl Maltz, "Forward: The Appeal of Originalism," 1987 *Utah Law Review* 773, 773.
[2] *Original Meaning Jurisprudence: A Sourcebook* (Report to the Attorney General by the Office
of Legal Policy, United States Department of Justice, 12 March 1987), 1. Although not a
scholarly work in the strict sense of the term, this booklet is a handy compilation of the major
theses of originalism and a prime example of the constitutional dimension of contemporary

nomination of Judge Robert Bork to the Supreme Court,[3] the originalism debate moved back out of public awareness and even out of most law reviews.[4] Nevertheless, the debate is reignited every time a nomination to a seat on the Supreme Court goes before the Senate. For example, in his opening statement at the confirmation hearings for Justice Ruth Bader Ginsburg in the summer of 1993, Senator Orrin Hatch set forth the standard originalist position:

The role of the judicial branch is to enforce the provisions of the Constitution and the laws we enact in Congress as their meaning was originally intended by the Framers. Any other philosophy of judging requires unelected Federal judges to impose their own personal views on the American people in the guise of construing the Constitution and Federal statutes.[5]

The claim that in constitutional adjudication we necessarily face the interpretive choice between the intentions of the Framers and the personal views of unelected federal judges, and that the former have a democratic legitimacy that the latter do not,[6] is central to originalism, and it is a claim that this book will examine in detail.

For now, however, the question is, why does the originalism debate over the proper standards of constitutional interpretation recur? The answer, I suggest, is twofold. First, as Chapter 1 will note, the contemporary originalism debate springs from an immediate, historically specific political context: the cultural struggle over the meaning and legacy of the 1960s waged by liberals and conservatives in the final third of the twentieth century. Yet,

American political conflict to which I just referred. It is a useful illustration of originalist themes, and I shall refer to it henceforth as *Sourcebook*.

[3] On the Bork nomination, see, among others, Robert H. Bork, *The Tempting of America: The Political Seduction of the Law* (New York: Simon & Schuster, 1990); Ethan Bronner, *Battle for Justice: How the Bork Nomination Shook America* (New York: W. W. Norton and company, 1989); and Patrick B. McGuigan and Dawn M. Weyrich, *Ninth Justice: The Fight for Bork* (Washington, DC: Free Congress Research and Education Foundation, 1990).

[4] See, however, Antonin Scalia, *A Matter of Interpretation: Federal Courts and the Law*, ed. Amy Gutmann (Princeton, NJ: Princeton University Press, 1997). The major symposia dealing with originalism in the 1990s have included the following: "Originalism, Democracy, and the Constitution," 19 *Harvard Journal of Law & Public Policy* 237–531 (1996); "Fidelity in Constitutional Theory," 65 *Fordham Law Review* 1247–1818 (1997); and "Textualism and the Constitution," 66 *George Washington Law Review* 1081–1394 (1998). During the early stages of the presidency of George W. Bush, the Federalist Society returned to the topic of originalism on a 2002 symposium panel entitled "Panel II: Originalism and Historical Truth," in "Law and Truth: The Twenty-First Annual National Student Federalist Society Symposium on Law and Public Policy," 26 *Harvard Journal of Law and Public Policy* vii–x, 1–237 (2003), at 67–107.

[5] *New York Times* (national edition), July 21, 1993, C26.

[6] For example, *Sourcebook* argues at 4 that "if the courts go beyond the original meaning of the Constitution, if they strike down legislative or executive action based on their personal notions of the public good or on other extra-constitutional principles, they usurp powers not given to them by the people."

second, while this debate may have been set off by a particular political context, its roots lie in the very nature of the American constitutional system itself. The contemporary originalism debate is a particular formulation of an ongoing concern with the nature of constitutional interpretation that stems from the fact that in the United States we live under a written constitution. Fundamental political conflict in the United States comes to constitutional expression not simply because of the peculiar feature of American political culture captured in Alexis de Tocqueville's famous dictum that "scarcely any political question arises in the United States which is not resolved, sooner or later, into a judicial question."[7] The truth of de Tocqueville's observation rests not on a mere idiosyncrasy of American political culture, but rather on what I suggest is the central feature of the American polity: We are a society constituted, which is to say ordered, by our fidelity to a fundamental text. The common bond of American society, as so many people have recognized, is not race, ethnicity, language, or religion, but the Constitution.

This common bond, however, is of a very special sort. The Constitution is a written document, but it is a written document with social reality. In philosophical terms, the Constitution is not just linguistic, but ontological. This is what we mean when we say, with deceptive simplicity and apparent redundancy, that the Constitution *constitutes*. The Constitution has a social reality in that it is not simply a legal document, as are so many written constitutions around the world that may or may not be in force. Rather, its social reality lies in the fact that through it we actually define who we are as a people. The Constitution certainly defines who we are as a people in a symbolic sense, as do the flag and other symbols of American nationhood. Yet to say that the Constitution constitutes is to argue that it defines who we are as a people not just in a symbolic sense, but, more significantly, in a substantive sense. We Americans are, I suggest, a people who live textually.

Given this special character of the Constitution, therefore, political conflict over principles basic to and definitive of American society quite naturally finds expression in conflict over interpretation of the fundamental text that formalizes those principles and renders them authoritative. As Gary McDowell has written, "the fact that the Constitution orders our politics means that, politically, a great deal hangs on the peg of interpretation; to change the Constitution's meaning through interpretation is to change our

---

7 Alexis de Tocqueville, *Democracy in America* (New York: Vintage Books, 1990), Vol. 1, 280. De Tocqueville's observation continues to ring true: Political controversies often do become constitutional controversies, as evinced by the issue of flag burning in the 1980s, and constitutional controversies often become political controversies, as with the issue of criminal procedure in the 1960s and after. For flag burning, see, e.g., *Texas v. Johnson*, 491 U.S. 397 (1989). As to the politicization of criminal procedure, see, e.g., Theodore H. White, *The Making of the President, 1968* (New York: Atheneum Publishers, 1969), passim, for the Republican assault on *Mapp v. Ohio*, 367 U.S. 643 (1961) and *Miranda v. Arizona*, 384 U.S. 436 (1966) in the 1968 presidential election.

politics."[8] "By controlling the meaning of a text," he says, "one can control – shape, mold, and direct – the affairs of that society bound by that text."[9] While I will proceed in this book with an argument against much of what McDowell intends by such a claim, I strongly affirm the claim itself.[10] The idea of controlling American society by controlling the meaning of its fundamental constitutive text is, I submit, precisely the core of the claim that we Americans are a people who live textually. And, no less important, this same idea explains the controversial nature of the originalism debate in contemporary American constitutional theory. As an argument about controlling the meaning of our fundamental constitutive text, the originalism debate is an argument about controlling the affairs of our society. That fact is what gives an apparently abstract jurisprudential controversy its concrete, partisan passion.

The originalism debate, however, is often erroneously conflated with the other, longer-standing debate traditionally occurring in constitutional theory: the debate over the legitimacy of judicial review, which subsumes within it the argument over judicial activism and judicial restraint.[11] The common thread between the two is their derivation from the proposition – the first principle of the American political system – that the Constitution is fundamental law. To grasp that principle, the central logic of American constitutional reasoning can be formulated in terms of what I call our "constitutional syllogism":

P_1:   If X is contrary to the Constitution, then X is null and void.
P_2:   X is contrary to the Constitution.
C: Therefore, X is null and void,

where X is an act of a federal, state, or local legislative, executive, or judicial body.[12] P_1 is the major premise of the constitutional syllogism and expresses

---

[8] Gary McDowell, "Introduction," in Gary L. McDowell, ed., *Politics and the Constitution: The Nature and Extent of Interpretation* (Washington, DC: National Legal Center for the Public Interest and The American Studies Center, 1990), xi.

[9] Ibid., x.

[10] Indeed, the intelligibility of this distinction between a written claim and what the author intended by the claim is central to the analysis that follows.

[11] In "Judicial Review and a Written Constitution in a Democratic Society," 28 *Wayne Law Review* 1 (1981), for example, Joseph Grano discusses many of the themes of the originalist debate but does so under the rubric of the justification and proper scope of judicial review. Michael Perry also appears to conflate the two questions, to some extent out of despair over the exhaustion of the debate over constitutional theory. See *The Constitution in the Courts: Law or Politics?* (New York: Oxford University Press, 1994).

[12] Much constitutional conflict, it should be noted, occurs around what we can call a "subsyllogism":

P_1:   If X is contrary to the Constitution, then X is null and void.
    $P_{1.1}$: If X fails test Q, then X is contrary to the Constitution.
    $P_{1.2}$: X fails test Q.
P_2:   X is contrary to the Constitution.

the proposition that within the American political system the Constitution counts as fundamental law. More than merely the major premise of the constitutional syllogism, however, P_1 is the first premise of the American political system itself, and throughout all constitutional controversies it remains unchallenged. P_2, for its part, is the minor premise of the syllogism and expresses the claim that a particular act of government is inconsistent with the powers granted by the Constitution. Given the major and minor premises of the constitutional syllogism, the conclusion necessarily follows that the particular act of government in question is null and void. What, then, is the source of controversy in constitutional interpretation if the conclusion necessarily follows from the premises of the syllogism? The problem is P_2, for it raises two central questions: First, who in the American political system is authorized to determine that X is contrary to the Constitution? Second, how – that is, by what criteria – does the authorized interpreter(s) determine that X is indeed contrary to the Constitution?[13] The question as to who in the American political system is authorized to determine that X is contrary to the Constitution initiates the debate over the legitimacy of judicial review and the complementary debate over judicial activism and judicial restraint.[14] By contrast, the question as to the criteria by which one determines that X is contrary to the Constitution is the foundation of the originalism debate.[15]

That is, much constitutional debate has to do with the proper tests to be applied to determine constitutionality, such as the various levels of scrutiny at issue in equal protection cases or the *Lemon* test at issue in many establishment clause cases.

[13] In *American Constitutional Interpretation* (Mineola, NY: Foundation Press, 1986), Walter Murphy, James Fleming, and William Harris point to a third central question of constitutional interpretation beyond "Who interprets?" and "How does one interpret?" – "What is the Constitution to be interpreted?" While it is helpful initially to distinguish between asking how and asking what, they are in fact two sides of the same question. To determine what counts as the Constitution is already to have committed to a particular "how," and to determine how one interprets the Constitution is already to have committed to a particular "what."

[14] As every first-year law student learns, in *Marbury v. Madison*, 5 U.S. 137 (1803), Marshall actually begged the central question at issue in the case. He argued for the validity and necessity of the status of the Constitution as fundamental law (P_1), which was not in dispute, whereas he merely asserted the validity and necessity of judicial review (the "Who?" question of P_2), which was at issue.

[15] These questions are related in that the former flows into the latter. Briefly, the controversy over the legitimacy of judicial review is often characterized in terms of the notions of "judicial activism" and "judicial restraint." Judicial activism and judicial restraint have to do with the willingness of courts to overturn the actions of elected bodies and officials. If one argues, as Alexander Bickel famously did, that insofar as it is a countermajoritarian force in our political system, judicial review "is a deviant institution in the American democracy (Alexander Bickel, *The Least Dangerous Branch* [New Haven, CT: Yale University Press, 1986], 18), then any exercise of judicial review would be presumptively illegitimate. If Congress passed a law appropriating funds for, say, operating expenses of cabinet departments, then, all things being equal, a court would be remiss if it failed to exercise restraint and allow the law to stand. However, if Congress passed a law mandating, simply and explicitly, that adherence to a particular religion is a condition of full participation in American citizenship, then, all

As the structure of constitutional reasoning, the constitutional syllogism as a whole expresses the idea of binding the future at stake in the concept of fundamental law. Behind all the various provisions of the American Constitution there stands a fundamental and widely acknowledged premise: The

things being equal, a court would be remiss if it failed to be activist and strike down the law. The propriety of judicial activism or judicial restraint is not an independent matter, therefore, but rather depends upon the more fundamental issue of the norms on the basis of which courts decide to overturn or ratify the actions of elected bodies and officials.

It is those norms of judicial review that implicate the originalism debate. Given what some consider the presumptive illegitimacy of judicial review, the precise determination of relevant norms becomes central to curbing judges' discretion in their exercise of such a countermajoritarian function as judicial review in matters affecting individual rights and liberties. Federal courts, and especially the Supreme Court, are regularly charged with invalidating state policies in these areas not on constitutional grounds, but rather on grounds that at bottom are nothing but the personal policy preferences of electorally unaccountable judges. Speaking for the Reagan administration's view of the 1984–5 Court's decisions in the areas of federalism, criminal justice, and religion, former Attorney General Edwin Meese claimed that "far too many of the Court's opinions were, on the whole, more policy choices than articulations of constitutional principle. The voting blocs, the arguments, all reveal a greater allegiance to what the Court thinks constitutes sound public policy than a deference to what the Constitution – its text and intention – may demand" (Edwin Meese III, Speech before the American Bar Association, July 9, 1985, Washington, DC, reprinted in Paul G. Cassell, ed., *The Great Debate: Interpreting Our Written Constitution* [Washington, DC: The Federalist Society, 1986], 9). At the more academic level of analysis, Michael Perry argued more broadly that "virtually all" of the Court's modern individual-rights decision making "must be understood as a species of policymaking, in which the Court decides, ultimately without reference to any value judgment constitutionalized by the framers, which values among competing values shall prevail and how those values shall be implemented" (Michael J. Perry, *The Constitution, the Courts, and Human Rights* [New Haven, CT: Yale University Press, 1982], 2). The conservative critique of contemporary Supreme Court jurisprudence argues that such policymaking is possible only to the extent that judges stray from the original meaning of constitutional provisions.

At the same time, however, we must bear in mind that if one were to reject judicial review in favor of some type of legislative review, one would still be faced with the distinct question of how one determines whether or not X is contrary to the Constitution. That is, if we argue that legislative judgments as to the constitutionality of bills under consideration are deemed to be final and not subject to judicial review, we still face the problem of how legislators, rather than judges, determine constitutionality. After all, legislators, no less than judges, are committed to the proposition that if X is contrary to the Constitution, then X is null and void. Had the Jeffersonian position that the legislature, rather than the Hamiltonian position that the judiciary, is authorized to make the determination that X is contrary to the Constitution won out, the question of criteria for making that determination remains. Thus, while the originalism debate and the debates over the legitimacy of judicial review and judicial activism are related in that they both derive from the Constitution's status as fundamental law, they are distinct in that they derive from different questions that arise in the basic constitutional syllogism. If most of the constitutional theory of the 1980s and early 1990s was devoted to the "How?" question, much of the theory since then, perhaps due to the apparent exhaustion of the debate, has been devoted to the "Who?" question. See, for example, Mark Tushnet, *Taking the Constitution Away from the Courts* (Princeton, NJ: Princeton University Press, 1999), and Cass Sunstein, *One Case at a Time: Judicial Minimalism on the Supreme Court* (Cambridge, MA: Harvard University Press, 1999).

purpose and very nature of a constitution – especially a written constitution – is its capacity to bind the future. Sanford Levinson explains this idea nicely:

Constitutions, of the written variety especially, are usefully viewed as a means of freezing time by controlling the future through the "hardness" of language encoded in a monumental document, which is then left for later interpreters to decipher. The purpose of such control is to preserve the particular vision held by constitutional founders and to prevent its overthrow by future generations.[16]

Walter Berns likewise adverts to this premise when he writes that the Framers "provided for a Supreme Court and charged it with the task, not of keeping the Constitution in tune with the times but, to the extent possible, of keeping the times in tune with the Constitution."[17] The concept of "binding capacity" is truly a strong point of originalism, for binding the future is, in American political thought, the very purpose of a written constitution in the first place. "Until the people have, by some solemn and authoritative act, annulled or changed the established form, it is binding upon themselves collectively, as well as individually," Hamilton wrote in Federalist 78.[18] Marshall echoed him in *Marbury*:

That the people have an original right to establish, for their future government, such principles as, in their opinion, shall most conduce to their own happiness, is the basis, on which the whole American fabric has been erected. The exercise of this original right is a very great exertion; nor can it, nor ought it to be frequently repeated. The principles, therefore, so established, are deemed fundamental. And as the authority, from which they proceed, is supreme, and can seldom act, they are designed to be permanent.[19]

Similarly, Raoul Berger points to Jefferson's comment that the purpose of a constitution is to "bind down those whom we are obliged to trust with power," doing so "by the chains of the Constitution."[20]

---

[16] Sanford Levinson, "Law as Literature," 60 *Texas Law Review* 373, 376 (1982). Similarly, Barry Friedman and Scott Smith write: "The search for the 'history' and 'traditions' of the people is precisely the right one for constitutional interpreters. The goal is always to identify in our history a set of commitments more enduring and less transient than immediate popular preference. This is the single most important function of a constitution – to limit present preferences in light of deeper commitments." "The Sedimentary Constitution," 147 *University of Pennsylvania Law Review* 1, 65 (1998).

[17] Walter Berns, *Taking the Constitution Seriously* (New York: Simon & Schuster, 1987), 236.

[18] *The Federalist Papers*, Clinton Rossiter, ed. (New York: New American Library, 1961), 470.

[19] *Marbury v. Madison*: 5 U.S. 137, 176 (1803). "The constitution," Marshall continued in the same place, "is either a superior, paramount law, unchangeable by ordinary means, or it is on a level with ordinary legislative acts, and like other acts, is alterable when the legislature shall please to alter it." Because the Constitution is indeed "superior, paramount law," it is binding on future generations because it cannot be changed easily or for light and transient causes.

[20] Cited in Raoul Berger, *Government by Judiciary: The Transformation of the Fourteenth Amendment* (Cambridge, MA: Harvard University Press, 1977), 252. Referring to this same idea

While the binding capacity of the Constitution comes into play in the area of structural principles such as federalism and the separation of powers, perhaps the prime example of that capacity is its role in the problematic relation between majority rule and individual rights. As fundamental law, the Constitution, supposedly above politics, is always drawn into political controversies between majority rule and individual rights precisely because of its binding function. Through this function the Constitution establishes the distinction, central to American political culture, between the sphere of matters subject to decision by majority rule, regardless of individual preferences to the contrary, and the sphere of matters subject to individual choice, regardless of majority preferences to the contrary. The Constitution binds contemporary majorities to respect this distinction and thereby not to act in certain ways, however democratically decided, vis-à-vis individuals. Robert Bork aptly distinguishes between these spheres in terms of what he has famously called the "Madisonian dilemma":

The United States was founded as a Madisonian system, which means that it contains two opposing principles that must be continually reconciled. The first principle is self-government, which means that in wide areas of life majorities are entitled to rule, if they wish, simply because they are majorities. The second is that there are nonetheless some things majorities must not do to minorities, some areas of life in which the individual must be free of majority rule. The dilemma is that neither majorities nor minorities can be trusted to define the proper spheres of democratic authority and individual liberty.... We have placed the function of defining the otherwise irreconcilable principles of majority power and minority freedom in a nonpolitical institution, the federal judiciary, and thus, ultimately, in the Supreme Court of the United States.[21]

As it attempts to reconcile these contending spheres, to police the boundary between two principles "forever in tension,"[22] the judiciary, which itself is never to make policy decisions, is always drawn into politics because it puts procedural and substantive limits on the policy decisions that can be made. It is the binding capacity of the Constitution that grounds the obligation of an otherwise democratic polity to accept and respect these limitations. Given the framework of a sphere of majority rule and a sphere of individual choice, the traditional problem, of course, is to decide what falls within each sphere. In analytical terms, the political question in such instances is always, does the Constitution bind a contemporary democratic majority to cede

---

of "the chains of the Constitution," Berger elsewhere makes the standard originalist argument about the binding capacity of the text: "In carrying out their purpose to curb excessive exercise of power, the founders used words to forge those chains. We dissolve the chains when we change the meaning of the words." See "Originalist Theories of Constitutional Interpretation," 73 *Cornell Law Review* 350, 353 (1988).

[21] Bork, *The Tempting of America*, 139.

[22] Ibid., 139.

decision-making power to the individual? The nature and extent of the Constitution's binding capacity, however, turn directly on the interpretation of the text. That is why Jefferson cautioned: "Our peculiar security is in the possession of a written constitution. Let us not make it a blank paper by construction."[23]

Jefferson's statement here returns us, therefore, to our initial point – viz., that while the contemporary originalism debate arose in a particular political context, its roots and recurrence lie in the very nature of the American constitutional system itself. That nature is quite simply the fact that "Our peculiar security is in the possession of a written constitution." The concern that we not make the Constitution "a blank paper by construction" illustrates the corollary fact that as long as we have a written constitution, we are going to have arguments over the nature of constitutional interpretation. Originalism is an interpretive theory advocated precisely as a way – indeed, the only way – to ensure that the Constitution will not be made a blank paper by construction. Its focus on the concept of original meaning is the crux of the theory: Whatever complexities it might involve and whatever forms it might take, originalism at its simplest holds that a constitutional provision means precisely what it meant to the generation that wrote and ratified it, and not, as nonoriginalism would contend, what it might mean differently to any subsequent generation. Originalists themselves, we will see, differ as to evidence of original meaning. For some, the original meaning is grounded in the intentions of the writers – the authors – of the Constitution, the position I shall call "hard originalism"; for others, the original meaning is grounded in the understanding of the ratifiers – the first readers – of the Constitution, the position I shall call "soft originalism." Both versions, however, subscribe to the more general principle that in constitutional interpretation the normative context of interpretation is that of those who wrote and ratified the language in question rather than that of any later interpreters.[24]

---

[23] Cited in Berger, *Government by Judiciary*, 364.

[24] This question of the proper normative context of constitutional interpretation has been with us from the ratification debates on and featured prominently in several early classic decisions of the Supreme Court. When Chief Justice Marshall writes in *Gibbons v. Ogden* that "the enlightened patriots who framed our constitution, and the people who adopted it, must be understood to have employed words in their natural sense, and to have intended what they have said," *Gibbons v. Ogden*: 22 U.S. 1, 187, 188 (1824), the normative interpretive context seems to be that of those who wrote and ratified the Constitution. Madison, for example, wrote that if "the sense in which the Constitution was accepted and ratified by the Nation...be not the guide in expounding it, there can be no security for a consistent and stable government, more than for a faithful exercise of its powers." Cited in Berger, *Government by Judiciary*, 364. Justice Scalia writes that "I take it to be a fundamental principle of constitutional adjudication that the terms in the Constitution must be given the meaning ascribed to them at the time of their ratification." *Minnesota v. Dickerson*, 508 U.S. 366, 379 (1990) (Scalia, J., concurring). On the other hand, when Marshall says in *Ogden v. Saunders* that the words of the Constitution "are to be understood in that sense

This principle manifests the interpretive problematic endemic to American constitutionalism, a problematic that involves the nature and authority of written texts and their interpretation. The political theory of American constitutionalism rests equally on two fundamental premises, the premises of constraint and consent. The first premise is that the purpose of a constitution, especially a written one, is to bind future generations to the vision of its founders, that is, to constrain the American people – individuals and institutions, citizens and government officials alike – to follow the principles of the Constitution rather than anything else. The second premise is that the binding of future generations to the vision of the founders is a democratically grounded and legitimated act of We the People, that is, that in some sense We the People have consented to be governed – bound – by the principles set forth in the Constitution. To speak of the Constitution's capacity to bind the future crucially presupposes the capacity of language, and especially the capacity of written texts, to structure human action, and this is to point to an important intersection between the social sciences' traditional interest in investigating social phenomena and the humanities' traditional interest in investigating language. That intersection is the grounding of human texts in human activity and the structuring of human activity by human texts, an interrelation I call "textuality."[25] Thus, an explanation of the binding capacity of the Constitution involves a theory of constitutional textuality – a theory of the ontology of language, if you will – because such binding capacity consists of a particular relation between the Constitution and American society.

If textuality is the key to binding capacity, then interpretation is the key to textuality. Whatever else it might be, in formal terms "constitutional interpretation" means interpretation of the Constitution, a statement that, far from being merely a banal tautology, implies the important substantive proposition that the constitutional text regulates – governs – the range of possible interpretations and thus constrains the interpreters. Interpretation must occur *in* the terms of the constitutional text – in the sense that the constitutional text provides the language of interpretation – and *within* the terms of the constitutional text – in the sense that the constitutional text constrains the range and substance of interpretation. An interpreter must

---

in which they are generally used by those for whom the instrument was intended," 25 U.S. (12 Wheat.) 213 (1827), 332, the normative interpretive context could be taken to be not that of those who "intended the instrument," but of those to whom the Constitution was addressed – and this category certainly includes future generations as well as the founding generation.

[25] In *The Interpretable Constitution* (Baltimore: Johns Hopkins University Press, 1993), Will Harris refers to the phenomenon I label textuality as "interpretability": "I will call the systematic connection between document and polity the interpretability of the Constitution, with the explicit claim that when we refer to constitutional interpretation we are invoking this connection" (5).

in principle be able to say, "Regardless of – indeed, at times contrary to – my own personal values, popular opinion, or any other factors, in my best judgment the Constitution requires X." In and of itself, the claim that in constitutional interpretation we should be bound by the text of the Constitution is an unobjectionable statement of the idea of binding the future at the very core of the concept of a constitution. To be a constitutionalist of the American variety, therefore, is necessarily to be a "textualist" in the broad sense that one ascribes authority to a particular written text.

Yet how does one guarantee that constitutional interpretation occurs in the terms and within the terms of the constitutional text? Originalism is a regulative theory of constitutional interpretation whose purpose is to provide such a guarantee; should there arise a distinction between the original understanding and a current understanding of a particular constitutional provision, the original understanding is the only authoritative, democratically legitimate, and legally binding understanding. That is, originalism argues that the necessary check on our understanding of the text of the Constitution is the original understanding of the text of the Constitution, and that in the absence of this – and *only* this – check there could be no fixed meaning, and thus no democratically legitimate way of binding future generations to the structure of the polity created by the founding generation. In this way originalism points to binding capacity as its very essence, and that is why there is such strength in its appeal.

However, the characteristic move of originalism is to conflate what, I will argue, are two distinct claims. Originalism translates the uncontroversial claim that in constitutional interpretation we should be bound by the text of the Constitution into the controversial claim that the original understanding of the constitutional text always trumps any contrary understanding of that text in succeeding generations. The reason this translation is controversial is that, to its proponents, originalism is synonymous with constitutionalism itself, such that to reject originalism is to reject constitutionalism. Underlying these claims is the relation between two propositions that I will explore in detail in the course of the book but that I can introduce here:

P_1: What binds the future is the constitutional text.
P_2: What binds the future is the original understanding of the constitutional text.

Originalism denies the possibility of distinguishing between P_1 and P_2. The proposition that what binds the future is the constitutional text and the proposition that what binds the future is the original understanding of the constitutional text are, for originalism, identical,[26] such that the denial of

---

[26] Justice Antonin Scalia, for example, asserts this identity by writing that it is "a fundamental principle of constitutional adjudication that the terms in the Constitution must be given the meaning ascribed to them at the time of their ratification." Scalia, concurring, in *Minnesota v.*

the latter necessarily amounts to a denial of the former. In other words, to deny the authoritativeness of the original understanding of the constitutional text is, for originalism, to deny the authoritativeness of the Constitution per se, and to deny the authoritativeness of the original understanding is to undermine the binding capacity of the Constitution. Thus, as a claim about the nature of constitutionalism, this is to argue that to reject originalism is to reject constitutionalism itself.

The position I seek to develop here, by contrast, is that P_1 and P_2 are in fact and necessarily separable. That is, the proposition that what binds the future is the constitutional text is a broader proposition than the narrower proposition that what binds the future is the original understanding of the constitutional text, such that we can uphold the former without being forced to accept the latter.[27] Crucially, I contend that we have to understand these propositions as distinct and separable if we are to account for both the democratic and binding character of the Constitution. The surprising paradox of originalism, I will argue, is that originalism, due to its assumptions about language and interpretation, in fact cannot explain the democratically grounded binding capacity of the Constitution on which it stakes its claim to theoretical and political validity. The purpose of a constitution may well be to get everything down on paper, in language, in order to bind future generations, but originalism's focus on the original understanding – that is, the writers' intentions or the ratifiers' understanding – in fact presupposes a marked lack of trust in the capacity of language to bind. We must infer from originalism's focus on original understanding that, despite its emphasis on the constitutional text, what binds us is not the language of the text but rather the understanding of the people who wrote and ratified the language of the text. The paradox here is that if originalism truly believed in the binding capacity of language that it affirms, it would lose its raison d'être: Originalism can claim to be a necessary guide to constitutional interpretation only because it denies the binding capacity of language that it purports to affirm.

At bottom, then, my purpose here is to "take the Constitution seriously," in the phrasing of Walter Berns,[28] and it is my perhaps surprising suggestion that doing so requires defending originalist goals – and constitutionalism generally – from originalism itself. Language, I will argue, simply does not function in the way originalism presupposes. Originalism's premises in both political and literary theory, I will argue, create a paradox: To the extent that

---

Dickerson, 113 S. Ct. 2130, 2939 (1993). Originalism, in other words, is the very essence of constitutionalism.

[27] This is the position, as Barry Friedman and Scott B. Smith aptly cite Alexander Bickel, that "fidelity is owed to the Constitution rather than to the Framers." "The Sedimentary Constitution," 147 *University of Pennsylvania Law Review* 1, 6 (1998). For originalism, by contrast, fidelity to the Constitution is necessarily fidelity to the Framers.

[28] Berns, *Taking the Constitution Seriously*.

the Constitution is binding, it is not democratic, and to the extent that it is democratic, it cannot be binding. While originalism sees binding character and democratic character as consistent, they are in fact, on originalism's political and literary premises, contradictory. I will argue, then, that originalism simultaneously affirms and denies the democratic and binding authority of the Constitution because it simultaneously affirms and denies the binding capacity of language. As the foundation of constitutionalism, originalism insists on the capacity of language to bind, yet originalism considers itself necessary because of (what it does not recognize as) its disbelief in the binding capacity of language. That is, originalism claims to be the only interpretive paradigm by which the Constitution democratically binds the future, but my contention here will be that the theory's *necessary* – if not always admitted – distinction between the constitutional text and the original understanding of that text actually undermines the democratic and binding character of the Constitution.

With an eye toward the truly voluminous literature on the originalism debate that has appeared since the mid-1970s, Michael Perry, one of our most consistently thoughtful constitutional theorists, claimed as long ago as 1991 that "the debate about the legitimacy of particular conceptions of constitutional interpretation – originalist, nonoriginalist, and nonoriginalist-textualist – is now largely spent."[29] Arguing that the originalism–nonoriginalism distinction has collapsed, that we should conceive their relation as "both/and" rather than "either/or," Perry wrote that

originalism entails nonoriginalism, that although we should all be originalists, we must all be nonoriginalists too: The originalist approach to constitutional interpretation necessarily eventuates in nonoriginal meanings; over time an originalist approach to the interpretation of a constitutional provision whose present meaning is different from – in particular, is fuller than – its original meaning, whose present meaning goes *beyond* the original meaning.[30]

As I will explain in the course of this book, I think Perry was right in saying that the originalism–nonoriginalism debate is spent, but he was right for the wrong reasons. We will do well to reconstruct and take another, closer look at the seemingly familiar dimensions of this debate,[31] a debate that will likely

[29] "The Legitimacy of Particular Conceptions of Constitutional Interpretation," 77 *Virginia Law Review* 669, 673 (1991). I explore his terminology *infra*. For another argument in the same direction, see Eric J. Segall, "A Century Lost: The End of the Originalism Debate," 15 *Constitutional Commentary* 411 (1998).

[30] Perry, "Legitimacy," 710.

[31] One commentator writes as recently as 2002 that "[t]he originalist debate has progressed without a clear statement of the doctrine or an adequate account of the different versions in which it can manifest itself." Aileen Kavanagh, "Original Intention, Enacted Text, and Constitutional Interpretation," 47 *American Journal of Jurisprudence* 255, 3 (2002). Indeed, despite the voluminous literature over the years, Kavanagh states, at 34, that "[m]uch of the confusion in the constitutional theoretical discussion of originalism has been caused by

reignite immediately – and ferociously – when one of the current justices announces his or her retirement and thus offers President George W. Bush his first opportunity to shape the Supreme Court. I will argue that originalism can neither be nor accomplish what its own self-understanding claims it is and does; the concept of original or Framers' intent[32] cannot function as the check on interpretation in the way originalists maintain. The mistaken argument of originalism is that *we* do not – and, indeed, cannot – decide

unclear terminology." However familiar, therefore, the originalism debate certainly can bear further examination.

[32] A terminological issue arises immediately when we mention the word "Framers." Raoul Berger maintains that the "intent of the Framers" is "the explanation that draftsmen gave of what their words were designed to accomplish, what their words mean." See "Originalist Theories of Constitutional Interpretation," 73 *Cornell Law Review* 350, 350–1 (1988). Leonard Levy writes that the term "original intent" "is commonly used and widely understood to mean what the Constitutional Convention understood or believed about the Constitution." *Original Intent and the Framers' Constitution* (New York: Macmillan Publishing Company, 1988), xiv. Strictly speaking, the term Framers should refer to those who wrote the original Constitution or its subsequent amendments, as distinct from those who ratified the original Constitution or its subsequent amendments. As Jack N. Rakove writes:

Intention connotes purpose and forethought, and it is accordingly best applied to those actors whose decisions produced the constitutional language whose meaning is at issue: the framers at the Federal Convention or the members of the First Federal Congress (or subsequent congresses) who drafted later amendments.... Original intention is thus best applied to the purposes and decisions of its authors, the framers.

Original Meanings: Politics and Ideas in the Making of the Constitution (New York: Vintage Books, 1997), 8. By contrast, Rakove continues, "understanding" "may be used more broadly to cover the impressions and interpretations of the Constitution formed by its original readers – the citizens, polemicists, and convention delegates who participated in one way or another in ratification" (Ibid). Most sophisticated commentators accept James Madison's assessment of the Convention's interpretive importance vis-à-vis that of the actual ratifiers: "As a guide in expounding and applying the provisions of the Constitution, the debates and incidental decisions of the Convention can have no authoritative character... [t]he legitimate meaning of the Instrument must be derived from the text itself; or if a key is to be sought elsewhere, it must not be in the opinions or intentions of the Body which planned and proposed the Constitution, but in the sense attached to it by the people in their respective State Conventions where it recd. all the Authority which it possesses." Cited in Christopher Wolfe, *The Rise of Modern Judicial Review* (New York: Basic Books, 1986), 34. The various sets of notes recorded at the Philadelphia Convention are thus taken to serve as guides to the way the Constitution was probably understood at the various state conventions.

In the interest of accuracy and precision, I have considered using the term "Founders" to refer generically to those who wrote and those who ratified the Constitution and its amendments, leaving "Framers" to refer to those who wrote – as in the foregoing citations from Berger and Rakove – and "ratifiers" to those who ratified the text. Nevertheless, such precision flies in the face of conventional usage. Consequently, I shall use Framers to refer collectively to those who wrote and ratified the Constitution or its subsequent amendments, clearly distinguishing between writers and ratifiers when necessary, and I shall use "original understanding" to refer to what both the writers and ratifiers of a constitutional provision considered it to mean.

what the Constitution means; rather, the Framers and/or the ratifiers decide, and our obligation is but to obey. Otherwise, goes the argument, the Constitution would have neither its necessary binding character nor its necessary democratic character. My goals in this book, then, are (1) to show why originalism makes such an argument, (2) to show why that argument does not work, and (3) to show why it does not matter to a successful account of the binding and democratic character of the Constitution that the originalist argument does not work. *We* – always and necessarily *we* – decide, and that is what grounds *both* the binding and democratic character of the Constitution.

That said, my argument against originalism thus may appear to be an argument for nonoriginalism, but it is my hope to contribute here to breaking out of that either–or dichotomy. It is neither the purpose nor, I hope, the consequence of my analysis here to make a case for nonoriginalism as conventionally understood. My suggestion is that the critique of originalism I offer amounts to the critique of nonoriginalism as well. That nonoriginalism is named and conceived in terms of originalism is not, I suggest, just coincidence.[33] If we in fact are *not* able to choose between reading the Constitution in original terms and reading it in contemporary terms, if in fact we can read the Constitution *only* in contemporary terms, then we cannot be originalists as opposed to nonoriginalists or nonoriginalists as opposed to originalists. Rather, while grounded in political conflict, they are bound together in their mutual opposition because their opposition is generated by a particular set of metatheoretical premises, premises about the nature of language, interpretation, and objectivity.[34] My argument will be that both originalists and

---

[33] As Lawrence Lessig has written:

> While originalists sometimes say that we must apply the principles of the Framers and Ratifiers to the circumstances of today, they more often behave as if the question were simply (and always), "How would the originals have answered this question then?" And while non-originalists usually claim that weight should be given to the historical meaning of the Constitution, rarely do they suggest just how this should be done. Thus, the extremism of the strict originalist (decide cases now as they would have been decided then) invites the extremism of the non-originalist (decide cases now as would be now morally the best), and in between these extremes is lost our understanding of what fidelity might be.

"Fidelity in Translation," 71 *Texas Law Review* 1165, 1171 (1993) (footnotes omitted). I discuss Lessig's notion of translation in Chapter 2.

[34] Let me be clear when I say that an argument over differing conceptions of language, interpretation, and objectivity underlies the originalism debate. At the beginning of this Introduction, I stated that controversies in American constitutional theory, as the legal expression of essentially political conflict, are the theoretical expression of intensely partisan, practical concerns. By that I mean to make a claim that avoids two types of reductionism. On the one hand, I do not take a Platonist position that sees politics as an epiphenomenon of abstract theory. On the other hand, I also reject what might be called a "legal-realist" position that sees theory as nothing more than an epiphenomenon of politics. Instead, while I see controversies in constitutional theory as grounded in political concerns, I consider those theoretical controversies to have an integrity of their own that makes them worth examining in their own right.

nonoriginalists, due to shared assumptions about the way language works, seem to think – at least unconsciously – that we need to impose a structure on constitutional discourse or else risk what I will call "semantic" – and thus political – anarchy. Consequently, a successful critique of originalism does not require that we opt for nonoriginalism. Instead, I hope to show that a critique of the fundamental premises of originalism dissolves the nonoriginalist alternative as well and forces a retheorization of the nature of constitutional interpretation as already and always structured.[35] If the concept of Framers' intent cannot function in the way that originalism requires, because it relies on misconceived assumptions about the nature of language, interpretation, and objectivity, then the conventional distinction between originalism and nonoriginalism can no longer stand.[36]

Instead, on the retheorization of constitutional interpretation I propose here, I will describe the Constitution not as originalist or nonoriginalist or, as Perry suggests, both, but as constitutive.[37] My project here is to argue that the constitutive character of the Constitution is the key to accounting successfully for both the democratic character and the binding capacity of the Constitution, and that it is what I will call an "interpretive" theory of constitutional textuality, rather than what I will call the "positivist" theory of textuality presupposed by originalism, that can explain that constitutive character satisfactorily.[38] The interpretive approach enables us to resolve the paradox of originalism in the broader concept of constitutive character, which is in the end the true political character of constitutional discourse, for only the interpretive approach allows us to explain the statement that we

[35] As David Couzens Hoy has written, "If originalism cannot be stated acceptably, then the need to formulate an explicitly anti-originalist theory disappears." "A Hermeneutical Critique of the Originalism/Nonoriginalism Distinction," 15 *Northern Kentucky Law Review* 479, 480–1 (1988). In other words, while originalism, as a self-conscious interpretive approach, can be said to have arisen historically in opposition to what its adherents believe to be the errors of nonoriginalist jurisprudence, nonoriginalism derives *logically* from premises it shares with originalism.

[36] There are, one might argue, three possible positions here: (1) constitutionalism (and law generally) necessitates originalism, (2) constitutionalism allows for originalism, but for nonoriginalism as well, and (3) constitutionalism is actually inconsistent with originalism and nonoriginalism. The originalist position is (1), the nonoriginalist position is (2), and my position is (3).

[37] Think of two football coaches and a third figure independent of the former two: One of the two coaches could advocate a run on the next play, while the other could advocate a pass. If they asked the third figure to settle the matter, and he said, "Okay, bunt," we would have a clear sense that the third figure has changed the game. That is the burden of my enterprise here – to change the game.

[38] I will, of course, define and explain these theories in detail, but I must sound a note of caution at the outset. Legal scholars are familiar with the term "interpretivist," but the term "interpretive" I employ here is quite distinct from and not at all equivalent to the former. I strongly urge the reader to bear that in mind while reading this book and resist the temptation to elide the two.

are a people who constitute ourselves as a people in and through the terms of a fundamental text.

My goal, therefore, is to engage and advance the literature of the originalism debate not by simply adding on to it but, rather, by working through that literature in order to reconceptualize it in a fundamental but hitherto largely unexplored manner. In other words, I will use a reexamination and critique of the originalism debate as a springboard for developing a positive theory of the nature of constitutionalism and constitutional interpretation. I will make an essentially philosophical argument here rather than a specifically legal one, because the originalism debate has been conducted – with rare exceptions, unknowingly – on the basis of philosophical assumptions about the nature of language, objectivity, and interpretation. More important, a reconsideration of the originalism debate in terms of the metatheory that underlies it will tell us something significant about what it means to live within the terms of a fundamental constitutive text. As a work of both analysis and synthesis, the plan of the book, specifically, is as follows. Chapter 1, "The Politics of Originalism," deals with the question of whether originalism is an essentially conservative approach to constitutional interpretation, concluding that this is not the case. Chapter 2, "The Concept of a Living Constitution," explores the question of whether the term "living Constitution" is, as originalism would argue, an oxymoron. Chapter 3, "Interpretivism and Originalism," traces the genealogy of the originalism debate back to the interpretivism debate and argues that the former is grounded in but not identical to the latter. Through reconstructing the genealogy of these debates, I shall map the logic of their interrelationship and argue that the conventional assumption of their conceptual equivalence itself rests on certain tacit and debatable premises about the nature of what I call constitutional textuality. Chapter 4, "The Paradox of Originalism," makes the argument that while originalism claims to be the only interpretive theory by which the Constitution can be seen to bind the future democratically, its premises in fact create a contradiction between the notion of binding the future and the principle of democratic consent. Chapter 5, "The Problem of Objectivity," explores the claim that the only guarantee of objectivity in constitutional interpretation is the anchor of original understanding, without which we are adrift in a sea of subjectivity. Chapter 6, "The Epistemology of Constitutional Discourse (I)," examines the deeper epistemological grounds of objectivity in constitutional interpretation, and Chapter 7, "The Epistemology of Constitutional Discourse (II)," takes a detailed and critical look at a recent sophisticated case for the literary theory that grounds originalism. The guiding theme of both chapters is the claim that, while originalism argues that we need a strong normative standard to prevent the Court from creating new rights unrelated to the text of the Constitution, there can be no such strong normative standard outside the discourse of constitutional interpretation. Rather, the discourse itself – the generation of arguments back and forth over particular

constitutional issues and assessments of the persuasiveness of those arguments – is its own normative standard. Constitutional interpretation is principled, with a normative bite, in the only way it can be – because we take it
as our task to explain what *the Constitution* means and not what we mean,
not what we would like it to mean, not what a popular majority wants, and
so on. That normative standard and bite thus can be nothing other than the
constitutive character of the Constitution, and Chapter 8, "The Ontology of
Constitutional Discourse (I)," begins the task of grounding both the binding
and democratic features of the Constitution in the constitutive character of
the text by exploring how the legacy of legal realism undercuts the possibility of explaining those features. Chapter 9, "The Ontology of Constitutional
Discourse (II)," completes the explanation of the constitutive character of
the Constitution through the use of John Searle's distinction between the
regulative and the constitutive. Both chapters argue that we structure our
social reality through our articulation of constitutional principle, but we articulate constitutional principle through structuring our social reality. That
is the sense of the constitutive character of the Constitution; constitutional
principle and social reality are not two separate, independent, and externally
connected items, but rather abstractions from our social ontology. Finally,
Chapter 10, "The Political Character of Constitutional Discourse," maintains by way of conclusion that not the originalist but rather what I call the
interpretive theory of constitutional interpretation allows us to understand
the essential nature of constitutional discourse as classical political theory
would have it – public deliberation over what constitutes the common good
under a written constitution.

Located at the intersection of law, political science, philosophy, and literary theory, then, this book is intended to be a work of constitutional theory
rather than, more narrowly, an argument about deciding cases.[39] It will not
argue for some alternative normative theory or method for deciding cases –
nor will it argue for or against a right to privacy, a right to abortion, the
limits of national powers in a federal system, and so on – but instead will
question the presupposition, on which originalism and nonoriginalism both
rest, that we need a normative theory in the first place. It is thus a descriptive
and analytical argument about the nature of constitutional interpretation, an
argument about what constitutional interpretation is and cannot not be.[40]

---

[39] As Stephen M. Griffin writes: "There are important theoretical questions about American
constitutionalism that have nothing to do with Supreme Court decisions. The nature of
American constitutionalism, the validity of the doctrine of popular sovereignty, and the
relationship of the Constitution to American political development are all examples. These
questions do not normally arise in any court case because they concern the appropriate
purpose and design of the constitutional system as a whole." *American Constitutionalism:
From Theory to Politics* (Princeton, NJ: Princeton University Press, 1996), 4.

[40] Richard Posner argues that constitutional theory is essentially normative: "the effort to
develop a generally accepted theory to guide the interpretation of the Constitution of the

Additionally, it is a work that uses a reconsideration of the originalism debate to illuminate the nature of American constitutionalism rather than, more narrowly, a work that is simply another study of originalism. Ultimately, then, its goals are to examine the phenomenon of "binding the future" central to the purpose of a constitution and yet not directly addressed by other works, to provide a concept of interpretive constitutional theory more systematic than one finds scattered about the present literature, and thus to contribute to moving constitutional theory past the originalism debate, and, finally, by reasserting the essentially constitutive character of the Constitution, to contribute to recent calls to put constitutions back into the empirical concerns of political science and social theory.[41]

United States." Richard A. Posner, "Against Constitutional Theory," 73 *New York University Law Review* 1, 1 (1998). My goal is, to the extent that the distinction is truly intelligible, not normative but descriptive: to explain the way constitutional interpretation works rather than to propose another alternative.

[41] In "A Constitutionalist Political Science," for example, Dennis J. Coyle suggests that "constitutionalism is, or at least should be, virtually synonymous with political science." *The Good Society*, Vol. 9, No. 1 (1999), 76–81, 76.

I

The Politics of Originalism

Beyond the primary issues of foreign policy and the economy, the main pre-occupation of American politics for approximately the past forty years has been an intense struggle over the social phenomena we have come to know generally under the rubric of "the sixties."[1] Considered culturally rather than chronologically – that is, as the sixties rather than as the 1960s – this period began with the civil rights movement, the rise of the New Left, and the Kennedy assassination in the early 1960s, continued with the evanescent counterculture of hippies and flower children in San Francisco and elsewhere from the mid-1960s until 1970, and ended with Richard Nixon's second inauguration and the cessation of the military draft in January 1973. We recall various slogans from this period, such as "Make love, not war" or "Tune in, turn on, drop out," but perhaps the most general and fundamental slogan, the one that, though less familiar, captured the ethos of the sixties, was this: "There will be respect for authority when authority is respectable." The defining theme of the sixties, at bottom, was the questioning of authority.[2] Post-sixties cultural politics in America has been marked by a reassertion of traditional authority.

Specifically, over the years since the sixties, we have witnessed the political ascendancy of a conservative counterrevolution against the liberalization the sixties wrought in various areas of American life, resulting in an ongoing

---

[1] For a recent discussion of this point, see Todd Gitlin, "Straight from the Sixties: What Conservatives Owe the Decade They Hate," *The American Prospect* (May–June 1996), 54–9.

[2] Amid a huge and still-growing literature, see Samuel Huntington, "Chapter III: The United States," in Michel J. Crozier, Samuel Huntington, and Joji Watanuki, eds., *The Crisis of Democracy: Report on the Governability of Democracies to the Trilateral Commission* (New York: New York University Press, 1975); James Davison Hunter, *Culture Wars: The Struggle to Define America* (New York: Basic Books, 1991), 49, and his later book, *Before the Shooting Begins: Searching for Democracy in America's Culture War* (New York: Free Press, 1994); and William J. Bennett, *The De-Valuing of America: The Fight for Our Culture and Our Children* (New York: Summit Books, 1992).

conflict between a peculiarly American cultural reformation and counter-reformation, sixties versus traditional culture. Where Theodore White wrote in 1969 of "the clash of its two great cultures,"[3] James Davison Hunter wrote in 1991 of the emergence of a culture war "over fundamentally different conceptions of moral authority, over different ideas and beliefs about truth, the good, obligation to one another, the nature of community, and so on."[4] This is a conflict, Hunter maintains, that is "ultimately a struggle over national identity – *over the meaning of America*, who we have been in the past, who we are now, and perhaps most important, who we, as a nation, will aspire to become in the new millennium."[5]

The cultural war over authority, then, has continued unabated.[6] As the events of the sixties shook the foundations of authority in various areas of American life, they stimulated in the process a torrent of theoretical speculation from the left, right, and center about basic political, social, and cultural values.[7] And, inevitably, this legitimation crisis manifested itself in the legal world as well. Robert Bork, for example, characterizes his failed nomination to a seat on the Supreme Court as "merely one battleground in a long-running war for control of our legal culture, which, in turn, was part of a larger war for control of our general culture."[8] Echoing the rhetoric of

---

[3] Theodore H. White, *The Making of the President, 1968* (New York: Atheneum Publishers, 1969), 34.

[4] Hunter, *Culture Wars*, 49.

[5] Ibid., 50.

[6] Thus, more recently, Elliott Abrams refers to the GOP as "the defender of public morals against the sixties generation," and Jeffrey Bell writes that "The acquittal of Bill Clinton is a stinging setback for conservatives in the values war that has been going on in one form or another since the 1960s." *The Weekly Standard*, February 22, 1999, 12. Two years later, barely six weeks after the Bush inauguration, cultural conservatives sounded a call to arms again: "Far from being over, the culture wars have just begun." Stanley Kurtz, "Push-Pull," *National Review*, March 5, 2001, 32–4, at 34. Most recently, in his bitter dissent in *Lawrence v. Texas*, 02–112 (2003), Justice Antonin Scalia writes that the Court "has largely signed on to the so-called homosexual agenda" in that it "has taken sides in the culture war, departing from its role of assuring, as neutral observer, that the democratic rules of engagement are observed" (slip opinion).

[7] As Sheldon Wolin presciently wrote in 1960, "most of the great statements of political philosophy have been put forward in times of crisis; that is, when political phenomena are less effectively integrated by institutional forms. Institutional breakdown releases phenomena, so to speak, causing political behavior and events to take on something of a random quality, and destroying the customary meanings that had been part of the old political world." *Politics and Vision* (Boston: Little, Brown and Company, 1960), 8. The literature in question is voluminous. For one example of the academic debates about liberalism, see the survey by Stephen Mulhall and Adam Swift, *Liberals and Communitarians* (Cambridge, MA: Blackwell Publishers, 1992).

[8] Robert H. Bork, *The Tempting of America: The Political Seduction of the Law* (New York: Simon & Schuster, 1990), 271. For the development of Bork's views in an even more extreme direction, see *Slouching Toward Gomorrah: Modern Liberalism and American Decline* (New York: Regan Books, 1996).

conservative intellectuals commonplace since the 1970s, Bork refers to the "wide disparity between the left-liberal values of the intellectual class and the dominant values of bourgeois culture,"[9] a disparity, he claims, of long standing. The conservative counterrevolution has prominently included a sustained political and theoretical attack on the jurisprudence of the federal judiciary generally[10] and of the Warren Court specifically, charging it with a "radical egalitarianism and expansive civil libertarianism" that are a "threat to the notion of limited but energetic government."[11] Bork characteristically puts the point dramatically:

The forces that would break law to a tame instrument of a particular political thrust are past midway in a long march through our institutions. They have overrun a number of law schools, including a large majority of America's most prestigious, where the lawyers and judges of the future are being trained. They have an increasing voice in our politics and in Congress. But the focus of the struggle, the commanding height sought to be taken, as indeed it partially has been, is control of the courts and the Constitution.[12]

Former Solicitor General Charles Fried advances the same claim:

The gradual development of constitutional law became an explosion of change in the Warren Court. With a liberal majority firmly in control in the middle sixties, the Warren Court caused a thick growth of rights and rights doctrine to grow up around what may originally have seemed like isolated decisions striking at extreme and uncivilized acts of government.[13]

Instead of standing for the impartial rule of law, Fried argues, "the federal courts had become political engines of the left-liberal agenda."[14] More recently, indicating the continuing persistence of the conservative critique, Lino Graglia has written that "the Court's controversial decisions over the last four decades have not been random in their political impact. On the contrary, their effect has been to enact the policy preferences of a small minority on the far left of the American political spectrum."[15]

[9] Bork, *The Tempting of America*, 242.

[10] In their 1980 platform, for example, the Republicans insisted on "the appointment of judges at all levels of the judiciary who respect traditional family values and the sanctity of innocent human life." *National Party Platforms of 1980*, compiled by Donald Bruce Johnson (Urbana: University of Illinois Press, 1982), 203. Reflecting the move toward assembling a majority electoral coalition around social rather than economic issues, the Republican platforms of the 1980s increasingly took on the tone of the Wallace platform of 1968.

[11] Speech by Attorney General Edwin Meese III before the American Bar Association, July 9, 1985, Washington, DC, reprinted in Paul G. Cassell, ed., *The Great Debate: Interpreting Our Written Constitution* (Washington, DC: The Federalist Society, 1986), 9.

[12] Bork, *The Tempting of America*, 3.

[13] *Order and Law: Arguing the Reagan Revolution* (New York: Simon & Schuster, 1991), 56.

[14] Ibid., 57.

[15] Lino Graglia, "Does Constitutional Law Still Exist?" *National Review*, June 26, 1995, 34. Continuing on the same page, he writes: "The vast majority of constitutional-law professors

In constitutional terms, this controversy over the Warren Court and its legacy concerns the nature and extent of federal limitations on the states' police power, and thus by implication the role of the federal courts. What the "hot-button" issues in contemporary domestic politics – race,[16] crime,[17] religion,[18] and sex[19] – have in common is that they all implicate the police power of the states; that is, the power of the states to enact legislation to provide for the health, safety, welfare, and morals of their populations. From the standpoint of the U.S. Constitution, the police power of the states, in contrast to federal powers, is plenary: Whereas, at least in principle, the federal government may do nothing except that for which warrant is found to be granted explicitly or implicitly by the U.S. Constitution, states may do anything except that which is found to be explicitly or implicitly prohibited by the U.S. Constitution.[20] Interpreting constitutional rights broadly, therefore, increases federal limitations on state police power through the intervention of federal courts, while interpreting rights narrowly decreases federal limitations on state police power and thus the corresponding intervention of federal courts in state matters. From the perspective of constitutional theory, accordingly, the liberalization of the sixties became possible because of new restrictions in the name of the U.S. Constitution on the power of the states to enforce traditional social orthodoxies. Thus, on the assumption, shared by both liberals and conservatives, that it provides a bulwark against the change represented by the liberalization of the sixties because it would require a narrower reading of constitutional rights, originalism has been the cutting edge of the conservative attack on the federal court decisions that helped to undermine the enforcement of traditional social orthodoxies.[21] Originalism is now seen as the interpretive approach that trims back such restrictions – restrictions alleged to be judge-made and therefore politically

---

in law schools and political-science departments, like the vast majority of all academics, media people, and others in our cultural elite, share the Supreme Court's liberal policy preferences." Writing in 1996, Graglia argues that "almost without exception, the effect of rulings of unconstitutionality over the past four decades has been to enact the policy preferences of the cultural elite on the far left of the American political spectrum." "It's Not Constitutionalism, It's Judicial Activism," 19 *Harvard Journal of Law & Public Policy* 293 (1996), 298.

[16] E.g., *Brown v. Board of Education*, 347 U.S. 483 (1954).
[17] E.g., *Mapp v. Ohio*, 367 U.S. 643 (1961), and *Miranda v. Arizona*, 384 U.S. 436 (1966).
[18] E.g., *Engel v. Vitale*, 370 U.S. 421 (1962), *Abington School Dist. v. Schempp*, 374 U.S. 203 (1963), *Edwards v. Aguillard*, 482 U.S. 578 (1987), and *Lee v. Weisman*, 112 S.Ct. 2649 (1992).
[19] E.g., *Griswold v. Connecticut*, 381 U.S. 479 (1965), *Roe v. Wade*, 410 U.S. 113 (1973), and *Bowers v. Hardwick*, 478 U.S. 186 (1986).
[20] The police power of a state, of course, can be limited by provisions of the state's own constitution.
[21] See, however, the discussion of the allegedly conservative character of originalism later in this chapter.

illegitimate – in order to free the police power of the states from post-*Brown* federal constitutional restraints and thereby reestablish traditional social orthodoxies.

Framed by the unusually ideological political climate of the early Reagan era, the originalism debate in contemporary American constitutional theory thus made a grand entrance onto the public stage as the centerpiece of the conservative jurisprudential agenda. The debate burst out of the confines of the legal academy and into public awareness in 1985 in the famous and extraordinary exchange between Attorney General Edwin Meese and Justice William Brennan. In a speech before the American Bar Association in Washington, D.C., in July of that year, Meese reviewed the Supreme Court's 1984–5 term, with particular attention to constitutional questions in the areas of federalism, criminal law, and religion.[22] Such a review of the Court's decisions, Meese suggested, revealed a lack of coherence that amounted to a "jurisprudence of idiosyncrasy":

Taken as a whole, the work of the term defies analysis by any strict standard. It is neither simply liberal nor simply conservative; neither simply activist nor simply restrained; neither simply principled nor simply partisan. The Court this term continued to roam at large in a veritable constitutional forest.[23]

Certainly, any incoherence or idiosyncrasy would conflict with the values of continuity and predictability central to a well-functioning legal system. The main point of Meese's observations, however, was much sharper than the charge of incoherence or idiosyncrasy, a charge he believed valid not just in 1984 but "generally true in recent years."[24] After all, the Court presumably could avoid incoherence and idiosyncrasy by issuing rulings of a uniformly and consistently liberal or conservative character. Meese's stated concern was precisely that the Court should avoid partisanship as well as incoherence and idiosyncrasy. The central point of his comments was that the Court's decisions during the 1984–5 term represented the articulation not of principle but of the justices' policy preferences:

In considering these areas of adjudication – Federalism, Criminal Law, and Religion – it seems fair to conclude that far too many of the Court's opinions were, on the whole, more policy choices than articulations of constitutional principle. The voting blocs,

---

[22] Here especially we see a prime example of my opening claim that, as the legal expression of essentially political conflict, controversies in American constitutional theory are the theoretical expression of intensely partisan, practical concerns. Edwin Meese certainly has been more of a political than scholarly figure, but when I refer to him, I do so as a way to move from the practical and partisan to the theoretical.

[23] Meese, July 9, 1985, speech in Cassell, *The Great Debate*, 3.

[24] Ibid.

the arguments, all reveal a greater allegiance to what the Court thinks constitutes sound public policy than a deference to what the Constitution – its text and intention – may demand.[25]

The only way to avoid both judicial policymaking and theoretical incoherence, Meese argued, was to adopt what he called the "Jurisprudence of Original Intention." "The text of the document and the original intention of those who framed it," he said, should be "the judicial standard in giving effect to the Constitution."[26] More broadly, he stated:

It is our belief that only "the sense in which the Constitution was accepted and ratified by the nation," and only the sense in which laws were drafted and passed provide a solid foundation for adjudication. Any other standard suffers the defects of pouring new meaning into old words, thus creating new powers and new rights totally at odds with the logic of our Constitution and its commitment to the rule of law.[27]

The logic of this argument is that constitutional interpretation can be grounded exclusively either in principle or in politics. The key originalist premise is that (neutral) principle is possible only within the interpretive paradigm of originalism. Consequently, our alternatives are originalist jurisprudence or political jurisprudence, the latter an oxymoron from the originalist perspective. Political jurisprudence is wrong because, as it violates the norm of separation of powers insofar as it gives policy-making power to unelected judges rather than to the electorally accountable political branches of government, its focus on preferences of unelected judges violates the norms of democratic accountability and principled decision making. Originalism, Meese maintained, is therefore the only jurisprudence that is consistent with the fundamental American requirements of democratic legitimacy and principled adjudication.

Yet in a speech three months later, in October 1985, to the Text and Teaching Symposium at Georgetown University, a speech remarkable in that a sitting Supreme Court justice replied to a political attack by an administration official, Justice Brennan argued sharply that originalism's self-styled fidelity to the intentions of the Framers was, in his oft-quoted phrase, "little more than arrogance cloaked as humility." Considered as a whole, his speech contained at least five principal lines of counterattack against Meese's claim of democratic legitimacy and principled adjudication. Three of those lines dealt with the nature and methodology of constitutional interpretation, while

[25] Ibid., 9.
[26] Ibid., 3.
[27] Ibid., 10. "The approach this administration advocates," he stated similarly in his speech to the Federalist Society's Lawyers Division later in 1985 (see footnote 41), "is rooted in the text of the Constitution as illuminated by those who drafted, proposed, and ratified it." *The Great Debate*, 35.

two dealt with more directly political arguments. The former appear in this lengthy passage:

There are those who find legitimacy in fidelity to what they call "the intentions of the Framers." In its most doctrinaire incarnation, this view demands that Justices discern exactly what the Framers thought about the question under consideration and simply follow that intention in resolving the case before them. It is a view that feigns self-effacing deference to the specific judgments of those who forged our original social compact. But in truth it is little more than arrogance cloaked as humility. It is arrogant to pretend that from our vantage we can gauge accurately the intent of the Framers on application of principle to specific, contemporary questions. All too often, sources of potential enlightenment such as records of the ratification debates provide sparse or ambiguous evidence of the original intention. Typically, all that can be gleaned is that the Framers themselves did not agree about the application or meaning of particular constitutional provisions, and hid their differences in cloaks of generality. Indeed, it is far from clear whose intention is relevant – that of the drafters, the congressional disputants, or the ratifiers in the states? – or even whether the idea of an original intention is a coherent way of thinking about a jointly drafted document drawing its authority from a general assent of the states. And apart from the problematic nature of the sources, our distance of two centuries cannot but work as a prism refracting all we perceive.[28]

Brennan's simplest charge here, which for now I shall merely state, is that the integrity and completeness of the documentary record on which originalists rely are highly problematic. This refers to the familiar historiographical problem of accurately determining who said and thought what at the Philadelphia convention and at the ratifying conventions in the states,[29] and to the theoretical problem of deciding how to weigh and sum differing and competing intentions and understandings once we do know what they were.[30]

Brennan's second charge in the foregoing passage is that originalist adjudication requires that judges determine and follow exactly what the Framers thought, or would have thought, about the issue at bar. Such a claim does indeed represent originalism "in its most doctrinaire incarnation," in Brennan's words, and in that form is vulnerable to attack as a straw-man argument. Robert Bork, like Meese, contends that "the only way in which the Constitution can constrain judges is if the judges interpret the document's words according to the intentions of those who drafted, proposed, and ratified its

---

[28] Speech by former Justice William J. Brennan, Jr., before the Text and Teaching Symposium at Georgetown University, October 12, 1985, Washington, D.C., reprinted in Cassell, *The Great Debate*, 14–15.

[29] See James H. Hutson, "The Creation of the Constitution: The Integrity of the Documentary Record," 65 *Texas Law Review* 1 (1986).

[30] Representative of the voluminous literature on this issue are Ronald Dworkin, "The Forum of Principle," in Ronald Dworkin, *A Matter of Principle* (Cambridge, MA: Harvard University Press, 1985), and Paul Brest, "The Misconceived Quest for the Original Understanding," 60 *Boston University Law Review* 204 (1980).

provisions and its various amendments."[31] Nevertheless, Bork's conception of originalist jurisprudence, which here he calls "intentionalism," escapes Brennan's charge:

It is important to be plain at the outset what intentionalism means. It is not the notion that judges may apply a constitutional provision only to circumstances specifically contemplated by the framers. In so narrow a form the philosophy is useless. Since we cannot know how the framers would vote on specific cases today, in a very different world from the one they knew, no intentionalist of any sophistication employs the narrow version just described.[32]

On Bork's view, originalist adjudication involves the commonplace practice of applying a general principle to a specific problem. Following John Hart Ely, he writes that

all an intentionalist requires is that the text, structure, and history of the Constitution provide him not with a conclusion but with a premise. That premise states a core value that the framers intended to protect. The intentionalist judge must then supply the minor premise in order to protect the constitutional freedom in circumstances the framers could not foresee. Courts perform this function all of the time.[33]

On the other hand, in Brennan's favor we must note that Bork's position here is somewhat disingenuous. Consider this syllogism:

Major premise: The Constitution prohibits cruel and unusual punishment.
Minor premise: The death penalty is cruel and unusual punishment.
Conclusion: The Constitution prohibits the death penalty.

If this is a fair representation of the reasoning Bork supports, then, clearly, both he and Brennan can disagree about the minor premise while both agree on the major premise. Bork is correct to say that a sophisticated originalist does not require that judges decide cases exactly the way the Framers would if they faced the same issues, but Brennan is correct to say that in determining the all-important minor premise, the originalist requires that judges ascertain and follow the Framers' understanding of the matter.

In other words, originalism says that *we* do not determine whether the minor premise can be subsumed under the major premise; rather, all we determine is whether from the perspective of the *Framers* – again, where Framers

---

[31] Robert Bork, Speech to the University of San Diego Law School, November 18, 1985, reprinted in Cassell, *The Great Debate*, 45.

[32] Ibid., 45–6.

[33] Ibid., 46. The reference to John Hart Ely is to *Democracy and Distrust* (Cambridge, MA: Harvard University Press, 1980), 2: "the work of the political branches is to be invalidated only in accord with an inference whose starting point, whose underlying premise, is fairly discoverable in the Constitution. That the complete inference will not be found – because the situation is not likely to have been foreseen – is generally common ground" (footnote omitted).

refers both to those who wrote and ratified the Constitution and its amendments – it can be so subsumed. At the same time, it is not clear that Bork's syllogism is inconsistent with Brennan's claim that "the burden of judicial interpretation is to translate 'the majestic generalities of the Bill of Rights, conceived as part of the pattern of liberal government in the eighteenth century, into concrete restraints on officials dealing with the problems of the twentieth century.'"[34] Conversely, Brennan is not far from Bork when he – Brennan – writes that "[e]ach generation has the choice to overrule or add to the fundamental principles enunciated by the Framers; the Constitution can be amended or it can be ignored. Yet with respect to its fundamental principles, the text has suffered neither fate."[35]

Brennan's third line of attack on originalism raises a fundamental issue about the nature and methodology of constitutional interpretation, an issue I once again will merely state here. This line of attack involved a brief hermeneutic critique of the interpretive approach characteristic of the jurisprudence of original intention. In his words:

We current Justices read the Constitution in the only way that we can: as Twentieth Century Americans. We look to the history of the time of framing and to the intervening history of interpretation. But the ultimate question must be, what do the words of the text mean in our time. For the genius of the Constitution rests not in any static meaning it might have had in a world that is dead and gone, but in the adaptability of its great principles to cope with current problems and current needs. What the constitutional fundamentals meant to the wisdom of other times cannot be their measure to the vision of our time. Similarly, what those fundamentals mean for us, our descendants will learn, cannot be the measure to the vision of their time.[36]

This contention is sufficiently imprecise to allow of two possible hermeneutic claims. The first is based on the premise that we are capable of reading the Constitution either as twenty-first-century – that is, contemporary – Americans or as eighteenth-century Americans, and states that we should read the Constitution as twenty-first-century Americans. Meese's claim in his speech implies the same premise, viz., that we are capable of reading the Constitution either as twenty-first-century Americans or as eighteenth-century Americans. His disagreement with Brennan lies in his argument that we should read the Constitution as eighteenth-century Americans. For an originalist this is the only responsible and legitimate interpretive choice, for to choose the alternative is to engage in a willful disregard of the rule of law. The second possible hermeneutic claim in Brennan's contention, however, is that there is no such choice between reading the Constitution as twenty-first-century Americans or as eighteenth-century Americans. Rather, we in the twenty-first century

---

[34] Brennan, 17, citing Justice Robert Jackson, *Board of Education v. Barnette*, 319 U.S. 624 (1943).
[35] Ibid., 17.
[36] Ibid.

are capable of reading the Constitution *only* as twenty-first-century Americans. Particularly in the first sentence of this passage, Brennan seems to make this latter hermeneutic claim, although the rest of the passage suggests that he is making the former.

Beyond these three lines of attack on originalism from the perspective of the nature and methodology of constitutional interpretation, the other two advanced by Brennan dealt with more directly political arguments. He argued, first, that the Constitution does not establish a purely majoritarian political system; that is, that it is wrong to suggest that "because ours is a government of the people's elected representatives, substantive value choices should by and large be left to them."[37] The purpose of the Constitution in general and the Bill of Rights in particular, he stated, is "to declare certain values transcendent, beyond the reach of temporary political majorities."[38] If originalism is equivalent to majoritarianism, Brennan argues, then it misunderstands the history on which it prides itself. Yet this too may be a straw-man argument, for Bork, to take just one case, clearly conceives the Madisonian dilemma to be posed by the juxtaposition of majority rule and individual rights.[39] In most issue domains, according to Bork, majorities are entitled to rule simply because they are majorities. In others, however, individuals are entitled to make their own decisions independently of the wishes of the majority. The existence of this latter domain for Bork would appear to be precisely Brennan's area in which certain values are declared transcendent, beyond the reach of temporary political majorities.

Finally and most directly, Brennan charged that despite protestations to the contrary, originalism carries a substantive political agenda:

Perhaps most importantly, while proponents of this facile historicism justify it as a depoliticization of the judiciary, the political underpinnings of such a choice should not escape notice. A position that upholds constitutional claims only if they were within the specific contemplation of the Framers in effect establishes a presumption

---

[37] Ibid., 15. "The great bulk of the Constitution," Meese's Office of Legal Policy argued by contrast, "is concerned with the structure of our political institutions. It addresses, not substantive issues and decisions, but procedures governing *how* and *by whom* those decisions are to be made." *Original Meaning Jurisprudence: A Sourcebook* (Report to the Attorney General by the Office of Legal Policy, United States Department of Justice, 12 March 1987), 26.

[38] Ibid., 16. Given Brennan's citation of Justice Jackson's *Barnette* opinion elsewhere in his speech, we may reasonably assume that here he had in mind this passage, at 638, from that opinion:

The very purpose of a Bill of Rights was to withdraw certain subjects from the vicissitudes of political controversy, to place them beyond the reach of majorities and officials and to establish them as legal principles to be applied by the courts. One's right to life, liberty, and property, to free speech, a free press, freedom of worship and assembly, and other fundamental rights may not be submitted to vote; they depend on the outcome of no elections.

[39] See "Neutral Principles and Some First Amendment Problems," 47 *Indiana Law Journal* 1 (1971).

of resolving textual ambiguities against the claim of constitutional right. It is far from clear what justifies such a presumption against claims of right. Nothing intrinsic in the nature of interpretation – if there is such a thing as the "nature" of interpretation – commands such a passive approach to ambiguity. This is a choice no less political than any other; it expresses antipathy to claims of the minority rights against the majority. Those who would restrict claims of right to the values of 1789 specifically articulated in the Constitution turn a blind eye to social progress and eschew adaptation of overarching principles to changes of social circumstance.[40]

Establishing "a presumption of resolving textual ambiguities against the claim of constitutional right," he argues here, means making the distinctly political choice that in cases of conflict between majority rule and individual rights, the latter must defer to the former. At the very least, Brennan implies, such a choice – and especially such an automatic choice – requires justification. More broadly, he rightly states here that the choice of a particular interpretive approach is "a choice no less political than any other," but at the same time his preferred interpretive approach is subject to the same requirement of justification.

In his speech a month after Brennan's, before the Federalist Society Lawyers Division in Washington, D.C., in November 1985, Meese responded to several of the foregoing points raised by Brennan. First, he rejected Brennan's narrow characterization of originalism by stating that the jurisprudence of original intention "does not view the Constitution as some kind of super-municipal code, designed to address merely the problems of a particular era – whether those of 1787, 1789, or 1868."[41] The authors of the 1987 report of the Reagan administration's Office of Legal Policy, reporting to Meese himself, rejected the narrow characterization of originalism as a caricature:

It is both artificial and unnecessary to ask how the framers would have decided the constitutional issues we face today. Modern society is vastly different from that which existed in the late eighteenth century. No one can possibly determine precisely how the framers would have viewed today's constitutional issues.[42]

---

[40] Ibid., 15. Although Brennan rightly states here that the choice of a particular interpretive approach is "a choice no less political than any other," he seems to maintain the view that his own approach is not political. Sheldon D. Pollack writes that much of the debate over the nature of constitutional interpretation

> leaves the impression that the fundamental problem of constitutional theory is the discovery (and justification as "legitimate") of an authentic method of reading the text. Yet, ultimately these disagreements share an underlying misperception of the problem as one of method and interpretation, rather than as a conflict of political choices.

"Constitutional Interpretation as Political Choice," 48 *University of Pittsburgh Law Review* 989, 990 (1987).

[41] Speech to the Washington, DC, chapter of the Federalist Society Lawyers Division, November 15, 1985, reprinted in Cassell, *The Great Debate*, 33.

[42] *Sourcebook*, 27.

The Constitution, both Meese and this report argued, establishes principles that transcend the particular circumstances in which they were adopted. Second, Meese argued that the documentary record is indeed sufficiently complete and precise to ground constitutional interpretation:

In short, the Constitution is not buried in the mists of time. We know a tremendous amount of the history of its genesis. The Bicentennial is encouraging even more scholarship about its origins. We know who did what, when, and many times why. One can talk intelligently about a "founding generation."[43]

We can, he maintained, clearly identify constitutional principles:

Our approach understands the significance of a written document and seeks to discern the particular and general principles it expresses. It recognizes that there may be debate at times over the application of these principles. But it does not mean these principles cannot be identified.[44]

Finally, Meese insisted that originalism is the only interpretive approach capable of depoliticizing the law. The jurisprudence of original intention, he maintained, involves

not an agenda of issues or a menu of results. At issue is a way of government. A jurisprudence based on first principles is neither conservative nor liberal, neither right nor left. It is a jurisprudence that cares about committing and limiting to each organ of government the proper ambit of its responsibilities. It is a jurisprudence faithful to our Constitution.[45]

In terms of its self-understanding, in other words, originalism is not first and foremost about the liberalization of the sixties, but rather about neutral principles and about keeping the judiciary within a clearly demarcated sphere of action in order to ensure that it does not step on the proper functions of the other branches of government.[46] Principle, Meese implies, is ideologically neutral; it is neither conservative nor liberal.

Yet is originalism neither conservative nor liberal? That is to say, is there in fact no politics of originalism? Originalists, according to Daniel Farber and Suzanna Sherry, "are committed to the view that original intent is not only relevant but authoritative, that we are in some sense obligated to follow the intent of the framers."[47] By writing and ratifying a constitution, the

---

[43] Cassell, *The Great Debate*, 33.
[44] Ibid., 36.
[45] Ibid., 40.
[46] *Sourcebook* argues at 4 that "if the courts go beyond the original meaning of the Constitution, if they strike down legislative or executive action based on their personal notions of the public good or on other extra-constitutional principles, they usurp powers not given to them by the people." Note the premise that anything other than the "original meaning" must be either "their personal notions of the public good" or "other extra-constitutional principles."
[47] Daniel A. Farber and Suzanna Sherry, *A History of the American Constitution* (St. Paul, MN: West Publishing Company, 1990), 374.

Framers clearly intended to establish a polity constituted and structured by a determinate set of procedural and substantive principles. The word "determinate" indicates that the Constitution creates one and only one of several possible political forms – it creates a polity of type X, so to speak, rather than, and thus distinct from, a polity of type A, B, or C. Michael Perry, in his earlier work a nonoriginalist who considered originalism to be a theoretically coherent position, describes it in this highly structured manner:

> According to originalism (in the soundest version I can imagine), in ratifying each constitutional provision, the ratifiers, on behalf of those they represented, constitutionalized – that is, they established as supremely authoritative for purposes of the legal system – a belief or set of beliefs about how government should be organized or about what government may, may not, or must do. They established a norm or set of norms about the structure or limits of government.[48]

The Framers established, in other words, *one* determinate set of norms as opposed to any other possible set of norms. As Sotirios Barber has written, "the Constitution is simply not compatible with any and every conceivable state of affairs."[49] It orders our world in a particular, determinate way.

The Constitution thus represents – constitutes – the intent of the Framers (once again, the writers and ratifiers) that subsequent generations live within and in accordance with a particular political structure. From one point of view, we are dealing here with a tautology: If the Constitution constitutes the intent of the Framers, then the claim that in constitutional interpretation we should be bound by the intent of the Framers amounts to the claim that in constitutional interpretation we should be bound by the Constitution. This is an assertion of the exclusively authoritative status of those principles constitutionalized by the writers and ratifiers, and as such it is an unobjectionable general statement of the idea of binding the future at the very core of the concept of a written constitution. However, the practical interpretive question is, whose understanding of that determinate set of principles by which the writers and ratifiers intended us to live is to count as authoritative? In its self-proclaimed fidelity to the written Constitution, originalism is a particular form of textualism that translates the claim that judges (and, in fact, all interpreters) should be bound by the constitutional text into the narrower claim that judges should be bound by the original understanding of the constitutional text.[50] To determine, for example, whether states have the

---

[48] Michael Perry, *Morality, Politics, and Law* (Oxford: West Publishing Company, 1988), 123.

[49] Sotirios Barber, *On What the Constitution Means* (Baltimore: Johns Hopkins University Press, 1984), 45.

[50] The textualist's originalism is not Framers'-intent originalism. Textualism looks, rather, for the meaning of the constitutional text that was understood or would have been understood by "the public" "at the time of the law's enactment" – to quote Robert Bork, who is very close to Scalia on this point. Or a little more accurately: It looks for the meaning as understood

power to criminalize abortion[51] or sodomy,[52] we appeal to our understanding of the Constitution. What originalists seek to do is to clinch an argument over the proper understanding of the Constitution by appealing to what they call original intent. The originalist concept of Framers' intent, specifically, ceases to be analytically equivalent to the Constitution itself and becomes instead an extrinsic check on how we read the constitutional text: The original understanding of clause or provision X, the understanding of those who wrote and ratified it, is to check our or any contemporary understanding of clause or provision X.

What is authoritative for originalists, in other words, is not the principles constitutionalized by the writers and ratifiers, but rather the writers' and ratifiers' own understanding of the principles they constitutionalized. Originalism, that is, holds that the "original meaning" of the constitutional text is privileged: The original understanding of the constitutional text always trumps any contrary understanding of that text in succeeding generations. Jefferson Powell puts this point succinctly:

> The central tenet of originalism as it is often understood is the existence of a clear demarcation between the original meaning of a constitutional provision and its subsequent interpretation. The originalist, we are told, is the interpreter who knows the difference and acknowledges it by according authority to the founders rather than to their successors.[53]

The determination of what counts as evidence of "the original meaning of a constitutional provision" is, of course, fundamental. With respect to the question of evidence of constitutional norms, one form of originalism looks to the private intentions of those who wrote the particular constitutional provisions as they did, while another form looks to the contemporaneous public understanding of the language comprising the document. With respect to the question of the source of constitutional norms, natural-rights originalism looks to nature (i.e., to the natural-rights philosophy of the Framers), while positivist originalism looks to convention (i.e., to the particular, historically contingent decisions the Framers made). Yet in any version, by ensuring that subsequent generations do not substitute their own purposes or understandings for those of the Framers, originalism is supposed to regulate the conduct

by the ratifying public; for the idea is that the law as understood by the ratifying public is alone the law that was democratically consented to. Textualism understands its mission to be keeping the Constitution as close as possible to the law that was "democratically adopted." Jed Rubenfeld, "Textualism and Democratic Legitimacy," 66 *George Washington Law Review* 1085, 1102–3 (1998).

51 *Roe v. Wade.*
52 *Bowers v. Hardwick.*
53 H. Jefferson Powell, "Rules for Originalists," 73 *Virginia Law Review* 659, 676 (1987). Also see Raoul Berger, "Originalist Theories of Constitutional Interpretation," 73 *Cornell Law Review* 350, 350–1 (1988), and Richard Saphire, "Enough About Originalism," 15 *Northern Kentucky Law Review* 513, 516 (1988).

of constitutional interpretation in order to guarantee that judges, unelected, do not impose their personal political and policy values upon the rest of us. As its proponents see it, therefore, originalism is a normative theory of constitutional interpretation whose purpose is to regulate adjudication in order to prevent constitutional interpretation from becoming political. The specter haunting all originalist theory is the thought of political judges unconstrained by constitutional principle. In view of that specter, Robert Bork, for example, argues that "The only way in which the Constitution can constrain judges is if the judges interpret the document's words according to the intentions of those who drafted, proposed, and ratified its provisions and its various amendments."[54] In other words, to originalists the only way we can have principled rather than political jurisprudence is by means of the interpretive approach of originalism.

Nevertheless, despite its claim of political neutrality, originalism is believed to serve a conservative political agenda grounded in the desire to free the police power of the states from post-*Brown* federal constitutional restraints.[55] Leonard Levy has written that originalism, as conservatives understand it,

allows no room for the right to an abortion, it validates the death penalty, it repudiates the *Miranda* warnings, it provides no protection to pornography, it disallows desecration of the flag, it prevents reverse discrimination, it permits government aid to religion on a non-preferential basis, and it safeguards nearly every plank in the conservative platform that might become involved in litigation.[56]

More recently, Scott Gerber argues that the conventional originalism of what he calls "conservative originalists" is unabashedly ideological:

Despite the methodological appeal of the conservatives' argument . . . their campaign for a jurisprudence of original intention should be seen for what it is: a quest for political results. Analyzing the conclusions to which the conservatives are led by originalism reveals that they are simply espousing politically conservative interpretations of the Constitution and labeling them "original intent." In effect, the conservatives are substituting conservative result-oriented jurisprudence for liberal result-oriented jurisprudence. (The conservatives' call for a jurisprudence of original intention is clearly a reaction to the liberal jurisprudence of the Warren Court.) They are seeking radically to change constitutional law to make it conform to their preferred conception of it.[57]

---

[54] Bork, Speech to the University of San Diego Law School, in Cassell, *The Great Debate*, 45. Also see Bork, "Neutral Principles and Some First Amendment Problems," 47 *Indiana Law Journal* 1 (1971).

[55] See, for example, the discussion of the incorporation debate later in this chapter.

[56] Leonard Levy, *Original Intent and the Framers' Constitution* (New York: Macmillan Publishing Company, 1988), 374.

[57] Scott Douglas Gerber, *To Secure These Rights: The Declaration of Independence and Constitutional Interpretation* (New York: New York University Press, 1995), 4–5. Gerber wishes to

Is originalism, then, an essentially conservative approach to constitutional interpretation? The originalist argument for originalism is that it is ideologically neutral, because it is principled rather than political jurisprudence,[58] whereas the conventional critique of this argument is that originalism is in fact a conservative doctrine that regularly produces conservative results. The question is somewhat tricky, of course, because of the slipperiness of the terms "conservative" and "liberal" in this context. Historically in Western politics, the broad rule of thumb was that the position that favors expanding the domain in which majorities rule was considered liberal, and the position that restricts that domain was considered conservative. This rule of thumb applied also to early American politics, as evinced by the fact that much of the *Federalist Papers* was devoted to the problem of preventing majority tyranny under a republican form of government.

By contrast, if we grant the premise that state enforcement of traditional social, moral, and religious orthodoxies is a conservative position, then during the Warren Court era of American politics in the twentieth century the position that favors restricting the domain of individual rights and letting majorities rule as much as possible came to be considered the conservative position and the reverse the liberal position. However, considered more broadly in terms of the customary distinction between economic and social issues in contemporary American politics, the term conservative can mean the position that favors both the restriction of government intervention and regulation in matters involving property rights and the expansion of government intervention and regulation in matters involving individual rights. Consequently, in the area of personal or individual rights, if an originalist approach yields a restriction of rights in favor of expanded majority rule, we tend to consider it conservative; if it yields an expansion of individual rights with a corresponding restriction of majority rule, we tend to consider it liberal. Conversely, in the area of property or economic rights, we tend to say that an approach that yields a restriction of individual rights in favor of expanded majority rule is liberal[59] and an approach that yields an expansion of individual rights with a corresponding restriction of majority rule is conservative.[60]

---

defend what he calls "liberal originalism," which he defines as grounded in the liberalism of the natural-rights theory of the Declaration of Independence, against both nonoriginalism and the conventional originalism of conservative originalists.

[58] See, e.g., Earl Maltz, "Forward: The Appeal of Originalism," 1987 *Utah Law Review* 773. He writes at 793 that "the association of originalism with conservatism is not inevitable. It is not originalism simpliciter that is nonneutral; the conservative 'tilt' exists only because of the perception that, freed from the constraints of originalism, activist judges would exercise their authority to favor liberal causes."

[59] E.g., New Deal cases such as *N.L.R.B. v. Jones & Laughlin Steel Corp.*, 201 U.S. 1 (1937).

[60] E.g., most famously, *Lochner v. New York*, 198 U.S. 45 (1905). Additionally, contemporary appeals to the takings clause, made by groups considered conservative, are an attempt to limit federal regulatory power over environmental matters.

Against this background, both Meese and Brennan, trading charges of politicizing constitutional adjudication, staked a claim to the position of principled rather than political jurisprudence. The crux of their disagreement is that Meese argued that originalism is a necessary condition of principled jurisprudence, such that without originalism a principled jurisprudence is impossible. Brennan, on the other hand, maintained that a principled jurisprudence is possible without originalism. Is originalism, then, a principled and ideologically neutral approach to constitutional interpretation or is it an essentially conservative approach to constitutional interpretation? Conservatives could argue that they are originalists irrespective of results for the reason that originalism is simply the only legitimate mode of adjudication.[61] This claim, however, raises the question of when an originalist interpretation might (1) yield a liberal result that (2) is accepted by conservatives. That is, in case of a conflict between originalist jurisprudence and conservative results, which does the conservative choose? If the latter, then critics such as Scott Gerber are right: Conservatives must be seen as "simply espousing politically conservative interpretations of the Constitution and labeling them 'original intent.'" On the other hand, conservatives might argue that originalism would never yield a liberal result, that the fact that supposedly originalist adjudication appears to yield a liberal result is evidence that it was not truly originalist. Bork, for example, states: "For the past half-century, whenever the Court has departed from the original understanding of the Constitution's principles, it has invariably legislated an item on the modern liberal agenda, never an item on the conservative agenda."[62] But if originalism indeed would and could never yield a liberal result, we have to ask how its advocates can make the distinction between principle and results that is the necessary foundation of their argument. Any claim that considerations of principle always yield results consistent with one's personal and political preferences necessarily invokes a healthy skepticism.

To the extent that conservative means a narrow reading of constitutional rights in favor of majority rule, then, originalism is conservative insofar as it favors government power over individual rights. But does originalism always favor government power over individual rights? Originalism

---

[61] "The philosophy of original understanding means that the ratifiers of the Constitution and today's legislators make the political decisions, and the courts do their best to implement them. That is not a conservative philosophy or a liberal philosophy; it is merely the design of the American Republic." Bork, *The Tempting of America*, 177.

[62] Ibid., 130. Bork grounds this claim on a crude sociological theory of the Court as a mouthpiece of the dominant class in society – a claim whose Marxist roots should discomfort him! More conventionally, he writes at 177: "When the Supreme Court was dominated by conservative activists, prior to the coming of the New Deal Court, adherence to original understanding and judicial self-restraint was urged by liberals. Since the Supreme Court of the past several decades has been more likely to create constitutional rights that liberals like, those views are likely to be espoused by conservatives."

sometimes favors individual rights over government power, and sometimes government power over individual rights, with the consequence that, at this level of abstraction, originalism is sometimes liberal and sometimes conservative. When the questions of individual rights and government power are viewed in context (i.e., more substantively), however, it appears that originalism is conservative when it supports the conservative focus on individual rights in such economic and property matters as government regulation and takings, and conservative when it supports the conservative preference for government enforcement of traditional social, moral, and religious orthodoxies. However, the key question is, what do originalists do if and when originalist jurisprudence yields liberal results – that is, decisions that favor individual rights over government power in matters of traditional social, moral, and religious orthodoxies? If we are to accept the originalist argument that originalism is ideologically neutral, concerned with principle rather than results, then we have to see at least one instance in which originalists acknowledge that a liberal result is generated by originalist interpretation and accept it as such. On the other hand, if we are to accept the conventional critique that originalism is in fact a conservative doctrine that regularly produces conservative results, we have to see that originalist adjudication never yields a liberal result. The incorporation controversy provides an interesting illustration of this problem.[63] In that argument over the relation between the Bill of Rights and the Fourteenth Amendment, we find an instance in which professedly originalist adjudication yields liberal results that are rejected by conservatives.

---

[63] At first glance, attempts by Robert Bork and other originalists to disown the decisions in *Dred Scott v. Sandford*, 60 U.S. 393 (1857), and *Brown v. Board of Education*, 347 U.S. 483 (1954), might appear to be similar illustrations of this problem. See Bork, *The Tempting of America*, 28–34 and 74–84, where he argues at 76, with no reference whatsoever to Raoul Berger's *Government By Judiciary*, that "the result in *Brown* is consistent with, indeed is compelled by, the original understanding of the fourteenth amendment's equal protection clause." Yet Bork runs afoul of Maltz's charge here regarding *Brown*:

> Diverse groups of both originalists and nonoriginalists have concluded that a strict application of originalist principles would lead to the conclusion that maintenance of "separate but equal" schools would not violate the Constitution. This conclusion is one most individuals attracted to the general theory of originalism would find extremely distasteful. As a result, many originalists distort their analysis to avoid being forced to argue that *Brown* should be overruled.

Maltz, "The Appeal of Originalism," 794 (footnotes omitted). The originalist view of *Brown* is not that originalism reaches a liberal result; rather, in view of the originalist commitment to the conservative position upholding government enforcement of traditional orthodoxies, an originalist in *Brown* would have upheld the traditional orthodoxy of segregation. To the extent that originalists are troubled by *Brown*, then, they personally disapprove of the *conservative* result generated by originalism. That is, here again, originalism generates not a liberal but a conservative result – but one of which many originalists disapprove politically.

It thus becomes necessary to save originalism from originalists themselves. Originalism is not necessarily a conservative position, where conservative connotes the position that concomitantly narrows the domain of constitutional rights and expands the domain of majority rule. As a brief examination of the incorporation controversy will show, originalist adjudication can sometimes have liberal rather than conservative implications, favoring individual rights rather than government power. The incorporation doctrine articulated and defended by Justice Hugo Black on originalist grounds was intended to provide a bulwark against the dangers of judicial subjectivity and political adjudication decried by originalists, and yet originalists reject the doctrine as inconsistent with original intent. This is not to say that Black could not have been wrong about the intentions of the framers of the Fourteenth Amendment; rather, the point is that he believed he could make the case for incorporation on originalist grounds. If originalists argue that Black was wrong, do they argue that he was wrong empirically, simply as a matter of historical accuracy, or do they argue that he was wrong theoretically, because incorporation is inconsistent in principle with original intent? Moreover, it is ironic that the originalist rejection of the incorporation doctrine raises the same arguments made against Black's position by Justice Felix Frankfurter, who defended what Black and contemporary originalists deride as highly subjective natural-law reasoning. Black is important because he is originalism's bulwark against the claim that originalism is nothing more than conservative politics; and he is interesting also because conservatives reject those views of his (e.g., incorporation) that would ground originalism's claim to be more than simply conservative politics.

The incorporation controversy is an example par excellence of the problem of determining the proper interpretive norms in constitutional jurisprudence. The question is, what are the appropriate assumptions that we must bring to bear in reading a particular provision of the Constitution? This problem has always been especially acute in the matter of the second sentence of the first section of the Fourteenth Amendment:

No state shall make or enforce any law which shall abridge the privileges or immunities of citizens of the United States; nor shall any state deprive any person of life, liberty, or property, without due process of law; nor deny to any person within its jurisdiction the equal protection of the laws.

The question of incorporation had to do, famously, with the nature of the interpretive relation between the Fourteenth Amendment and the Bill of Rights. This problem was stated succinctly by Justice John M. Harlan (II) in *Duncan v. Louisiana*: "Where does the Court properly look to find the specific rules that define and give content to such terms as 'life, liberty, or property' and 'due process of law'?"[64] After the Court in *The Slaughterhouse*

---

[64] 391 U.S. 145, 174 (1968).

Cases[65] interpreted very narrowly any restraint that the privileges or immunities clause of the Fourteenth Amendment might impose on the states, the first major case dealing with the reach of the due process clause was *Twining v. New Jersey* in 1908. At issue in *Twining* was a state law allowing a jury to draw an unfavorable inference from a criminal defendant's failure to testify and deny the evidence presented against him. The general question, according to the Court, was "whether such a law violates the Fourteenth Amendment, either by abridging the privileges or immunities of citizens of the United States, or by depriving persons of their life, liberty or property without due process of law."[66]

Twining's first claim was that the privileges or immunities clause, in essence, incorporated the protections found in the Bill of Rights on the grounds that

the "privileges and immunities of citizens of the United States," protected against state action by [the Fourteenth Amendment], include those fundamental personal rights which were protected against National action by the first eight Amendments; that this was the intention of the framers of the Fourteenth Amendment, and that this part of it would otherwise have little or no meaning and effect.[67]

Following both *Barron v. Baltimore*[68] and *Slaughterhouse*, the Court denied the privileges or immunities claim with the argument that "the exemption from compulsory self-incrimination is not a privilege or immunity of National citizenship guaranteed by this clause of the Fourteenth Amendment against abridgment by the States."[69] With the failure of this argument, Twining's incorporation argument shifted to his due process claim. It is here that the Court staked out the basic parameters of the modern incorporation controversy. The due process claim, the Court held,

requires separate consideration, for it is possible that some of the personal rights safeguarded by the first eight Amendments against National action may also be safeguarded against state action, because a denial of them would be a denial of due process of law. . . . If this is so, it is not because those rights are enumerated in the first eight Amendments, but because they are of such a nature that they are included in the conception of due process of law."[70]

The argument here, to recur in the future, was that while they may overlap, the Bill of Rights and the due process clause are in principle two conceptually distinct sets of rights against government – the former valid against the federal government, the latter against state governments. It is worthwhile

[65] 83 U.S. 36 (1873).
[66] *Twining v. New Jersey*, 211 U.S. 79, 91 (1908).
[67] Ibid., 93.
[68] 32 U.S. 243 (1833).
[69] Ibid., 99.
[70] Ibid.

noting that in addressing Twining's due process claim, the Court took what today would be called an originalist approach:

One aid to the solution of the question is to inquire how the right was rated during the time when the meaning of due process was in a formative state and before it was incorporated in American constitutional law. Did those who then were formulating and insisting upon the rights of the people entertain the view that the right was so fundamental that there could be no due process without it?[71]

After a discussion of the history of due process, the Court concluded: "The inference is irresistible that it has been the opinion of constitution makers that the privilege, if fundamental in any sense, is not fundamental in due process of law, nor an essential part of it." Justice Harlan (I), in dissent, argued that both clauses protected Twining's claim, but he did so also in historical – that is, originalist – terms. Thus, originalism may not lead to unanimity.

The next major development in the theory of incorporation came in 1937 in *Palko v. Connecticut*, in which appellant Palko challenged a Connecticut statute that allowed the state to appeal the outcome of a criminal trial as a violation of the Fourteenth Amendment, saying that the effect of a new trial was to place him in double jeopardy for the same offense. Palko claimed that "whatever is forbidden by the Fifth Amendment is forbidden by the Fourteenth also."[72] The reason, according to the Court, was this broader claim: "Whatever would be a violation of the original bill of rights (Amendments I to VIII) if done by the federal government is now equally unlawful by force of the Fourteenth Amendment if done by a state."[73] The Court rejected this claim. Surveying numerous cases in which the Court enforced and did not enforce immunities found in the Bill of Rights against the states, Justice Benjamin Cardozo argued that "In these and other situations immunities that are valid as against the federal government by force of the specific pledges of particular amendments have been found to be implicit in the concept of ordered liberty, and thus, through the Fourteenth Amendment, become valid as against the states."[74] The question, then, is not whether a claimed immunity is found within the Bill of Rights, but, rather, whether it is "implicit in the concept of ordered liberty," "of the very essence of a scheme of ordered liberty," or, in the words of *Snyder v. Massachusetts*, a "principle of justice so rooted in the traditions and conscience of our people as to be ranked as fundamental."[75]

If *Twining* and *Palko* constitute the prehistory of the incorporation controversy, it is in the debate between Justices Hugo Black and Felix Frankfurter

[71] Ibid., 107.
[72] *Palko v. Connecticut*, 302 U.S. 319, 322 (1937).
[73] Ibid., 323.
[74] Ibid., 324–5.
[75] *Snyder v. Massachusetts*, 291 U.S. 97, 105 (1934).

in the 1946 case of *Adamson v. California*[76] that we find the most enlightening expression of the major interpretive issues. In *Adamson*, the appellant challenged certain provisions of California law that "permit the failure of a defendant to explain or to deny evidence against him to be commented upon by court and by counsel and to be considered by court and jury."[77] The Court essentially reaffirmed the holdings in *Twining* and *Palko*, finding against Adamson's claim on the grounds that (1) the Bill of Rights was not relevant to his claim under due process and (2) the due process claim fails because the privilege at issue does not fall within the meaning of due process. The interesting element of the case consists of Frankfurter's concurrence and Black's dissent.

The due process clause of the Fourteenth Amendment, as we have seen, mandates that no state shall deprive any person of life, liberty, or property without due process of law. The problem, however, has been the question of what properly counts as "due process of law" within the meaning of the Constitution. Where do we look to ascertain that meaning? Black's view, as is well know, is that due process of law means nothing more and nothing less than those protections found in the Bill of Rights, the first eight amendments to the Constitution. Using traditional constitutional language, this is the argument that the Fourteenth Amendment "totally incorporates" the protections of the Bill of Rights and makes them constitutionally enforceable against the states. In Black's words:

> My study of the historical events that culminated in the Fourteenth Amendment, and the expressions of those who sponsored and favored, as well as those who opposed its submission and passage, persuades me that one of the chief objects that the provisions of the Amendment's first section, separately, and as a whole, were intended to accomplish was to make the Bill of Rights applicable to the states. With full knowledge of the import of the *Barron* decision, the framers and backers of the Fourteenth Amendment proclaimed its purpose to be to overturn the constitutional rule that case had announced.[78]

Black makes this claim on what we today would call originalist grounds. He writes, citing *Ex parte Bain*, 121 U.S. 1, 12, that "'It is never to be forgotten that, in the construction of the language of the Constitution..., as indeed in all other instances where construction becomes necessary, we are to place ourselves as nearly as possible in the condition of the men who framed that instrument.'"[79] From that perspective, he argues that the history of the Fourteenth Amendment

conclusively demonstrates that the language of the first section of the Fourteenth Amendment, taken as a whole, was thought by those responsible for its submission to

---

[76] 332 U.S. 46 (1946).
[77] Ibid., 48.
[78] Ibid., 71–2, dissenting opinion.
[79] Ibid., 72, dissenting opinion.

the people, and by those who opposed its submission, sufficiently explicit to guarantee that thereafter no state could deprive its citizens of the privileges and protections of the Bill of Rights.[80]

In this light, he argues, the problem with cases like *Twining* is that "Neither the briefs nor opinions in any of these cases . . . make reference to the legislative and contemporary history for the purpose of demonstrating that those who conceived, shaped, and brought about the adoption of the Fourteenth Amendment intended it to nullify this Court's decision in *Barron v. Baltimore, supra,* and thereby to make the Bill of Rights applicable to the States."[81] In both *Twining* and *Adamson,* Black continued, "the Court explicitly declined to give weight to the historical demonstration that the first section of the Amendment was intended to apply to the states the several protections of the Bill of Rights."[82]

The reason Black championed this "total-incorporationist" view was his concern that the Court would see itself as "endowed by the Constitution with boundless power under 'natural law' periodically to expand and contract constitutional standards to conform to the Court's conception of what at a particular time constitutes 'civilized decency' and 'fundamental liberty and justice.'"[83] Such "natural law" theory, according to Black, "degrade[s] the constitutional safeguards of the Bill of Rights and simultaneously appropriate[s] for this Court a broad power which we are not authorized by the Constitution to exercise."[84] The natural law formula, according to Black, was the idea that due process of law can be ascertained by invoking indefinite phrases like "implicit in the concept of ordered liberty" or "liberties that are deeply rooted in this nation's history and tradition." Any such idea, Black argued, partakes of natural law and is "a violation of our Constitution, in that it subtly conveys to courts, at the expense of legislatures, ultimate power over public policies in fields where no specific provision of the Constitution limits legislative power."[85] "I fear to see the consequences," he wrote, "of the Court's practice of substituting its own concepts of decency and fundamental

---

[80] Ibid., 74–5, dissenting opinion. To present proof of this claim, Black, as is well known, attached to his dissent an appendix purporting to survey the history of the Fourteenth Amendment. See *Adamson,* 92–123. Equally well known, Charles Fairman shortly thereafter published a refutation of Black's historical claims. "Does the Fourteenth Amendment Incorporate the Bill of Rights? 2 *Stanford Law Review* 5 (1949). Fairman is commonly taken to have won the argument, but for a dissenting view see Michael Kent Curtis, *No State Shall Abridge: The Fourteenth Amendment and the Bill of Rights* (Durham, NC: Duke University Press, 1986). I make no effort to assess the competing historical accounts here; what is important is the common appeal to history in the first place.

[81] Ibid., 73, dissenting opinion.

[82] Ibid., 74, dissenting opinion.

[83] Ibid., 69.

[84] Ibid., 70.

[85] Ibid., 75.

justice for the language of the Bill of Rights as its point of departure in interpreting and enforcing that Bill of Rights."[86]

Justice Frankfurter, by contrast, argued that the due process clause could not be read as simply incorporating the first eight amendments to the Constitution. The total-incorporation position, he argued *on originalist grounds*, was contrary to text and history:

> Those reading the English language with the meaning which it ordinarily conveys, those conversant with the political and legal history of the concept of due process, those sensitive to the relations of the States to the central government as well as the relation of some of the provisions of the Bill of Rights to the process of justice, would hardly recognize the Fourteenth Amendment as a cover for the various explicit provisions of the first eight Amendments.[87]

At the same time, Frankfurter opposed the idea of selective incorporation as well, doing so for the same reason that Black proposes total incorporation – the danger of judicial subjectivity:

> There is suggested merely a selective incorporation of the first eight Amendments into the Fourteenth Amendment. Some are in and some are out, but we are left in the dark as to which are in and which are out. Nor are we given the calculus for determining which go in and which stay out. If the basis of selection is merely that those provisions of the first eight Amendments are incorporated which commend themselves to individual justices as indispensable to the dignity and happiness of a free man, we are thrown back to a merely subjective test.[88]

In a sense, of course, selective incorporation was not really an interpretive approach. Black was the only incorporationist strictly speaking, since he saw the Fourteenth Amendment as designed to incorporate the Bill of Rights. The other justices were by intention not incorporationists at all, but rather accidental or coincidental incorporationists, since they saw the due process clause as having an independent potency. That is, the due process clause is to be read not in terms of which rights protected by the Bill of Rights are to be included in it and which are not, but rather in terms of what rights, in the *Palko* formulation, are deemed so fundamental that they are implicit in the concept of ordered liberty. Due process is thus in principle a concept distinct from the idea of the Bill of Rights; that is its independent potency. And it is that notion of independent potency that was central to Frankfurter's position. The power of the due process clause stems, in Frankfurter's view, from a more general, less textual source:

> The Amendment neither comprehends the specific provisions by which the founders deemed it appropriate to restrict the federal government nor is it confined to them. The Due Process Clause of the Fourteenth Amendment has an independent potency,

---

[86] Ibid., 89.
[87] Ibid., 63, concurring opinion.
[88] Ibid., 65, concurring opinion.

precisely as does the Due Process Clause of the Fifth Amendment in relation to the Federal Government.[89]

The question, of course, is the origin and nature of the norms that constitute that "independent potency." Frankfurter's approach to determining the content of this concept was this:

And so, when, as in a case like the present, a conviction in a State court is here for review under a claim that a right protected by the Due Process Clause of the Fourteenth Amendment has been denied, the issue is not whether an infraction of one of the specific provisions of the first eight Amendments is disclosed by the record. The relevant question is whether the criminal proceedings which resulted in conviction deprived the accused of the due process of law to which the United States Constitution entitled him. Judicial review of that guaranty of the Fourteenth Amendment inescapably imposes upon this Court an exercise of judgment upon the whole course of the proceedings in order to ascertain whether they offend those canons of decency and fairness which express the notions of justice of English-speaking peoples even toward those charged with the most heinous offenses. These standards of justice are not authoritatively formulated anywhere as though they were prescriptions in a pharmacopoeia. But neither does the application of the Due Process Clause imply that judges are wholly at large. The judicial judgment in applying the Due Process Clause must move within the limits of accepted notions of justice and is not to be based upon the idiosyncrasies of a merely personal judgment.[90]

From this perspective, then, whether the criterion is that a norm must be "a fundamental principle of liberty and justice which inheres in the very idea of free government and is the inalienable right of a citizen of such a government,"[91] "implicit in the concept of ordered liberty,"[92] or fall within

---

[89] Ibid., 66, concurring opinion.

[90] Ibid., 67–8, concurring opinion. Compare Frankfurter's opinion for the Court in *Wolf v. Colorado*, 338 U.S. 25, 27 (1949):

Due process of law thus conveys neither formal nor fixed nor narrow requirements. It is the compendious expression for all those rights which the courts must enforce because they are basic to our free society. But basic rights do not become petrified as of any one time, even though, as a matter of human experience, some may not too rhetorically be called eternal verities. It is of the very nature of a free society to advance in its standards of what is deemed reasonable and right. Representing as it does a living principle, due process is not confined within a permanent catalogue of what may at a given time be deemed the limits or the essentials of fundamental rights.

To rely on a tidy formula for the easy determination of what is a fundamental right for purposes of legal enforcement may satisfy a longing for certainty but ignores the movements of a free society. It belittles the scale of the conception of due process. The real clue to the problem confronting the judiciary in the application of the Due Process Clause is not to ask where the line is once and for all to be drawn but to recognize that it is for the Court to draw it by the gradual and empiric process of "inclusion and exclusion."

Frankfurter here entertains the notion of a living Constitution. See Chapter 2.

[91] *Twining v. New Jersey*, 211 U.S. 78, 106 (1908).

[92] *Palko v. Connecticut*, 302 U.S. 319, 325 (1937).

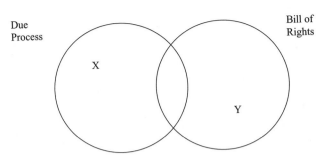

Due
Process

Bill of
Rights

X

Y

FIGURE I

"those canons of decency and fairness which express the notions of justice
of English-speaking peoples," due process is a concept independent of the
particular provisions of the Bill of Rights.

Frankfurter's position, then, was that there may be some overlap between
two independent domains: those rights protected against state infringement
by the due process clause and those protected against federal infringement
by the Bill of Rights. Consider the following figures. Figure I represents
Frankfurter's position. We see two overlapping circles, one of which is due
process and the other of which is the Bill of Rights. A claim X falling into
the area on the left would be a due process right that is not also one of those
within the Bill of Rights. A claim Y falling into the area on the right would
be a right protected by the Bill of Rights but not by due process. An example
of the latter would be the protection against self-incrimination denied in
Twining and *Adamson* or the double-jeopardy protection denied in *Palko*.
Figure 2, by contrast, represents Black's position, which was that there is, in
effect, only one circle: Those rights protected against state infringement by
the due process clause include nothing more and nothing less than the rights
protected against federal infringement by the Bill of Rights. Anything falling
within the Bill of Rights falls within due process, and anything falling within
due process falls within the Bill of Rights. Finally Figure 3 represents a third

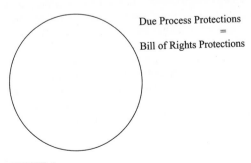

Due Process Protections
=
Bill of Rights Protections

FIGURE 2

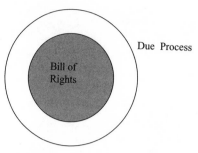

FIGURE 3

position in *Adamson*, one that thus far has had no development since that initial mention – that of Justice Frank Murphy. "I agree," he wrote, "that the specific guarantees of the Bill of Rights should be carried over intact into the first section of the Fourteenth Amendment. But I am not prepared to say that the latter is entirely and necessarily limited by the Bill of Rights."[93] In terms of Figure 3, then, all of the protections of the Bill of Rights fall within the ambit of due process, but there are elements within the broader concept of due process that are not within the Bill of Rights.

The central debate, though, was between Frankfurter and Black. It is worth noting that both claimed to argue their positions on originalist grounds, and both sought to justify their positions as the only way to avoid judicial subjectivity. Their argument continued five years after *Adamson* in *Rochin v. California*, 342 U.S. 165 (1951), the case dealing with the admissibility of evidence of illegal drug activity seized by pumping the offender's stomach. In this instance, however, both Black and Frankfurter agreed that the evidence was seized unconstitutionally, but, interestingly, for contrasting reasons that throw light on their theories of the due process clause. In his famous phrase, Frankfurter stated that stomach pumping is "conduct that shocks the conscience."[94] Writing for the Court, he reaffirmed his interpretive approach to the due process clause:

Regard for the requirements of the Due Process Clause "inescapably imposes upon this Court an exercise of judgment upon the whole course of the proceedings [resulting in a conviction] in order to ascertain whether they offend those canons of decency and fairness which express the notions of justice of English-speaking peoples even toward those charged with the most heinous offenses." *Malinski v. New York*, [324 U.S. 401 (1945)], at 416–417. These standards of justice are not authoritatively formulated anywhere as though they were specifics. Due process of law is a summarized constitutional guarantee of respect for those personal immunities which, as Mr. Justice Cardozo twice wrote for the Court, are "so rooted in the traditions and

---

[93] 332 U.S. 46, 124 (1946), dissenting opinion.
[94] 342 U.S. 165, 172 (1951).

conscience of our people as to be ranked as fundamental," *Snyder v. Massachusetts,* 291 U.S. 97, 105, or are "implicit in the concept of ordered liberty." *Palko v. Connecticut,* 302 U.S. 319, 325.[95]

"Due process of law," Frankfurter continued, "as a historic and generative principle, precludes defining, and thereby confining, these standards of conduct more precisely than to say that convictions cannot be brought about by methods that offend 'a sense of justice.'"[96] Nevertheless, he argued that this interpretive criterion does not amount to a license for judicial subjectivity:

The vague contours of the Due Process Clause do not leave judges at large. We may not draw on our merely personal and private notions and disregard the limits that bind judges in their judicial function. Even though the concept of due process of law is not final and fixed, these limits are derived from considerations that are fused in the whole nature of our judicial process.... These are considerations deeply rooted in reason and in the compelling traditions of the legal profession.[97]

Such an approach, Frankfurter concluded, "is not to be derided as resort to a revival of 'natural law.'"[98]

For his part, Black agreed that pumping Rochin's stomach violated the due process clause, but not because that action was conduct that shocks the conscience. Rather, it violated the due process clause because it violated the Fifth Amendment's privilege against self-incrimination. Black's concern, as in *Adamson,* was judicial subjectivity:

What the majority hold is that the Due Process Clause empowers this Court to nullify any state law if its application "shocks the conscience," offends "a sense of justice" or runs counter to the "decencies of civilized conduct." The majority emphasize that these statements do not refer to their own consciences or to their sense of justice and decency.[99]

Black's position, however, was that such statements could in truth refer to nothing other than the justices' own consciences or sense of justice and decency. Instead, he maintained, "faithful adherence to the specific guarantees in the Bill of Rights insures a more permanent protection of individual liberty than that which can be afforded by the nebulous standards stated by the majority."[100] "I long ago concluded," Black warned, "that the accordion-like

---

[95] Ibid., 169.
[96] Ibid., 173.
[97] Ibid., 170–1.
[98] Ibid., 171.
[99] Ibid., 175, concurring opinion.
[100] Ibid., 175, concurring opinion.

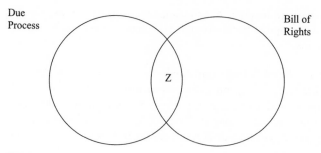

FIGURE 4

qualities of this philosophy must inevitably imperil all the individual liberty safeguards specifically enumerated in the Bill of Rights."[101]

In graphical terms, then, consider Figure 4, a version of Figure 1: Rochin's claim Z falls within the middle area of this figure, the area of overlap between protections grounded in the Bill of Rights and those grounded in due process. Frankfurter can thus agree with Black that the claim should be protected because of its due process pedigree, while Black can agree with Frankfurter because of its origin in the Bill of Rights.

By 1961, though Frankfurter was still on the Court, his due process position had been taken over by Justice John M. Harlan (II), who wrote in *Poe v. Ullman*, 337 U.S. 497 (1961), that "Again and again this Court has resisted the notion that the Fourteenth Amendment is no more than a shorthand reference to what is explicitly set out elsewhere in the Bill of Rights."[102] Harlan's fundamental interpretive norms were history and tradition:

Due process has not been reduced to any formula; its content cannot be determined by reference to any code. The best that can be said is that through the course of the Court's decisions it has represented the balance which our Nation, built upon postulates of respect for the liberty of the individual, has struck between that liberty and the demands of organized society. If the supplying of content to this Constitutional concept has of necessity been a rational process, it certainly has not been one where judges have felt free to roam where unguided speculation might take them. The balance of which I speak is the balance struck by this country, having regard to what history teaches are the traditions from which it developed as well as the traditions from which it broke. That tradition is a living thing. A decision of this Court which radically departs from it could not long survive, while a decision which builds on what has survived is likely to be sound. No formula could serve as a substitute, in this area, for judgment and restraint.[103]

---

[101] Ibid., 177, concurring opinion.
[102] *Poe v. Ullman*, 337 U.S. 497, 541 (1961), dissenting opinion.
[103] Ibid., 542, dissenting opinion.

Over time, more and more of the immunities found in the Bill of Rights were taken over as valid against the states through the due process clause of the Fourteenth Amendment, as summarized in *Duncan v. Louisiana*,[104] the decision that held that the right to trial by jury guaranteed by the Sixth Amendment in federal proceedings is also guaranteed in state criminal cases by the due process clause. Black concurred with this decision on his total-incorporation grounds and wrote principally to take issue with Harlan's dissent that critiqued his position. Black again attacked what appeared to him to be the subjectivity of the Frankfurter–Harlan approach. In Harlan's view, according to Black,

the Due Process Clause is treated as prescribing no specific and clearly ascertainable constitutional command that judges must obey in interpreting the Constitution, but rather as leaving judges free to decide at any particular time whether a particular rule or judicial formulation embodies an "immutable principl[e] of free government" or is "implicit in the concept of ordered liberty," or whether certain conduct "shocks the judge's conscience" or runs counter to some other similar, undefined and undefinable standard. Thus due process, according to my Brother Harlan, is to be a phrase with no permanent meaning, but one which is found to shift from time to time in accordance with judges' predilections and understandings of what is best for the country.[105]

Black's concern, once again, was the danger of judicial subjectivity. Every such test, he continued, "depends entirely on the particular judge's idea of ethics and morals instead of requiring him to depend on the boundaries fixed by the written words of the Constitution. Nothing in the history of the phrase 'due process of law' suggests that constitutional controls are to depend on any particular judge's sense of values."[106]

In all of the foregoing cases in which Black took part, we see that the originalist perspective that grounded his theory of total incorporation supported, whether in dissent (*Adamson*) or concurrence (*Rochin, Duncan*), an expansion of individual rights against state infringement. Thus, if the concept of constitutional liberalism refers since the 1930s to the subordination of government power to individual rights, then originalism in Black's hands yielded liberal results in these cases. However, in *Griswold v. Connecticut*, 381 U.S. 479 (1965), we see Black's originalism turn conservative in the sense of subordinating individual rights to government power. If in cases like *Adamson* Black dissented because the Court allowed a state to fall below a constitutionally required minimum, he dissented in *Griswold* because, in his view, the Court sought to force the states to uphold as rights more than the constitutionally required minimum. He stated:

---

[104] 391 U.S. 145 (1968).
[105] Ibid., 168, concurring opinion.
[106] Ibid., 169, concurring opinion.

While I completely subscribe to the holding of *Marbury v. Madison*, 1 Cranch 137, and subsequent cases, that our Court has constitutional power to strike down statutes, state or federal, that violate commands of the Federal Constitution, I do not believe that we are granted power by the Due Process Clause or any other constitutional provision or provisions to measure constitutionality by our belief that legislation is arbitrary, capricious or unreasonable, or accomplishes no justifiable purpose, or is offensive to our own notions of "civilized standards of conduct." Such an appraisal of the wisdom of legislation is an attribute of the power to make laws, not of the power to interpret them.[107]

Here we see the core elements of the contemporary originalist argument: In the absence of an originalist anchor, the Court will (1) trespass into the legitimate policy-making domains of the political branches of government and (2) have no constitutional compass but the personal values of the justices who happen to sit on the Court at any given time. On grounds that remained unchanged since *Adamson*, Black stated that "I like my privacy as well as the next one, but I am nevertheless compelled to admit that government has a right to invade it unless prohibited by some specific constitutional provision."[108] Whether dissenting from the Court's limitation of constitutional protections in *Adamson* or dissenting from the Court's expansion of constitutional protections in *Griswold*, Black took his interpretive bearings for the due process clause from the specific constitutional provisions of the Bill of Rights, doing so on the grounds that this is what the framers and ratifiers of the Fourteenth Amendment intended. Originalist adjudication, then, is not necessarily the conservative jurisprudence it appears to be today; it can yield liberal as well as conservative results.

Yet what is interesting is that although Black always defended the theory of total incorporation on originalist grounds and maintained that it was the only defense against judicial subjectivity and judicial imperialism in Fourteenth Amendment jurisprudence, contemporary originalists subject it to sharp attack. Since 1925, Meese stated in the first of his famous 1985 speeches,

a good portion of constitutional adjudication has been aimed at extending the scope of the doctrine of incorporation. But the most that can be done is to expand the scope; nothing can be done to shore up the intellectually shaky foundation upon which the doctrine rests. And nowhere else has the principle of federalism been dealt so politically violent and constitutionally suspect a blow as by the theory of incorporation.[109]

Note the claim that incorporation rests on an "intellectually shaky foundation." Meese was concerned here to mount a strong defense of federalism against what he regarded as the illegitimate encroachment of federal

---

[107] 381 U.S. 479, 513 (1965), dissenting opinion.
[108] Ibid., 510, dissenting opinion.
[109] Cassell, *The Great Debate*, 8.

power in general, and a strong defense of the autonomy of the states' police power against constitutional restrictions imposed by the federal judiciary in particular.

Our view is that federalism is one of the most basic principles of our Constitution. By allowing the States sovereignty sufficient to govern, we better secure our ultimate goal of political liberty through decentralized government. We do not advocate States' rights; we advocate States' responsibilities. We need to remember that state and local governments are not inevitably abusive of rights. It was, after all, at the turn of the century the States that were the laboratories of social and economic progress – and the federal courts that blocked their way. We believe that there is a proper constitutional sphere for state governance under our scheme of limited, popular government.[110]

Meese's defense of federalism here is interesting for two reasons. First, it is an echo of the criticism of the total-incorporation position by both Justice Frankfurter and Justice Harlan. In *Adamson*, for example, Frankfurter wrote: "A construction which gives to due process no independent function but turns it into a summary of the specific provisions of the Bill of Rights would . . . tear up by the roots much of the fabric of law in the several States, and would deprive the States of opportunity for reforms in legal process designed for extending the area of freedom."[111] Similarly, Harlan, in *Duncan*, argued on federalism grounds against the extension of Sixth Amendment requirements upon the states, writing that "I have raised my voice many times before against the Court's continuing undiscriminating insistence upon fastening on the States federal notions of criminal justice, and I must do so again in this instance."[112] The irony of Meese's reiteration of the federalism argument advanced by Frankfurter and Harlan is that, as we saw earlier, their approach to the due process clause involved the very natural law reasoning that Black and contemporary originalists criticize as subjective, idiosyncratic, and the motor of judicial imperialism.

At the same time, the second reason Meese's – and Frankfurter's and Harlan's – defense of federalism is interesting is that it is at bottom a renewal of the division of opinion in the *Slaughterhouse Cases* over whether the adoption of the Civil War amendments amounted to a fundamental constitutional shift or merely a minor adjustment in the nature of American federalism. To recall briefly, the opinion of the Court, written by Justice Samuel Miller, was that the Civil War amendments effected no such radical change:

The argument, we admit, is not always the most conclusive which is drawn from the consequences urged against the adoption of a particular construction of an instrument. But when, as in the case before us, these consequences are so serious, so

---

[110] Ibid., 5.
[111] 332 U.S. 46, 67 (1946), concurring opinion.
[112] 391 U.S. 145, 173 (1967), dissenting opinion.

far-reaching and pervading, so great a departure from the structure and spirit of our institutions; when the effect is to fetter and degrade the State governments by subjecting them to the control of Congress in the exercise of powers heretofore universally conceded to them of the most ordinary and fundamental character; when, in fact, it radically changes the whole theory of the relations of the State and Federal governments to each other and of both these governments to the people, the argument has a force that is irresistible in the absence of language which expresses such a purpose too clearly to admit of doubt.

We are convinced that no such results were intended by the Congress which proposed these amendments, nor by the legislatures of the States which ratified them.[113]

By contrast, the dissenters held precisely that the nature of American federalism had undergone a profound alteration. Justice Stephen Field argued that the matter in question was "whether the recent amendments to the Federal Constitution protect the citizens of the United States against the deprivation of their common rights by State legislation. In my judgment, the fourteenth amendment does afford such protection, and was so intended by the Congress which framed and the States which adopted it."[114] In the words of Justice Joseph Bradley:

Admitting, therefore, that formerly the States were not prohibited from infringing any of the fundamental privileges and immunities of citizens of the United States, except in a few specified cases, that cannot be said now, since the adoption of the fourteenth amendment. In my judgment, it was the intention of the people of this country in adopting that amendment to provide National security against violation by the States of the fundamental rights of the citizen.[115]

Note the appeal to original intent in all three of these citations on both sides of the issue. Arguing against a fundamental change in the nature of American federalism, Miller, as we have seen, states: "We are convinced that no such results were intended by the Congress which proposed these amendments, nor by the legislatures of the States which ratified them." Arguing for such a fundamental change, we again have seen, Field refers to what was "intended by the Congress which framed and the States which adopted it," and Bradley refers to "the intention of the people of this country in adopting that amendment." To the extent, then, that contemporary originalists such as Meese advocate a narrowing of constitutional limitations on the police power of the states, they echo the position taken by the *Slaughterhouse* majority in 1873, whereas Justice Black's incorporation doctrine echoes the position of the *Slaughterhouse* dissenters.

---

[113] *Slaughterhouse Cases*, 83 U.S. 36, 78 (1873).
[114] Ibid., 89. Field argued, at 96, that on the majority's reading, in fact, the Fourteenth Amendment "was a vain and idle enactment, which accomplished nothing and most unnecessarily excited Congress and the people on its passage."
[115] Ibid., 121–2.

The ground of the contemporary conservative attack on the incorpora-tion doctrine, therefore, can be seen plausibly as either of two indepen-dent factors: one of two competing theories of post–Fourteenth Amendment federalism or one of two competing accounts of original intent. In either case, despite his originalism, Bork, for one, recognizes in Black's position the fact that while the incorporation doctrine might expand the Court's power to limit state attempts to enforce traditional orthodoxies – the source of complaint for originalists like Meese – the doctrine also serves, as Black's dissent in *Griswold* indicates, to limit the Court's power as well. "Among Black's reasons," he writes, "was *the desire to end judicial legislation under the due process clause* by substituting the provisions of the Bill of Rights for the vague formulas used in substantive due process."[116] Granting the validity of Black's claim to originalist methodology, we can see that orig-inalism can support both individual rights against government power in some circumstances and government power against individual rights in other circumstances.

Thus, contrary to critics of originalism, who claim that it is essentially conservative, and contrary to advocates of originalism, who claim that it is ideologically neutral but who nevertheless seem to take a liberal result as prima facie and convincing evidence that the adjudication could not have been truly originalist, the example of Justice Black's incorporation doctrine suggests that originalism at times will yield liberal as well as conservative results. From this perspective, it is the fixity of the Constitution that allows, given the variability of circumstances, the variability of originalist results as either liberal or conservative.[117] Inversely and ironically, to hold that origi-nalist invariability yields conservative results presupposes the variability of the Constitution itself, which the advocates of originalism claim to oppose through their adherence to that very interpretive approach. From the origi-nalist perspective, any interpretive approach to the Constitution that is not originalist necessarily lands an interpreter in the land of the living Constitu-tion, a land where there are no limits on government because the text means anything to anyone. Nonoriginalist constitutional interpretation, from this perspective, is either overtly unprincipled, in that it does not care to provide justification for a given reading of the text, or else is unprincipled in effect be-cause the search for justificatory interpretive principles outside the text can result ultimately in nothing beyond the personal values of the interpreter.

---

[116] *The Tempting of America*, 94; emphasis added.
[117] As Madison wrote in Federalist 37: "All new laws, though penned with the greatest technical skill, and passed on the fullest and most mature deliberation, are considered as more or less obscure and equivocal, until their meaning be liquidated and ascertained by a series of particular discussions and adjudications." James Madison, *The Federalist Papers*, Clinton Rossiter, ed. (New York: New American Library, 1961), No. 37, 229. So too with the meaning of the Constitution: We determine its meaning in the process of conceptualizing in constitutional terms the issues we raise.

The emphasis on the binding character of the Constitution is the essential originalist insight, one that remains central to the American political and constitutional tradition. Originalists, however, see the binding character of the Constitution as incompatible with any notion of a "living Constitution." It is to this issue that we now turn.

2

The Concept of a Living Constitution

One of the most familiar dimensions of the originalism debate in contemporary American constitutional theory is the conflict over the concept of a "living Constitution." Justice Antonin Scalia, for example, writes that "the Great Divide with regard to constitutional interpretation is not that between Framers' intent and objective meaning, but rather that between *original* meaning (whether derived from Framers' intent or not) and *current* meaning."[1] Despite claims that originalism is "neither conservative nor liberal, neither right nor left,"[2] originalism is typically considered a conservative jurisprudence that is committed to rejecting the legitimacy of the concept of a living Constitution. Nonoriginalism, by contrast, is commonly understood to be the very theory of a living Constitution. The originalism debate can thus be neatly encapsulated in terms such as those of commentator Gregory Bassham:

Conservatives, such as Robert Bork, Chief Justice William Rehnquist, Justice Antonin Scalia, and former Attorney General Edwin Meese, have argued that constitutional meaning is forever fixed by the original intent of the framers and that courts should hold government action unconstitutional only if that action clearly violates that original intent. Liberals, such as Ronald Dworkin, Michael Perry, Leonard Levy, and retired Justice William Brennan, have countered that the Constitution is a living document and that courts should interpret its broadly based guarantees in the light of changing circumstances, values, and needs.[3]

---

[1] Antonin Scalia, *A Matter of Interpretation: Federal Courts and the Law*, ed. Amy Gutmann (Princeton, NJ: Princeton University Press, 1997), 38.

[2] Speech by Attorney General Edwin Meese III before the Federalist Society Lawyers Division, November 15, 1985, Washington, DC, reprinted in Paul G. Cassell, ed., *The Great Debate: Interpreting Our Written Constitution* (Washington, DC: The Federalist Society, 1986), 40.

[3] Gregory Bassham, review of Graham Walker, *Moral Foundations of Constitutional Thought*, in *Review of Politics*, Vol. 53, No. 4. (Fall 1991), 718.

On the conventional originalist account, "living" is counterposed to "fixed" or "permanent." Insofar as originalists thereby oppose the idea of permanence to the idea of changing circumstances, as we see in this passage, it is clear, then, that originalists indeed consider "living Constitution" to be equivalent to "changing permanence" and therefore, like "substantive due process," the contradiction in terms we call an oxymoron. Nonoriginalists, of course, would disagree.

Nevertheless, the issue of whether or not living Constitution amounts to a self-contradiction is more complicated, and thus more interesting, than a simple "yes" or "no" might suggest. For one thing, while originalists conventionally argue that living Constitution is indeed an oxymoron, there are originalists who claim that the concept is important, meaningful, and legitimate. More fundamentally, either answer unavoidably embodies a complex but implicit set of assumptions about the nature of constitutional interpretation, assumptions more often obscured than revealed in discussions of the concept of a living Constitution in terms of metaphors uncritically accepted and loosely employed. The question admits of no immediate answer until we unpack and reexamine the disparate ideas embedded in the phrase living Constitution. That is what I propose to do in this chapter.

Specifically, I want to argue that while the concept of a living Constitution forms a fault line dividing originalism and nonoriginalism,[4] it is a concept more interesting than it might thereby appear, for besides nonoriginalists, some originalists try to lay claim to it as well. So what is at stake here? By looking freshly at the ordinary uses and descriptions of the term, that is what I want to find out. The fight over possession of the term represents a struggle to account for the enduring nature of the Constitution. That is, it involves competing accounts of how we can say, in the words of a federal appellate court, that "our Constitution is a living reality, not parchment preserved under glass."[5] In this chapter I want to sketch the outlines of an argument about the continuing reality of the American Constitution. In

---

[4] Beyond the originalist debate, legal historian Morton J. Horwitz characterizes the concept of a living Constitution as one of two competing metaphors in an argument

> between an eighteenth century Newtonian Constitution and a nineteenth century Darwinian Constitution. The Newtonian view of the universe was of a perfect machine set in motion by a deist God at the beginning of time. Everything subsequent was determined by the operation of physical laws, present at the beginning and themselves never changing. The Newtonian Constitution corresponded to these physical laws, and like them was meant to last for all time. The Newtonian world view of the framers certainly encouraged this sort of imagery. By contrast, the Darwinian ideal of the nineteenth century, the idea of evolution, supposed the unfolding of gradual but inevitable change in the Constitution. As society changed, the Constitution would also change, adapting to the environment in which it functioned.

"The Meaning of the Bork Nomination in American Constitutional History," 50 *University of Pittsburgh Law Review* 655, 657 (1989).

[5] *Shanley v. Northeast Independent School District*, 462 F.2d 960, 972 (1972).

brief, the argument is as follows. When we begin to examine the concept of a living Constitution, our initial claim is that originalism considers the meaning of the Constitution to be fixed, while nonoriginalism considers that meaning to be changeable. Against nonoriginalism I want to argue that the meaning – that is, the values constitutionalized by the writers and ratifiers of constitutional provisions – is fixed; against originalism, I want to argue that our understanding, our interpretation, of that meaning is changeable. The key to this claim, of course, is the intelligibility of the distinction between meaning and understanding, for without this distinction originalism can explain the fixed character of the Constitution but not its enduring character, while nonoriginalism can explain its enduring character but not its fixed character. In the special terms I have stipulated, I want to argue the essentially Burkean notion that the Constitution endures by changing. Indeed, in view of the fact that Marshall says it is the nature and purpose of a written constitution to endure for the ages, the phrase living Constitution turns out to be redundant rather than oxymoronic.

"Our characteristic contemporary metaphor," Thomas Grey wrote in 1975, "is 'the living Constitution' – a constitution with provisions suggesting restraints on government in the name of basic rights, yet sufficiently unspecific to permit the judiciary to elucidate the development and change in the content of those rights over time."[6] Grey's statement posits the fundamental tension at issue in the concept of a living Constitution: restraint – or, more precisely, constraint – and development and change. Erwin Chemerinsky, a living-Constitution advocate, expresses this succinctly: "The very existence of a Constitution creates the tension between constraint and flexibility. A Constitution exists, above all, to entrench certain values, protecting them from easy change by social majorities."[7] Formulating this same tension in terms of relevance versus authority, Archibald Cox argues that the interpretive task is to "[keep] the Constitution a living instrument relevant to a constantly changing society while also preserving the authority of the original document and constitutional traditions of the past."[8] The focus of accounts of the concept of a living Constitution, however, tends to be more on the flexibility side of the tension rather than on the constraint.[9] Despite recognizing

---

[6] Thomas Grey, "Do We Have an Unwritten Constitution?" 27 *Stanford Law Review* 703, 709 (1975).

[7] "The Constitution Is Not 'Hard Law': The Bork Rejection and the Future of Constitutional Jurisprudence," 6 *Constitutional Commentary* 29, 37 (1989) (footnote omitted).

[8] Archibald Cox, "The Role of the Supreme Court: Judicial Activism or Self-Restraint?" 47 *Maryland Law Review* 118, 119 (1987).

[9] To some commentators the former factor simply overwhelms the latter. Henry T. Miller, for example, writes that a living Constitution is a document "chameleon-like in its complexion, which changes to suit the needs of the times and whims of the interpreters." See "Constitutional Fiction: An Analysis of the Supreme Court's Interpretation of the Religion Clauses," 47 *Louisiana Law Review* 169, 194 (1986).

this tension, for example, Chemerinsky himself wrote in an earlier article that the concept of a living Constitution is grounded "on the reality that modern society cannot possibly be governed by the specific views of individuals who lived two centuries ago."[10] He associates the concept with the need to focus on the abstract intent of the Framers, for "[i]f the Constitution's meaning is defined only by the drafters' specific views, the Constitution could not govern the modern world."[11] As Marshall Breger describes this view, the term living Constitution refers to the proposition that we must view "the normative provisions of the constitutional text – equal protection and due process – as evolving in meaning and reflecting the moral progress of our civilization."[12] The rationale of nonoriginalist constitutional interpretation, as Morton J. Horwitz puts it, is "the idea that the Constitution is a changing document that needs to evolve to deal with the different needs of a changing society."[13]

Terms such as "evolve" and "adapt" run through references to the concept of a living Constitution, a document understood to be a governing text that evolves to meet changing circumstances and whose meaning changes to give expression to the fundamental values of each generation.[14] According to Robert Sedler, for example, to say that the Constitution is a living document is to say that "its meaning must change to give expression to the fundamental values of each generation."[15] And that meaning is said to change through a process of evolution. David Anders writes that "The phrase 'living

---

[10] Erwin Chemerinsky, "The Supreme Court, 1988 Term: Forward: The Vanishing Constitution," 103 *Harvard Law Review* 43, 92 (1989).

[11] Ibid., 92.

[12] Marshall J. Breger, "Introductory Remarks: Conference on Statutory Interpretation: The Role of Legislative History in Judicial Interpretation," 1987 *Duke Law Journal* 362, 364 (1987) (footnote omitted).

[13] Horwitz, "The Meaning of the Bork Nomination," 658. "The argument about a living Constitution versus originalism," Horwitz goes on to suggest at 663, "is parallel to the question of modern and adaptable religion versus the old time religion." Originalism in constitutional discourse, he says, "is the equivalent of religious fundamentalism." Cf. Gordon Wood, "The Fundamentalists and the Constitution," *New York Review of Books*, February 18, 1988, 33–40.

[14] Beyond those sources cited in the text, see such phrasing in, e.g., Morton J. Horwitz, "The Warren Court and the Pursuit of Justice," 50 *Washington & Lee Law Review* 5, 5 (1993); Arthur S. Miller, "The President and Faithful Execution of the Laws," 40 *Vanderbilt Law Review* 389, 391 (1987); Daniel Shaviro, "An Economic and Political Look at Federalism in Taxation," 90 *Michigan Law Review* 895, 951 (1992) (note 225); Laura Oren, "The State's Failure to Protect Children and Substantive Due Process: Deshaney in Context," 68 *North Carolina Law Review* 659, 689 (1990); Louis Fisher, "Constitutional Interpretation by Members of Congress," 63 *North Carolina Law Review* 707, 717 (1985); Abner J. Mikva, "How Well Does Congress Support and Defend the Constitution?" 61 *North Carolina Law Review* 587, 608 (1983).

[15] "The Legitimacy Debate in Constitutional Adjudication: An Assessment and A Different Perspective," 44 *Ohio State Law Journal* 93, 107 (1983).

Constitution' refers to the premise that the Constitution's meaning should evolve with time."[16] The reason the Constitution's meaning should evolve, on this view, is the argument that only through an evolving meaning can the Constitution endure. Thus, in the words of Richard Fallon:

> The Constitution was written to endure through different historical ages, and part of the task of constitutional interpretation is to produce a body of law adequate to the present day. The familiar metaphor of a "living Constitution" suggests that our legal culture assumes a close connection between legal interpretation in general, and constitutional interpretation in particular, and an evolving ideal of justice.[17]

The concept of justice, in this sense, refers particularly to the equal protection and due process clauses of the Fourteenth Amendment. Marshall Breger, for example, states that living Constitution refers to the proposition that we must view "the normative provisions of the constitutional text – equal protection and due process – as evolving in meaning and reflecting the moral progress of our civilization."[18] Douglas Hsiao writes simply that "the Constitution is a living, changing document."[19] Another writer understands the notion of a living Constitution as a document that is "to be interpreted through reasoned elaboration in light of changing understanding and circumstances."[20] In still another formulation, the Constitution is a "living, breathing document that ha[s] to be interpreted in accordance with the times."[21]

It is the connection between the concept of a living Constitution and the idea of a changing, evolving meaning that associates the concept with nonoriginalism and distinguishes it from the jurisprudence of original intent. According to Daniel Conkle, for example, "the Constitution is a living, growing document, capable of being read in a way not envisioned or intended by its framers and ratifiers at all."[22] Jay Schlosser puts the opposition starkly:

> Living constitutionalists believe that the Constitution should expand and contract so as to more accurately reflect the views of the current society. On the other hand,

---

[16] "Justices Harlan and Black Revisited: The Emerging Dispute Between Justice O'Connor and Justice Scalia Over Unenumerated Fundamental Rights," 61 *Fordham Law Review* 895, 904 (1993) (note 70).

[17] Richard H. Fallon, Jr., "A Constructivist Coherence Theory of Constitutional Interpretation," 100 *Harvard Law Review* 1189, 1213–14 (1987) (footnotes omitted).

[18] Breger, "Introductory Remarks," 364. The footnote omitted here refers to the discussion of cruel and unusual punishment in *In re Winship*, 397 U.S. 358, 359 (1970).

[19] Douglas H. Hsiao, "Invisible Cities: The Constitutional Status of Direct Democracy in a Democratic Republic," 41 *Duke Law Journal* 1267, 1303 (1992).

[20] Sylvia A. Law, "Abortion Compromise – Inevitable and Impossible," 1992 *University of Illinois Law Review* 921, 928 (1992).

[21] J. Steven Beckett, "Whatever Happened to the Bill of Rights? A Criminal Defense Lawyer's Perspective," 1992 *University of Illinois Law Review* 213, 217 (1992).

[22] "Toward a General Theory of the Establishment Clause," 82 *Northwestern University Law Review* 1115, 1191 (1988) (footnote omitted).

original intent interpretivists feel the Constitution should retain the intent the framers had when constructing it.[23]

Marjorie Kornhauser draws the same distinction similarly:

In theory, originalists look at the text, the framers' intent, and the underlying purpose at the time of the Constitution's adoption. Nonoriginalists, on the other hand, assert that the Constitution is a living document meant to deal with conditions unforeseen at the time of its adoption; they look not just to original text, intent, and purpose, but to evolving concepts and norms as well.[24]

While originalists decry what they consider the substitution of contemporary values for writers' and ratifiers' values in constitutional interpretation, Lawrence Marshall defends this understanding of living Constitution as both necessary and welcome. In his words:

Consistent with the notion of the Constitution as a living document, definitions and applications of terms like "due process," "cruel and unusual punishment," and "unreasonable search and seizure" evolve over time. The specter of judges inserting content into these phrases is not an unfortunate or inevitable by-product of the framers' poor drafting or lack of foresight; it is a critical part of the process of breathing life into a document originated by those long dead.[25]

Harold Koh justifies such a position by distinguishing between a rigid literalism he ascribes to originalism and a flexible pragmatism that views the Constitution as a living document that must adapt to modern times.[26]

---

[23] Jay Schlosser, "The Establishment Clause and Justice Scalia: What the Future Holds for Church and State," 63 *Notre Dame Law Review* 380, 387 (1988) (note 55).

[24] Marjorie E. Kornhauser, "The Constitutional Meaning of Income and the Income Taxation of Gifts," 25 *Connecticut Law Review* 1, 4. (1992)

[25] "Contempt of Congress: A Reply to the Critics of an Absolute Rule of Statutory Stare Decisis," 88 *Michigan Law Review* 2467, 2478 (1990) (footnote omitted). See also Richard S. Kay's formulation in a review of books on the Bork nomination, 84 *Northwestern University Law Review* 1190, 1200 (1990).

[26] Harold Koh, 41 *Duke Law Journal* 122, 128 (1991) (note 34). See also Philip A. Hamberger:

Commentators have frequently assumed that constitutional law inevitably changes or at least should change with developments in American society – a position traditionally espoused under the rubric of a "living constitution." From this point of view, both new applications of the Constitution and changes in the nature of our society may require alterations in the rules and generalizations that comprise much of our constitutional law. As America has developed, so too, it is said, has our understanding of due process and other constitutional categories. This assumption – that constitutional law must change with society – is closely related to another assumption, that constitutional texts and the law interpreted from them are, in their nature, relatively indeterminate. To meet changing circumstances (without frequent resort to the amendment process), constitutional law allegedly must be flexible; and for constitutional law to be flexible, the Constitution must, in one way or another, be indeterminate.

"The Constitution's Accommodation of Social Change," 88 *Michigan Law Review* 239, 242–3 (1989). Hamburger's position here is that "neither Federalists nor Anti-Federalists thought it appropriate for constitutional law to change in adaptation to social developments." Ibid., at 242.

Perhaps the sharpest contrast between originalism and the living Constitution of nonoriginalism can be found by attending to the views of Arthur Selwyn Miller, one of the foremost adherents of the concept of a living Constitution, who sees the term as "a label to describe the ways in which the formal Constitution has been progressively updated, as different exigencies confronted succeeding generations of Americans."[27] Recalling the tension between constraint and flexibility, we can see that Miller comes down resoundingly on the side of the latter:

Constitutions, including the American (the oldest written instrument extant), are always in a state of becoming. They are not static or frozen in time. Rather, they are open-ended, continuously being updated to meet the exigencies of succeeding generations.... Just as each generation of intellectuals writes its own history, so each generation rewrites the Constitution – not wholesale, of course, for law is not made that way, but incrementally, bit by bit, more like the slow building of a coral reef than a volcanic explosion.[28]

The suggestion that each generation rewrites the Constitution, if it is meant literally, is the most radical version of the concept of a living Constitution, the version that contrasts most sharply with the originalist emphasis on fixity and permanence. Miller himself explicitly states the consequence for the jurisprudence of original intent:

The necessary implication is that the intentions of the Founding Fathers cannot control the resolution of modern problems. At best, those intentions are but one of the criteria of constitutional argument – even if they are ascertainable, which in most (perhaps all) present-day instances they are not. The Constitution's purported immutable principles of law and justice are cast in such high-level abstraction that each generation of judges (and scholars) can pour what it will into them. The words of the ancient charter remain the same but their content changes through time.... Not one of the great generalities of the Constitution has even had a fixed meaning: not due process of law nor equal protection of the laws, not interstate commerce nor taxing and spending, not freedom of speech nor unreasonable searches and seizures, to name but a few. Not that they are entirely unlimited in their application; rather, a rigid or fixed definition cannot be given, else the Constitution would be ossified and ultimately ignored.[29]

The idea that some, if not all, of the provisions of the Constitution have no fixed meaning, that the content of the document changes as each generation of interpreters pours into it what it will, amounts to a living Constitution with a vengeance. "The dead hand of the past," Miller says in what amounts to a response to this charge, "cannot guide the course of contemporary decisions."[30]

---

[27] "Pretense and Our Two Constitutions," 54 *George Washington Law Review* 375, 379 (1986).
[28] Arthur Selwyn Miller, *The Modern Corporate State: Private Governments and the American Constitution* (Westport, CT: Greenwood Press, 1976), 5–6.
[29] Ibid., 6–7.
[30] Ibid., 7.

The originalist rejection of the concept of a living Constitution, by contrast, stems from the argument that it is precisely the purpose of a written constitution to enable "the dead hand of the past" to guide contemporary affairs. More precisely, this argument is that the raison d'être of a written constitution is to entrench the fundamental values of the founding generation and privilege them over the fundamental values of subsequent generations. Originalists argue that the notion of nonoriginalist constitutional interpretation characteristic of the phrase living Constitution contradicts the very concept of a constitution itself. From their perspective, to accept constitutionalism is necessarily to accept originalism; to reject originalism is necessarily to reject constitutionalism itself.[31] For example, referring to the idea of a changing constitution, one whose terms "necessarily change in meaning over time, so that each new generation must interpret them afresh for itself," Richard Epstein writes that "the idea that constitutions must evolve to meet changing circumstances is an invitation to destroy the rule of law. If the next generation can do what it wants, why bother with a constitution to begin with, when it is only an invitation for perpetual revision?"[32]

If nonoriginalists employ the concept of a living Constitution to lean slightly or, apparently as in the case of Arthur Miller, almost fully in the direction of flexibility, then originalists reject that metaphor and move partially or entirely toward the opposite pole of constraint. Reviewing Raoul Berger's *Death Penalties: The Supreme Court's Obstacle Course*, Gary McDowell, for example, writes as if he were responding directly to Miller's statement that each generation of interpreters pours into the Constitution what it will:

The idea of a permanent constitution has been replaced by the idea of a living constitution, a constitution whose substantive meaning depends more upon time and circumstance than upon clearly discernible political principles. This notion of a living constitution has encouraged the belief that the Constitution is merely an "old bottle" into which the courts are able – and obligated – to "pour new wine."[33]

---

[31] Curiously, originalism is not about the American Constitution per se. Its adherents argue that the very concept of a constitution, whatever its substantive content, requires fidelity to the original intent.

[32] Richard Epstein, *Takings: Private Property and the Power of Eminent Domain* (Cambridge, MA: Harvard University Press, 1985), 24. Similarly, Herman Belz writes that the notion of a living Constitution is "fundamentally antagonistic to the founding project of written constitutionalism." Herman Belz, *A Living Constitution or Fundamental Law? American Constitutionalism in Historical Perspective* (Lanham, MD: Rowman & Littlefield Publishers, 1998), 8. Note the exclusive disjunction in Belz's title: a living Constitution or fundamental law – not both.

[33] "Book Review: Death Penalties: The Supreme Court's Obstacle Course" by Raoul Berger, Reviewed by Gary L. McDowell, 51 *George Washington Law Review* 624, 629 (1983) (footnote omitted).

The concept of a living Constitution, McDowell argues, is inconsistent with the very nature and purpose of a written constitution:

To argue that a written constitution is made viable only by ignoring both its literal text and original purpose is, in effect, to argue that the idea of a written constitution is meaningless. The truth of the matter is that the idea of a written Constitution is not meaningless – but it is occasionally frustrating. And therein lies the permanent conflict. For a written constitution will always impede each generation's quest for moral and political progress: It is the means whereby political principles can hedge in popular passions.[34]

Citing the principal author of the Constitution himself, McDowell appeals to James Madison's belief that we must read the Constitution in the sense in which it was accepted and ratified by the nation. "In that sense alone," Madison wrote to Henry Lee in 1824,

it is the legitimate Constitution. And if that be not the guide in expounding it, there can be no security for a consistent and stable, more than for a faithful exercise of its powers. If the meaning of the text be sought in the changeable meaning of the words composing it, it is evident that the shape and attributes of the Government must partake of the changes to which the words and phrases of all living languages are constantly subject. What a metamorphosis would be produced in the code of law if all its ancient phraseology were to be taken in its modern sense.[35]

McDowell speaks for all originalists when he draws from this statement the claim that the meaning of the Constitution is not living or evolving, but fixed and permanent.

Justice Antonin Scalia similarly opposes the idea of an evolving, changing Constitution, doing so in terms of a focus on the role of a constitution in preventing or slowing change. In "Originalism: The Lesser Evil," Scalia says that nonoriginalists wrongly derive from Marshall's statement that "it is a constitution we are expounding"[36] the implication that interpretation of the document must change over time. Rather, he writes,

[t]he real implication was quite the opposite: Marshall was saying that the Constitution had to be interpreted generously because the powers conferred upon Congress under it had to be broad enough to serve not only the needs of the federal government originally discerned but also the needs that might arise in the future. If constitutional interpretation could be adjusted as changing circumstances required, a broad initial interpretation would have been unnecessary.[37]

---

34 Ibid., 626 (footnote omitted).
35 9 *The Writings of James Madison*, 191 (G. Hunt, ed., 1900–10), cited by McDowell at 51 *George Washington Law Review* 624, 629 (1983).
36 *McCulloch v. Maryland*, 17 U.S. 316, 407 (1819).
37 Antonin Scalia, "Originalism: The Lesser Evil," 57 *Cincinnati Law Review* 849, 853 (1989). As he writes more recently, "It certainly cannot be said that a constitution naturally suggests changeability; to the contrary, its whole purpose is to prevent change – to embed certain

Any adaptation to new circumstances, according to Scalia, is the duty and province of the political branches. He argues that if the Constitution were "a novel invitation to apply current societal values, what reason would there be to believe that the invitation was addressed to the courts rather than to the legislature?" The legislature, he says, would seem to be "a much more appropriate expositor of social values."[38] The broader consideration for Scalia, however, is the role of the Constitution in limiting the power of democratic majorities. It is not a nonoriginalist living Constitution, but rather only originalist interpretation that is capable of providing such a bulwark:

At an even more general theoretical level, originalism seems to be more compatible with the nature and purpose of a Constitution in a democratic system. A democratic society does not, by and large, need constitutional guarantees to insure that its laws will reflect "current values." Elections take care of that quite well. The purpose of constitutional guarantees... is precisely to prevent the law from reflecting certain *changes* in original values that the society adopting the Constitution thinks fundamentally undesirable. Or, more precisely, to require the society to devote to the subject the long and hard consideration required for a constitutional amendment before those particular values can be cast aside.[39]

On Scalia's view, in other words, the concept of a living Constitution amounts to nothing less than a rejection of constitutionalism. As such, a living Constitution from an originalist perspective is indeed an oxymoron.

Beyond McDowell and Scalia, we can find noteworthy originalist critiques of the concept of a living Constitution in an article by Walter Berns, in a *Sourcebook* prepared by the Office of Legal Policy in the Meese Justice Department, and in a famous article by Chief Justice William Rehnquist. As an originalist, Berns rejects the concept of a living Constitution because it is "a protean constitution, one whose meaning is not fixed."[40] He characterizes the argument for a living Constitution in this way:

We are told that it is unreasonable – even foolish – to expect that the Framers could have written a Constitution suitable alike for a society of husbandmen and a society of multinational corporations, to say nothing of one as well adapted to the age of the musket and sailing ship as to the age of intercontinental nuclear-tipped missiles. As the problems have changed, the argument goes, so must the manner in which they

---

rights in such a manner that future generations cannot readily take them away." *A Matter of Interpretation*, 40.

[38] Scalia, "Originalism: The Lesser Evil," 854.

[39] Ibid., 862.

[40] Walter Berns, "Do We Have a Living Constitution?" *National Forum*, Vol. LXIV, No. 4 (Fall 1984), 29. Berns rejects the concept, that is, except to say that Americans "have an experience of stable, constitutional government. In that sense, we surely have 'a living Constitution'" (ibid.).

are confronted and solved, and the Constitution cannot be allowed to stand in the way.[41]

Yet, according to Berns, the permanent meaning of the Constitution allows for adapting governmental powers to new circumstances. Contrary to living-Constitution theorists, he writes, "[Chief Justice John] Marshall did not say that the Constitution should be adapted to the various crises of human affairs; he said that the powers of Congress are adaptable to meet those crises."[42] The overriding originalist premise, according to Berns, was the concern of Marshall and the founding generation "not to keep the Constitution in tune with the times but, rather, to keep the times, to the extent possible, in tune with the Constitution."[43] This directly contradicts Miller's view of the role of the Supreme Court:

> The Supreme court has had the main chore of updating the Constitution through time. This was its great historical function – that of legitimating constitutional change, accomplished by putting new content into the unchanging words of the document. The litigable, interpretable parts of the Constitution, deliberately written in cryptic language, enabled the Court in succeeding generations to alter the content of the terms.[44]

Whereas Miller here suggests that the role of the Court is to keep the Constitution in tune with the times, Berns sees the Court as keeping the times in tune with the Constitution. The prominence of the value of constraint is clear.

Among the various ways the Reagan administration articulated its jurisprudential agenda, the publication of *Original Meaning Jurisprudence: A Sourcebook*, cited in earlier chapters, presents a strong critique of the concept of a living Constitution. The booklet's call to arms is clear: "The most basic issue facing constitutional scholars and jurists today is whether federal courts should interpret and apply the Constitution in accordance with its original meaning."[45] Like McDowell, this *Sourcebook* argues against ideas such as those we find in Miller's writings of an evolving Constitution and the Supreme Court as a continuing constitutional convention. According to Miller, "the great and continuing function of the Court has been to act as a continuing constitutional convention, to update the fundamental law, to make it relevant in different times and for different peoples."[46] "If courts

---

[41] Ibid., 31.

[42] Ibid., 30.

[43] Ibid., 30. See also Walter Berns, *Taking the Constitution Seriously* (New York: Simon & Schuster, 1987), 236.

[44] Miller, *The Modern Corporate State*, 13. Cf. Arthur Selwyn Miller, "Notes on the Concept of the 'Living' Constitution," 31 *George Washington Law Review* 881, 917–18 (1963).

[45] *Original Meaning Jurisprudence: A Sourcebook* (Report to the Attorney General by the Office of Legal Policy, United States Department of Justice, 12 March 1987), 1.

[46] Ibid., 14.

apply an 'evolving' meaning," the *Sourcebook* argues to the contrary, "they are no longer interpreting our basic charter as ratified, and no longer carrying out the will of the governed. Acting instead as a 'continuing constitutional convention,' they are no longer interpreting at all, but amending and inventing."[47] The emphasis of the *Sourcebook* is on the concept of a fixed and permanent, not a changeable, living, Constitution:

The very purpose of committing the Constitution to writing, and of carefully choosing its words, was to establish certain rules and precepts as our fundamental law. We can thus presume that the language of the Constitution does have a fixed and ascertainable meaning. The founders did not intend future courts to infuse their words with meaning, but to discover and apply the meaning as originally understood and reflected in the text.[48]

What, however, about the conventional trump card of living-Constitution advocates – the ongoing appearance of new circumstances unknown to the Framers? Arguing, for example, against Chief Justice William Howard Taft's majority opinion in *Olmstead v. United States*[49] that the Fourth Amendment could not cover wiretapping telephone lines because telephones were unknown at the time of the ratification of the amendment, Justice Louis Brandeis wrote in dissent that since the time of Chief Justice Marshall,

this Court has repeatedly sustained the exercise of power by Congress, under various clauses of that instrument, over objects of which the Fathers could not have dreamed. . . . Clauses guaranteeing to the individual protection against specific abuses of power must have a similar capacity of adaptation to a changing world. It was with reference to such a clause that this Court said in Weems v. United States, 217 U.S. 349, 373: "Legislation, both statutory and constitutional, is enacted, it is true, from an experience of evils, but its general language should not, therefore, be necessarily confined to the form that evil had theretofore taken. Time works changes, brings into existence new conditions and purposes. Therefore a principle to be vital must be capable of wider application than the mischief which gave it birth. This is peculiarly true of constitutions."[50]

Yet the *Sourcebook* originalists have no problem with Brandeis's view here, distinguishing between a clause's fixed meaning and its changing application: "We can properly apply the fourth amendment to wiretaps, not because its original meaning is irrelevant . . . , but because the plain original meaning of 'unreasonable searches and seizures' is broad enough to encompass electronic surveillance."[51]

---

[47] Ibid., 4–5 (footnotes omitted).
[48] Ibid., 23.
[49] 277 U.S. 438 (1928).
[50] *Olmstead v. United States*, 277 U.S. 438, 472–3.
[51] *Sourcebook*, 24.

It is in this foregoing sense that Chief Justice Rehnquist, in a famous article entitled "The Notion of a Living Constitution,"[52] endorses a limited usage of the term living Constitution. "The framers of the Constitution wisely spoke in general language," he writes, "and left to succeeding generations the task of applying that language to the unceasingly changing environment in which they would live."[53] This usage of living Constitution centers on the idea of general principles that transcend the particular circumstances of their adoption and are capable of application to new circumstances unforeseen by their adopters. Rehnquist considers this a version of living Constitution that is legitimate, grounding it in this celebrated passage by Justice Oliver Wendell Holmes:

When we are dealing with words that also are a constituent act, like the Constitution of the United States, we must realize that they have called into life a being the development of which could not have been foreseen completely by the most gifted of its begetters. It was enough for them to realize or to hope that they had created an organism; it has taken a century and has cost their successors much sweat and blood to prove that they created a nation. The case before us must be considered in the light of our whole experience and not merely in that of what was said a hundred years ago.[54]

The Constitution "lives" in Rehnquist's first, Holmesian sense, in that it is capable of addressing new problems beyond the foresight of the Framers. "Merely because a particular activity may not have existed when the Constitution was adopted, or because the framers could not have conceived of a particular method of transacting affairs," Rehnquist writes, "cannot mean that general language in the Constitution may not be applied to such a course of conduct."[55] It is important to note, however, that what changes and adapts in this sense of living Constitution is not the meaning of constitutional principles but their application. According to the Court in *South Carolina v. United States*, for example:

The Constitution is a written instrument. As such its meaning does not alter. That which it meant when adopted it means now. Being a grant of powers to a government its language is general, and as changes come in social and political life it embraces in its grasp all new conditions which are within the scope of the powers in terms conferred. In other words, while the powers granted do not change, they apply from generation to generation to all things to which they are in their nature applicable. This in no manner abridges the fact of its changeless nature and meaning.

---

[52] William H. Rehnquist, "The Notion of a Living Constitution," 54 *Texas Law Review* 693 (1976).

[53] Ibid., 694.

[54] *Missouri v. Holland*, 252 U.S. 416, 433 (1920). Cited in part by Rehnquist, "The Notion of a Living Constitution," at 694.

[55] Ibid.

Those things which are within its grants of power, as those grants were understood when made, are still within them, and those things not within them remain still excluded.[56]

Constitutional principles on this view, therefore, are permanent and fixed, whereas the application of those principles allows for development; and this is a distinction based upon the claim that there is a fundamental distinction between *identifying* a principle and *applying* that principle.

Rehnquist is more concerned in his article, however, to attack what he considers to be the conventional meaning of living Constitution, although as Rehnquist uses the phrase it is not obviously pertinent. That is, Rehnquist, drawing on a U.S. district court brief, defines living Constitution as the position that "nonelected members of the federal judiciary may address themselves to a social problem simply because other branches of government have failed or refused to do so."[57] In more detail, he writes that this second sense of the phrase is

based upon the proposition that federal judges, perhaps judges as a whole, have a role of their own, quite independent of popular will, to play in solving society's problems. Once we have abandoned the idea that the authority of the courts to declare laws unconstitutional is somehow tied to the language of the Constitution that the people adopted, a judiciary exercising the power of judicial review appears in a quite different light. Judges then are no longer the keepers of the covenant; instead they are a small group of fortunately situated people with a roving commission to second-guess Congress, state legislatures, and state and federal administrative officers concerning what is best for the country.[58]

As Rehnquist conceives this argument, living-Constitution advocates claim that "if the states' legislatures and governors, or Congress and the President, have not solved a particular problem, then the federal court may act."[59] Originalism, to the contrary, contends that under the separation of powers the courts are not to act as policymakers, even in the case of default by the political branches. According to Rehnquist, living-Constitution advocates ascribe this default function to the courts in order "to make the Constitution relevant and useful in solving the problems of modern society."[60] The Constitution is a living document, then, insofar as it remains "relevant and useful." It is worth noting, however, that while Rehnquist attacks the concept

---

[56] *South Carolina v. United States*, 199 U.S. 437, 448–9 (1905). The Court goes on here to set forth, at 450, the central principle of what we now call originalism: "To determine the extent of the grants of power we must, therefore, place ourselves in the position of the men who framed and adopted the Constitution, and inquire what they must have understood to be the meaning and scope of those grants."

[57] Rehnquist, "The Notion of a Living Constitution," 695.

[58] Ibid., 698.

[59] Ibid., 700.

[60] Ibid., 698–9.

of a living Constitution insofar as it is a rationale for judicial activism – the real target of his article – the "permanent" Constitution advocated by originalism is itself a prescription for judicial activism. If it really is the duty of the Supreme Court to keep the times in tune with the Constitution, then the Court will continually expend a great deal of effort on reining in the political branches as they constantly attempt to adapt to changing circumstances.[61] In that sense, then, rejecting the living Constitution in favor of the permanent Constitution does not necessarily eliminate the possibility of the judicial activism decried by originalism.

So, based upon this survey of originalists and nonoriginalists, can we conclude that the term living Constitution is an oxymoron? Well, not yet. It is significant to note, in the first place, that while originalists generally attack the concept of a living Constitution, there are originalists who wish to affirm some legitimate dimension to it. Rehnquist, as we just saw, accepts the concept if it is employed to mean the Holmesian description of the Constitution – although, in another place, one might question whether Rehnquist grasps what is arguably the critique of originalism implicit in the passage he cites. In any case, Rehnquist is not the only originalist who holds on, however tenuously, to the use of a living Constitution. For example, as we saw in the Introduction, in his opening statement at the confirmation hearings for Justice Ginsburg in the summer of 1993, Senator Orrin Hatch set forth the originalist argument about the fixity of original intent.[62] Nevertheless, in his review of Robert Bork's *The Tempting of America*, Hatch also praises the living character of the Constitution:

Ours is a living Constitution. It lives because the genius of its enduring principles continues to apply to today as our fundamental law. Those who reject the Constitution as written treat it as dead. For them, enlightened judges must set aside the dusty language of by-gone generations. These skeptics forget that the living Constitution has protected American liberties for more than two centuries.[63]

Significantly, however, what living means to Hatch is not "changing" or "evolving," but "enduring."[64] Perhaps not coincidentally, we find this same

---

[61] "Legislatures respond to changing circumstances and changing needs, and as they do so they are as likely as not to get further and further away from the original spirit and purposes of the Constitution. A court that owes its duty to the Constitution is not solely concerned with the immediate needs of society, and therefore cannot defer unduly to legislative judgments." Charles A. Reich, "The Living Constitution and the Court's Role," in Stephen Parks Strickland, ed., *Hugo Black and the Supreme Court* (Indianapolis: The Bobbs-Merrill Company, 1967), 155.

[62] See footnote 5 in the Introduction.

[63] Orrin Hatch, "Book Review: *The Dangers of Political Law: The Tempting of America: The Political Seduction of the Law*, by Robert H. Bork," 75 *Cornell Law Review* 1338, 1354 (1990).

[64] For John O. McGinnis, the Constitution "lives" and endures because it corresponds to enduring characteristics of human nature. When the Court returns, he argues, to the Framers' view of human nature, confirmed by modern evolutionary biology, "the Constitution – far

distinction and equivalence advanced by the originalist authors of the *Sourcebook*:

Ironically, non-interpretivists have used the phrase "a living Constitution" to describe their approach to constitutional adjudication. But the Constitution is truly living only for those who believe that its original meaning should control its application. It remains vibrant only for those who appreciate the genius underlying its enduring principles; who respect its place as our fundamental law; and who recognize that, while its provisions may be applied to new circumstances as our society changes, its meaning remains fixed and timeless. It is the non-interpretivists, on the other hand, who treat the Constitution as dead, as a dusty relic whose meaning is to be ignored and replaced by the latest trends in social theory, or by the moral predilections of individual federal judges.[65]

Here too the Constitution is living in the sense that it "remains vibrant," has "enduring principles," and is "timeless" in the sense that it does not become a dated, "dusty relic." At the same time, this passage states that the Constitution's meaning "remains fixed," a quality not inconsistent with the special sense in which it is a living document.

Where, then, are we at this point? The conventional originalist view, we have seen, counterposes living to fixed or permanent. The only legitimate sense of living Constitution, a few originalists argue, is that of an enduring Constitution, one that remains meaningful and relevant generation after generation and does not become mere parchment under glass. Nonoriginalists' concept of a living Constitution, on the other hand, is at first glance a document understood, as we have seen, to be a governing text that evolves to meet changing circumstances and whose meaning changes to give expression to the fundamental values of each generation. Yet I would suggest that while they have let their terminology get away from them in their uncritical use of metaphorical language such as evolving, changing, and adapting, nonoriginalists too are engaged in explaining the enduring character of the Constitution. That is, both originalists and nonoriginalists would agree, I believe, that the Constitution has endured and should continue to endure. The difference between them is that what nonoriginalists see as the necessary condition of enduring meaning – viz., the Constitution's capacity to evolve and adapt to changing circumstances – originalists see instead as the dissolution of meaning. Put differently, although superficially the term living

from being a dead hand – will be a living hand beckoning us back to government that better reflects the constraints of human nature. In fact, the original Constitution turns out to be a living Constitution because it was founded on an accurate assessment of the living organism that generates our politics." "The Original Constitution and Our Origins," 19 *Harvard Journal of Law & Public Policy* 251, 261 (1996).

[65] *Sourcebook*, 5. At 1, note 1, this booklet considers "interpretivism" to be synonymous with "originalism" and "original meaning jurisprudence," and "noninterpretivism" to be synonymous with "nonoriginalism." I will argue in Chapter 3 that these terms, while related, are distinct.

Constitution distinguishes and polarizes originalism and nonoriginalism, at a deeper level it is the phenomenon both interpretive theories are trying to explain. The difficulty in explaining the enduring character of the Constitution is that any interpretive theory also must explain the equally important binding character of the Constitution.

That is, any explanation of American constitutionalism must be able to account for both the enduring character and the binding character of the Constitution. The Scylla of constitutional interpretation is that the Constitution might be conceived as so fixed that it becomes out of date, inapplicable, irrelevant; the Charybdis is that it might be conceived as so flexible and living that it ceases to bind. In order to examine the relation between these two factors, we must recall what it is reasonable to consider *the* first principle of American constitutional law and theory. This principle is Chief Justice John Marshall's famous admonition in *McCulloch v. Maryland* that in considering the controversies of constitutional interpretation, "we must never forget that it is a *constitution* we are expounding."[66] On the evidence of Marshall's seminal opinions in *McCulloch* and *Marbury v. Madison*,[67] we can say that this principle embodies two central propositions, propositions from which the originalism debate ultimately derives. First, because it is intended to endure for generations to come, the Constitution is necessarily a highly general document that continually requires interpretation. Marshall writes in *McCulloch*:

The subject is the execution of those great powers on which the welfare of a nation essentially depends. It must have been the intention of those who gave these powers, to insure, as far as human prudence could insure, their beneficial execution. This could not be done by confiding the choice of means to such narrow limits as not to leave it in the power of Congress to adopt any which might be appropriate, and which were conducive to the end. This provision is made in a constitution intended to endure for ages to come, and, consequently, to be adapted to the various crises of human affairs. To have prescribed the means by which government should, in all future time, execute its powers, would have been to change, entirely, the character of the instrument, and give it the properties of a legal code. It would have been an unwise attempt to provide, by immutable rules, for exigencies which, if foreseen at all, must have been seen dimly, and which can be best provided for as they occur.[68]

Despite apparent similarities, the Constitution is not simply a statute, nor is it even a so-called super-statute; it has neither the limited focus and purpose of a statute nor the concrete specificity and detail of a statute.[69] While a

---

[66] *McCulloch v. Maryland*, 17 U.S. 316, 407.
[67] *Marbury v. Madison*, 5 U.S. 137 (1803).
[68] *McCulloch v. Maryland*, 17 U.S. 316, 407.
[69] A statute is a law enacted by a legislature, generally for the purpose of solving social problems and setting down general principles or rules covering specifically defined situations (e.g., tax policy, traffic rules). "An act of the legislature declaring, commanding, or prohibiting

statute usually involves highly technical legal language that often requires professional expertise in its construction, Marshall suggests, a constitution must be general because it is essentially a political document that must be accessible to the citizens of the polity it constitutes. In his well-known words:

A constitution, to contain an accurate detail of all the subdivisions of which its great powers will admit, and of all the means by which they may be carried into execution, would partake of the prolixity of a legal code, and could scarcely be embraced by the human mind. It would probably never be understood by the public. Its nature, therefore, requires, that only its great outlines should be marked, its important objects designated, and the minor ingredients which compose those objects be deduced from the nature of the objects themselves.[70]

As the word "deduced" suggests, interpretation is thus inextricably at the heart of understanding the Constitution, for in order to endure for the ages the document must be written at a level of generality sufficient to allow for application to changing circumstances.[71] Recall Justice Brandeis's citation of *Weems* in *Olmstead* noted previously: "'Time works changes, brings into existence new conditions and purposes. Therefore a principle to be vital must

something; a particular law enacted and established by the will of the legislative department of government; the written will of the legislature, solemnly expressed according to the forms necessary to constitute it the law of the state." *Black's Law Dictionary*, 5th ed. (St. Paul, MN: West Publishing Company, 1978), 1265.

[70] *McCulloch v. Maryland*, 17 U.S. 316, 407. In like manner, Justice Joseph Story discussed the necessary generality of the Constitution in *Martin v. Hunter's Lessee*:

The constitution unavoidably deals in general language. It did not suit the purposes of the people, in framing this great charter of our liberties, to provide for minute specifications of its powers, or to declare the means by which those powers should be carried into execution. It was foreseen that this would be a perilous and difficult, if not an impracticable, task. The instrument was not intended to provide merely for the exigencies of a few years, but was to endure through a long lapse of ages, the events of which were locked up in the inscrutable purposes of Providence. It could not be foreseen what new changes and modifications of power might be indispensable to effectuate the general objects of the charter; and restrictions and specifications, which, at the present, might seem salutary, might, in the end, prove the overthrow of the system itself. Hence its powers are expressed in general terms, leaving to the legislature, from time to time, to adopt its own means to effectuate legitimate objects, and to mould and model the exercise of its powers, as its own wisdom, and the public interests, should require.

14 U.S. 304, 326–7 (1816).

[71] Indeed, the Constitution is not just necessarily general, given its political character, but also unavoidably general, given its legal character: "All new laws, though penned with the greatest technical skill and passed on the fullest and most mature deliberation, are considered as more or less obscure and equivocal, until their meaning be liquidated and ascertained by a series of particular discussions and adjudications." James Madison, *The Federalist Papers*, Clinton Rossiter, ed. (New York: New American Library, 1961), No. 37, 229.

be capable of wider application than the mischief which gave it birth. This is peculiarly true of constitutions.'"[72]

The second proposition embodied in the principle that "it is a *constitution* we are expounding" is closely related to the first one. The reason a constitution must endure, the reason it must be capable of being understood by the public, is that it is intended to be *binding*. Within the American political system the Constitution occupies a unique position: It is fundamental law. Madison referred to this idea in Federalist 53,[73] but the concept of fundamental law was articulated most prominently by Hamilton and Marshall in the context of discussing the legitimacy of judicial review. Thus, Hamilton wrote in Federalist 78:

A constitution is, in fact, and must be regarded by the judges as, a fundamental law. It therefore belongs to them to ascertain its meaning as well as the meaning of any particular act proceeding from the legislative body. If there should happen to be an irreconcilable variance between the two, that which has the superior obligation and validity ought, of course, to be preferred; or, in other words, the Constitution ought to be preferred to the statute, the intention of the people to the intention of their agents.[74]

Though Hamilton's focus was on the role of judges, we see here that the necessary premise of judicial review is that it is the very nature of any constitution worthy of the name to be fundamental law. "There is no position," Hamilton wrote, "which depends on clearer principles than that every act of a delegated authority, contrary to the tenor of the commission under which it is exercised, is void. No legislative act, therefore, contrary to the Constitution, can be valid."[75] Similarly, Marshall held in *Marbury* that "all those who have framed written constitutions contemplate them as forming the fundamental and paramount law of the nation, and consequently the theory of

---

[72] See footnote 50.

[73] Writing that the federal government would be limited by "the authority of a paramount Constitution," he stated that "The important distinction so well understood in America between a Constitution established by the people and unalterable by the government, and a law established by the government and alterable by the government, seems to have been little understood and less observed in any other country." *The Federalist Papers* (No. 53), 331.

[74] Ibid., 467. Hamilton addressed this issue, he said, because "[s]ome perplexity respecting the rights of the courts to pronounce legislative acts void, because contrary to the Constitution, has arisen from an imagination that the doctrine would imply a superiority of the judiciary to the legislative power" (ibid., 466–7).

[75] Ibid., 467. Thomas Paine made this same point: "A constitution is a thing *antecedent* to a government, and a government is only the creature of a constitution. The constitution of a country is not the act of its government, but of the people constituting a government.... A constitution, therefore, is to a government what the laws made afterward by that government are to a court of judicature. The court of judicature does not make the laws, neither can it alter them; it only acts in conformity to the laws made, and the government is in like manner governed by the constitution." Thomas Paine, *The Rights of Man* (New York: Viking Penguin, 1984), 71.

every such government must be, that an act of the legislature, repugnant to the constitution, is void."[76] This, he said, is what it means to have a written constitution.

Given this concept of fundamental law, then, grounded by Hamilton and Marshall in a theory of constitutionalism, we can formulate the central logic of American constitutional reasoning in terms of what in the Introduction I called our constitutional syllogism:

> Premise 1:   If X is contrary to the Constitution, then X is null and void.
> Premise 2:   X is contrary to the Constitution.
> Conclusion: Therefore, X is null and void,

where X is an act of a federal, state, or local legislative, executive, or judicial body. Allowing for the "Who?" and "How?" problems raised by Premise 2,[77] we can see that as the structure of constitutional reasoning, the constitutional syllogism as a whole expresses the idea of binding the future at stake in the concept of fundamental law. What does "binding the future" mean? It means that there are limits on the structure and powers of government that the ordinary processes of government are powerless to alter. The central point running through all originalist writings is that the Constitution is supposed to provide limits on government through the fixity of its meaning. This is an important point, for it is the essential originalist insight: The whole point of having a constitution as fundamental law is to bind the future. This, in and of itself, is neither conservative nor liberal in the ordinary political sense of those terms. Walter Berns has written that the Framers "provided for a Supreme Court and charged it with the task, not of keeping the Constitution in tune with the times but, to the extent possible, of keeping the times in tune with the Constitution."[78] The key to "keeping the times in tune with the Constitution," he claims, is the necessarily *written* nature of the Constitution, for "at the time of our founding most Americans would have agreed with Tom Paine that 'an unwritten constitution is not a constitution at all.'"[79] Madison, Berns writes, gives us the reason: "'The legitimate meaning of the Instrument [of government] must be derived from the text itself,' and that meaning can be confidently ascertained only when the text can be read and not merely recalled."[80] The written, that is, textual, character of the Constitution is, therefore, asserted to be the central precondition of the document's binding capacity, and the belief in the binding capacity of a written constitution, the ability of a text to control the future, is an essential component not just of the American judicial tradition, but

---

[76] *Marbury v. Madison*, 5 U.S. 137, 177.
[77] See Introduction, 4–6.
[78] Berns, *Taking the Constitution Seriously*, 236.
[79] Ibid., 70.
[80] Ibid., 76 (footnote omitted). Text in brackets inserted by Berns.

of the American political tradition as a whole. This is the initial premise of all American constitutional interpretation, and denying it places one outside the bounds of legitimate constitutional debate.[81]

So, when we ask whether living Constitution is an oxymoron, we are asking whether a living Constitution can be a binding Constitution. Some living-Constitution advocates, we noted at the outset, suggested that they are aware of the tension between constraint and flexibility. Beyond those commentators already cited in this regard, even Arthur Miller indicates, perhaps unintentionally, that this tension exists:

> How, then, does the Constitution change through time? Whenever an authoritative text exists through time, the language of which remains substantially intact, there is a need for exegesis through a continuing process of interpretation to update the basic document to new conditions. Necessarily that exegesis has to be articulated in terms of a "living" text or document if the original version, often considered to be sacred, is to be preserved while simultaneously permitting its application to new conditions and new situations.[82]

Reference here to an "authoritative text" and to a need to preserve the "original version" exhibits, even if dimly, an awareness of the binding function of the Constitution. Yet, as we saw, Miller and other nonoriginalists tend to lose sight of the binding function in their emphasis on the living character of the document. In the context of a discussion of hermeneutics, for example, Sheldon Pollack argues that the concept of a living Constitution regards the text as a "forum for pronouncing contemporary values as constitutional values, to be born anew with each successive progression of 'human experiences,'" and that is "bound by nothing other than the contemporary conceptual and moral framework of 'living' justices."[83] Given statements such as these, originalists understandably and legitimately ask what remains of the binding function of the Constitution. Indeed, if the text is in fact a "forum for pronouncing contemporary values as constitutional values," there is not even a "there" – substantive content – there in the Constitution that could be enduring.

By all appearances, then, it would seem that the originalist argument of a living Constitution really is an oxymoron. The Constitution lives in the sense that it endures, but, in order to bind, it cannot live in the sense that it changes or evolves. Nevertheless, I do not believe that the originalist argument wins the day here – but neither do I believe that the nonoriginalist living-Constitution arguments we have seen thus far win the day themselves.

---

[81] The argument that the purpose of a written constitution is to bind the future, and that it is capable of doing so, necessarily challenges, of course, the current deconstructionist argument that texts are inherently indeterminate.

[82] Miller, *The Modern Corporate State*, 9.

[83] "Constitutional Interpretation as Political Choice," 48 *University of Pittsburgh Law Review* 989, 1008 (1987).

Both sides hint – nonoriginalists dimly so, originalists quite surprisingly so – at the distinction between meaning and understanding, a distinction necessary to account for the fact that the Constitution both binds and endures. Given this distinction, not only is a living Constitution a constitution, but also the Constitution must be living to be a constitution. The key difference here is that between a changing Constitution, on the one hand, and changing understandings or interpretations of a permanent Constitution, on the other, and it is fundamental for grasping the nature, the legitimacy, and – yes – the necessity of a concept of a living Constitution.

In nonoriginalist writings such as the representative sample cited earlier, that difference is mostly overlooked, with the result that commentators rather loosely and uncritically talk about a changing and evolving Constitution. This provides, as we have seen, a very easy target for originalist attacks. In some living-Constitution writings that themselves are not unrepresentative, however, one can find a subtle but definite and important distinction between a changing Constitution and changing understandings of a permanent Constitution. Thus, while Morton Horwitz off-handedly but all the more revealingly mentions the "idea of a 'living' or changing constitution,"[84] suggesting a terminological equivalence, Barry Friedman argues that "the very idea of a living Constitution requires that its language be spacious, accommodating varying interpretations over time."[85] In another instance, Martin H. Redish and Karen L. Drizin write: "We do not mean to suggest that interpretations of the Constitution may not change over time. Given the broad constitutional language and acceptance of the Constitution as a 'living' document, such changes are not precluded."[86] Or again, talking about the concept of a living Constitution, Philip Hamburger writes:

Commentators have frequently assumed that constitutional law inevitably changes or at least should change with developments in American society – a position traditionally espoused under the rubric of a "living constitution." From this point of view, both new applications of the Constitution and changes in the nature of our society may require alterations in the rules and generalizations that comprise much of our constitutional law. As America has developed, so too, it is said, has our understanding of due process and other constitutional categories.[87]

---

[84] "The Constitution of Change: Legal Fundamentality without Fundamentalism," 107 *Harvard Law Review* 32, 41 (1993). As the title of this article indicates, Horwitz suggests – persuasively – a parallel with religion: "Originalists and constitutional literalists are fundamentalists. The argument about a living Constitution versus originalism is parallel to the question of modern and adaptable religion versus the old time religion." "The Meaning of the Bork Nomination," 655, 663.

[85] "Dialogue and Judicial Review," 91 *Michigan Law Review* 577, 649 (1993) (footnote omitted).

[86] "Constitutional Federalism and Judicial Review: The Role of Textual Analysis," 62 *New York University Law Review* 1, 29 (1987) (note 110).

[87] "The Constitution's Accommodation of Social Change," 88 *Michigan Law Review* 239, 242–3 (1989). Hamburger goes on to suggest that to meet changing circumstances constitutional

In all of these cases, the commentators speak of changing interpretations rather than a changing Constitution, a distinction that preserves the idea of a fixed or permanent Constitution that is subject to differing and, one hopes, improving understanding. At the same time, one must still acknowledge the preponderance of talk in nonoriginalist writings about a changing Constitution, talk that gets those living-Constitution advocates into political and theoretical trouble.

While I suggested that nonoriginalists dimly hint at the distinction between meaning and understanding, I also said that originalists themselves draw such a distinction, albeit implicitly, and that it is surprising that they do so. When emphasizing the distinction between the Constitution and constitutional law, as Reagan's Attorney General Meese did in a speech published as "The Law of the Constitution"[88] and as Gary McDowell did in his Berger review cited earlier,[89] originalists get more than they bargained for. They argue for the claim that our understanding changes and, presumably, improves, and that is what living-Constitution advocates really mean despite their loose terminology. To explain this at least unusual if not alarming claim, I first must set out a brief analysis of the structure of the essential originalist argument.

If my characterization of originalism is fair and accurate, as I think it is, then we can say that the premise that underlies and unites all forms of the theory is the normative status of the interpretive context of 1787. Specifically, the characteristic and controversial move of originalism is its translation of the claim that in constitutional interpretation we should be bound by the text of the Constitution – the essential originalist insight – into the proposition, generally definitive of originalism in all of its specific forms, that the original understanding of the constitutional text always trumps any contrary understanding of that text in succeeding generations. Let me try to present this in a somewhat more formal manner. In defining originalism in the Introduction, I distinguished between two claims:

P_1: What binds the future is the constitutional text.
P_2: What binds the future is the original understanding of the constitutional text.

Originalism, I said, denies the possibility of such a distinction, while I do not. What differences are in play here? I argue that Proposition 2 is a narrower claim than Proposition 1 in that we can deny the authoritativeness of the original understanding of the Constitution and yet still affirm the authoritativeness of the Constitution – that is, the text – itself. Originalism, in

---

law must be flexible, and that such flexibility requires that the Constitution must be relatively indeterminate. Without being able to pursue this here, I would suggest simply that the distinction between meaning and understanding might be a way around this claim.

[88] Edwin Meese, "The Law of the Constitution," 61 *Tulane Law Review* 979 (1987).
[89] 51 *George Washington Law Review* 624, 629.

contrast, sees Proposition 1 and Proposition 2 as identical, such that the denial of the authoritativeness of the original understanding of the Constitution necessarily amounts to a denial of the authoritativeness of the Constitution itself.

How does all this relate to conventional nonoriginalism and its concept of the living Constitution? First, nonoriginalists reject, as I just did, Proposition 2, the claim that what binds the future is the original understanding of the constitutional text. Yet – and here is the key – if nonoriginalists tacitly accept the originalist premise that Proposition 1 and Proposition 2 are equivalent, then their rejection of the claim that what binds the future is the original understanding of the constitutional text necessarily implies, as originalists maintain, the rejection of the claim that what binds the future is the constitutional text. It is precisely this that enables originalists to claim that, in its usual sense, the concept of a living Constitution is an oxymoron – and conventional nonoriginalists seem to fall right into this trap. Yet if one were, as I propose, to reject this premise of equivalence and argue that we can deny the authoritativeness of the original understanding of the Constitution and yet still affirm the authoritativeness of the Constitution itself, then we have the possibility of talking about a binding and enduring Constitution in nonoriginalist terms.

An interesting way of representing this argument is to ask whether the writers and ratifiers of a given constitutional provision could have been mistaken about its meaning. If we answer that they could indeed be mistaken about it, then we seem to be committed to saying that the text constitutionalized certain principles – *not* the writers' and ratifiers' understanding of those principles – and that any understanding of those principles is relative to changing circumstances and is capable of improvement. But this is simply to assert the distinction between meaning and understanding that differentiates between a changing Constitution and changing understandings of a permanent Constitution. The consequence, significantly, is that nonoriginalism and the concept of a living Constitution become legitimate. On the other hand, if we answer that the writers and ratifiers could not be mistaken about the meaning of the Constitution, as I think originalism would argue, then we are committed to saying that the text constitutionalized, not certain principles per se, but specifically the original understanding of those principles. This, however, is to deny the distinction between meaning and understanding, but the surprise is that such a denial undermines the difference between the Constitution and constitutional law controversially, but I think properly, advocated by former Attorney General Meese.

Briefly, the distinction between the Constitution and constitutional law is, according to Meese, a necessary distinction "essential to maintaining our limited form of government."[90] On the one hand, the Constitution is the

---

[90] Meese, "The Law of the Constitution," 979, 981.

binding, authoritative norm in American society. "The Constitution," he says on this point, "is – to put it simply but one hopes not simplistically – the Constitution. It is a document of our most fundamental law."[91] The distinction in question is this:

Constitutional law, on the other hand, is that body of law that has resulted from the Supreme Court's adjudications involving disputes over constitutional provisions or doctrines. To put it a bit more simply, constitutional law is what the Supreme Court says about the Constitution in its decisions resolving the cases and controversies that come before it.[92]

It is not inaccurate, I suggest, to say that the argument here is that constitutional law represents the Court's understanding of the meaning of the Constitution as it applies in particular cases. If that is so, then Meese's concern is to distinguish between the meaning of the Constitution, which is always authoritative, and the Court's understanding of that meaning, which is fallible. Thus, citing Charles Warren, he writes that "what's most important to remember is that [h]owever the Court may interpret the provisions of the Constitution, it is still the Constitution which is the law and not the decision of the Court."[93] The assumption of fallibility, according to Meese, is crucial:

The Supreme Court would face quite a dilemma if its own constitutional decisions really were the supreme law of the land, binding on all persons and governmental entities, including the Court itself, for then the court would not be able to change its mind. It could not overrule itself in a constitutional case.[94]

By thus distinguishing between the Constitution and constitutional law and establishing the fallibility of the Court, Meese then reaches his goal: "If a constitutional decision is not the same as the Constitution itself, if it is not binding in the same way that the Constitution is, we as citizens may respond to a decision with which we disagree."[95] That is, beyond the parties to a particular case, everyone – ordinary citizens and governmental officials alike – is bound first and foremost by the Constitution itself and not by the Court's understanding of the Constitution.

Now, put succinctly, my argument is that the necessary condition of validly proclaiming a distinction between the Constitution and constitutional law is the assumption that our understanding of the Constitution is subject to correction, revision, and improvement. Yet this assumption must imply that we can have a changing understanding of a fixed document, which is the relation

---

[91] Ibid., 981.
[92] Ibid., 982.
[93] Ibid., 983, referring to Charles Warren, *The Supreme Court in United States History* (Boston: Little, Brown and Company, 1923), 460–71.
[94] Ibid., 983.
[95] Ibid., 985.

Meese asserts between constitutional law and the Constitution. Thus, if an originalist comes up with historical evidence that radically revises the way we see the Constitution, has the meaning changed or has our understanding changed (and improved)? The originalist would have to say the latter; that is, that not the Constitution but rather our understanding changed. In other words, it is not that we have chosen to ignore the Constitution; instead, we claim to have a better understanding of what it means in the circumstances at hand.

If this is the case, however, it undercuts the usual attack by originalists on constitutional decisions with which they disagree. Consider the argument by Thomas Grey, with whom we began this discussion, that much of our settled contemporary constitutional law is incompatible with originalist jurisprudence.[96] Assuming the inconsistency of such things as fundamental-rights adjudication and incorporation with originalist interpretation, as Grey does, we have two alternatives. On the one hand, we can accept the norms of originalist interpretation and tear the offending decisions out of the fabric of our settled law, an admittedly radical approach. On the other hand, we can reject the norms of originalist interpretation and seek to justify the decisions at issue by some other, nonoriginalist interpretive theory. Grey, to recall, adopts in this article the latter alternative. But what about the initial assumption that fundamental-rights adjudication and the incorporation doctrine are inconsistent with originalist interpretation? By accepting this, Grey gives the game away right at the start. One could argue instead that they are not inconsistencies but rather better understandings of the meaning of the Constitution as it is applied in the particular circumstances. In this sense, *Brown v. Board of Education,*[97] for example, is not an illegitimate and nonoriginalist departure from *Plessy v. Ferguson;*[98] instead, it is simply but importantly a better understanding of the meaning of equal protection than the *Plessy* Court had. In a second example, the Court itself implies this notion of a changing and improving understanding of a fixed meaning in *Wallace v. Jaffree,* a 1985 religion-clause case:

Just as the right to speak and the right to refrain from speaking are complementary components of a broader concept of individual freedom of mind, so also the individual's freedom to choose his own creed is the counterpart of his right to refrain from accepting the creed established by the majority. *At one time it was thought that this right*

[96] Grey, "Do We Have an Unwritten Constitution?" 27 *Stanford Law Review* 703 (1975). Grey, to recall, uses the term "interpretivist" where I use "originalist." For a similar argument focused upon Justice Antonin Scalia's originalism, see Cass R. Sunstein, "Justice Scalia's Democratic Formalism," 107 *Yale Law Journal* 529 (1997), who writes at 564 that from Scalia's perspective "most of modern constitutional law, now taken as constitutive of the American constitutional tradition by Americans and non-Americans alike ... is illegitimate and fatally undemocratic."

[97] 347 U.S. 483 (1954).
[98] 163 U.S. 537 (1896).

merely proscribed the preference of one Christian sect over another, but would not require equal respect for the conscience of the infidel, the atheist, or the adherent of a non-Christian faith such as Islam or Judaism. But when the underlying principle has been examined in the crucible of litigation, the Court has unambiguously concluded that the individual freedom of conscience protected by the First Amendment embraces the right to select any religious faith or none at all. This conclusion derives support not only from the interest in respecting the individual's freedom of conscience, but also from the conviction that religious beliefs worthy of respect are the product of free and voluntary choice by the faithful, and from recognition of the fact that the political interest in forestalling intolerance extends beyond intolerance among Christian sects – or even intolerance among "religions" – to encompass intolerance of the disbeliever and the uncertain.[99]

Simply put, the Court claims that we understand the meaning of the religion clauses better now than we did at an early time, and that is not to say that the meaning itself has changed. And, as a last example here, we could ask, did the meaning of the Declaration of Independence change, disallowing the slavery that many people did not consider inconsistent with its principles in 1776, or did people come to understand that meaning differently, and better, by deciding that slavery was indeed inconsistent with the Declaration? Clearly, I suggest, most people would accept the latter explanation.

An interesting attempt to theorize this notion of the Constitution as a text with a fixed meaning subject to potentially changing understandings appears in Lawrence Lessig's articles "Fidelity in Translation"[100] and "Understanding Changed Readings: Fidelity and Theory."[101] Pointing to the brute fact that readings of the Constitution change, Lessig writes with particular regard to the changed readings of the New Deal that most commentators "have assumed that unless one could show either (1) that the readings of the Constitution for the forty years before the New Deal had been wrong, or (2) that some political act sufficed to authorize this judicial transformation, then (3) the changed readings of the New Deal would remain unjustified. Given the choices, a few pick (2), most follow (1), and the balance (conservatives or cynics) choose (3)."[102] If readings of the Constitution prior to the New Deal were indeed wrong, then certainly changed readings afterward could be conceptualized as a return to the correct, original meaning of the text, whereas if the readings were not wrong, then any changed readings would be, as in Lessig's third category, unjustified. Those in his second category, most prominently Bruce Ackerman in *We the People I: Foundations*,[103] accept that the readings of the Constitution prior to the New Deal were indeed correct but wish to justify and legitimize those changed readings nevertheless.

---

[99] 472 U.S. 38, 52–3 (1985), (emphasis added).
[100] 71 *Texas Law Review* 1165 (1993).
[101] 47 *Stanford Law Review* 395 (1995).
[102] "Understanding Changed Readings," 400.
[103] Cambridge, MA: Belknap Press of Harvard University Press (1991).

By contrast, if nonoriginalists accept the originalists' premise that controversial readings of the Constitution are indeed nonoriginalist but seek to justify them anyway, Lessig proposes a way to reject that initial premise. He wants to argue that "we have long recognized cases where, in the face of changes in context, the proper act of fidelity is a changed reading of the constitutional text – constitutional change, that is, without constitutional amendment."[104] Such phrasing, of course, raises in its presumably unintended carelessness a red flag, for the notion of constitutional change without constitutional amendment invites the originalist charge of illegitimacy that Lessig wants to rebut. He is more accurate – and, indeed, wants – to talk of "a changed reading of the constitutional text" as something distinct from constitutional change without constitutional amendment. The central concept Lessig employs to develop and justify this distinction is the concept of translation. "If context matters to meaning," he writes, understanding context as "that range of facts, or values, or assumptions, or structures, or patterns of thought that are relevant to an author's use of words to convey meaning,"[105] "and if contexts may change, then the reader focused on fidelity needs a way to *neutralize* or *accommodate* the effect that changing context may have on meaning. Fidelity, that is, needs a way of reading that preserves meaning despite changes in context."[106] It is context, in brief, that necessitates translation, for the task of translation "is always to determine how to change one text into another text, while preserving the original text's meaning."[107]

The problem posed by changing interpretive contexts, Lessig writes, is the opening of an interpretive gap:

Between the context of writing and the context of reading, then, there may arise an interpretive gap. And it is this gap that suggests the general problem that gives rise to the subject of this essay. When the interpretive gap is small – when the context of writing is very similar to the context of reading – the confusion caused by differences between contexts may also be quite small. Reading can proceed as if context did not matter. Judges can say interpretation begins as always with the text read as if interpretation really did involve just a text that is read. When contexts remain alike they may also remain invisible.

But when the gap is not small – when the differences between contexts become quite large – then reading cannot proceed as if context did not matter. Or at least it cannot so proceed if contextualism is correct and the aim of the reader is something like interpretive fidelity. For if contextualism is correct, and a change in context is ignored, the reader may rewrite the writer's original meaning.[108]

---

[104] "Understanding Changed Readings," 400.
[105] "Fidelity in Translation," 1178.
[106] Ibid., 1177.
[107] Ibid., 1173.
[108] Ibid., 1176.

It is against this background that Lessig argues that interpretive change can actually constitute interpretive fidelity. Because, in his words, "[t]he interpreter of fidelity seeks *readings* of legal *texts* in the current interpretive *context* that preserve the *meaning* of an earlier reading in an earlier context,"[109] it follows that

[i]f meaning is a function of text in context, then it should be clear that in at least some cases, a changed reading could be consistent with fidelity. For some changed readings simply accommodate changes in context, by aiming to find a reading in the new context that has the same meaning as a different reading had in a different context.[110]

Lessig's main argument, therefore, is "(1) that change in light of changed presuppositions is the essence of fidelity; and (2) that refusing to change in light of changed circumstances would be infidelity.... Sometimes change is essential for fidelity."[111]

To make that argument, Lessig distinguishes between interpretive approaches he calls "one-step" fidelity and "two-step" fidelity. The one step of the former and the first of the two steps of the latter are, he says, the same: reading the text in its original context. For the one-step approach, however, this one step suffices:

For with this first step, the one-step believes the problem of fidelity both begins and ends – that once we find meaning in the originating context (the context of writing) we simply apply that meaning in the context of application (the context of reading) as if any differences between the context of writing and the context of reading just did not matter. Fidelity, the one-step believes, means applying the original text *now* the same as it would have been applied *then*.[112]

The problem with one-step fidelity, Lessig argues, is that it does not distinguish between the original context of meaning and the original context of the application of that meaning. His explanation is somewhat less than felicitous, but his point is clear enough:

If we speak of the application's meaning, then we must consider the application itself to be a text. And as with any text, its meaning is a function of its context. Here, then, begins the problem faced by the two-step. For while contextualism teaches that we read the original text in the original context, we have no choice but to make an application, not in the original context, but in the current context. If the original and current contexts differ, then the meaning of the same application in the two contexts may differ as well.[113]

---

109 "Understanding Changed Readings," 410.
110 Ibid., 403.
111 "Fidelity in Translation," 1217.
112 Ibid., 1183 (footnote omitted).
113 Ibid., 1184.

The problem with one-step fidelity, in other words, is that it "fails to preserve meaning across interpretive contexts. It fails because, although sensitive to the effects of context upon meaning in the *original* context, it is blind to the effects of context upon the *application* meaning in the *application* context." [114] Consequently, Lessig maintains, there is a risk that one-step fidelity, of which at least some forms of originalism are examples, "by ignoring changes in context, changes rather than preserves meaning. In these cases, the one-step originalist defeats rather than advances fidelity." [115]

By contrast, according to Lessig, two-step fidelity seeks to translate, and thus preserve, the original meaning of the text in its original context into the equivalent meaning as applied in a later, current context. At length, he writes:

What distinguishes the two-step fidelitist from the one-step is that the two-step seeks a way to preserve the meaning of the *application* in just the way the one-step agrees we should preserve the meaning of the *text*. The one-step and two-step read a text against its original context so that its meaning in the original context is preserved; the two-step reads the meaning of the application *as applied in the current context* so that the meaning of the application is the same in the original and current context. Thus, while the one-step applies the text now and here just as it would have been then and there, the two-step asks how to apply the text now and here so as to preserve the meaning of an application then and there – how, that is, to make the meaning of the current application equivalent to the meaning of an original application, or alternatively, how to *translate* the original application into the current context. [116]

This is why the concept of translation appears to Lessig to have such rich potential, for he says that "translation is that process by which texts in one language are transformed into texts of another language, by constructing a text in the second language with the same meaning as the text in the first." [117] In the domain of legal interpretation, he writes: "The legislature *said* X, and the two-step, respecting the change in interpretive contexts, wants to *say* Y, because only Y will mean now what X meant then. The two-step seeks a practice that empowers her to change in the name of fidelity, and translation is the model for any such practice." [118] In the manner of true

---

[114] Ibid., 1189.

[115] Ibid., 1188.

[116] Ibid., 1184–5 (footnotes omitted). As he states in his later article: "What changes across contexts is the *application*, or as I will call it, the *reading* of the legal text in context. What the lawyer or court does is find a *reading* a legal text [*sic*] in a new context, so as to preserve the meaning of an earlier reading of the legal text in an earlier context." "Understanding Changed Readings," 402.

[117] "Fidelity in Translation," 1189.

[118] Ibid., 1192. "If meaning is a function of text in context, then it should be clear that in at least some cases, a changed reading could be consistent with fidelity. For some changed readings simply accommodate changes in context, by aiming to find a reading in the new context that has the same meaning as a different reading had in a different context." "Understanding Changed Readings," 403.

Burkean conservatism, then, Lessig argues that at times it is only change that allows for preservation; interpretive change can actually be the only way to ensure interpretive fidelity. The concept of translation appears useful because it involves both creativity – putting the meaning of a text written in one language into another language – and constraint – *preserving* the meaning of a text written in one language as it comes to appear in another language.[119]

Lessig's use of the concept of translation is an extremely interesting, if not ingenious, attempt to develop a theory of what I have called in this chapter the distinction between the fixed meaning of a text and the potentially variable understandings of that text.[120] It purports to save originalist goals from originalism itself. Nevertheless, it is worth noting that at least in one crucial respect Lessig's concept of translation remains locked within the originalist premises he seeks to escape: He holds, perhaps unintentionally, to the essentially positivist foundations of originalism.[121] Consider this description Lessig gives of the basic task of legal interpretation: "Like the interlanguage translation of texts, interpretation in law proceeds first by understanding the sense or meaning of the text at issue in its original context (familiarity); the problem of fidelity is how to preserve that significance in the current context (equivalence)."[122] As legal interpreters, in other words, our job is to understand the meaning of the text in its original context and then, separately, *apply* that meaning in the current context.

Yet consider next the concept of translation that Lessig borrows from Reuben Brower and endorses in his argument:

For in every act of reading or understanding, we read what was said against the background of some context, find a meaning, and carry that meaning into a context of our own. If these interpretive contexts differ, not just in language but also "by

---

[119] That constraint, Lessig holds, rests on what he calls "structural humility" and "humility of capacity." See "Fidelity in Translation," 1251–63.

[120] At the end of his lengthy article, however, Lessig startles us with the comment that the distance between the Framers' time and our time has possibly become too great even for translation to work. "Perhaps," he writes in his penultimate paragraph,

> it is time to rewrite our Constitution, written in a language long lost and forgotten, with ideals and expectations too far from the ordinary ken of constitutional readers, in a language we once again understand, with a meaning that is once again our own. We are like the person who finds himself at the store, with a list he can no longer make out, struggling to reconstruct what it must have been that he wanted to buy; at some point it may make sense simply to decide again what he wants, to rewrite the list, to give up the obsession that it must be the same as the old list, to move on.

"Fidelity in Translation," 1268. The explosive political potential of this strategy is mind-boggling. If the Constitution provides the framework within which we argue and negotiate our political differences, Lessig's suggestion opens up the probability of differences and conflicts of an even more fundamental nature.

[121] I will treat this issue at length in Chapters 6 and 7 on the question of what I call the "epistemology of constitutional discourse."

[122] Lessig, "Fidelity in Translation," 1211.

distance in space and time within a single language," then, in a sense, translation of some form always occurs. Commonsense translation is just a special case of the process of translation that occurs everywhere.[123]

Lessig's citation of Brower here, however, proves too much. It says, essentially, that all reading, all understanding, is interpretation. Indeed, Lessig states that "Every act of communication, the theorist of translation asserts, is an act of translation."[124] Yet Lessig said, as I noted in the preceding paragraph, that we first read the original meaning and then translate it in order to apply it to the present situation. But to read and understand the original meaning in the first place already requires, by Brower's account, translation. Lessig smuggles in the notion, characteristic of the epistemologically positivist premises of originalism, of the brute facticity of meaning: We *discover* meaning and then, in the act of application, we *interpret* it.

At least in this form, whether or not it would be Lessig's considered view, the assumption here is that one can determine the originating context independently of the context of application and vice versa. Lessig would have done well to have consulted an article by David Couzens Hoy entitled "A Hermeneutical Critique of the Originalism/Nonoriginalism Distinction."[125] In the context of a critique of Michael Perry's *Morality, Politics, and Law*,[126] Hoy writes: "The idea that there is a sharp distinction between original meaning and present meaning arises, I believe, from believing that there is also a distinction between understanding the meaning of a text, and applying that meaning in a present context."[127] On the basis of such a belief, says Hoy, the interpretive process is understood to involve two distinct steps:

The first moment of interpretation is to ascertain the *meaning* of the text. The second, separate moment is then to ascertain its *significance*. The meaning of the text is what we grasp in the moment of understanding the text, and the text's significance is generated in the second, separate moment of applying that initial understanding to the present situation.[128]

By contrast, Hoy argues, "[Hans-Georg] Gadamer's notion of application describes a prior cognitive operation where we first find the text to be saying something to us. In finding that the text is at all intelligible, the moment of application, as Gadamer understands it, has already taken place for us."[129] Thus, the understanding–application distinction is on this view impossible. We do not, and cannot, first understand what the text means and then,

---

[123] Ibid., 1190 (footnotes omitted), citing Reuben A. Brower, Introduction to Reuben A. Brower, ed., *On Translation* (Oxford: Oxford University Press, 1966), 3.

[124] "Fidelity in Translation," 1190.

[125] 15 *Northern Kentucky Law Review* 479 (1988).

[126] For my own critique of Perry, see especially Chapter 6.

[127] Hoy, "A Hermeneutical Critique of the Originalism/Nonoriginalism Distinction," 491.

[128] Ibid., 492 (footnote omitted).

[129] Ibid., 493.

independently, apply it to the present context. Understanding and application are strictly a package deal. "If understanding always involves interpretation and application," Hoy writes, "then the originalist theory that we should ascertain the original meaning by itself before seeing how it pertains to our present cases is an artificial characterization of what understanding the law involves."[130] In this light, by maintaining that we first determine the meaning of a text in its original context and then translate that meaning into the current context in order to apply it, Lessig remains firmly within the originalist premises he seems to attempt to escape. Nevertheless, he offers a sophisticated if flawed account of the distinction between meaning and understanding.

To maintain the distinction between the Constitution and constitutional law, then, we have to consider the Constitution to be the fixed meaning and constitutional law to be our potentially variable understanding (interpretation). That leaves us able to revise the latter in terms of the former. Distinguishing between meaning and understanding acknowledges the fallibility of the latter and allows for the possibility of criticizing the Court in particular and of democratic constitutional discourse in general. My claim is that both originalism and conventional nonoriginalism fail to grasp the significance of this point. If conventional nonoriginalism, so to speak, absorbs the Constitution into constitutional law, such that the Constitution becomes nothing more than what the judges say it is, then originalism typically absorbs constitutional law into the Constitution, with the consequence that originalist interpretation is not just an understanding of the meaning of the Constitution, but the Constitution itself, such that if we disagree with the originalist interpretation we are breaching the boundaries of legitimate constitutional interpretation. We must therefore be careful about the notion of a "constantly changing society" that comes up in arguments over the concept of a living Constitution. The premise of constitutionalism is the idea that the problems of politics and government endure throughout social change, yet neither originalism nor conventional nonoriginalism gives sufficient attention to the difference between new problems and new forms of old problems. Where originalism seems to focus on old problems and conventional nonoriginalism on ostensibly new problems, the concept of a living Constitution presupposes the notion of new forms of old problems.

In that light, perhaps the only meaningful and legitimate sense of a living Constitution lies in the position that Charles Reich ascribes to Justice Hugo Black in "The Living Constitution and the Court's Role." Black, of course, claimed to reject the idea of a living Constitution:

I realize that many good and able men have eloquently spoken and written, sometimes in rhapsodical strains, about the duty of this Court to keep the Constitution in tune

---

[130] Ibid., 497.

with the times. The idea is that the Constitution must be changed from time to time and that this Court is charged with a duty to make those changes. For myself, I must with all deference reject that philosophy.[131]

For Black, whom originalists generally claim as one of their own, the concept of a living Constitution threatened to make the Constitution mean both less than it does (e.g., *Adamson v. California*) and more than it does (e.g., *Griswold v. Connecticut*), in that it could mean failing to protect as rights some claims that *are* rights and protecting as rights claims that are not rights. Nevertheless, Reich makes a persuasive case that Black's judicial philosophy points implicitly to a workable concept of a living Constitution that provides the only coherent account of how the document remains both enduring and binding. Reich sets out Black's approach in this passage:

By "faithful adherence" Black has demanded adherence to the spirit and objectives of the Bill of Rights, rather than to any particular interpretation of its provisions. His approach is functional in nature. He asks what a given provision of the Bill of Rights was designed to accomplish – what evils it was intended to prevent. Then he seeks to give the provision a meaning which will, in a contemporary setting, accomplish the same general purposes and prevent the same kinds of evils.[132]

I would qualify this description by saying that, following Reich, when Black asks "what a given provision of the Bill of Rights was designed to accomplish," he is inquiring into the meaning of the provision; and when Black "seeks to give the provision a meaning which will, in a contemporary setting, accomplish the same general purposes and prevent the same kinds of evils," he is not "giving a meaning" but rather proposing his understanding of the meaning. The former is fixed; the latter is variable.

If that is Black's approach to constitutional adjudication, then Reich lays out the rationale that justifies it in this central passage:

How can a dynamic conception of a constitution be squared with a literal one? The answer is that in a dynamic society the Bill of Rights must keep changing in its application or lose even its original meaning. There is no such thing as a constitutional provision with a static meaning. If it stays the same while other provisions of the Constitution change and society itself changes, the provision will atrophy. That, indeed, is what has happened to some of the safeguards of the Bill of Rights. A constitutional provision can maintain its integrity only by moving in the same direction and at the same rate as the rest of society. In constitutions, constancy requires change.[133]

As paradoxical as this argument sounds, it is essentially the Burkean notion of preservation through change, as opposed to the standard originalist concept of the Constitution that amounts to standing athwart history, yelling

[131] *Griswold v. Connecticut*, 381 U.S. 479, 522 (Black, dissenting) (1965).
[132] Reich, 139.
[133] Ibid., 141–2.

"Stop!" The Burkean preservation-through-change concept of a living Constitution is more truly conservative, Reich's characterization of Black's philosophy implies, than the concept of the permanent Constitution advocated by contemporary conservatives. In Reich's words again:

Thus it is paradoxical but true that Justice Black's constitutional philosophy, although it embodies motion and change, is in a large sense devoted to maintaining the Bill of Rights in its original significance. What he has really sought in the language and history of the Bill of Rights is its spirit and purpose, and these he has tried to keep constant. Moving almost by instinct, he has developed a functional doctrine of an unchanging Bill of Rights.[134]

Yet, significantly, it follows that just as a person heading up on a down escalator can stay in the same place only by moving forward, the preservation of the original meaning of the Constitution in the face of continual social change requires an active Supreme Court:

To obey the law, to preserve it in any true sense, surely can mean nothing less than to keep its spirit functioning – to see that it continues to achieve the objectives for which it was originally designed. This takes more than a passive Court. It requires a Court that sees, understands, and creates – and then actively enforces the law in its current setting so that it becomes a reality for the people. Only when given life by such a Court can the law "rule."[135]

Is the Court, then, a continuing constitutional convention in the sense that Walter Berns opposes? No. *In keeping the times in tune with the Constitution, on this conception, the Court is keeping the Constitution in tune with the times. These are thus not opposed positions, as originalism and conventional nonoriginalism presume, but rather two sides of the same coin.*

So, finally, is living Constitution an oxymoron? The burden of my discussion and argument has been this: Against originalists I would say, no, living Constitution is not an oxymoron; against conventional nonoriginalists I would say, no, it is not an oxymoron – but not in the sense and for the reasons they think. Significantly, this plays out in the distinction I draw between interpretivism and originalism, to which we now turn.

---

[134] Ibid., 142.
[135] Ibid., 160.

3

Interpretivism and Originalism

The essential insight of the originalist paradigm in contemporary American constitutional theory is the proposition that the purpose of a constitution is to bind the future to a fixed, fundamental norm. Particularly noteworthy is the suggestion that it is the function of a constitution to stand as a bulwark against at least some aspects of historical change. A constitution, that is, exists not to facilitate change, for change is the norm. Rather, a constitution, insofar as it binds the future to a fixed, fundamental norm, exists to manage change, that is, to impose a structure on change, to channel it in some prescribed manner in accordance with that fixed, fundamental norm.[1]

We thus encounter here the political manifestation of the classic philosophical problem of the relationship between permanence and change: The principle of permanence is represented by the Constitution, and the principle of change is represented by majority rule. In a constitutional democracy, where society is governed for the most part but not entirely by majority rule, a constitution plays a dual role. At one level, it secures to popular majorities and their representatives a space in which they may act freely to legislate certain rules and policies binding on everyone in society regardless of one's values or preferences to the contrary. In this sense we can say that a constitution enables or empowers majority rule, and thus does accommodate change. However, more fundamentally, a constitution establishes the outer boundaries of the space within which popular majorities may act. The key to a constitution's capacity to establish boundaries and thus structure and channel historical change is its written, textual character and its concomitant fixity of meaning.

---

[1] "Adherence to the text and original understanding arguably constrains the discretion of decisionmakers and assures that the Constitution will be interpreted consistently over time." Paul Brest, "The Misconceived Quest for the Original Understanding," 60 *Boston University Law Review* 204, 204 (1980).

Originalism plants its flag on this notion of fixity of meaning. Should there arise a distinction between the original understanding and a current understanding of a particular constitutional provision, the original understanding is the authoritative, legally binding understanding. The characteristic and controversial move of originalism is to translate the broad principle that interpreters should be bound by the constitutional text into the narrower principle, generally definitive of originalism in its particular forms, that interpreters should be bound by the writers' and ratifiers' understanding of the constitutional text. Originalism, that is, holds that the "original understanding" of the Constitution is privileged: The original understanding of the constitutional text in the writing-and-ratifying generation always trumps any different understanding of that text in succeeding generations. Jefferson Powell puts this point succinctly:

> The central tenet of originalism as it is often understood is the existence of a clear demarcation between the original meaning of a constitutional provision and its subsequent interpretation. The originalist, we are told, is the interpreter who knows the difference and acknowledges it by according authority to the founders rather than to their successors.[2]

As we shall see, the determination of what counts as evidence of "the original meaning of a constitutional provision" is, of course, fundamental. Originalists themselves differ as to evidence of original understanding. For some, original understanding is grounded in the intentions of the framers – the authors – of particular constitutional provisions, the position I shall call "hard originalism"; for others, original understanding is grounded in the understanding of the ratifiers – the first readers – of particular constitutional provisions, the position I shall call "soft originalism."[3] Both versions, however, subscribe to the more general principle that in constitutional interpretation the normative context of interpretation is that of those who wrote and ratified the language in question rather than that of any later interpreters. That is, originalism argues that the necessary check on our understanding of the text of the Constitution is the original understanding of the text of

---

[2] H. Jefferson Powell, "Rules for Originalists," 73 *Virginia Law Review* 659, 676 (1987). Also see Raoul Berger, "Originalist Theories of Constitutional Interpretation," 73 *Cornell Law Review* 350, 350–1 (1988), and Richard Saphire, "Enough about Originalism," 15 *Northern Kentucky Law Review* 513, 516 (1988).

[3] Cass Sunstein suggests that there are two forms of originalism, hard and soft, but his use of these terms is somewhat different from my own. See Cass Sunstein, "Five Theses on Originalism," 19 *Harvard Journal of Law & Public Policy* 311 (1996). "For the hard originalist," he writes at 312, "we are trying to do something like go back in a time machine and ask the Framers very specific questions about how we ought to resolve very particular problems." "For the soft originalist," he continues at 313, "it matters very much what history shows; but the soft originalist will take the Framers' understanding at a certain level of abstraction or generality."

the Constitution. By ensuring that subsequent generations do not substitute their own purposes or understandings for those of the original writers and ratifiers, originalism is supposed to regulate the conduct of constitutional interpretation in order to guarantee that judges, unelected, do not enforce their personal values against the rest of us. In this way, the appeal of originalism arises from its emphasis on binding capacity as its specific essence and as that of constitutionalism generally. The written, that is, textual, character of the Constitution is, therefore, asserted to be the central precondition of the document's binding capacity, and the belief in the binding capacity of a written constitution, the ability of a text to control the future, is an essential component not just of the American judicial tradition, but of the American political tradition as a whole.

Given this essential character of constitutionalism, it is not surprising to find references to the ideas of fundamental norm and fixed meaning in Supreme Court cases prior to what we today understand as the originalism debate. A few such cases are illustrative. First, in perhaps the most infamous case in U.S. Supreme Court history, *Dred Scott v. Sandford*,[4] Chief Justice Roger Taney, justifying the opinion of the Court, articulated at length the contrast between the permanence of constitutional meaning and the variability of majority rule:

No one, we presume, supposes that any change in public opinion or feeling, in relation to this unfortunate race, in the civilized nations of Europe or in this country, should induce the court to give to the words of the Constitution a more liberal construction in their favor than they were intended to bear when the instrument was framed and adopted. Such an argument would be altogether inadmissible in any tribunal called on to interpret it. If any of its provisions are deemed unjust, there is a mode prescribed in the instrument itself by which it may be amended; but while it remains unaltered, it must be construed now as it was understood at the time of its adoption. It is not only the same in words, but the same in meaning, and delegates the same powers to the Government, and reserves and secures the same rights and privileges to the citizen; and as long as it continues to exist in its present form, it speaks not only in the same words, but with the same meaning and intent with which it spoke when it came from the hands of its framers, and was voted on and adopted by the people of the United States. Any other rule of construction would abrogate the judicial character of this court, and make it the mere reflex of the popular opinion or passion of the day.[5]

Although contemporary originalists scramble to dissociate themselves from Taney's reasoning in *Dred Scott*,[6] this justification of that reasoning – with

---

[4] 60 U.S. 393 (1857).
[5] Ibid., 426.
[6] In Robert Bork's treatment of *Dred Scott* on pages 28–34 of *The Tempting of America: The Political Seduction of the Law* (New York: Simon & Schuster, 1990), for example, he refers not once to this passage. The decision resulted, in his view, not from originalist reasoning, but rather from Taney's "transformation of the due process clause from a procedural to a substantive requirement" (31). This, Bork continues, "was the first appearance in American

its reference to the rule that the Constitution "must be construed now as it was understood at the time of its adoption" and to the view that "as long as it continues to exist in its present form, it speaks not only in the same words, but with the same meaning and intent with which it spoke when it came from the hands of its framers" – represents the essential themes of originalism.

We find such themes in other early cases as well. In the 1905 case of *South Carolina v. United States*,[7] the Court dealt with the question of state-government immunity to federal taxation of South Carolina's business activity as a dealer of alcoholic beverages. In the context of his opinion for the Court, Justice David Brewer stated the basic originalist argument as to the Constitution's fixed, unchanging meaning:

> The Constitution is a written instrument. As such its meaning does not alter. That which it meant when adopted it means now. Being a grant of powers to a government its language is general, and as changes come in social and political life it embraces in its grasp all new conditions which are within the scope of the powers in terms conferred. In other words, while the powers granted do not change, they apply from generation to generation to all things to which they are in their nature applicable. This in no manner abridges the fact of its changeless nature and meaning. Those things which are within its grants of power, as those grants were understood when made, are still within them, and those things not within them remain still excluded.[8]

The key phrase here is the Constitution's "changeless nature and meaning." To maintain this fixed meaning of the powers granted to Congress, the Court argued, "we must, therefore, place ourselves in the position of the men who

constitutional law of the concept of 'substantive due process,' and that concept has been used countless times since by judges who want to write their personal beliefs into a document that, most inconveniently, does not contain those beliefs" (31). Similarly, former Attorney General Edwin Meese attributes the *Dred Scott* decision not to adherence to originalist interpretation but to its rejection:

> In the 1850's, the Supreme Court under Chief Justice Roger B. Taney read blacks out of the Constitution in order to invalidate Congress' attempt to limit the spread of slavery. The *Dred Scott* decision, famously described as a judicial "self-inflicted wound," helped bring on the civil war. There is a lesson in this history. There is danger in seeing the Constitution as an empty vessel into which each generation may pour its passion and prejudice.

Speech before the Washington, DC, chapter of the Federalist Society Lawyers Division, November 15, 1985, in *The Great Debate: Interpreting Our Written Constitution*, ed. Paul G. Cassell (Washington, DC: The Federalist Society, 1986), 37. Among originalists only Harry V. Jaffa, to my knowledge, has called attention to this originalist passage in Taney's opinion, and he attributes the political, moral, and constitutional disaster of the decision not to reliance on original intent, but to reliance on a faulty conception of original intent. See "What Were the 'Original Intentions' of the Framers of the Constitution of the United States?," 10 *University of Puget Sound Law Review* 351 (1987).

[7] 199 U.S. 437 (1905).
[8] Ibid., 448–9. In the very next sentence of this passage, Brewer cites the Taney passage in *Dred Scott* we have just examined.

framed and adopted the Constitution, and inquire what they must have understood to be the meaning and scope of those grants."[9]

The most famous articulation of these themes by the Court prior to the contemporary originalism debate appears, of course, in the New Deal cases.[10] In *Home Building & Loan Association v. Blaisdell*,[11] the Court in 1934 upheld the Minnesota Mortgage Moratorium Law of 1933 against a contract-clause challenge. Writing for the Court, Chief Justice Charles Evans Hughes stated his classic rejection of originalist interpretation:

If by the statement that what the Constitution meant at the time of its adoption it means to-day, it is intended to say that the great clauses of the Constitution must be confined to the interpretation which the framers, with the conditions and outlook of their time, would have placed upon them, the statement carries its own refutation.[12]

By contrast, Justice George Sutherland, joined in dissent by Justices Willis Van Devanter, James McReynolds, and Pierce Butler, wrote that a constitutional provision "does not admit of two distinctly opposite interpretations. It does not mean one thing at one time and an entirely different thing at another time."[13] The way to insure this fixity of meaning, he continued, is to follow this strict standard of interpretation:

The whole aim of construction, as applied to a provision of the Constitution, is to discover the meaning, to ascertain and give effect to the intent, of its framers and the people who adopted it.... As nearly as possible we should place ourselves in the condition of those who framed and adopted it.[14]

The same themes appear in *West Coast Hotel Co. v. Parrish*,[15] in which the Court in 1937 overruled its earlier understanding of due process in *Adkins v. Children's Hospital*[16] and upheld a state minimum-wage law for women

---

[9] Ibid., 450.

[10] Interestingly, in his 1985 Federalist Society speech cited in footnote 6, Meese justified the decisions upholding the New Deal as being essentially originalist in character:

[T]he decisions of the New Deal and beyond that freed Congress to regulate commerce and enact a plethora of social legislation were not judicial adaptations of the Constitution to new realities. There were in fact removals of encrustations of earlier courts that had strayed from the original intent of the Framers regarding the power of the legislature to make policy.

Cassell, *The Great Debate*, 38. Nevertheless, he leaves unremarked the fact that it was the *dissenters* rather than the majorities in these decisions who understood themselves to be, in our terms, originalists. Yet see Justice Clarence Thomas's concurring opinion in *U.S. v. Lopez*, 93–1260 (1996), where he renews the New Deal dissenters' originalist objections.

[11] 290 U.S. 398 (1934).

[12] Ibid., 442–3.

[13] Ibid., 448–9.

[14] Ibid., 453.

[15] 300 U.S. 379 (1937).

[16] 261 U.S. 525 (1923).

against a due-process challenge. In dissent, Justice Sutherland appealed to what we today would call originalism:

It is urged that the question involved should now receive fresh consideration, among other reasons, because of "the economic conditions which have supervened"; but the meaning of the Constitution does not change with the ebb and flow of economic events. We frequently are told in more general words that the Constitution must be construed in the light of the present. If by that it is meant that the Constitution is made up of living words that apply to every new condition which they include, the statement is quite true. But to say, if that be intended, that the words of the Constitution mean today what they did not mean when written – that is, that they do not apply to a situation now to which they would have applied then – is to rob that instrument of the essential element which continues it in force as the people have made it until they, and not their official agents, have made it otherwise.[17]

Putting the point forcefully and succinctly, Sutherland wrote: "The meaning of the constitution is fixed when it is adopted, and it is not different at any subsequent time when a court has occasion to pass upon it."[18] The reason for this fixity of meaning, he made clear, is the role of the Constitution as a limit on majority rule:

If the Constitution, intelligently and reasonably construed in the light of these principles, stands in the way of desirable legislation, the blame must rest upon that instrument, and not upon the court for enforcing it according to its terms. The remedy in that situation – and the only true remedy – is to amend the Constitution.[19]

Sutherland concludes this argument by stating that the role of a court in this situation "is to declare the law as written, leaving it to the people themselves to make such changes as new circumstances may require."[20] Until such a point is reached, the meaning of the Constitution remains fixed and unchanged.

Against the background of such historical antecedents as the foregoing, it is clear that the fundamental issue that underlies constitutional theory is whether and how a fixed text – that is, a text of determinate, unchanging meaning – can accommodate the change endemic to the world it attempts to order and govern.[21] In contemporary constitutional theory, a period of approximately the last quarter-century that I would characterize as having begun with the appearance in 1975 of Thomas Grey's seminal article "Do We

---

[17] 300 U.S. 379, 402–3 (1937).
[18] Ibid., 404, citing Thomas Cooley, *A Treatise on Constitutional Limitations* (Boston: Little, Brown and Company, 1868), 55.
[19] 300 U.S. 379, 404 (1937).
[20] Ibid.
[21] To phrase the question in this manner obviously entails rejecting the claims of deconstructionism and poststructuralism. To the extent that such theories deny the possibility of texts of fixed, determinate, unchanging meaning, they necessarily deny the very possibility of constitutionalism as I have described it here.

Have an Unwritten Constitution?,"[22] this fundamental issue has appeared in two conceptualizations: the debate between interpretivism and noninterpretivism, and the debate between originalism and nonoriginalism. Generally speaking, interpretivism is the position that judges may enforce only those norms found to be explicit or clearly implicit in the text of the Constitution, while noninterpretivism is the position that judges may enforce additional norms not found within the text. Originalism is the position that judges must enforce constitutional norms only as they were understood by those who wrote and ratified them, while nonoriginalism is the position that judges may enforce such norms as they are understood in the present.

It has been the conventional but, I suggest, unexamined assumption in contemporary constitutional theory that these two debates are on all fours with each other. That is, commentators have assumed that interpretivism and originalism are conceptually equivalent, and that noninterpretivism and nonoriginalism are conceptually equivalent. My argument, however, is that the originalism debate in contemporary constitutional theory stems from, but is not equivalent to, the interpretivism debate of the late 1970s. In other words, I want to argue that the originalism–nonoriginalism debate and the interpretivism–noninterpretivism debate, though related, are distinct structures of argument, even if most originalists consider the concepts equivalent and thus synonymous. This assumption is captured in former Attorney General Edwin Meese's famous 1985 statement that any nonoriginalist standard of adjudication "suffers the defect of pouring new meaning into old words, thus creating new powers and new rights totally at odds with the logic of our Constitution and its commitment to the rule of law."[23] The idea here of pouring new meaning into old words, or new wine into an old bottle, is central, for it suggests that not to read the Constitution in terms of original intent is necessarily not to read the Constitution – that is, that collection of norms or principles "constitutionalized" by the writers and ratifiers – at all. As the Reagan Justice Department's Office of Legal Policy put the matter, "[u]nlike those who interpret the Constitution according to its original meaning, noninterpretivists contend that courts should decide constitutional issues under standards not found in the Constitution."[24] Through reconstructing the genealogy of these debates, I shall map the logic of their interrelationship and argue that this assumption of conceptual equivalence itself rests on certain tacit and debatable premises about the nature of what I call "constitutional

---

[22] Thomas Grey, "Do We Have an Unwritten Constitution?" 27 *Stanford Law Review* 703 (1975).

[23] Speech by Attorney General Edwin Meese III before the American Bar Association, July 9, 1985, Washington, DC, in Cassell, *The Great Debate*, 10.

[24] *Original Meaning Jurisprudence: A Sourcebook* (Report to the Attorney General by the Office of Legal Policy, United States Department of Justice, 12 March 1987), 7. Throughout this booklet the authors call interpretation of the Constitution in terms of its original meaning, interpretivism, and interpretation in any other terms noninterpretivism.

textuality." In order to understand the originalism debate accurately and fully, we have to understand why and how it is not identical to the interpretivism debate, and my theme will be that, in the American polity, disagreement over the meaning of a common text is considered legitimate, while attempts to import norms from outside that text is considered illegitimate.

The interpretivism–noninterpretivism debate concerned the relation between the written Constitution and the source of norms governing judicial review. In 1975 Thomas Grey posed the essential dichotomy:

In reviewing laws for constitutionality, should our judges confine themselves to determining whether those laws conflict with norms derived from the written Constitution? Or may they also enforce principles of liberty and justice when the normative content of those principles is not to be found within the four corners of our founding document?[25]

These alternative conceptions of the norms governing judicial review became well known in the work of John Hart Ely as the contrasting positions of interpretivism and noninterpretivism,

the former indicating that judges deciding constitutional issues should confine themselves to enforcing norms that are stated or clearly implicit in the written Constitution, the latter the contrary view that courts should go beyond that set of references and enforce norms that cannot be discovered within the four corners of the document.[26]

The essential claim of interpretivism, Ely continued, is "its insistence that the work of the political branches is to be invalidated only in accord with an inference whose starting point, whose underlying premise, is fairly discoverable in the Constitution."[27] Grey, too, wrote that "What distinguishes the exponent of the pure interpretive model is his insistence that the only norms used in constitutional adjudication must be those inferable from the text – that the Constitution must not be seen as licensing courts to articulate and apply contemporary norms not demonstrably expressed or implied by the framers."[28] Similarly, in his 1982 book *The Constitution, the Courts, and Human Rights*, Michael Perry meticulously set out the same distinction. "The Supreme Court engages in *interpretive* review," he wrote,

when it ascertains the constitutionality of a given policy choice by reference to one of the value judgments of which the Constitution consists – that is, by reference to a value judgment embodied, though not necessarily explicitly, either in some particular

---

[25] Grey, "Do We Have an Unwritten Constitution?" 703.
[26] John Hart Ely, *Democracy and Distrust* (Cambridge, MA: Harvard University Press, 1980), 1 (footnote omitted).
[27] Ibid., 1–2 (footnote omitted).
[28] Grey, "Do We Have an Unwritten Constitution?" 706, footnote 9.

provision of the text of the Constitution or in the overall structure of government ordained by the Constitution.[29]

By contrast, he continued, "The Court engages in *noninterpretive* review when it makes the determination of constitutionality by reference to a value judgment other than one constitutionalized by the framers."[30] Interpretivism, then, is the view that it is exclusively the Constitution that is the authoritative source of norms to be used in judicial review, whereas noninterpretivism is the view that in at least certain classes of cases some set of supplementary, extraconstitutional norms is authoritative also.

It is important to understand that in this initial formulation of interpretivism and noninterpretivism, the disagreement has both normative and empirical – that is, prescriptive and descriptive – dimensions. Grey argued in his article that "very little of our constitutional law of individual rights has any firm foundation in the model of judicial review which traces from *Marbury v. Madison* to the jurisprudence of Mr. Justice Black."[31] Were we to adopt interpretivism as our guide, he said, we would have to throw out substantial chunks of settled as well as unsettled law, grounded in the equal-protection clause of the Fourteenth Amendment and the due-process clauses of the Fifth and Fourteenth Amendments, covering issues from abortion and birth control to sexual and possibly even racial discrimination. Grey himself argued against such a move:

I do not think that the view of constitutional adjudication outlined by [interpretivist] commentators is sufficiently broad to capture the full scope of legitimate judicial review. It seems to be that the courts do appropriately apply values not articulated in the constitutional text, and appropriately apply them in determining the constitutionality of legislation.[32]

However, Grey begs the question here by referring to "legitimate judicial review," for the legitimacy of modern judicial review is precisely what is in question. Accepting the proposition that there is a disjunction or inconsistency between the controversial holdings of modern judicial review and interpretivist theory, Grey is faced with the question as to whether we throw out the model or throw out the controversial holdings. If interpretivism is empirical, then it is descriptively false: As an explanatory model, Grey argues, it does not satisfactorily account for the methods and results of modern judicial review. In this empirical sense, then, the interpretivist model is inaccurate and must be discarded in favor of noninterpretivism.

---

[29] Michael J. Perry, *The Constitution, the Courts, and Human Rights* (New Haven, CT: Yale University Press, 1982), 10.

[30] Ibid., 11.

[31] Grey, "Do We Have an Unwritten Constitution?" 718.

[32] Ibid., 705.

On the other hand, however, an interpretivist could agree, regretfully, that interpretivism is empirically false but would argue that the model is first and foremost a normative one. Consequently, given the claim of an inconsistency between the controversial holdings of modern judicial review and interpretivist theory, the interpretivist would say so much the worse for the former. That is, interpretivism is first and foremost a normative theory: While it does not describe what the Court has done, it prescribes what the Court ought to do. This, then, is the sense in which both interpretivism and originalism are regulative theories whose purpose is to guarantee that constitutional interpretation will remain bound by the text of the Constitution. The specter haunting both theories is the thought of political judges unconstrained by constitutional principle. In view of that specter, Bork, for example, argues that "The only way in which the Constitution can constrain judges is if the judges interpret the document's words according to the intentions of those who drafted, proposed, and ratified its provisions and its various amendments."[33] For interpretivism, the only source of constitutional principle is the text of the Constitution itself; for originalism, the only source of constitutional principle is the original understanding of the text of the Constitution itself.

In the time since Grey posed these alternative conceptions of judicial review, the contrast between interpretivism and noninterpretivism became the conventional discourse in constitutional theory that framed the issue of grounds for the exercise of judicial review. Many commentators viewed the conflict between interpretivism and noninterpretivism as a newer version of the older conflict between positive-law and natural-law conceptions of the Constitution. This was evident in Grey's account:

For the generation that framed the Constitution, the concept of a "higher law," protecting "natural rights," and taking precedence over ordinary positive law as a matter of political obligation, was widely shared and deeply felt. An essential element of American constitutionalism was the reduction to written form – and hence to positive law – of some of the principles of natural rights. But at the same time, it was generally recognized that written constitutions could not completely codify the higher law. Thus in the framing of the original American constitutions it was widely accepted that there remained unwritten but still binding principles of higher law. The ninth amendment is the textual expression of this idea in the federal Constitution.[34]

---

[33] Bork, Speech to the University of San Diego Law School, in *The Great Debate*, 45. Also see Bork, "Neutral Principles and Some First Amendment Problems," 47 *Indiana Law Journal* 1 (1971).

[34] Grey, "Do We Have an Unwritten Constitution?" 715–16. See also Grey's development of this point in "Origins of the Unwritten Constitution: Fundamental Law in American Revolutionary Thought," 30 *Stanford Law Review* 843, 843 (1978). Cf. Ely: "The interpretivism–noninterpretivism dichotomy stirs a long-standing debate that pervades all of law, that between 'positivism and natural law.'" *Democracy and Distrust*, 1, footnote. Also see Gary C.

The Constitution and its provisions, from the natural-law position, must be interpreted as grounded in, understandable in terms of, and perhaps even correctable by certain fundamental principles that are not explicitly part of the written text of the document, but that are as much a part of the Constitution – and enforceable as such – as the written text. The contrary, positive-law position is that the historical lack of agreement on the meaning and content of "fundamental principles" or "natural rights" leads to the conclusion that the only possible ground for the consensus necessary for the existence of a functioning society is that set of positive conventions explicitly accepted by the members of that society.

The classic discussion of this issue, of course, was the debate between Justices Samuel Chase and James Iredell in the famous 1798 case of *Calder v. Bull.*[35] The oft-cited opinions of these justices are commonly taken to be a disagreement over the propriety of natural-law-based constitutional interpretation, but Iredell, in fact, appears on a careful reading to have argued past Chase. It is not at all obvious in this familiar passage that Chase advocated recurrence to some body of natural law counterposed to positive law. He wrote:

I cannot subscribe to the omnipotence of a state legislature, or that it is absolute and without control; although its authority should not be expressly restrained by the constitution, or fundamental law of the state.... The legislature may enjoin, permit, forbid and punish; they may declare new crimes, and establish rules of conduct for all its citizens in future cases; they may command what is right, and prohibit what is wrong; but they cannot change innocence into guilt, or punish innocence as a crime; or violate the right of an antecedent lawful private contract; or the right of private property. To maintain that our federal or state legislature possess such powers, if they had not been expressly restrained, would, in my opinion, be a political heresy altogether inadmissible in our free republican governments.[36]

The Constitution and its provisions, in other words, must be interpreted as grounded in and thus correctable by certain fundamental principles that are not explicitly part of the written text of the document. In claiming that "[a]n act of the legislature (for I cannot call it a law), contrary to the great first principles of the social compact, cannot be considered a rightful exercise of legislative authority," Chase argues that the "great first principles of the social compact"[37] are as much a part of the Constitution – and enforceable

---

Leedes, "A Critique of Illegitimate Noninterpretivism," 8 *University of Dayton Law Review* 533, 537–8 (1983).

[35] *Calder v. Bull,* 3 Dallas 386 (1798). Grey cites this case in "Do We Have an Unwritten Constitution?" 708, footnote 21.

[36] *Calder v. Bull,* 3 Dallas 386, 387–8 (1798).

[37] Ibid., 388. This appears to be what Grey was getting at. "The Constitution is not an *ex nihilo* creation," he wrote in a later article, "but is conceived as expressing an underlying unwritten act or arrangement, just as a written contract is meant to embody an agreement, and a will the testator's intentions about his estate. But the Constitution is meant to express

as such – as the written text. The "text" to be interpreted, however, is not natural law, in the sense of a universal moral code binding on all peoples in all places at all times, but rather the principles of the social compact comprising specifically American society, which grounds the Constitution.

Justice Joseph Story, for example, refers to these background assumptions in the rules for interpretation he discusses in his *Commentaries*. "In construing the constitution of the United States," he writes, "we are, in the first instance, to consider, what are its nature and objects, its scope and design, as apparent from the structure of the instrument, viewed as a whole, and also viewed in its component parts."[38] This statement, in and of itself, does appear to focus on the text of the Constitution itself, independent of any such background assumptions at issue in Chase's argument. Yet Story emphasizes the necessity of viewing the constitutional text in terms of the purposes for which it was written and adopted:

But a constitution of government, founded by the people for themselves and their posterity, and for objects of the most momentous nature, for perpetual union, for the establishment of justice, for the general welfare, and for a perpetuation of the blessings of liberty, necessarily requires, that every interpretation of its powers should have a constant reference to these objects.[39]

In this sense, the Preamble, to which Story here refers, stands as the "great first principles of the social compact" that underlie and justify the Constitution. Those principles, therefore, provide the necessary interpretive context: "The constitution of the United States," Story maintains, "is to receive a reasonable interpretation of its language, and its powers, keeping in view the objects and purposes, for which those powers were conferred."[40]

Contrary to this position, Iredell talks about natural justice. If the national or a state legislature, he writes,

shall pass a law, within the general scope of their constitutional power, the court cannot pronounce it to be void, merely because it is, in their judgment, contrary to the principles of natural justice. The ideas of natural justice are regulated by no fixed standard; the ablest and the purest men have differed upon the subject; and all that the court could properly say, in such an event, would be, that the legislature (possessed of an equal right of opinion) had passed an act which, in the opinion of the judges, was inconsistent with the abstract principles of natural justice.[41]

---

an arrangement vastly more complex than those underlying most legal documents: the web of society's basic institutions and ideals, its 'unwritten constitution.'" "The Constitution as Scripture," 37 *Stanford Law Review* 1, 16 (1984) (footnote omitted).

38 Joseph Story, *Commentaries on the Constitution of the United States*, (Boston: Hilliard, Gray, and Company, 1833), Vol. I, 136.

39 Ibid., Vol. I, 141.

40 Ibid., 139.

41 *Calder v. Bull*, 398–9.

On this view of the matter, to be sure, as opposed to Chase's view that the term "the Constitution" necessarily includes, at least in the minds of the Framers, an unwritten, "natural" dimension as well and as much as a written, "positive" dimension, Iredell's view is that the term "the Constitution" necessarily includes *only* the written, "positive" dimension. Given the historical lack of agreement on the content of the principles of natural justice, Iredell's position suggests, the only possible ground for the consensus necessary for the existence of a functioning society is that set of positive conventions explicitly accepted by the members of that society. Yet if my account of Chase is correct, then Iredell's critique is beside the point, for Chase talks about the "great first principles of the social compact" rather than speculative notions of natural justice. At the same time, Iredell's underlying concern *is* on the mark. Whether our "text" is natural law, the political theory of the Constitution, or just the Constitution – that is, the document – itself, the problem is objectivity in interpretation. If "the ideas of natural justice are regulated by no fixed standard" – if, that is, there is no natural, given standard of correctness – then any standard of correctness must be conventional, and in American society that is the role of the Constitution itself.

Interestingly, once the originalism debate superseded the interpretivism debate, this Chase–Iredell argument recurred not between originalists and nonoriginalists, but within originalism itself. The crux of the conflict is Harry Jaffa's famous claim that the Constitution embodies the principles of the Declaration of Independence.[42] In its most recent originalist manifestation, Lino Graglia takes the Iredell position against the Chase position he ascribes to Jaffa. Graglia writes that "The Constitution incorporates natural law because, according to Jaffa, it incorporates the Declaration of Independence."[43] At greater length, he offers what is at bottom the Iredellian critique:

It is very important, Jaffa agrees with Bork, that judges stick to enforcing positive law in order to avoid the danger of having unelected government officials substitute their policy views for the views of the elected representatives of the people. This

---

[42] See Jaffa's article "What Were the "Original Intentions" of the Framers of the Constitution of the United States?" where at 363 he writes:

As the "fundamental *act* of Union," the Declaration was and remains the fundamental legal instrument attesting to the existence of the United States. From it all subsequent acts of the people of the United States, including the Constitution, are dated and authorized. It defines at once the legal and the moral personality of that "one People" (who are said to be a "good people") who separated themselves from Great Britain and became free and independent. It thereby also defines the source and nature of that authority that is invoked when "[w]e the people of the United States" ordained and established the Constitution.

"For these reasons," he continues at 363, "the Declaration remains the most fundamental dimension of the law of the Constitution." See also Jaffa's *Original Intent and the Framers of the Constitution: A Disputed Question* (Chicago: Regnery Gateway, 1994).

[43] Lino Graglia, "Jaffa's Quarrel with Bork: Religious Belief Masquerading as Constitutional Argument," 4 *Southern California Interdisciplinary Law Journal* 705, 708 (1995).

danger is avoided, however, Jaffa apparently thinks, when the positive law (here, the Constitution) simply enacts the natural law. Natural law then becomes positive law, and a judge who decides cases on the basis of his understanding of the principles of natural law is simply performing the ordinary judicial function of interpreting and applying law. It would be abhorrent for a judge to import ideas and principles into the Constitution from the outside, Jaffa says, but for a judge to decide constitutional cases on the basis of natural law presents no problem, because natural law is part of the Constitution. All of which, of course, is utter confusion.[44]

In response, Jaffa writes that Graglia identifies original intent "with a legal positivism that is completely alien to the thought of the Founding generation."[45] By contrast, echoing Chase, Jaffa writes that "Contrary to Graglia – and Thrasymachus – the American Revolution is rooted in the conviction that there is a non-arbitrary standard of just and unjust, right and wrong, rooted in man's nature as a rational being."[46]

Against this background, we can see that what was at bottom a debate over the fixed or changeable character of the Constitution became trapped in the spatial metaphor of "the four corners of the document," popularized by Grey and Ely, which generated the accompanying metaphor of an "unwritten Constitution." In such a discourse, how one conceived the contrast between interpretivism and noninterpretivism depended upon how one conceived the Constitution, for the contrast takes a different shape depending upon whether one understands the Constitution to have a written dimension alone or to have both a written and an unwritten dimension. To grasp this point, we must bear in mind that at one level the term "the Constitution" functioned generally as the normative standard of judicial review, while at another level the term "the Constitution" functioned as a specific conception of what comprises that normative standard of judicial review. Thus, on the one hand, we could maintain that what we mean by the term "the Constitution" includes the written text and only the written text, such that only those norms that are stated or clearly implicit in the written text are judicially cognizable and enforceable. The Constitution exists as a written document complete in and of itself, on this view, without any claim that it necessarily must be seen as an embodiment, however incomplete and imperfect, of some broader, higher, unwritten set of moral or political principles. Thus, "the Constitution" equals the text. On the other hand, we could maintain that what we mean by the term "the Constitution" includes both the written text and a set of unwritten, broader, higher moral or political principles on which the written text must be seen to rest. Here the Constitution exists as a written document that necessarily represents a particular and thus incomplete and imperfect

44 Ibid., 707–8.
45 Harry Jaffa, "Graglia's Quarrel with God: Atheism and Nihilism Masquerading as Constitutional Argument, 4 *Southern California Interdisciplinary Law Journal* 715, 716 (1995).
46 Ibid., 726.

embodiment of a broader, higher law without which the written text is ultimately incomprehensible, with the consequence that both the written and the unwritten dimensions of the Constitution are judicially cognizable and enforceable.[47] Thus, "the Constitution" equals text-plus.

If we were indeed to argue that the Constitution had both a written and an unwritten dimension, we would still face the task of explaining what type of relation might hold between these dimensions. The vagueness of the spatial concepts used to demarcate this relation reveals its problematic character. The question would be, is the unwritten dimension "in addition to" the written dimension, or is it "behind" or "beyond" the written dimension? Gary Jacobsohn, for one, strongly defends the latter position, arguing that

the written Constitution was meant to embody the natural rights commitments of the framers. Therefore, judicial appeals to "higher law" are not justifiable when they lead to a distinction between written and unwritten constitutions, but they are justifiable insofar as they help explicate and illuminate the written words of the Constitution itself. From this perspective the positivists are correct in their insistence upon the exclusive authority of the written document, but fundamentally misguided in their understanding of the nature of this document, since, as we have seen, the written words do not preclude a natural rights content. Judges who accept the intermediate position stated above will not feel free to invoke ideas of natural justice that are not grounded in the constitutional text. Yet neither will they read that text as if it were a business contract or, worse, as an "unprincipled" document. If the Constitution is a set of rules and procedures, it is so in part because it flows out of a coherent and knowable, not arbitrary or ever-mutable, set of philosophic presuppositions.[48]

It is certainly legitimate and important to claim that the Constitution is a principled document with a substantive meaning of its own, but there is a persistent ambiguity in the claim that "the written Constitution contains

---

[47] The best statement of the idea that the Constitution can be only an incomplete and imperfect embodiment of important principles is perhaps Justice Harlan's dissent in *Poe v. Ullman*:

> Due process has not been reduced to any formula; its content cannot be determined by reference to any code. The best that can be said is that through the course of this Court's decisions it has represented the balance, which our nation, built upon postulates of respect for the liberty of the individual, has struck between that liberty and the demands of organized society.

367 U.S. 497, 542 (1961). In contrast, Robert Bork echoes Justice Black's response to this idea when he argues that "the judge who looks outside the Constitution always looks inside himself and nowhere else." "The Struggle Over the Role of the Court," *National Review*, September 17, 1982, 1138.

[48] Gary Jacobsohn, *The Supreme Court and the Decline of Constitutional Aspiration* (Totowa, NJ: Rowman & Littlefield, 1986), 75. Jacobsohn seems to reverse his argument, however, by claiming here that judges who accept his position "will not feel free to invoke ideas of natural justice that are not grounded in the constitutional text." He wants to claim that the constitutional text is grounded in ideas of natural justice, whereas his statement here claims that ideas of natural justice are grounded in the constitutional text.

within it the principles of justice for which the noninterpretivist seeks external justification."[49] Given the theory of textuality that Jacobsohn employs here, the ambiguity lies in trying to reject noninterpretivism's purported search for principles "outside" or "external to" the Constitutional text while maintaining that the constitutional text embodies the natural-rights commitments of the framers. Grounding the constitutional text in natural-rights principles sounds rather like the noninterpretivism Jacobsohn wants to reject, and grounding natural-rights principles in the constitutional text sounds rather like the positivism he wants to reject.

In light of this ambiguity in the meaning of the Constitution, the noninterpretivist position – that is, the view that judges may legitimately enforce norms not found to be stated or clearly implicit in the written text of the Constitution – could have both a strong and a weak sense. On the one hand, if what we mean by the term "the Constitution" includes the written text and only the written text, then noninterpretivism would consist of the argument that while the Constitution includes only those norms stated or clearly implicit in the written text of the document, judges nevertheless may enforce additional, *extraconstitutional* norms.[50] In this strong sense, noninterpretivism agrees with what interpretivism defines as the Constitution and simply argues that in at least certain classes of cases some set of supplementary, extraconstitutional norms are authoritative also.[51] Yet if we assume that both interpretivism and noninterpretivism accept the identical concept of the Constitution, then one is hard put, as interpretivists have been quick to note, to avoid questions about the legitimacy of noninterpretivism in the American constitutional tradition. Noninterpretivists would be ascribing constitutional status to something other than the Constitution when in the American political tradition only the Constitution has constitutional status. The simple claim that constitutional interpretation consists of interpretation of the constitutional text is the key to the legitimacy of anything purporting to be constitutional interpretation. Against the strong sense of noninterpretivism, consequently, interpretivism clearly won the war.[52]

---

[49] Ibid., 92.
[50] This is the position that Michael Perry wanted to defend in his first work in constitutional theory. His concern, he wrote, is to justify "the legitimacy of constitutional policymaking (by the judiciary) that goes *beyond* the value judgments established by the framers of the written Constitution (extraconstitutional policymaking)." *The Constitution, the Courts, and Human Rights*, ix.
[51] Indeed, one could argue that noninterpretivists were driven to that position because they were in effect committed to an originalist understanding of the Constitution.
[52] This is why there is such strength in the appeal of interpretivism or originalism. "Even results which are patently inconsistent with originalism are often couched in rhetoric about the intent of the framers. Moreover, one cannot read a broad range of constitutional cases without reaching the conclusion that originalism has in fact been an important influence on the development of constitutional doctrine (although admittedly not the only influence). Thus in order to forego originalist analysis one must also be willing to abandon a major part

On the other hand, if what we mean by the term "the Constitution" includes both the written text and a set of unwritten, broader, higher moral or political principles on which the written text must be seen to rest, then noninterpretivism might consist of the argument that because the Constitution has an unwritten dimension as well as the written dimension that contains certain stated and clearly implicit norms, judges may legitimately enforce the unwritten norms as well due to the fact that *they are themselves constitutional* rather than extraconstitutional. On this view, in other words, the constitutional text rests upon a foundation of unwritten moral and political principles that the Constitution expresses and within which alone the Constitution makes sense. In this weak sense, then, what is called noninterpretivism is actually a position that certainly supports interpreting the Constitution; it simply disagrees with what interpretivism defines as the Constitution.

Understanding this point lays bare the logic of the transition to the terminology of originalism and nonoriginalism, because for the weak sense of noninterpretivism what is now clearly at stake is *how* we are properly to interpret the exclusively authoritative constitutional text and not *whether* to consider the constitutional text exclusively authoritative. Once we no longer take as necessary the assumption that interpretivism and noninterpretivism presuppose an identical concept of the Constitution, noninterpretivism in the weak sense turns into a form of interpretivism and their conflict becomes one between competing types or schools of *constitutional* interpretation – that is, of interpretation of the constitutional text. Conflict over the proper principles of constitutional interpretation is in fact not truly about whether the Constitution is the fundamental normative standard in the American political system. Rather, granting the Constitution's authoritative status, the interpretative problem is over the questions, just what counts as the Constitution and just what counts as constitutional interpretation? Whatever disagreements might arise among various readers of the Constitution, they are disagreements about how the Constitution is to be interpreted, not whether it is to be interpreted – that is, the issue is one of interpretation rather than fidelity.[53] Consequently, as some commentators recognized, there is, strictly speaking, no such thing as the strong sense of noninterpretivism in American

---

of the American judicial tradition." Earl Maltz, "The Failure of Attacks on Constitutional Originalism," 4 *Constitutional Commentary* 43, 44 (1987).

[53] "The theories that are generally classed as 'noninterpretive'...are plainly interpretivist in any plausible sense. They disregard neither the text of the Constitution nor the motives of those who made it; rather they seek to place these in the proper context. 'Noninterpretive' theorists argue that the commitment of our legal community to this particular document, with these provisions enacted by people with those motives, presupposes a *prior* commitment to certain principles of political justice which, if we are to act responsibly, must therefore be reflected in the way the Constitution is read and enforced. That is the antithesis of a clean slate argument, and a paradigm of the method of interpretation. It disregards neither text nor original intention, but rather proposes a theory to teach us how to discover what the former means and what the latter is." Ronald Dworkin, *A Matter of Principle* (Cambridge,

constitutional interpretation.[54] The issue, rather, becomes the argument between originalist interpretation of the constitutional text and nonoriginalist interpretation of the constitutional text; it is an argument not over the notion of an unwritten Constitution, but rather one over the nature of the proper interpretive context in which to read the written Constitution. The spatial metaphor of which norms fall within and which fall outside of the four corners of the document led the debate, wrongly, into the question of whether or not to interpret the Constitution rather than into the question of how to interpret the Constitution.[55]

Because Grey really was concerned with the latter question, he later regretted its conceptualization as the former as a distortion of his initial argument. Writing in 1984, he stated: "We are all interpretivists; the real arguments are not over whether judges should stick to interpreting, but over what they should interpret and what interpretive attitudes they should adopt."[56] Thus, reformulating the issue he had raised in his initial article, he stated that "The question is whether the constitutional text should be the sole source of law for purposes of judicial review, or whether judges should supplement the text with an unwritten constitution that is implicit in precedent, practice, and conventional morality."[57] In more detail, he wrote:

It is common to call the opposing schools of thought on the question "interpretivist" and "noninterpretivist," but this distorts the debate. If the current interest in interpretive theory, or hermeneutics, does nothing else, at least it shows that the concept of interpretation is broad enough to encompass any plausible mode of constitutional adjudication. We are all interpretivists; the real arguments are not over whether judges should stick to interpreting, but over what they should interpret and what

---

MA: Harvard University Press, 1985), 35. Cf. Richard B. Saphire, "Judicial Review in the Name of the Constitution," 8 *University of Dayton Law Review* 745, 799 (1983).

54 "'Interpretivism' fell out of favor when everybody apparently began to realize that its opposite – noninterpretivism – was incoherent, since few judges or scholars seem to suggest (or at least to concede) that, in constitutional adjudication, one should be doing something other than interpreting the Constitution." Saphire, "Enough about Originalism," 515, note 7.

55 Thus, when a critic rejects the reasoning in a given case – say, the announcement of a right to privacy in *Griswold v. Connecticut*, 381 U.S. 479 (1965). – the interpretivist objection would be simply that the Court has invoked some value not to be found within the four corners of the Constitution in order to strike down the legislative provision at issue. In other words, assuming that the text contains values "a" through "m," the interpretivist would object to an opinion by saying that the Court has invoked value "p," not to be found within the text. An originalist objection, on the other hand, would focus on constitutional provision X and say that the Court has wrongly read X in terms of contemporary understandings rather than the original understanding. From the former perspective, the criticism is that the Court has (improperly) added something to the Constitution; from the latter, the criticism is that the Court has wrongly interpreted what everyone accepts as being a particular provision of the Constitution.

56 Thomas Grey, "The Constitution as Scripture," 37 *Stanford Law Review* 1, 1 (1984).

57 Ibid.

interpretive attitudes they should adopt. Repenting past errors, I will therefore use the less misleading labels "textualists" and "supplementers" for, respectively, those who consider the text the sole legitimate source of operative norms in constitutional adjudication, and those who accept supplementary sources of constitutional law.[58]

Nevertheless, Grey's new distinction between textualists and supplementers was a distinction without a difference from his original categories of interpretivism and noninterpretivism. Despite the insight that the presumed equivalence between interpretivism–noninterpretivism and originalism–nonoriginalism does not hold because the alternative conceptual pairs derive from different questions, still at stake in Grey's attempted reformulation is his initial interpretivist–noninterpretivist distinction between text and text-plus.

The earliest prominent use of "originalism" and "nonoriginalism," to be sure, shows the imprint of the interpretivism–noninterpretivism debate in its suggestion that what is at stake is the authoritativeness of the constitutional text rather than how we go about interpreting an authoritative text. In the literature of contemporary constitutional theory the classic account of these contending positions is the 1980 article by Paul Brest entitled "The Misconceived Quest for the Original Understanding," which introduced the term "originalism." Brest offers a bifurcated definition of originalism, exhibiting rather than resolving the ambiguity of the concept, as "the familiar approach to constitutional adjudication that accords binding authority to the text of the Constitution or the intentions of the adopters."[59] By the "intentions of the adopters" Brest means what Christopher Wolfe calls their "historical set of expectations,"[60] and thus the intentionalist originalist seeks evidence of constitutional norms in the subjective expectations and, one might argue, even the mental states of the authors of the text. The textualist, by contrast, focuses, as we have seen, on the public understanding of the language of the Constitution. Referring to Blackstone's rules of legal interpretation, Wolfe points to what he says "must be kept in view throughout the process of interpretation: the intention of the lawgiver that is being sought is the intention as expressed in the words of the law, not some intention that exists outside of or despite the words of the law."[61] Textualism, therefore, focuses

---

[58] Ibid.

[59] Brest, "The Misconceived Quest for the Original Understanding," 204 (footnote omitted). In "Forward: The Appeal of Originalism," 1987 *Utah Law Review* 773, at 773, Earl Maltz defined originalism as "the theory that in constitutional adjudication judges should be guided by the intent of the Framers," and in his first footnote attributed the term to Paul Brest of Stanford and maintained that it is essentially the same theory as what others have called interpretivism.

[60] Christopher Wolfe, *Judicial Activism: Bulwark of Freedom or Precarious Security?* (Pacific Grove, CA: Brooks/Cole Publishing Company, 1991), 3.

[61] Christopher Wolfe, *The Rise of Modern Judicial Review: From Constitutional Interpretation to Judge-Made Law* (New York: Basic Books, 1986), 18–19.

on the language of a constitutional provision as the primary evidence of constitutional norms. An originalist theory, on this view, anchors the fixity of constitutional meaning in either the text of the Constitution or the intentions of those who wrote and ratified it.

On this basis, Brest lays out a typology that begins with these definitions of the forms of strict originalism:

The most extreme forms of originalism are "strict textualism" (or literalism) and "strict intentionalism." A strict textualist purports to construe words and phrases very narrowly and precisely. For the strict intentionalist, "the whole aim of construction, as applied to a provision of the Constitution, is ... to ascertain and give effect to the intent of its framers and the people who adopted it."[62]

In moderate originalism, on the other hand,

[t]he text of the Constitution is authoritative, but many of its provisions are treated as inherently open textured. The original understanding is also important, but judges are more concerned with the adopters' general purposes than with their intentions in a very precise sense.[63]

Finally, what Brest calls nonoriginalism "accord[s] the text and original history presumptive weight, but do[es] not treat them as authoritative or binding. The presumption is defeasible over time in the light of changing experiences and perceptions."[64] Central to all of these formulations by Brest

---

[62] Brest, "The Misconceived Quest for the Original Understanding," 204, citing *Home Building & Loan Association v. Blaisdell*, 290 U.S. 398, 453 (1934).

[63] Ibid., 204–5. "Open texture" is a term used by H. L. A. Hart:

Whichever device, precedent or legislation, is chosen for the communication of standards of behaviour, these, however smoothly they work over the great mass of ordinary cases, will, at some point where their application is in question, prove indeterminate; they will have what has been termed an *open texture*. So far we have presented this, in the case of legislation, as a general feature of human language; uncertainty at the borderline is the price to be paid for the use of general classifying terms in any form of communication concerning matters of fact. Natural languages like English are when used irreducibly open textured.

The Concept of Law (Oxford: Oxford University Press, 1961), 124–5. Compare Madison's statement in Federalist 37 that "no language is so copious as to supply words and phrases for every complex idea, or so correct as not to include many equivocally denoting different ideas." *The Federalist Papers*, Clinton Rossiter, ed. (New York: New American Library, 1961), 229.

[64] Brest, "The Misconceived Quest for the Original Understanding," 205. Moderate originalism and nonoriginalism, according to Brest, differ in this way:

The moderate originalist acknowledges that the text and original history are often indeterminate and that the elaboration of constitutional doctrine must often proceed by adjudication based on precedent, public values, and the like. But adjudication may not proceed in the absence of authorization from some original source, and when the text or original history speaks clearly it is binding. The nonoriginalist treats the text and original history as presumptively binding and limiting, but as neither a necessary nor sufficient condition for constitutional decisionmaking.

is the contrast between a public and a private conception of constitutional textuality. For the textualist, the constitutional text is public language, in that its meaning is established socially:

> That an interpreter must read a text in the light of its social as well as linguistic context does not destroy the boundary between textualism and intentionalism. Just as the textualist is not concerned with the adopters' idiosyncratic use of language, she is not concerned with their subjective purposes. Rather, she seeks to discern the purposes that a member of the adopters' society would understand the provision to encompass.[65]

Textual meaning on this conception is tied to generally accepted language usage among members of the society at the time the text is written. For the intentionalist, on the other hand, the constitutional text is essentially a private language, in that it is nothing but a representation of the mental states of writers and ratifiers:

> By contrast to the textualist, the intentionalist interprets a provision by ascertaining the intentions of those who adopted it. The text of the provision is often a useful guide to the adopters' intentions, but the text does not enjoy a favored status over other sources.[66]

For the intentionalist, then, the true meaning of the Constitution is not the constitutional text but rather a historically fixed and ascertainable set of mental states that stand, so to speak, behind the text. "The referent of a text understood as (simply) the linguistic embodiment of past normative judgments," Michael Perry has written, "is, in a sense, 'behind' the text. One must look behind the text to the original meaning if one is to understand the text."[67] Although the thrust of his article dealt with the nature of interpretation of the constitutional text, Brest's definitions themselves – and particularly that of nonoriginalism – imply instead that, as in the interpretivism–noninterpretivism debate, the binding authority of the text still was at issue.[68]

Ibid., 237 (footnote omitted). Brest is concerned to argue in this article that while moderate originalism is a coherent and workable mode of constitutional decision making, whereas strict originalism is not, nonoriginalism is preferable to moderate originalism in serving the ends of constitutional government. "The only difference between moderate originalism and nonoriginalist adjudication," he writes at 229, "is one of attitude toward the text and original understanding. For the moderate originalist, these sources are conclusive when they speak clearly. For the nonoriginalist, they are important but not determinative."

[65] Ibid., 208 (footnote omitted).

[66] Ibid., 209 (footnote omitted).

[67] Michael J. Perry, "The Authority of Text, Tradition, and Reason: A Theory of Constitutional 'Interpretation,'" 58 *Southern California Law Review* 551, 559 (1985).

[68] In *Original Intent and the Constitution* (Lanham, MD: Rowman & Littlefield Publishers, Inc., 1992), Gregory Bassham offers a more philosophically rigorous account of the kinds of distinctions Brest presented in his classic article. Originalists, he notes at 28, "agree on some generalized level that the Constitution's original 'intent' is binding. They disagree, however, about how best to conceptualize that intent – some emphasizing textual meaning, others

Of course, for originalism the binding authority of the text and the fixity of constitutional meaning are necessarily always at issue. As understood by originalism, however, in what is the fixity of constitutional meaning anchored? Here is where the terminology of the originalism debate has changed, shifting, though not always clearly, toward greater refinement under the pressure of criticism of the theory. On the one hand, the premise

intended meaning, still others publicly understood meaning and so forth." Critical of aspects of Brest's account of the necessary distinctions among varieties of originalism, however, Bassham argues that "intentionalism is a sounder, more defensible approach to constitutional adjudication than textualism is" (51). From that basis, noting that "*Both* strict and moderate intentionalism clearly confront massive evidentiary difficulties" (54), Bassham concludes that, "on balance, . . . moderate intentionalism is a more defensible form of originalism than either textualism or strict intentionalism" (56). Moderate intentionalism "seeks to determine, not the framers' scope beliefs, but rather the legal principles or propositions the framers understood themselves to be enacting" (84). At footnote 110 (157) Bassham states that "[t]he view that I call moderate intentionalism is close, I believe, to the view Michael Perry terms 'sophisticated originalism,'" and I shall discuss Perry's view in Chapter 6.

Thus, on the one hand, the purpose of Bassham's analysis is to prove that "originalism is not the 'basket case' critics often allege it to be. On the contrary, in its most defensible form originalism is an attractive, coherent, and basically workable theory, rooted in widely shared notions of political legitimacy" (95). Almost immediately after making that claim, however, Bassham takes it back. Given the (debatable) claim that much of contemporary, settled constitutional doctrine is essentially nonoriginalist in nature,

any "originalist" theory that fails to attack the roots of the current constitutional order effectively subordinates original intent to precedent, and this ceases to be a genuine form of originalism at all. Originalists, by definition, are committed to the primacy of original intent. But stones that the Constitution's builders rejected have now become foundation stones of a constitutional order very different from, and in many ways far grander than, that which the framers envisioned. And to that earlier vision we cannot and should not seek to return. (100)

Even in its most defensible form, Bassham ultimately concludes, originalism is indefensible:

In sum, even sophisticated originalism, the soundest and most attractive form of originalism, is ultimately indefensible. Although sophisticated originalism is able to avoid many of the objections commonly leveled against other forms of the theory, it remains vulnerable to three standard criticisms: (1) that it would produce excessive instability and discontinuity in constitutional doctrine; (2) that it accords insufficient weight to the value of adhering to deeply entrenched and widely accepted nonoriginalist precedent; and (3) that it fails to recognize that there may be times when the Court is justified in departing from original intent in order to make good on those larger purposes and aspirations that have linked Americans from the founding generation to our own. (106–7)

Bassham turns out to be, in the end, after all of his concern to distinguish the varieties of originalism better than Brest and others had done, to be something of a nonoriginalist:

Evolution by interpretation, as well as by occasional formal amendment, is inevitable if a constitution is to continue to speak to the future with the same relevance and moral force with which it spoke to the past. For only in this way can a short and basically unchanging written charter of government remain responsive to continually evolving conditions and needs. (103)

that underlies and unites all of the various forms of the theory is clearly that originalists always look to the particular historical period in which a given constitutional provision was written and ratified, whether the 1780s, the 1860s, or any other relevant period. At the same time, given this central premise, the phrase "various forms of the theory" indicates that there are two central conflicts within originalism itself, conflicts structured around the two key issues of (1) the source of constitutional norms and (2) the evidence of constitutional norms. Regarding the source of constitutional norms, we can distinguish among originalists those we can call "positivists" and those we can call "natural-rights theorists." Regarding the question of evidence of constitutional norms, we can distinguish between those who emphasize the intentions of the framers or writers of constitutional provisions and those who emphasize the understanding of the ratifiers of particular constitutional provisions.

The central question as to the source of constitutional principles is whether or not the Constitution can be understood to embody a unified, coherent moral and political theory. "Some lawyers, many judges, and perhaps most academic commentators," Henry Monaghan writes in "Our Perfect Constitution," "view the constitution as authorizing courts to nullify the results of the political process on the basis of general principles of political morality not derived from the constitutional text or the structure it creates."[69] Nevertheless, he argues, we must understand the Constitution not as "manifest[ing] a unified, coherent conception of political justice," but rather as a document characterized by the "unprincipled, and imperfect, nature of an enactment produced by compromise."[70] The Constitution, he says, should be seen as a super-statute: "Like important statutes, the constitution emerged as a result of compromises struck after hard bargaining."[71] For Monaghan, therefore,

Courts, he maintains at 102, "may sometimes be justified in rejecting the original understanding when this understanding clearly is no longer responsive to contemporary values and needs." Bassham's analysis, while informative, ultimately does not speak to my own concerns here, for it offers in the end a nonoriginalist critique of originalism, whereas I shall try to provide an exit from that either–or dichotomy. What *is* important to my own account is a reference Bassham makes early in his book (5) to a theory of meaning:

In addition to the inertia of precedent and the power of the traditional conception of judicial authority, a semantical theory that for centuries served as the standard account of how words achieve sense and reference may also have contributed to the long dominance of originalism in this country. According to that theory, verbal meaning is, focally, what philosophers of language now call speaker's meaning: that meaning which the person or persons, who made use of the words, intended to convey to others, whether he used them correctly, skillfully, logically or not.

I address this issue in Chapters 6 and 7.

[69] Henry Monaghan, "Our Perfect Constitution," 56 *New York University Law Review* 353, 353 (1981).

[70] Ibid., 391, 393.

[71] Ibid., 392.

the Constitution is not a perfect document, defined as one that embodies a unified and coherent moral and political theory, but an imperfect document, a bundle of compromises that do not stand under any broad, unifying principle.

This latter position is the positivist view that the Constitution consists simply of a number of separate, discrete, and incompletely interrelated provisions that do not add up to anything more than the particular will and preferences of a constitutional majority. Chief Justice Rehnquist, in two well-known passages, takes the starkly conventionalist standpoint of legal positivism:

> If [a democratic] society adopts a constitution and incorporates in that constitution safeguards for individual liberty, these safeguards indeed do take on a generalized moral rightness or goodness. They assume a general social acceptance neither because of any intrinsic worth nor because of any unique origins in someone's idea of natural justice but instead simply because they have been incorporated in a constitution by the people. . . .
>
> Beyond the Constitution and the laws in our society, there simply is no basis other than the individual conscience of the citizen that may serve as a platform for the launching of moral judgments. There is no conceivable way in which I can logically demonstrate to you that the judgments of my conscience are superior to the judgments of your conscience, and vice versa.[72]

And Bork, as we saw in his discussion of the Madisonian dilemma, argues that "in wide areas of life majorities are entitled to rule, if they wish, simply because they are majorities." The Constitution, from the positivist perspective, is, strictly speaking, an unprincipled document – there is no general organizing principle that rationalizes the specific principles that happen to have been chosen to go into the text. The content of the Constitution is simply the conventionalist choice of a particular historical (super)-majority that, in Monaghan's words, consists of "simply a series of separate and incompletely related provisions which, taken together, are insufficiently expressive of the substantive values of a twentieth-century liberal democracy."[73]

If we say, however, that the Constitution does indeed embody a unified and coherent moral and political theory in terms of which we can understand the inclusion of the specific provisions of the text, then the question is, which theory? Adapting Monaghan's argument, we can say that in contrast to his own position of constitutional imperfectionism, there are two categories of constitutional perfectionism. The focus of Monaghan's critique in his article was what we would call nonoriginalism. He attacked those "due substance" theorists who claim that the Constitution expresses a unified, coherent conception of political justice defined in terms of the values of

---

[72] Rehnquist, "The Notion of a Living Constitution," 54 *Texas Law Review* 693, 704 (1976).
[73] Monaghan, "Our Perfect Constitution," 391.

twentieth-century liberal democracy. Such theorists, he argues, assert "that there is a clear and substantial connection between the constitution and *current* conceptions of political morality."[74] The key point here is twofold: Monaghan rejects nonoriginalism both because he rejects the search for any unified and coherent moral and political theory and because he rejects any appeal to contemporary norms in constitutional interpretation. Similarly, Gary Jacobsohn argues that the "higher law" advocates he discusses claim that the moral theory at issue is some contemporary twentieth-century moral theory.[75]

But where Monaghan rejects the search for any coherent moral theory, Jacobsohn says, along with Harry Jaffa, that there is indeed a unifying moral and political theory at issue, and that theory is the natural-rights moral theory of the Framers. Or, as Scott Gerber writes, the Constitution "establishes a framework of government through which certain underlying philosophical principles are to be advanced. And those philosophical principles are the natural-rights principles of the Declaration of Independence."[76] The natural-rights position, in other words, argues that the Constitution does embody a unified and coherent moral and political theory, but argues that it is the theory of the writers and ratifiers. Christopher Wolfe, for example, argues that the Constitution architectonically embodies a broad conception of politics and justice:

The important point to emphasize is that the Constitution is not just a grab bag of different provisions. It is a constitution, that is, a fundamental law that establishes the great outlines of our government and in which, therefore, a coherent conception of government may be discerned by attention to the whole and its parts. Knowledge of this conception of government is a valuable aid in interpreting provisions of the Constitution, especially where the limits of language and men have resulted in some ambiguity.[77]

With an eye toward not only positivist originalism but also what he considers the illegitimacy of nonoriginalism, Harry Jaffa offers the succinct statement that "if it can be said that Justice Brennan's Constitution is one of 'overarching principles' uncontrolled by the actual text, so it might be ventured that

---

[74] Ibid., 358.
[75] Thus Bork, while a positivist rather than natural-rights originalist, argues in agreement with the latter that "today's constitutional cognoscenti...would have judges remake the historic Constitution from such materials as natural law, conventional morality, prophetic vision, the understanding of an ideal democracy, or what have you." *The Tempting of America*, 6.
[76] Scott Douglas Gerber, *To Secure These Rights: The Declaration of Independence and Constitutional Interpretation* (New York: New York University Press, 1996), 15.
[77] Wolfe, *The Rise of Modern Judicial Review*, 62–3.

Mr. Meese's Constitution is a text without overarching principles."[78] In like manner, Jacobsohn argues that

the Constitution is a written document within which are embodied principles of natural justice intended by its framers to be relevant to constitutional interpretation. Implicit in our approach is a dual challenge: first to the positivists, who dismiss natural rights as irrelevant to the Constitution, and second to the "higher lawyers," who claim the appropriateness of going outside the Constitution for determining adjudicative outcomes.[79]

"If the Constitution is a set of rules and procedures," Jacobsohn adds later in his text, "it is so in part because it flows out of a coherent and knowable, not arbitrary or ever-mutable, set of philosophic presuppositions."[80]

In Monaghan's schema, then, his own position is an originalist imperfectionism, which he opposes to a nonoriginalist perfectionism. But natural-rights originalism is a third position: It is, in Monaghan's terms, an originalist perfectionism. Despite their differences, however, what makes both the positivist position and the natural-rights position versions of originalism is the fact that they both ascribe authoritative status to the social-historical context of 1787. Monaghan, Chief Justice Rehnquist, Lino Graglia, and Robert Bork, among others, line up on the positivist side of the conflict, while Christopher Wolfe, Gary Jacobsohn, Scott Gerber, Hadley Arkes, and Harry Jaffa, among others, line up on the natural-rights side. The positivist originalist privileges the particular historical decisions taken in Philadelphia and the ratifying conventions, while the natural-rights originalist privileges the natural-rights theory associated with the Framers' generation.[81]

The second issue that divides originalists has to do with the evidentiary problem of interpretive guidelines for ascertaining constitutional norms. Whether we consider those norms to be grounded in convention or in nature, the interpreter faces the task of determining what counts as evidence for the

---

[78] Jaffa, "What Were the 'Original Intentions" of the Framers of the Constitution of the United States?" 358.

[79] Jacobsohn, *The Supreme Court and the Decline of Constitutional Aspiration,* 5.

[80] Ibid., 75.

[81] Jaffa puts the matter nicely, if somewhat apocalyptically:

In asking what were the original intentions of the Founding Fathers, we are asking what principles of moral and political philosophy guided them. We are not asking their personal judgments upon contingent matters. We are asking what were those principles – those truths "applicable to all men and all times" – to which they subscribed. The crisis of American constitutionalism–the crisis of the West – lies in the denial that there are any such principles or truths. It is no less a crisis in the heart of American conservatism than of American liberalism.

Jaffa, "What Were the 'Original Intentions" of the Framers of the Constitution of the United States?" 386.

values the writers and ratifiers constitutionalized. As suggested earlier, we can distinguish between those who emphasize the intentions of the framers or writers of constitutional provisions and those who emphasize the understanding of the ratifiers of particular constitutional provisions. Here the use of the term "intentions" somewhat obscures the matter. Wolfe, for example, writes that the intention of the Framers can be understood "either as an historical set of expectations or as a determinate meaning of the language."[82] These are not the same thing. Whereas the initial anchor of constitutional meaning in originalism was the concept of original intent,[83] criticism of the subjectivism and psychologism in the idea of intent led to its replacement by the concept of original understanding as the anchor of constitutional meaning. Bork, for example, makes this shift in *The Tempting of America*. In the mid-1980s, he argued that "only by limiting themselves to the historic intentions underlying each clause of the Constitution can judges avoid becoming legislators, avoid enforcing their own moral predilections, and ensure that the Constitution is law."[84] His focus here is on what we normally call the intentions of the Framers. By the time of the appearance of *The Tempting of America* in 1990, however, he maintains that originalists "do not seek the subjective intent of the Framers but rather the objective meaning that constitutional language had when it was adopted."[85] In detail, he writes:

Though I have written of the understanding of the ratifiers of the Constitution, since they enacted it and made it law, that is actually a shorthand formulation, because what the ratifiers understood themselves to be enacting must be taken to be what the public of that time would have understood the words to mean. It is important to be clear about this. The search is not for a subjective intention. If someone found a letter from George Washington to Martha telling her that what he meant by the power to lay taxes was not what other people meant, that would not change our reading of the Constitution. Nor would the subjective intentions of all the members of a ratifying convention alter anything.... As Professor Henry Monaghan of Columbia has said, what counts is what the public understood. Law is a public act. Secret reservations or intentions count for nothing. All that counts is how the words used in the Constitution would have been understood at the time. The original understanding is thus manifested in the words used and in secondary materials, such as debates at

[82] Wolfe, *Judicial Activism*, 3.

[83] Raoul Berger, for example, maintains that original intention is "the explanation that draftsmen gave of what their words were designed to accomplish, what their words mean." See "Originalist Theories of Constitutional Interpretation, 73 *Cornell Law Review* 350, 350–1 (1988).

[84] Robert Bork, Speech to the University of San Diego Law School, November 18, 1985, in Cassell, *The Great Debate*, 52. At 45 he wrote: "The only way in which the Constitution can constrain judges is if the judges interpret the document's words according to the intentions of those who drafted, proposed, and ratified its provisions and its various amendments."

[85] Bork, *The Tempting of America*, 218.

the conventions, public discussion, newspaper articles, dictionaries in use at the time, and the like.[86]

The standard of constitutional meaning, in other words, is not what went through the minds of the Framers as they wrote and ratified the particular constitutional provisions they did, but rather the contemporaneous public understanding of the language comprising the document. "The intent to be given effect," according to the Office of Legal Policy in 1987, "is the objective intent as expressed in the words of the law being construed," for "[o]ur fundamental law is the text of the Constitution as understood by the ratifying society, not the subjective views of any group or individual."[87]

It is revealing, however, that textualism and intentionalism can appear to run together. Consider this statement by Richard Kay:

It is true that the determination of a shared intention calls for judgments about the psychological states of people long dead, but it will rarely be necessary to investigate these things directly. The concern is simply which of two contesting interpretations is more likely consistent with the original intention. The answer will often be presumptively clear from the language the constitution-makers chose. Beyond that, it will be enough in most cases to learn what people, at the time, *generally* meant when they used certain language and what people involved in the process of enactment thought was at issue.[88]

Kay begins here with a reference to the "psychological states of people long dead," which suggests the subjective approach of intentionalism, but he advances the claim that at issue is "what people, at the time, *generally* meant when they used certain language and what people involved in the process of enactment thought was at issue," which suggests the public-language approach of textualism. What this elision reveals is that, as in the case of the first axis of positivism and natural-rights theory, both the intentionalist and textualist forms of originalism on the second axis center on the people of 1787. As Kay goes on to write, "the task of seeking the original intentions

---

[86] Ibid., 144, footnote omitted. See also Justice Scalia's discussion of intent:

> We look for a sort of "objectified" intent – the intent that a reasonable person would gather from the text of the law, placed alongside the remainder of the *corpus juris*. . . . And the reason we adopt this objectified version is, I think, that it is simply incompatible with democratic government, or indeed, even with fair government, to have the meaning of a law determined by what the lawgiver meant, rather than by what the lawgiver promulgated. . . . It is the *law* that governs, not the intent of the lawgiver.

> Antonin Scalia, *A Matter of Interpretation: Federal Courts and the Law*, ed. Amy Gutmann (Princeton, NJ: Princeton University Press, 1997), 17.

[87] *Original Meaning Jurisprudence: A Sourcebook* (Report to the Attorney General by the Office of Legal Policy, United States Department of Justice, 12 March 1987), 14 and 17.

[88] Richard S. Kay, "Adherence to the Original Intentions in Constitutional Adjudication: Three Objections and Responses," 82 *Northwestern University Law Review* 226, 250 (1988) (footnote omitted).

involves an attempt to recreate the perspectives of the constitution-makers – their values, their needs, and even what we would consider their misconceptions."[89] Similarly, whether intentionalist or textualist, according to Brest, the interpreter acts at least in the first instance as an historian who "must immerse herself in the world of the adopters to try to understand constitutional concepts and values from their perspective."[90]

This notion of immersing ourselves in the world(s) of the writers and ratifiers of constitutional provisions in order to gain *their* perspective on constitutional questions is the crux of the matter. Whether one emphasizes drafters' intention or ratifiers' understanding as evidence of constitutional norms, or supports positivist or natural-rights sources of constitutional norms, an originalist by definition takes as normative the interpretive context of the time of ratification rather than that of any subsequent or contemporary period. The originalist, then, translates the claim that in constitutional interpretation we should be bound by the text of the Constitution into the claim that either the writers' intention or the ratifiers' understanding of the constitutional text always trumps any contrary understanding of that text in succeeding generations.

The reason this translation is controversial is that, to its proponents, originalism is synonymous with constitutionalism itself, such that to reject originalism is to reject constitutionalism. This is the basis on which an originalist equates originalism and interpretivism. The logic involves a path of reasoning very much like this:

1. Binding capacity is central to constitutionalism;
2. originalism is central to the possibility of binding capacity;
3. to reject originalism is to reject the possibility of binding capacity;
4. to reject the possibility of binding capacity is to reject constitutionalism;
5. consequently, to reject originalism is to reject constitutionalism.

The fundamental claim in this reasoning, of course, is the second, viz., that originalism is central to the possibility of binding capacity. Underlying that claim, I suggest, is the relation, central to my argument, between these two familiar propositions:

P_1: What binds the future is the constitutional text.
P_2: What binds the future is the original understanding of the constitutional text.

Originalism, I have claimed, denies the possibility of distinguishing between P_1 and P_2. The proposition that what binds the future is the constitutional text and the proposition that what binds the future is the original

---

[89] Ibid., 252.
[90] Brest, "The Misconceived Quest for the Original Understanding," 218.

understanding of the constitutional text are *identical*, such that the denial of the latter necessarily amounts to a denial of the former. In other words, to deny the authoritativeness of the original understanding of the constitutional text is to deny the authoritativeness of the Constitution per se. Nonoriginalist constitutional interpretation, from this perspective, is either overtly unprincipled, in that it does not care to provide justification for a given reading of the text, or else is unprincipled in effect because the search for justificatory interpretive principles outside the text can result ultimately in nothing beyond the personal values of the interpreter.

Consequently, from an originalist perspective, rejecting the original understanding necessarily pushes an interpreter beyond the text, for the text can mean nothing other than either the writers' intention or the ratifiers' understanding. If one presumes that the meaning of a text is what the author understood himself to be saying in that text, then originalism is correct to say that there is no text without reference to authorial intention in the constitutional text. Or, alternatively, if one presumes that the meaning of a text is what the original readers of the text understood it to be saying, then originalism is correct to say that there is no text without reference to the original readers' understanding of the constitutional text. Not to interpret the Constitution in terms of either alternative is, on such a view, not to interpret the Constitution at all, for the Constitution, so this argument goes, cannot be a constitutional text at all if we ignore the grounds of objective meaning. Without a grounding in the original understanding, the meaning of the Constitution loses any character of objectivity and becomes nothing more than each reader's interpretation of it over time. This undermines the very concept of a constitution because it undermines the distinction between constitutional and extraconstitutional norms and thus eliminates the capacity of a constitutional text to bind. Consequently, because from the originalist perspective the text can be only what the writers and ratifiers understood it to be, nonoriginalist constitutional interpretation is necessarily noninterpretivist; the idea of nonoriginalist interpretivism is oxymoronic. Thus, given that perspective, Gary McDowell maintains quite logically that "The question today is not so much how to read the Constitution as *whether* to read the Constitution."[91] Yet this conclusion follows only from originalist premises, in particular those about the nature of language. It tells us more about originalism than it does about the character of constitutional interpretation per se.

From a perspective that is not originalist – which is not to say that it is conventionally nonoriginalist – on the other hand, nonoriginalism in these terms is not the view that judges should not be bound by the original intention

---

[91] Gary L. McDowell, "The Politics of Original Intention," in Robert A. Goldwin and William A. Schambra, eds., *The Constitution, the Courts, and the Quest for Justice* (Washington: AEI: 1989), 1–2.

or understanding, but rather that the original intention or understanding as lodged in the constitutional text holds no a priori privileged position over any contrary interpretation of that text in succeeding generations. It is not that the text is not "authoritative or binding," to use Brest's words, but rather that the writers' or ratifiers' interpretation of the constitutional text is not authoritative or binding. Where Brest's analysis still bears the imprint of the interpretivism debate by suggesting that what he calls textualism is a form of originalism, I would argue to the contrary that originalism is a form of textualism, in that originalism is an interpretive theory as to how to read a text. Recalling the two propositions just given, this is the view that P_1 and P_2 are not identical – that, in other words, we can affirm that what binds the future is the constitutional text without being committed to saying that what binds the future is either the writers' intention in or the ratifiers' understanding of the constitutional text. The central question in constitutional interpretation on such a view is not "what is the writers' or ratifiers' understanding of the meaning of the text?" but, rather, "what is the meaning of the text?" The former can help to illuminate the latter, but ultimately we – or any interpreter – have to answer the latter question directly.

To summarize, then, the move in contemporary constitutional theory from the terminology of interpretivism–noninterpretivism to that of originalism–nonoriginalism clarifies the fact that the fundamental argument is about textual interpretation. The interpretivism–noninterpretivism debate was, as we have seen, an argument over the extent to which norms explicit or clearly implicit in the constitutional text govern constitutional interpretation exclusively. Whereas the strong sense of noninterpretivism argues that in at least some cases extraconstitutional norms may supplement constitutional norms in governing constitutional interpretation, interpretivism argues that solely constitutional norms may govern constitutional interpretation. The originalism–nonoriginalism debate is, in terms of the logic of constitutional theory, not equivalent to but rather the successor to this debate. The originalism–nonoriginalism conflict is an interpretivist argument over how to interpret the constitutional text, in that nonoriginalism as well as originalism presumes that only norms explicit or clearly implicit in the constitutional text govern constitutional interpretation. Thus, while the interpretivism–noninterpretivism debate is a modern version of the debate between positive law and natural law, the originalism–nonoriginalism debate is not – it is a debate about interpreting positive law.[92] As such, more specifically, the issue

---

[92] By arguing that much of what the Court does is a "revolutionary" modification of the Constitution rather than an interpretation of the existing text, Robert Justin Lipkin in *Constitutional Revolutions: Pragmatism and the Role of Judicial Review in American Constitutionalism* (Durham, NC: Duke University Press, 2000) threatens to reopen the interpretivism debate transcended in the early 1990s.

becomes the argument between originalist interpretation and nonoriginalist interpretation of the constitutional text.[93] It is the argument between the original understanding of the Constitution and subsequent generations' understanding. Of course, such a formulation presumes the intelligibility of the distinction between original and subsequent understanding, to which I will turn in Chapter 6. For now, having clarified the evolution of the interpretivism debate into the originalism debate, we must attend more closely to the latter.

[93] And the common element here, I would emphasize, is the text. As Jonathan Macey argues, "we are all originalists after a fashion. This is because the very act of engaging in constitutional interpretation, whether by judges or law professors or legislators, is the act of being engaged in the process, however abstract, of figuring out what the Framers' wishes were. In engaging in judicial review, a judge is recognizing that the Constitution is the supreme law of the land, an idea that is only possible from an originalist point of view." Jonathan R. Macey, "Originalism as an 'Ism,'" 19 *Harvard Journal of Law & Public Policy* 301, 308 (1996). The originalism debate, therefore, is an argument within the interpretivist framework.

4

The Paradox of Originalism

A survey of the voluminous literature on the originalism debate in contemporary American constitutional theory suggests that the arguments for the originalist paradigm of constitutional interpretation tend to fall into two general categories: literary and political. The literary argument advanced by originalists is, simply, that reading a text obviously involves nothing more and nothing less than attempting to discover what the author was trying to communicate. Originalists themselves differ as to evidence of the original understanding of the Constitution. For some, original understanding is grounded in the intentions of the Framers – the authors – of the Constitution, the position I call hard originalism; for others, original understanding is grounded in the understanding of the ratifiers – the first readers – of the Constitution, the position I call soft originalism. Raoul Berger writes:

A constitution is a written document, and as John Selden, the seventeenth century sage, observed, "a man's wryting has but one true sense, which is that which the Author meant when he writ it." This is the essence of communication. It is for the writer to explain what his words mean; the reader may dispute the proposition, but he may not insist in the face of the writer's own explanation that the writer meant something different.[1]

On this view, which is that of hard originalism, the author of a text controls the meaning, and the reader's task can be nothing other than to enter into the mind of the author. Similarly, Lino Graglia argues that "interpreting a document means to attempt to discern the intent of the author; there is no other 'interpretive methodology' properly so called."[2] This, he suggests, is simply common sense: "Originalism is less a philosophy than a definition of 'interpretation,' and a plainer, more conventional, or less esoteric definition

---

[1] Raoul Berger, "Originalist Theories of Constitutional Interpretation," 73 *Cornell Law Review* 350, 353 (1988).
[2] Lino A. Graglia, "'Interpreting' the Constitution: Posner on Bork," 44 *Stanford Law Review* 1019, 1024 (1992) (footnote omitted).

does not seem possible."[3] "The difference between writing and reading (or between making and interpreting a law)," Graglia says, "is that the writer seeks to communicate with the reader while the reader seeks to understand the writer's communication."[4]

Summarizing broadly, we can say that the political argument for originalism subdivides into three principal points. First, as Earl Maltz writes, the preference for originalism "is grounded on the concept of law."[5] Having a government of law and not men means, on this view, that we require neutrality in the derivation, definition, and application of principle in adjudication.[6] Central to originalism is the claim that in constitutional adjudication we necessarily face the interpretive choice between the views of those who wrote and ratified the provision in question and the personal views of unelected federal judges. Consequently, judges can adjudicate neutrally only if they base their decisions on the former, the Framers' views. As Robert Bork has stated:

When a judge finds his principle in the Constitution as originally understood, the problem of the neutral derivation of principle is solved. The judge accepts the ratifiers' definition of the appropriate ranges of majority and minority freedom. The Madisonian dilemma is resolved the way that the founders resolved it, and the judge accepts the fact that he is bound by that resolution as law. He need not, and must not, make unguided value judgments of his own.[7]

We have, in other words, a zero-sum choice in interpreting the Constitution (or any other written text): the reader's personal values or those of the authors/ratifiers. Since neutrality among ourselves in cases of conflicting interpretations requires a common standard, the only such standard available to us is that provided by the original meaning of the text. Only in this way, originalists claim, can law be neutral.

The second principal political argument advanced in favor of originalism is that this interpretive approach is necessary to preserve the separation of powers dictated by the Constitution. According to Bork:

The judicial role [of adherence to neutrality in the derivation, definition, and application of principle] corresponds to the original understanding of the place of courts in our republican form of government. The political arrangements of that form of

---

3 Ibid., 1029.
4 Ibid., 1024. However, Graglia seems unaware of any possible inconsistency between this view and the one he endorses from Bork, viz., that originalism is the view "that judges should interpret the Constitution to mean what those who adopted it understood it to mean" (1019, footnote omitted).
5 Earl Maltz, "The Failure of Attacks on Constitutional Originalism," 4 *Constitutional Commentary* 43, 53 (1987).
6 See, for example, Robert Bork, *The Tempting of America: The Political Seduction of the Law* (New York: Simon & Schuster, 1990), Chapter 7.
7 Ibid., 146.

government are complex, its balances of power continually shifting, but one thing our constitutional orthodoxy does not countenance is a judiciary that decides for itself when and how it will make national policy, when and to what extent it will displace executives and legislators as our governors.[8]

"No other method of constitutional adjudication," he continues, "can confine courts to a defined sphere of authority and thus prevent them from assuming powers whose exercise alters, perhaps radically, the design of the American Republic."[9] Similarly, Graglia writes that "Originalism is a virtual axiom of our legal-political system, necessary to distinguish the judicial from the legislative function."[10] At stake here is the idea that the function of the judiciary is to interpret law rather than to make law, with the implication that only originalist adjudication enables courts to maintain the distinction. Without such a distinction, according to originalism, courts necessarily stray out of the judicial realm and improperly into the legislative and executive domains. Such straying, moreover, must be prevented both across the branches of the federal government and between the proper domains of the federal and state governments. As Maltz writes,

federal judges are required to invalidate actions inconsistent with limitations imposed by the framers. At the same time, however, where other government actors act consistently with the original understanding, the federal courts should defer to their decisions; the same legitimate authority that established the courts themselves requires judges to respect the specific grants of power to Congress and the reservation of powers to the states in the Tenth Amendment.[11]

Indeed, it is the belief that federal courts have improperly interfered in the police powers of the states in such major social issues as race, religion, crime, and sexual behavior that has spawned the contemporary originalism debate.[12]

The third, and perhaps most important, principal political point advanced by advocates of originalism is the democracy argument. In Maltz's words:

The most plausible defense of originalism rests on a single axiom: The framers of the Constitution had legitimate authority to make political decisions that would bind future governmental decisionmakers until superseded by judgments made through the process specified in the Constitution itself.[13]

This is the most interesting, supposedly the most powerful, but actually the most problematic of the three arguments for originalism. If the democracy

---

[8] Ibid., 153.
[9] Ibid., 155.
[10] Graglia, "Posner on Bork," 1019 (footnote omitted).
[11] Maltz, *Rethinking Constitutional Law: Originalism, Interventionism, and the Politics of Judicial Review* (Lawrence: University Press of Kansas, 1994), 20.
[12] See Chapter 1.
[13] Maltz, *Rethinking the Constitution*, 20.

argument is considered to be simply a majoritarian argument, then it is easily challenged, even by originalists. The democracy argument has to do with accountability: In essence, the originalist argues that since judges are not accountable to contemporary electoral majorities, they must be accountable to the Framers. Inversely, if they are not accountable to the Framers, they are not accountable at all, and thus are undemocratic. In this sense, the "rule of law" argument seems to be another version of the democracy argument. When we say a government of laws and not men, we're saying that the criteria or norms on the basis of which judges decide cases cannot be their own values – that would be the rule of men – but have to be norms with democratic legitimacy. At the same time that originalism defends itself on the basis of the democracy argument, however, the whole notion of binding the future itself is antidemocratic, because surely allowing a contemporary majority to rule itself the way it wishes is more democratic than mandating that a contemporary majority must yield to a past (super)majority. Even if we say that the contemporary majority, if it achieves supermajority status, is perfectly free to change the fundamental law, it can do so legitimately only in terms of procedures set down by the Framers. So the paradox of originalism involves the democracy argument, that in one sense originalism stakes its claim to legitimacy – and it is a political claim – on the basis of the democratic argument, yet to the extent that it justifies binding capacity it is making an antidemocratic argument. In other words, the democracy argument contradicts the binding argument, and the binding argument contradicts the democracy argument.

Here, then, is Maltz again:

> Although it is probably the most popular defense of originalism, the appeal to democratic theory is also the easiest to dismiss. The Constitution itself plainly establishes rights which are inconsistent with the basic concept of majoritarian rule. The existence of these rights cannot be reconciled with "democracy" by pointing out that the Constitution itself was adopted through a democratic process; clearly, the principle of majority rule must refer to contemporary majorities, not those which existed in 1787.[14]

The Constitution, obviously, is not a purely majoritarian document; Madison's entire concern in Federalist 10 was with the problem of how to limit the power of democratic majorities in a society governed by majority rule. That was the antimajoritarian thrust of the Madisonian dilemma captured by Bork:

> A Madisonian system is not completely democratic, if by "democratic" we mean completely majoritarian. It assumes that in wide areas of life majorities are entitled

---

[14] Maltz, "The Failure of Attacks on Constitutional Originalism," 52 (footnote omitted). Maltz's preferred defense of originalism is the concept of law noted earlier: "The originalist position is not grounded on democracy. It is grounded on the concept of law" (53).

to rule for no better reason than that they are majorities.... The model has a counter-majoritarian premise, however, for it assumes that there are some areas of life a majority should not control. There are some things a majority should not do to us no matter how democratically it decides to do them. These are areas properly left to individual freedom, and coercion by the majority in these aspects of life is tyranny.[15]

This is the sense in which we are a liberal or constitutional, rather than a majoritarian, democracy. As Murphy, Fleming, and Harris note, the United States "is a political hybrid of constitutionalism and democracy, that is, a constitutional democracy. Its formal political structures and the political theories on which they are based combine rule by popularly chosen representatives with government limited by institutional checks on their power."[16]

The bounded majoritarianism of such a system stems from the thesis of constitutionalism that "[t]here are some fundamental rights that government may not trample on, even with the active support of the overwhelming majority of the population, whether aggregated individually or by groups."[17] As Robert McKay notes in an essay on liberal democracy, we have not a pure but rather a bounded majoritarianism:

The teachings of liberal democracy point ambiguously in several directions. We are told that decisional authority rests with the people and their chosen representatives (some elected, some appointed by those elected), and majoritarian democracy requires respect for their views. We are also reminded that those spokespersons of the majoritarian impulse may not transgress the more or less ill-defined limits imposed by constitutional text.[18]

The majority rules, in other words, but not over everything. To defend originalism as an interpretive approach that maximizes the domain of majority rule, therefore, presupposes that by the design of the Constitution majority rule is a good in and of itself. Yet it is clearly part of the original design of the republic that majority rule is circumscribed; the original understanding was that the new polity was not a majoritarian democracy. "Direct democracy and majoritarianism," Stephen Macedo writes, "were decisively rejected by the Framers, and the system of government established by

[15] Robert Bork, "Neutral Principles and Some First Amendment Problems," 47 *Indiana Law Journal* 1, 2–3 (1971). Interestingly, Bork's claim that "there are some things a majority should not do to us no matter how democratically it decides to do them" does not cohere with his general view that there is no principled way to decide among competing values except by majority rule. He leaves himself no other ground except a majority's decision that there are some things a majority should never do.

[16] Walter Murphy, James E. Fleming, and William F. Harris II, *American Constitutional Interpretation* (Mineola, NY: Foundation Press, 1986), 23.

[17] Ibid., 27.

[18] Robert B. McKay, "Judicial Review in a Liberal Democracy," 121–44 in J. Roland Pennock and John W. Chapman, eds., *Liberal Democracy* (Nomos XXV) (New York: New York University Press, 1983), 123.

the Constitution embodies this rejection."[19] The Constitution is not purely democratic: It subordinates ordinary majorities to the requirement of extraordinary majorities, and it subordinates contemporary majorities to past majorities.

Accepting this, however, still leaves us with the possibility of a modified majoritarian argument. Granting that we are not a fully majoritarian democracy, the originalist can argue that activist judges improperly infringe on the decision-making domain left to majority rule. Constitutionalism, Graglia says, has to do with limits on the people's lawmaking power, whereas activist judicial review has to do with giving lawmaking power to unelected judges:

> Because the Constitution places few restrictions on self-government and few of them are controversial, American legislators have little occasion and are little tempted to enact unconstitutional laws. Judicial review confined to invalidating enactments actually prohibited by the Constitution would thus result in very few judicial invalidations of popular choices.[20]

The strongest majoritarian form of the democracy argument, then, is that unelected judges must not invade those areas left to majority rule. Originalists commonly consider *Roe v. Wade*[21] to exemplify such judicial imperialism, but in doing so they usually beg the question as to whether the abortion decision is properly subject to majority rule in the first place. "Judicial invalidation of the elected representatives' policy choices," according to Graglia, "should be permitted only when (as would very rarely be the case) the choice is clearly disallowed by the Constitution."[22]

In reality, the democracy argument is not a majoritarianism thesis, but instead is more fundamentally and powerfully the consent argument of classical liberalism. In an essay on the concept of liberal democracy, Frederick G. Whelan gives a nice summary of this relationship:

> Modern democratic theory is an outgrowth of a longer tradition of political thought that focuses on consent as the requisite foundation of government. Consent theory characteristically takes political and legal obligation as the central issue of political theory, and it asserts that (at least in the public realm) only an individual's consent... can create a valid obligation for him. It follows that governmental authority is legitimate, and subjects are obligated to obey it, only if they have consented to its existence in some fashion.[23]

---

[19] Stephen Macedo, *The New Right vs. the Constitution* (Washington, DC: Cato Institute, 1987), 28 (footnote omitted).

[20] Graglia, "Posner on Bork," 1032 (footnote omitted).

[21] 410 U.S. 113 (1973).

[22] Graglia, "Posner on Bork," 1044 (footnote omitted).

[23] Frederick G. Whelan, "Prologue: Democratic Theory and the Boundary Problem," 13–47 in Pennock and Chapman, eds., *Liberal Democracy* (Nomos XXV), 24–5.

What creates the Madisonian dilemma of bounded majority rule in the first place? The answer, as Bork sees clearly, can be nothing but consent. His argument in "Neutral Principles" must be understood to be that in some sense an extraordinary majority has consented to the principle embedded in our Madisonian system that a simple majority shall not be permitted to do certain things. "Society consents," he states, "to be ruled undemocratically within defined areas by certain enduring principles believed to be stated in, and placed beyond the reach of majorities by, the Constitution."[24] Similarly, in *The Tempting of America*, Bork writes: "The orthodoxy of our civil religion, which the Constitution has aptly been called, holds that we govern ourselves democratically, except on those occasions, few in number though crucially important, when the Constitution places a topic beyond the reach of majorities."[25] Walter Berns puts this same point in especially revealing terms: "The Constitution derives its binding authority – binding on the governed and the government alike – only from the fact that it is an act of the people in their constituting capacity."[26] The legitimacy of the Constitution, that is, is rooted in the fact that (in some sense) We the People have consented to it; the binding power of the text is grounded in our consent to it.

It is fair to suggest that almost no one across the spectrum of constitutional debate would object to these principles. The particular point of originalism, however, is to claim that only originalist interpretation is consistent with the principle of democratic consent. "In truth," Bork writes, "only the approach of original understanding meets the criteria that any theory of constitutional adjudication must meet in order to possess democratic legitimacy."[27] That is, the originalist argument is that it is the only interpretive theory that is adequate to a liberal democracy; only it can explain how and why the Constitution democratically binds the future. In the words of the Meese Justice Department: "Interpretation of the Constitution according to its original meaning is the only approach that takes seriously the status of our Constitution as fundamental law, and that permits our society to remain self-governing."[28] The phrase "our Constitution as fundamental law" refers to the binding power of the text, and the phrase "permits our society to remain self-governing" points to the grounding of the text in democratic consent. American constitutionalism is a liberal constitutionalism, and these

---

[24] Bork, "Neutral Principles," 3.

[25] Bork, *The Tempting of America*, 153.

[26] Walter Berns, *Taking the Constitution Seriously* (New York: Simon & Schuster, 1987), 236–7.

[27] Bork, *The Tempting of America*, 143. Also, at 163–4: "In both its vindication of principle against democratic majorities and its vindication of democracy against unprincipled judicial activism, the philosophy of original understanding does better by far than any other theory of constitutional adjudication can."

[28] *Original Meaning Jurisprudence: A Sourcebook* (Report to the Attorney General by the Office of Legal Policy, United States Department of Justice, 12 March 1987), 3.

are indeed its two central premises: The purpose of a constitution is to bind the future, and government is legitimate only when it is based on the consent of the governed.

Against this background, the principal concern of this chapter is to explore the way the liberal foundations of American constitutionalism "Locke" it into a problem. On the one hand, liberalism historically has affirmed the principle that the ultimate ground of legitimacy – authority – for a political system is the consent of the governed. On the other hand, however, the notion of binding the future appears to contradict the principle of consent that grounds the legitimacy of the political system. In the face of this paradox, originalism claims to be the only interpretive theory by which the Constitution can be seen to bind the future democratically. Yet originalism, I want to suggest, actually exacerbates rather than solves this conundrum, because of the particular way it privileges the past over the present. Consider this statement by Graglia:

> All judicially enforced constitutionalism limits majority rule. To the extent of this limitation, judicial review constitutes government of the living by the dead and, therefore, requires justification. When a judge invalidates a law that contravenes no clear and definite constitutional restriction a different and much more serious problem arises. In such a case, government is not by the dead but by judges, very much alive, who are not subject to electoral control.[29]

The claim that in constitutional adjudication we necessarily face the interpretive choice between the intentions of the Framers and the personal views of unelected federal judges, and that the former have a democratic legitimacy that the latter do not,[30] is central to originalism. Graglia acknowledges that "government of the living by the dead" requires justification, but he does not pursue this issue. Yet when he argues that a much more serious problem is government "by judges, very much alive, who are not subject to electoral control," he glosses over the fact that the dead likewise are not subject to electoral control. If it is illegitimate for judges' personal values to bind us, because we did not consent to such values and have no electoral control over them – a claim with which I have no quarrel – then we have to deal with the fact that we did not consent to the Framers' values and have no electoral control over them either (other than by amending the Constitution to alter or repeal specific provisions – but see the later discussion).

We would seem to face, in other words, an unpleasant set of alternatives: Either we are bound without our consent or we have not consented and thus

---

[29] Graglia, "Posner on Bork," 1020-1 (footnote omitted).

[30] For example, *Sourcebook* argues at 4 that "if the courts go beyond the original meaning of the Constitution, if they strike down legislative or executive action based on their personal notions of the public good or on other extra-constitutional principles, they usurp powers not given to them by the people." Beyond the question of democratic consent, of course, this is an appeal to the separation-of-powers argument as well.

are not bound. As Paul Brest explains this problem:

> According to the political theory most deeply rooted in the American tradition, the authority of the Constitution derives from the consent of its adopters. Even if the adopters freely consented to the Constitution, however, this is not an adequate basis for continuing fidelity to the founding document, for their consent cannot bind succeeding generations. We did not adopt the Constitution, and those who did are dead and gone.[31]

How can we plausibly be said to consent to a constitution we did not participate in ratifying? How do we explain that we are bound by our own consent? Originalists seem always to assume this rather than explain it. Recall the statement by Berns previously cited: "The Constitution derives its binding authority . . . only from the fact that it is an act of the people in their constituting capacity." "An act of the people in their constituting capacity" is the key phrase, for which we need an adequate account. Indeed, according to commentator Samuel Freeman:

> [Originalists] maintain that the constitution is democratic because it was established by our forebears in the supermajoritarian procedure that ratified the Constitution. But democratic sovereignty does not reside in some of the ancestors of some living Americans. It resides in the present body of citizens. Any account of constitutional interpretation must show why *existing* people, conceived of as free, equal, and independent, should *accept* and *endorse* the inherited Constitution.[32]

My argument is that originalism conceives this constituting capacity not as continuous but as a discrete historical moment (1787, 1868, etc.), yet to avoid the problem of consent this constituting capacity must be not in the past, but in an "omnipresent."

The problem, then, is that in making the argument from consent in order to justify the legitimacy of constitutionalism and limit judicial review, originalism threatens to prove too much.[33] The originalist conception of

---

[31] Paul Brest, "The Misconceived Quest for the Original Understanding," 60 *Boston University Law Review* 204, 225 (1980) (footnotes omitted).

[32] Samuel Freeman, "Original Meaning, Democratic Interpretation, and the Constitution," *Philosophy and Public Affairs*, Vol. 21, No. 1 (Winter 1992), 12. He continues at 15: "[I]f we take the primary role of a written constitution in a democracy to be its role as the public charter among sovereign citizens, providing terms for civic justification that they could reasonably accept and agree to, then straightaway we are confronted with a puzzle as to why the *only* kinds of considerations that are relevant to deciding what that document requires should be the intentions and understandings of those who wrote or ratified it. Indeed, it is not clear why *their* intentions and beliefs should carry any weight at all."

[33] Recall Edmund Burke's criticism of liberal natural-rights theory:

> Whilst they are possessed by these notions, it is vain to talk to them of the practice of their ancestors, the fundamental laws of their country, the fixed form of a constitution whose merits are confirmed by the solid text of long experience and an increasing public strength

liberal consent threatens the legitimacy of constitutionalism itself, because the idea of consent as a discrete historical act undermines the possibility of an idea of consent as ongoing, the idea necessary to legitimate the constitutional system. The key to solving the explanatory problem is this: "Given the questionable authority of the American Constitution," according to Brest, "it is only through a history of continuing assent or acquiescence that the document could become law."[34] The idea of the "dead hand of the past" is inconsistent with the idea of consent. We need a concept of the omnipresent, but all originalism can give us is the dead hand of the past. In order to affirm the binding role, for purposes of interpretation originalists must claim that We the People consist of the founders rather than any subsequent generation. Yet to affirm the democratic principle, We the People must include the founding and all subsequent generations. These, then, are the ideas I will explore in the remaining pages of this chapter.[35]

and national prosperity. They despise experience as the wisdom of unlettered men; and as for the rest, they have wrought underground a mine that will blow up, at one grand explosion, all examples of antiquity, all precedents, charters, and acts of parliament.

Edmund Burke, *Reflections on the Revolution in France*, ed. J. G. A. Pocock (Indianapolis: Hackett Publishing Company, 1987), 50–1.

[34] Brest, "The Misconceived Quest for the Original Understanding," 225 (footnotes omitted).

[35] My analysis and use of the notion of We the People would, of course, appear to implicate the work of Bruce Ackerman in his books of that title. In *We the People: Foundations* (Cambridge, MA: Belknap Press of Harvard University Press, 1991), from which I draw the following citations, Ackerman introduces the concept of a dualist Constitution. This concept, which parallels Hamilton's distinction in Federalist 78 between the people and their representatives, "seeks to distinguish between two different decisions that may be made in a democracy. The first is a decision by the American people; the second, by their government" (6). Ackerman employs this concept to develop a general theory of transformative moments in (American) constitutional regimes, a theory that attempts to present an account of the mechanisms of constitutional change through which We the People appear on the scene in contradistinction from ordinary, transient popular majorities and elites. In summary form, his account of the nonamendment mechanism of constitutional change is this:

Decisions by the People occur rarely, and under special constitutional conditions. Before gaining the authority to make supreme law in the name of the People, a movement's political partisans must, first, convince an extraordinary number of their fellow citizens to take their proposed initiative with a seriousness that they do not normally accord to politics; second, they must allow their opponents a fair opportunity to organize their own forces; third, they must convince a majority of their fellow Americans to support their initiative as its merits are discussed, time and again, in the deliberative fora provided for "higher lawmaking." It is only then that a political movement earns the enhanced legitimacy the dualist Constitution accords to decisions made by the People. (6)

In terms of that model of constitutional change, whose mechanism includes what he calls in Chapter 10 the "signaling phase," the "proposal phase," the "mobilized popular-deliberation phase," and the "legal-codification phase," Ackerman wants to argue that "both Reconstruction Republicans and New Deal Democrats appear as the equals of the Founding Federalists in creating new higher lawmaking processes and substantive solutions in the name of We the People of the United States" (58).

The liberal foundations of originalism in particular and American constitutional theory in general are evident in Berns's discussion of the constituting capacity of the American people noted earlier. We constituted ourselves as a people, according to Berns, through the Declaration of Independence:

An organic law is an organizing or constituting law, and the Declaration is the first such American law because, according to the political theory informing it, before there can be legitimate government, there must be a people, a people to institute it, and before there can be a people there must be a compact among persons who, by nature, are free and independent – which is to say, independent of each other.[36]

The liberal character of this description should be obvious. "By virtue of this compact, freely entered into by everyone with everyone," he continues, "the naturally free and independent individuals are transformed into or constituted a social entity, a people, or a society, and it is this society that institutes and empowers government."[37] In this Lockean formulation, Berns sees the Declaration as the first compact and the Constitution as the second. The fundamental premise that lies behind all of the various elements comprising the liberal tradition is the idea that authority is not natural, but conventional. In contrast to the medieval assumption that there is an a priori moral order to the universe, a structure within which everyone and everything has its place, classical liberalism, particularly in its Hobbesian formulation, begins with the idea of atomistic, antagonistic, free-floating individuals defined and existing independently of any a priori structure. Imagine, if you will, a connect-the-dots picture. In those terms, whereas the medieval tradition can be said to have emphasized the consecutive numbers that order the dots and thus form a picture, the liberal tradition posits the existence of the dots only,

With regard to the question of what should count as the norms for judicial review, Ackerman wants to defend the considered judgment of We the People against both the elected representatives of current majorities, which he calls the "monist position," and the claims of abstract moral or political theory, which he calls the "foundationalist position." Pointing to the Burkean notion of the Constitution as a historically rooted tradition and language of politics, Ackerman writes:

This sense of an ongoing tradition of discourse eluded the first two schools we have considered. The monistic democrat worships at the altar of the Present – he supposes that he knows all he needs to know about democratic rule if he simply consults the last statutory word approved by Congress. The foundationalist seeks to escape the limits of time altogether – he hopes to define some ahistorical State of Nature of Original Position to serve as a constitutional platform from which to pass judgment on history's passing show. (23)

While my discussion of the Burkean character of our Constitution will have some elements in common with Ackerman's work, at bottom his concern is principally with the question of when and how the considered judgment of We the People has been expressed and incorporated into our constitutional tradition. My attention to and use of the notion of We the People will be, I submit, distinct from Ackerman's.

[36] Berns, *Taking the Constitution Seriously*, 23.
[37] Ibid., 27.

without the ordering numbers. There is no natural human authority beyond the sovereign individual; less clearly than for Hobbes, for Locke the natural state of humankind is not political, therefore, but rather prepolitical. Individuals, in Locke's terms, are in "*a state of perfect freedom* to order their actions, and dispose of their possessions and persons, as they think fit, within the bounds of the law of nature, without asking leave, or depending upon the will of any other man."[38] The key idea is the absence of any a priori human authority: "Men living together according to reason, without a common superior on earth, with authority to judge between them, is *properly the state of nature.*"[39] From this premise that all authority is conventional follow the principles of individualism, liberty, equality, and, most important, consent. In the absence of any a priori moral order to the human world, all that exists is the individual; there are no political institutions to which the individual is naturally subordinate. All individuals, consequently, are by nature morally and politically equal, and they thereby have equal title to their liberty.

If, therefore, authority is conventional rather than natural, then that means that authority exists only by convention or agreement, and that is to say that authority is grounded on consent. Analytically, consent requires the following:

Consent means deliberate choice by the people among alternatives on an ongoing and regular basis; every law and policy is supposed to reflect the will of the majority expressed through the democratic process, while the participation of all the citizens reflects their general consent to the procedural norms of democracy and the constitution of the state in which these are embodied.[40]

Prior to an act of consent, people are in a prepolitical condition. Locke writes that "all men are naturally in that state, and remain so, till by their own consents they make themselves members of some politic society."[41] His statement on the act of consent is lengthy but well known:

Men being, as has been said, by nature, all free, equal, and independent, no one can be put out of this estate, and subjected to the political power of another, without his own consent. The only way whereby any one divests himself of his natural liberty, and puts on the *bonds of civil society*, is by agreeing with other men to join and unite into a community for their comfortable, safe, and peaceable living one amongst another, in a secure enjoyment of their properties, and a greater security against any, that are not of it. This any number of men may do, because it injures not the freedom of the rest; they are left as they were in the liberty of the state of nature. When any number

---

38 John Locke, *Second Treatise of Government*, ed. C. B. Macpherson (Indianapolis: Hackett Publishing Company, 1980), 8.

39 Ibid., 15. Similarly: "The *natural liberty* of man is to be free from any superior power on earth, and not to be under the will or legislative authority of man, but to have only the law of nature for his rule" (17).

40 Whelan, "Democratic Theory," 25.

41 Locke, *Second Treatise*, 13–14.

of men have so *consented to make one community or government*, they are thereby presently incorporated, and make *one body politic*, wherein the *majority* have a right to act and conclude the rest.[42]

The individual, from the liberal perspective, is legitimately subject only to that authority established and accepted by personal consent: "The *liberty of man*, in society, is to be under no other legislative power, but that established, by consent, in the common-wealth; nor under the dominion of any will, or restraint of any law, but what that legislative shall enact, according to the trust put in it."[43] And what a group of individuals consent to is the establishment of a society that will be governed by majority rule: "And thus every man, by consenting with others to make one body politic under one government, puts himself under an obligation, to every one of that society, to submit to the determination of the majority, and to be concluded by it."[44] Those who do not so consent do not form part of that society, just as in the ratification of the Constitution each state could consent to the new scheme for itself but could not bind other states to do the same (nine states were needed to put the Constitution into effect, not for all states, but only for those that ratified it). Once unanimous consent sets up a society, then the majority will establish a particular form of government. The majority-rule idea is central to democracy but not to liberalism itself. Locke said we could consent to a monarchy or oligarchy: "[T]he community may make compounded and mixed forms of government, as they think good."[45] We tend, however, to run the two together, such that we assume that democracy involves consent. Actually, we could say that while democracy involves consent, consent does not necessarily imply democracy, as Locke suggests. Hence even the bounded majoritarianism of the American polity rests on consent.

When pushed far enough, however, the consent argument threatens constitutionalism itself. Thomas Jefferson exhibits the logical extreme to which the argument from consent can go. To the question as to "[w]hether one generation of men has a right to bind another," he wrote in a letter to James Madison, "that no such obligation can be transmitted I think very capable of proof."[46] One generation is completely independent of another, he argues. In detail, he states that

no society can make a perpetual constitution, or even a perpetual law. The earth belongs always to the living generation. They may manage it then, and what proceeds from it, as they please, during their usufruct. They are masters too of their own persons, and consequently may govern them as they please. But persons and property

---

[42] Ibid., 52.
[43] Ibid., 17.
[44] Ibid., 52.
[45] Ibid., 68.
[46] Jefferson letter to James Madison, 6 September 1789, in "Letters of Thomas Jefferson," http://odur.let.rug.nl/~usa/P/tj3/writings/brf/jefl81.htm, 444.

make the sum of the objects of government. The constitution and the laws of their predecessors extinguished them, in their natural course, with those whose will gave them being. This could preserve that being till it ceased to be itself, and no longer. Every constitution, then, and every law, naturally expires at the end of 19 years. If it be enforced longer, it is an act of force and not of right.[47]

Similarly, thirty-five years later, Jefferson wrote:

Can one generation bind another, and all others, in succession forever? I think not.... A generation may bind itself as long as its majority continues in life; when that has disappeared, another majority is in place, holds all the rights and powers their predecessors once held, and may change their laws and institutions to suit themselves. Nothing then is unchangeable but the inherent and unalienable rights of man.[48]

The problem here exists at two levels. First, we – even Jefferson, if not John C. Calhoun – generally recognize the right of a contemporary majority to bind a contemporary minority, as evidenced by the ratification of the Constitution. While each state had to ratify the document for itself and could not be bound by a majority of the other states, within each state it was uncontroversial that a majority of the state's convention delegates could bind a minority of those delegates. Thus, while at one extreme Delaware's, New Jersey's, and Georgia's conventions voted unanimously to ratify, at the other 52 percent of Rhode Island's delegates bound the remaining 48 percent, and 53 percent each of Massachusetts', Virginia's, and New York's delegates bound the remaining 47 percent in favor of the new Constitution.[49] We recognize these majorities' rights to bind these minorities because we say that the minorities' initial agreement to participate in the ratification process bound them to the result even if their side lost. But, at the second level, why can a past majority bind a present majority? We know that we did not participate in the ratification process. This is what originalism has to explain in order to justify the democratic foundations of constitutionalism.

An example of the way the historicist consent argument of originalism actually eats away at the foundations of the constitutionalism that argument is intended to protect can be found in a revealing, not at all idiosyncratic article by Joseph Grano entitled "Judicial Review and a Written Constitution in a Democratic Society."[50] Using the term interpretivism as a synonym for originalism, Grano seeks to argue for interpretivism/originalism by laying

---

[47] Ibid., 451–2. For a critique of Jefferson's view here, see Jed Rubenfeld, "Textualism and Democratic Legitimacy," along with responses from Lilian Bevier, Michael McConnell, and Frank Easterbrook, in *66 George Washington Law Review* 1085 (1998).

[48] Letter to John Cartwright, 5 June 1824, in *The Political Writings of Thomas Jefferson*, ed. Edward Dumbauld (Indianapolis: Bobbs-Merrill Company, 1955), 126.

[49] Thomas A. Bailey and David M. Kennedy, *The American Pageant*, 8th ed. (New York: D. C. Heath & Company, 1987), 144 (my own calculations).

[50] Joseph Grano, "Judicial Review and a Written Constitution in a Democratic Society," 28 *Wayne Law Review* 1 (1981).

out arguments against noninterpretivism/nonoriginalism. Taking as a given the core principle of American constitutional design, he writes that "I start from the premise that the binding nature of our written Constitution must be taken as given."[51] Yet at the same time Grano states the claim that threatens to vitiate this principle: "Written constitutions are difficult to justify because of the problem of consent."[52] The difficulty, specifically, "is that a written constitution restrains not only the generation that adopts it, but subsequent generations as well, and restraint without assent is antithetical to the concept of self-government."[53] This, of course, is the argument that challenges constitutionalism itself. Despite his originalism, Grano invokes the famous metaphor used by nonoriginalists to attack originalists:

Some of our contemporary problems demonstrate the difficulty of being governed by the dead hand of the past. Racial preference for minority groups is one of our most wrenching moral issues. At the constitutional level, abundant scholarship has explored whether racial preference policies violate the fourteenth amendment's equal protection clause, a clause added to the Constitution in 1868. The more fundamental question, however, is why today's generation should be restricted on this issue by what people wrote and thought more than a century ago.[54]

Grano, however, has no theoretical or normative argument to offer on this question. Rather, he takes refuge in a practical, prudential position:

I am not advocating, therefore, that we revolt and discard our written Constitution; nor am I advocating that we hold a constitutional convention to repeal the Constitution. Whether or not the framers had a right to impose the Constitution on us, we have lived remarkably well under it, and the need for drastic action is not apparent. The point of my argument is that we should appreciate that the right to impose constitutional restraints on future generations is dubious.[55]

The Constitution, in other words, is like the bumblebee: By the laws of aerodynamics, it should not be able to fly – but it does.

What Grano wants to do with this conclusion, though, is to undermine noninterpretivism (nonoriginalism, recall, in his terms). In brief, he suggests that because constitutionalism itself has at best a questionable legitimacy, we consequently should be originalists because that interpretive approach will keep constitutional restraints on majority rule to a minimum. The problem with noninterpretivism is that it adds constitutional restraints:

My argument, in short, is that because written constitutions are difficult to justify, they should be limited in scope. Noninterpretivism should be rejected because it is

[51] Ibid., 4.
[52] Ibid., 51.
[53] Ibid., 51.
[54] Ibid., 52–3.
[55] Ibid., 58–9.

a methodology of constitutional expansion, a methodology that, in effect, increases the number of restraints imposed by the Constitution.[56]

That claim is fair enough, but Grano grounds it with a much more radical – radically Jeffersonian, if you will – argument:

Whether the issue be abortion, the right of the family or unrelated individuals to share living quarters, the right of a brother to marry a sister, or the right to a greater share of the wealth, every noninterpretivist decision recognizing one of these claims adds, in effect, a new provision to the written constitution and thereby imposes an additional moral restraint on subsequent generations. Every such decision assumes that if the moral position taken is not the last word, it is nevertheless presumptively correct and should bind our successors unless they can obtain the necessary super-majority to amend the Constitution.[57]

The reasoning is simple and clear: (1) If we adopt noninterpretivism (nonoriginalism), then we increase the number of constitutional restraints on majority rule; therefore (2), if we should not increase the number of constitutional restraints on majority rule, then we should reject noninterpretivism in favor of interpretivism (originalism). This argument is precisely Graglia's point:

The function of originalism is to minimize the conflict between judicial review and democracy; that conflict ordinarily arises only when judicial review is used to invalidate a choice made in the political process. The Court's refusal to intervene in the political process may be inconsistent with constitutionalism, but it is rarely inconsistent with democracy. If the end is democracy, that end is served when judge-restraining originalism permits the results of the democratic political process to stand.[58]

For Grano, therefore, "*Roe v. Wade* is as wrong as the proposed constitutional amendment to protect the fetus, and for the same reason: it seeks to bind succeeding generations to our generation's thinking, or at least to the thinking of a segment of it."[59] But this is a remarkable statement, for it attacks not just decisions originalists consider judicial activism, but also the recommended originalist solution to dissatisfaction with the meaning of the Constitution: formal amendments. Recall Justice George Sutherland's famous originalist dissent in *West Coast Hotel v. Parrish*:

It is urged that the question involved should now receive fresh consideration, among other reasons, because of "the economic conditions which have supervened"; but the meaning of the Constitution does not change with the ebb and flow of economic events. We frequently are told in more general words that the Constitution must be construed in the light of the present. If by that it is meant that the Constitution is made up of living words that apply to every new condition which they include,

---

[56] Ibid., 51.
[57] Ibid., 59 (footnote omitted).
[58] Graglia, "Posner on Bork," 1026 (footnotes omitted).
[59] Joseph Grano, "Judicial Review," 59.

the statement is quite true. But to say, if that be intended, that the words of the Constitution mean today what they did not mean when written – that is, that they do not apply to a situation now to which they would have applied then – is to rob that instrument of the essential element which continues it in force as the people have made it until they, and not their official agents, have made it otherwise.[60]

The Court, Sutherland maintained, must respect the fixed, original meaning of the Constitution[61] and leave it, democratically, to the people to change if they wish: "What a court is to do, therefore, is *to declare the law as written*, leaving it to the people themselves to make such changes as new circumstances may require."[62] As represented by Sutherland, then, the originalist position on constitutional change is this:

If the Constitution, intelligently and reasonably construed in the light of these principles, stands in the way of desirable legislation, the blame must rest upon that instrument, and not upon the court for enforcing it according to its terms. The remedy in that situation – and the only true remedy – is to amend the Constitution.[63]

Yet what is remarkable about Grano's claim is that it throws into question, for just the same reason, the legitimacy of even formal constitutional amendments. Grano would certainly agree with Sutherland's caution to the courts: "The judicial function is that of interpretation; it does not include the power of amendment under the guise of interpretation."[64] But his concern for democratic legitimacy undermines the amendment process as well. Just as much as courts, the Constitution, along with any amendments formally added to it, "denies the majority the right to choose between radical change and the force of tradition."[65]

Grano, therefore, in effect supports originalism at the cost of undermining the democratic legitimacy of the Constitution itself. Any binding power, apparently, is suspect:

In summary, noninterpretivism should be rejected not only for the reasons previously discussed in this article, but also because it permits our generation (or a segment of it) to impose its views on generations yet to come. Instead of doing this, we should leave our children the freedom to govern themselves and to define justice in accordance with their own conceptions.[66]

Grano's position amounts to a claim much like this: We should adopt originalism because constitutionalism itself is problematic in terms of consent,

---

[60] 300 U.S. 379, 402–3 (1937).
[61] "The meaning of the constitution is fixed when it is adopted, and it is not different at any subsequent time when a court has occasion to pass upon it." Ibid., 404.
[62] Ibid.
[63] Ibid.
[64] Ibid.
[65] Grano, "Judicial Review and a Written Constitution," 52.
[66] Ibid., 60.

and we therefore should not compound the problem, which afflicts the Framers themselves, by adding, as it were, fingers to the dead hand of the past. Yet this refutation of nonoriginalism proves too much, for it is essentially a refutation of originalism as well.

Precisely what, then, creates this problem for originalism even as it remains only dimly acknowledged by originalists? In and of itself, the claim that in constitutional interpretation we should be bound by the text of the Constitution is an unobjectionable statement of the idea of binding the future at the very core of the concept of a constitution. The characteristic and controversial move of originalism, we have seen, is the translation of this claim into the principle, generally definitive of originalism in its particular forms, that the original understanding of the constitutional text always trumps any contrary understanding of that text in succeeding generations. Originalism is a regulative theory of constitutional interpretation whose purpose is to provide such a guarantee; should there arise a distinction between the original understanding and a current understanding of a particular constitutional provision, the original understanding is the authoritative, legally binding understanding. As Maltz writes:

> The primary distinction between originalism and other theories lies in their perceptions of the mutability of constitutional meaning. Originalists view the meaning of the Constitution as having been fixed in 1789, while adherents to other interpretive strategies see it as open-ended. From this perspective, it makes little difference if the body with authority to fix the original understanding is the drafters, the ratifiers, or the people as a whole; the key point is that once settled – by whatever body – it would not evolve over time as circumstances change.[67]

Recall my earlier observation that originalists themselves differ as to evidence of original understanding. For some, original understanding is grounded in the intentions of the Framers – the authors – of the Constitution, the position I call hard originalism; for others, original understanding is grounded in the understanding of the ratifiers – the first readers – of the Constitution, the position I call soft originalism. Both versions, however, subscribe to the more general principle that in constitutional interpretation the normative context of interpretation is that of those who wrote and ratified the language in question rather than that of any subsequent interpreters. That is, originalism argues that the necessary check on our understanding of the text of the Constitution is the writers' and ratifiers' understanding of that text. In this way originalism points to binding capacity as its very essence, and that is why there is such strength in its appeal.

The originalist, then, translates the claim that in constitutional interpretation we should be bound by the text of the Constitution into the claim that the original understanding of the constitutional text always trumps any contrary

---

[67] Maltz, *Rethinking the Constitution*, 26–7.

understanding of that text in succeeding generations. The reason this translation is controversial is that, to its proponents, originalism is synonymous with constitutionalism itself. Graglia, for example, argues as follows:

Because the Constitution derived its legal authority only when it was ratified at state conventions, judges should take it to mean what it was understood to mean by the ratifiers or, more generally, the people they represented. In its clearest and strongest form this originalist position reduces to the tautology that no law should be held unconstitutional unless it is prohibited by the Constitution; that is, unless it is in fact inconsistent with the Constitution as understood by those who made it authoritative.[68]

The key move in this argument is the identification of the phrase "prohibited by the Constitution" with the phrase "inconsistent with the Constitution as understood by those who made it authoritative." Here again is originalism's rejection of any distinction between these two propositions:

P$_1$: What binds the future is the constitutional text.
P$_2$: What binds the future is the original understanding of the constitutional text.

What this means, however, is that it is not the text, but rather a particular, historically specific reading of the text, that is binding. For example, Bork writes: "The principles of the actual Constitution make the judge's major moral choices for him. When he goes beyond such principles, he is at once adrift on an uncertain sea of moral argument."[69] As it stands, this claim is unobjectionable. Yet what Bork actually means is that "the principles of the actual Constitution" *as understood by the writers and ratifiers* "make the judge's major moral choices for him."[70] Again, originalists – on the one hand – deny the possibility of distinguishing between the principles of the actual Constitution and the principles of the actual Constitution as understood by the Framers, but – on the other hand – their concern to make this identification makes sense only on the assumption that, as an empirical matter, one could indeed understand the principles of the Constitution differently from the way the writers and ratifiers understood them. Consequently, we must infer from originalism's focus on the original understanding that, despite its emphasis on the constitutional text, what binds us is not the language of the

---

[68] Graglia, "Posner on Bork," 1023–4.

[69] Bork, *The Tempting of America*, 252.

[70] Similarly, Gary McDowell writes: "At the most basic level, a jurisprudence of original intention is a recourse to the basic principles underlying the Constitution. The need is to take seriously the text of the Constitution and the principles that undergird that text." Gary L. McDowell, "The Politics of Original Intention," in Robert A. Goldwin and William A. Schambra, eds., *The Constitution, the Courts, and the Quest for Justice* (Washington, DC: AEI, 1989), 3. This claim too is unobjectionable as it stands. It is the addition of "as understood by the Framers" that makes the difference.

text but rather the people who wrote and ratified the language of the text. Additionally, for originalism, all we can ask is what the writers and ratifiers said about provision X – not whether they were right about provision X.

My contention, then, is that originalism simultaneously affirms and denies the democratic and binding authority of the Constitution, because it simultaneously affirms and denies the binding capacity of language. That is, originalism claims to be the only theory by which the Constitution democratically binds the future,[71] but the theory's distinction between the constitutional text and the original intention or understanding actually undermines the democratic and binding character of the text.[72] The paradox here is that if originalism truly believed in the binding capacity of language that it affirms, it would lose its raison d'être. That is, originalism can claim to be a necessary guide to constitutional interpretation only because it denies the binding capacity of language that it purports to affirm. Oddly enough, as Berns, for example, insists on the central importance of the writtenness of the Constitution by citing Thomas Paine's statement that "an unwritten constitution is not a constitution at all,"[73] his insistence empties that writtenness of content at the same time. The problem at issue here is simply this: The focus on the authoritativeness of the written text in originalism constantly dissolves that text into an unwritten meta-text standing behind it. The original understanding becomes, so to speak, a kind of Cliff Notes or Monarch Notes for the Constitution. Even Graglia unwittingly reveals this implication. "If the Constitution can be 'interpreted' to authorize the court to enforce natural justice," he argues, "there would be no need to refer to the Constitution in 'constitutional' cases; the only remaining question would be the meaning of natural justice, not the meaning of the Constitution."[74] This is true, but the same problem afflicts originalism as well. Substituting appropriately, this statement reads: "If the Constitution can be 'interpreted' to authorize the court to enforce the Framers' intent, there would be no need to refer to the Constitution in 'constitutional' cases; the only remaining question would be the meaning of the Framers' intent, not the meaning of the Constitution."

---

71 "Interpretation of the Constitution according to its original meaning is the only approach that takes seriously the status of our Constitution as fundamental law, and that permits our society to remain self-governing." *Sourcebook*, 3.

72 Note the distinction between language and meaning: "The most authoritative evidence of original meaning is the specific language used by the framers and ratifiers in the document. This wording was carefully chosen, usually after much reflection and debate, and we may reasonably presume that it conveys an ascertainable meaning. A court should interpret the words of the Constitution according to their plain and natural import in their general and popular use at the time the provision at issue was ratified." *Sourcebook*, 9. Language on this view does not so much constitute meaning itself as provide evidence of meaning.

73 Berns, *Taking the Constitution Seriously*, 70.

74 Graglia, "Posner on Bork," 1029.

As much as originalism opposes both the older legal realism and the new deconstructionism, it is at one with them in asserting – implicitly, to be sure – the essential indeterminacy of the text. The basic originalist position is that without the governance of the original understanding, the text of the Constitution means whatever each and every reader wants it to mean. As we earlier saw Bork state: "The only way in which the Constitution can constrain judges is if the judges interpret the document's words according to the intentions of those who drafted, proposed, and ratified its provisions and its various amendments."[75] Now, put simply *we*, in 2005 or in 2099, are capable of reading the text of the Constitution and coming to some understanding of what we think it means; but originalism argues that unless we subordinate our reading to the governance of the original understanding, our reading will necessarily be subjective and perverse. The contrast between *our* reading and *their* (i.e., the Framers') reading is the key point, for originalism is caught in the trap of insisting upon the distance between "them" and "us" in order to maintain the Constitution's binding character while denying any distance between "them" and "us" in order to maintain the Constitution's democratic character.

"The Constitution," again according to Berns, "derives its binding authority – binding on the governed and the government alike – only from the fact that it is an act of the people in their constituting capacity."[76] Both originalist and nonoriginalist alike affirm this proposition. Yet despite this general notion of We the People, the problem is this: Given the distinction between original and contemporary interpretive contexts, then, on the one hand, if *their* reading is binding on us, we can understand the binding character of the Constitution but how do we plausibly explain it as a democratic system of self-governance? On the other hand, if *we* are fully as much a part of We the People as *they* are, we can understand the democratic character of the Constitution, but how do we account for any binding capacity of a text that we read in our own interpretive context? The only way to make the text both democratic and binding is to conceptualize an ongoing – not a past – act of constituting, but originalism's insistence on the distance between the original and subsequent interpretive contexts leaves the theory trapped in the inability to account for anything other than solely a past act of constituting.

Like Berns, Christopher Wolfe also appeals to democratic legitimacy in upholding his preference for originalism:

Judicial review simply gave effect to the will of the people contained in the Constitution over the more transient popular will represented by the legislature (and executive) at a given moment. Thus, the very nature of judicial review kept it quite limited. To the extent that it was undemocratic, that was accounted for primarily

---

[75] Bork, *The Great Debate: Interpreting Our Written Constitution*, Paul G. Cassell, ed. (Washington, DC: The Federalist Society, 1986), 45.
[76] Berns, *Taking the Constitution Seriously*, 236–7.

by the nation's commitment to the principle of constitutionalism, whereby present majorities are limited by earlier extraordinary majorities.[77]

Wolfe's phrase "the nation's commitment to the principle of constitutionalism" and Berns's phrase "an act of the people in their constituting capacity" are crucially important here. Originalism bases its democracy argument on the principle of consent embedded in such phrases, but it locates and isolates that commitment or act of the people in 1787, 1868, and so on. Yet to avoid the problem of consent this constituting capacity must be not in the past, but in an omnipresent. Indeed, the idea of tacit consent is a kind of omnipresent. Wolfe is admirably aware of the role of tacit consent in originalism's democracy argument:

Tacit consent is a necessary part of any democratic theory, at least when the principle of constitutionalism is involved. Otherwise, there would have to be a rule such as Thomas Jefferson proposed, that every generation or so the laws (including the Constitution) automatically expire, thus requiring the new generation to make its consent to the laws explicit.[78]

The idea of tacit consent, of course, goes back at least to Locke. In his well-known, if lengthy, statement:

Every man being, as has been shewed, *naturally free*, and nothing being able to put him into subjection to any earthly power, but only his own *consent*; it is to be considered, what shall be understood to be a *sufficient declaration* of a man's *consent, to make him subject* to the laws of any government. There is a common distinction of an express and a tacit consent, which will concern our present case. No body doubts but an express *consent*, of any man entering into any society, makes him a perfect member of that society, a subject of that government. The difficulty is, what ought to be looked upon as a *tacit consent*, and how far it binds, i.e. how far any one shall be looked on to have consented, and thereby submitted to any government, where he has made no expressions of it all. And to this I say, that every man, that hath any possessions, or enjoyment, of any part of the dominions of any government, doth thereby give his *tacit consent*, and is as far forth obliged to obedience to the laws of that government, during such enjoyment, as any one under it. . . .[79]

Of course, for either express or tacit consent to be meaningful, people must have a real alternative in a "love it or leave it" situation, and this becomes questionable where not all borders are open (places people want to go to are not open, and places that are open are where no one wants to go) and when one recognizes the fact that our identities are socially embedded and thus not easily transplanted to a new environment. Nevertheless, what is often overlooked in considering Locke's theory of tacit consent is his caution, a

77 Christopher Wolfe, *Judicial Activism: Bulwark of Freedom or Precarious Security?* (Pacific Grove, CA: Brooks/Cole Publishing Company, 1991), 14.
78 Ibid., 55–6 (footnote omitted).
79 Locke, *Second Treatise*, 63–4.

few paragraphs later, that while tacit consent can oblige one to obey the law, it cannot make one a member of the sovereign citizenry:

> But submitting to the laws of any country, living quietly, and enjoying privileges and protection under them, *makes not a man a member of that society.* ... And thus we see, that *foreigners*, by living all their lives under another government, and enjoying the privileges and protection of it, though they are bound, even in conscience, to submit to its administration, as far forth as any denison; yet do not thereby come to be *subjects or members of that common-wealth*. Nothing can make any man so, but his actually entering into it by positive engagement, and express promise and compact.[80]

This compares to Jefferson's view of intergenerational relations: "We seem not to have perceived that, by the law of nature, one generation is to another as one independent nation to another."[81] It would appear from this that only express consent, and not tacit consent, can make one a member of We the People. The consent problem is thereby even more difficult. In brief, originalism relies on but does not adequately theorize the concept of "an act of the people in their constituting capacity."

Originalists, then, are "Locke'd" into a dilemma. It is well to say that the reason we should not allow judges any discretion is that they are un-elected and not electorally accountable – that is, that we did not and cannot consent to their actions. Yet when originalists see the interpretive context as a zero-sum choice between the personal values of the judge and the values constitutionalized by the Framers, and claim that the former are illegitimate because they are not based on our consent, whereas the latter are legitimate because they are, originalists must account successfully for the concept of consent. But how did/do we consent to the latter? Originalists see our con-stituting capacity as a discrete historical act. If that is indeed the case, then originalism, far from being the theory that grounds the democratic legitimacy of the Constitution, actually undermines it. As Freeman suggests:

> For originalists argue, in effect, that interpretation is to proceed from a different perspective, the historically specific point of view of our ancestors. We are to imagine ourselves in the framers' or ratifiers' situation, endowed with their particular interests and partial concerns, and ask, What values and principles are understood to be implicit in the Constitution from *this* position? My claim is, whether we conceive of originalism as a theory of interpretation or of adjudication ... this ancestral attitude is ruled out by democratic interpretation of the Constitution. It subordinates the permanent and shared interests of democratic citizens in their freedom and equal status to someone else's parochial interests, loyalties, and personal moral values.[82]

---

[80] Ibid., 65.

[81] Jefferson, Letter to James Madison in "Letters of Thomas Jefferson," 450.

[82] Freeman, "Original Meaning, Democratic Interpretation, and the Constitution," 28 (footnote omitted).

My argument is that only by conceiving our constituting capacity as an omnipresent activity – that is, always going on – can we resolve the consent dilemma. Our ongoing consent is that we continuously reaffirm the terms of constitutional debate set out by the Framers through our own active participation in that debate. If, on the other hand, our only role is passively to receive instruction from the Framers, then consent becomes problematic.

This, then, is the central idea of originalism: Constitutional interpretation is ultimately constitutional history. Lest this proposition appear to be too rash, consider Justice Antonin Scalia's description of the originalist task:

But what is true is that it is often exceedingly difficult to plumb the original understanding of an ancient text. Properly done, the task requires the consideration of an enormous mass of material – in the case of the Constitution and its Amendments, for example, to mention only one element, the records of the ratifying debates in all the states. Even beyond that, it requires an evaluation of the reliability of that material – many of the reports of the ratifying debates, for example, are thought to be quite unreliable. And further still, it requires immersing oneself in the political and intellectual atmosphere of the time – somehow placing out of mind knowledge that we have which an earlier age did not, and putting on beliefs, attitudes, philosophies, prejudices and loyalties that are not those of our day. It is, in short, a task sometimes better suited to the historian than the lawyer.[83]

An originalist himself, Scalia appreciates the difficulties endemic in originalist analysis, and this brings us to the nature of the problems that commentators have ascribed to the theory. Briefly drawing upon and combining the insights of two writers, we can say provisionally that originalism rests upon four key assumptions around which most criticism of the theory has developed. First, Larry Simon argues that originalism in any of its forms necessarily presupposes three claims:

First, there existed as a matter of psychological and historical reality a collective state of mind (however defined) of the real group of people who participated in the drafting and/or adoption of the original Constitution and each of its amendments, and this state of mind determines the meanings that these people as a group intended various constitutional provisions to have. Second, judges and scholars today can, by historical research, come to reasonably reliable and certain understandings about this state of mind as it relates to a substantial number of important provisions in the Constitution. Third, the meanings supplied by research into this state of mind are authoritative – if not descriptively (because the courts do not in fact give the

---

[83] Antonin Scalia, "Originalism: The Lesser Evil," 57 *University of Cincinnati Law Review* 849, 856–7 (1989). *Sourcebook* states at 9 that "[c]ontemporaneous dictionaries, records of the ratification debates and the Philadelphia Convention, and other historic sources are usually helpful in determining the general and popular use of constitutional language at the time it was ratified."

Constitution these meanings) then normatively (that is, the document ought to be given these meanings).[84]

In a nutshell, Simon argues that originalism rests on the factual reality of historical intent, the possibility of reliably retrieving that intent, and the normative binding power of that intent. To these three claims, however, we must add a fourth, put forward by Jefferson Powell:

> The central tenet of originalism as it is often understood is the existence of a clear demarcation between the original meaning of a constitutional provision and its subsequent interpretation. The originalist, we are told, is the interpreter who knows the difference and acknowledges it by according authority to the founders rather than to their successors.[85]

This claim, in essence, is the logically prior premise of the claim that it is possible reliably to retrieve the factual, historical intent of the Framers: It is the hermeneutic point that there is a clear, recognizable distinction between (original) meaning and interpretation. Only on that basis can one plausibly say that there is an intent that we can identify as (1) original and (2) authoritative.

Without rehearsing the detail necessary to explore the issue thoroughly, I simply want to outline the two general categories of criticism that commentators have made of originalism.[86] The first category points to the family of problems we can call "empirical" or, more precisely, "historiographical"; these have to do with the practicalities of actually establishing the set of historical decisions and events that for originalism constitute the complex fact we call original intent.[87] When we say that originalism stands for the

---

[84] Larry Simon, "The Authority of the Constitution and Its Meaning: A Preface to a Theory of Constitutional Interpretation," 58 *Southern California Law Review* 603, 636 (1985) (footnotes omitted).

[85] H. Jefferson Powell, "Rules for Originalists," 73 *Virginia Law Review* 659, 676 (1987).

[86] In presenting the following brief outline, I draw on Ronald Dworkin, "The Forum of Principle," in *A Matter of Principle* (Cambridge, MA: Harvard University Press, 1985), 33–71; Daniel Farber, "The Originalism Debate: A Guide for the Perplexed," 49 *Ohio State Law Journal* 1085 (1989); and Richard S. Kay, "Adherence to the Original Intentions in Constitutional Adjudication: Three Objections and Responses," 82 *Northwestern University Law Review* 226 (1988). For similar attention to the problems with the theory, see Brest, "The Misconceived Quest for the Original Understanding," 209–17.

[87] Although I regret the length of the following citation, it is instructive, I think, to recognize that so much of the historiographical category of criticism was anticipated by Justice Story:

§406. It is obvious, however, that contemporary interpretation must be resorted to with much qualification and reserve. In the first place, the private interpretation of any particular man, or body of men, must manifestly be open to much observation. The constitution was adopted by the people of the United States; and it was submitted to the whole upon a just survey of its provisions, as they stood in the text itself. In different states and in different conventions, different and very opposite objections are known to have prevailed; and might well be presumed to prevail. Opposite interpretations, and different explanations of different

proposition that constitutional adjudication must be guided by the intent of the Framers, our initial historiographical questions must be, who counts as the Framers and what counts as their intentions? In regard to the former question, we might start with the Philadelphia Convention for an answer, looking at who attended the proceedings. Here, however, a number of subsidiary issues arise: Among other questions, do we count among the Framers only those men who remained at the Convention for its entire session? Do we include everyone who stayed or only those who ultimately supported and signed the document? How do we assess the status of those who, according to the record, participated only infrequently, if at all, vis-à-vis those who were most active? Does everyone who signed the document have equal status or do those members of the Committee of Style who actually wrote the final draft have a privileged position? Additionally, what, in regard to time or history itself, was the founding period? When did it begin, as far as interpretive norms are conceived: May 1787; September 17, 1787? When did it end: At the moment of ratification? At the death of Chief Justice John Marshall in 1834?

Even if we could satisfactorily identify the Framers, we then would have to identify their intentions, a twofold problem. First, what counts as an individual's intentions in enacting legal language: what the wording means to him or what he understands the wording to mean to others? What

provisions, may well be presumed to have been presented in different bodies, to remove local objections, or to win local favour. And there can be no certainty, either that the different state conventions in ratifying the constitution, gave the same uniform interpretation to its language, or that, even in a single state convention, the same reasoning prevailed with a majority, much less with the whole of the supporters of it. In the interpretation of a state statute, no man is insensible of the extreme danger of resorting to the opinions of those, who framed it, or those who passed it. Its terms may have differently impressed different minds. Some may have implied limitations and objects, which others would have rejected. Some may have taken a cursory view of its enactments, and others have studied them with profound attention. Some may have been governed by a temporary interest or excitement, and have acted upon that exposition, which most favoured their present views. Others may have seen lurking beneath its text, what commended it to their judgment against even present interests. Some may have interpreted its language strictly and closely; others from a different habit of thinking may have given it a large and liberal meaning. It is not to be presumed, that, even in the convention, which framed the constitution, from the causes above-mentioned, and other causes, the clauses were always understood in the same sense, or had precisely the same extent of operation. Every member necessarily judged for himself; and the judgment of no one could, or ought to be, conclusive upon that of others. The known diversity of construction of different parts of it, as well of the mass of its powers, in the different state conventions; the total silence upon many objections, which have since been started; and the strong reliance upon others, which have since been universally abandoned, add weight to these suggestions. Nothing but the text itself was adopted by the people.

Commentaries on the Constitution of the United States (Boston: Hilliard, Gray and Company, 1833), Vol. 1, 388–9. The last sentence of this passage – "Nothing but the text itself was adopted by the people" – is quoted often in the literature, but the context is very important.

effect he hopes the language will have or what effect he actually expects it to have? Further, how do we assess the significance of the difference between intending not to do X and not intending to do X? Finally, how concrete or abstract do we take the individual Framer's intention to be (think of equal protection regarding female Americans as opposed to black Americans as a class)? Even if we could satisfactorily answer these questions about the intention of an individual, however, the second side of Framers' intent comes into play: Originalism's focus is not on the intention of an individual, but of a group called the Framers. A group intention is even more complex than an individual intention, for it requires that we solve what is called the "summing problem" in determining a collective intention. The Constitution is the product of not one individual but a group of individuals, whose coexistence in the same period of history and likely general similarities in matters of social class and outlook should not detract from the diversity ubiquitous in human affairs. When we say "the intent of the Framers," we cannot mean simply the intent of Madison or Hamilton or Wilson; we must mean the intent of the collectivity we call the Framers.[88]

Here, however, we vastly expand the problem. Assuming that we can solve the difficulties endemic in identifying the Framers and their intentions at the Philadelphia Convention, the problem remains that, as a matter of political legitimacy, all the Convention did was simply to propose a document that could become authoritative only if it was ratified by the people of the United States. Consequently, the intention at issue in originalism, strictly speaking, must be that of the ratifiers – informed by that of the writers, the authors, but ultimately that of the ratifiers. Yet granting that the ground of the authoritativeness of the Constitution is its ratification by the state conventions has the effect of multiplying the historiographical problems of identifying Framers' intent we have noted by a factor of 13.[89] It is for this reason that originalists often fall back on the argument that "[a]lthough the intention of the ratifiers, not the Framers, is in principle decisive, the difficulties of ascertaining the intent of the ratifiers leaves little choice but to accept the intent of the Framers as a fair reflection of it."[90]

Many originalists, to paraphrase Justice Scalia, recognize these problems but nevertheless affirm originalism as "the lesser evil" because "it's the best we can do."[91] On the other hand, many critics argue that, if constitutional

---

[88] For all the nonoriginalist critiques of the search for subjective intentions, there is perhaps no better critique than that of Justice Scalia, no nonoriginalist himself, in *Edwards v. Aguillard*, 482 U.S. 578, 636–8 (1987).

[89] We see the immensity of such problems in the Story passage cited in footnote 87.

[90] Monaghan, "Our Perfect Constitution," 56 *New York University Law Review* 353, 375 (1981) (footnote 130).

[91] One further historiographical problem has been the question of whether originalism itself was intended by the Framers and ratifiers to be the guiding theory of constitutional interpretation. See H. Jefferson Powell, "The Original Understanding of Original Intent," 98 *Harvard Law*

interpretation is indeed, as originalism claims, constitutional history, this is a rather shaky foundation for the weight the theory must place on the historical record. More significantly and radically, critics of originalism conclude from a survey of its historiographical problems that the factual, historical foundation on which the theory relies is simply unavailable in the form on which the theory insists. In the words of Ronald Dworkin, "there is no such thing as the intention of the Framers waiting to be discovered, even in principle. There is only some such thing waiting to be invented."[92]

If, in this brief survey of criticism, we grant for the sake of argument the premise that it is indeed possible to overcome the empirical, historiographical problems in identifying what originalism calls the intent of the Framers, we still confront the second category of criticism that commentators have made of the theory. This has to do with problems we can call "theoretical" and "normative." The theoretical problem, to which I can only refer here, takes off from the idea just cited from Dworkin that the Framers' intent is not so much discovered as it is constructed. It is the hermeneutic point that while we can have an understanding of the past, such understanding is not objective in the sense that originalism demands. Richard Kay, we have noted, writes that "the task of seeking the original intentions involves an attempt to recreate the perspectives of the constitution-makers – their values, their needs, and even what we would consider their misconceptions."[93] This is fair enough, but he immediately goes on to say that we do this "by consciously suppressing our contemporary preconceptions and values, and attempting to reconstruct those of our subject."[94] The hermeneutic argument of Hans-Georg Gadamer, David Hoy, and others is that such an act is not only empirically but also theoretically impossible. We do not think ourselves into the world of the Framers; we think the Framers into our world.[95]

The normative problem in this second category of criticism is, in essence, the "So what?" question. If we grant the possibility, at least in principle, of both solving the historiographical problems in originalism and attaining the purely objective account of Framers' intent in the sense that originalism demands, the question still remains of why the Framers' intent should be authoritative. The originalist answer is that "[i]nterpretation of the Constitution according to its original meaning is the only approach that takes seriously the status of our Constitution as fundamental law, and that permits our

Review 885 (1985) and, in reply, Charles Lofgren, "The Original Understanding of Original Intent?" 5 *Constitutional Commentary* 77 (1988). While there is admittedly some circularity in relying on original intent to ground the theory of originalism, it may be similarly problematic to rely on original intent to reject originalism.
[92] Ronald Dworkin, "The Forum of Principle," 39. See also Chapter 6.
[93] Kay, "Adherence to the Original Intentions," 252.
[94] Ibid.
[95] See Chapter 6.

society to remain self-governing."[96] As Bork has written, "only the approach of original understanding meets the criteria that any theory of constitutional adjudication must meet in order to possess democratic legitimacy."[97] The argument for the authoritative status of Framers' intent, in other words, is that only if constitutional interpretation is guided by the intent of the Framers can we plausibly speak of both the democratic and binding character of the text. This, at long last, is where we find the paradox of originalism: Originalism simultaneously affirms and denies the democratic and binding authority of the Constitution, because it simultaneously affirms and denies the binding capacity of language. Originalism claims to be the only theory by which the Constitution democratically binds the future, but the theory's distinction between the constitutional text and the original understanding actually undermines the democratic and binding character of the text. So, once again, the only way to make the text both democratic and binding is to conceptualize an ongoing – not a past – act of constituting, but originalism's insistence on the distance between the original and subsequent interpretive contexts leaves the theory trapped in the inability to account for anything other than solely a past act of constituting.

It is instructive in this regard to recall Walter Lippmann's distinction between "The People as voters" and *"The People"*:

> Because of the discrepancy between The People as voters and *The People* as the corporate nation, the voters have no title to consider themselves the proprietors of the commonwealth and to claim that their interests are identical with the public interest. A prevailing plurality of the voters are not *The People*.[98]

Whereas the People as voters, according to Lippmann, are merely the aggregate of all the individuals living within the United States at a particular moment, *"The People* are a corporation, an entity, that is to say, which lives on while individuals come into it and go out of it."[99] Significantly, Lippmann writes,

> it makes no sense to describe "The People of the United States" who ordained and established the Constitution as the inhabitants of the United States on that particular June 21, 1788, when the Constitution was established and ordained. Between sunrise and sunset of that historic day the persons composing *The People* had changed. In thirty years they had changed greatly; and in a hundred years, entirely.[100]

Yet what, according to Lippmann, it makes no sense to do, originalism implicitly does. In order to argue that the Constitution is grounded democratically, originalism relies, as Berns's statement suggests, on a concept of the

---

[96] *Sourcebook*, 3.
[97] Bork, *The Tempting of America*, 143.
[98] Walter Lippmann, *The Public Philosophy* (New York: New American Library, 1955), 34.
[99] Ibid., 35.
[100] Ibid., 34–5.

People: with regard to the Founding generation and our contemporary generation, we are they and they are we. Yet in order to ground the binding capacity of the Constitution, originalism relies on an idea of the Framers very much like Lippmann's concept of the people: We are *not* they and they are *not* we. It may well be that originalism is considered the "conservative" jurisprudence, but the interpretive theory of Constitutional textuality is consistent with the conservative notion of the People that Lippmann uses here. The only way to make the text binding is through an ongoing, not a past, act of constituting, and yet the positivism of originalism's theory of Constitutional textuality requires that there can be only past, never ongoing, acts of constituting.[101] Making somewhat the same point, Philip Bobbitt has written that "Historical arguments draw legitimacy from the social contract negotiated from an original position," whereas "textual arguments rest on a sort of ongoing social contract, whose terms are given their contemporary meanings continually reaffirmed by the refusal of the People to amend the instrument."[102] Therefore, while originalism asserts both the democratic and binding character of the Constitution, its assertion of the one undermines the other.

Additionally, the further implication of originalist principles is that the mere passage of time weakens both, for the binding capacity, grounded in a specific, historical, authoritative act, is decreasingly binding as time goes on. According to Bork, "particular respect is due to precedents set by courts within a few decades of a provision's ratification since the judges of that time presumably had a superior knowledge of the original meaning of the Constitution."[103] Though in this passage he is discussing originalism in regard to the claims of precedent, the point of importance here is the assumption that the further away we move in time from the writing and ratification of a particular provision or text as a whole, the weaker its meaning becomes for us. The implication is that as the original meaning becomes less and less clear and distinct, the passage of time gradually dissolves the democratic and binding character of the Constitution. Yet this is not at all where originalism wants to go.

Moreover, despite its democratic pretensions, originalism makes constitutional interpretation the province of an expert elite composed of historians. Seeing the Constitution as a social discourse makes us all interpreters, and thus makes constitutional discourse more democratic. Yet, at best, the originalist would ask the citizen not what she thinks the Constitution means, but what she thinks the Framers thought the Constitution means. A truly democratic interpretive paradigm, by contrast, would account for the binding character of the Constitution but still retain the principle that all of

[101] See Chapter 6.
[102] Philip Bobbitt, *Constitutional Fate* (New York: Oxford University Press, 1982), 26.
[103] Bork, *The Tempting of America*, 157.

us – not just judges and lawyers, to be sure, but individual citizens as well – are entitled to be constitutional interpreters. Drawing on Alexander Bickel, John Rawls captures the essence of liberal constitutionalism:

In a democratic society, then, it is recognized that each citizen is responsible for his interpretation of the principles of justice and for his conduct in the light of them. There can be no legal or socially approved rendering of these principles that we are always morally bound to accept, not even when it is given by a supreme court or legislature. Indeed each constitutional agency, the legislature, the executive, and the court, puts forward its interpretation of the constitution and the political ideals that inform it. Although the court may have the last say in settling any particular case, it is not immune from powerful political influences that may force a revision of its reading of the constitution. The court presents its doctrine by reason and argument; its conception of the constitution must, if it is to endure, persuade the major part of the citizens of its soundness. The final court of appeal is not the court, nor the executive, nor the legislature, but the electorate as a whole.[104]

From this perspective, the real binding force of the Constitution, the central characteristic of constitutionalism according to originalism, is its constitutive character. The element of consent is present in this constitutive character in that we are actively self-constituting political subjects and political objects simultaneously. Where the originalist believes that the Framers constitute us, my more radically democratic position is that we constitute the Framers as Framers. We take into account the Framers' views when we read the Constitution, but ultimately we have to decide how to weigh those views and to determine what we will take to be the meaning of the document. As Freeman writes: "This does not mean we cannot be influenced by the *reasons* the founders had for constitutional provisions; but when we are, it cannot be because *they* held them, but because these considerations impress us as good reasons anyone could accept in his or her capacity as equal citizen."[105]

To be perfectly clear, though, my argument does not maintain that the Constitution is not both democratic and binding; it suggests instead that originalism cannot provide the account of that dual character on which it stakes its claim to legitimacy. At the same time, it is not my purpose to argue for the consequent superiority of something called nonoriginalism. If originalism emphasizes the binding character of the Constitution at the unintended cost of threatening its democratic (i.e., consent) character, then conventional nonoriginalism, by rejecting the notion of the dead hand of the past, emphasizes the democratic character of the Constitution at the cost of threatening its binding character. Rather, my concern is to show that the originalism debate in contemporary constitutional theory ultimately turns on competing

---

[104] John Rawls, *A Theory of Justice* (Cambridge, MA: Belknap Press of Harvard University Press, 1971), 390 (footnote omitted). To suggest the aptness of this citation is certainly not to suggest that the Constitution is simply Rawlsian theory before its time.

[105] Freeman, "Original Meaning, Democratic Interpretation, and the Constitution," 28.

conceptions of language, interpretation, and objectivity, conceptions known as interpretive, on the one hand, and preinterpretive or positivist, on the other. While originalism sees binding character and democratic character as consistent, they are in fact, on originalist premises, contradictory. The interpretive approach enables us to resolve the paradox in the broader concept of constitutive character, which is in the end the true political character of constitutional discourse. Yet it is the postpositivist interpretive approach rather than the positivism of originalism that can account for this constitutive capacity. If I am right, then the dissolution of originalism will result not in the victory of nonoriginalism – for, like originalism, conventional nonoriginalism too rejects the constitutive character of language – but rather in the dissolution of nonoriginalism as well. At that point, we can get down to the serious business of arguing for what we consider the best interpretation of the Constitution by an appeal to the authority of neither the Framers nor contemporary moral theory, but of the fundamental text itself. Then, and only then, does constitutional argument become the truly social discourse of the American polity. To establish this, however, we turn now to the issue of language, interpretation, and objectivity.

5

The Problem of Objectivity

The originalism debate in contemporary American constitutional theory can be usefully understood as a three-dimensional phenomenon. The first and most immediate dimension of this debate is practical and political: The contemporary originalism debate springs from the historically specific political context of the cultural struggle over the sixties waged by liberals and conservatives in the final quarter of the twentieth century. The second dimension of the debate is theoretical and jurisprudential: The originalism debate in contemporary American constitutional theory is a particular formulation of an ongoing concern with the nature of constitutional interpretation that stems from the fact that we live under a written constitution. As long as we have a written constitution, we are going to have arguments over the nature of constitutional interpretation. Thus, while the contemporary originalism debate may have been set off by a particular political context, its roots lie in the very nature of the American constitutional system itself. An opponent of originalism would be wrong to dismiss it as nothing more than theoretical cover for a purely partisan, political agenda, for it is a powerful normative account of the binding capacity that we consider to be central to the very concept of a written constitution. The third dimension of the debate, however, is rather more abstract but nonetheless interesting: It is a metatheoretical argument over textuality and the nature of language, interpretation, and objectivity. The key to this metatheoretical issue is the concept of the "interpretive turn."

In outline form, the argument I am pursuing is, first, that originalism rests on what I call a positivist theory of textuality; second, that the positivist premise of originalism undermines originalism's claim to be able to account for both the binding capacity and democratic legitimacy of the Constitution; third, that the interpretive turn undermines this positivist theory of textuality; and fourth, that the interpretive turn reconciles the binding capacity and democratic legitimacy of the Constitution. In what follows, I want to unpack the concept of the interpretive turn in contemporary constitutional theory. That turn has two principal components: the thesis of antifoundationalism, in contrast with the foundationalism of the positivist theory, and the thesis of the constitutive character of the Constitution, in contrast with the purely regulative character allowed by the positivist theory. My focus here is on the former thesis, that is, on the interpretive argument that for metatheoretical reasons originalism can neither be nor accomplish what its own self-understanding claims it is and does; the concept of original understanding or Framers' intent[1] cannot function as the check on interpretation in the way originalists maintain. That said, my general argument against originalism thus may appear to be an argument for nonoriginalism, but my position is more radical. My argument is that the critique that undermines originalism does the same thing to nonoriginalism.

The way to begin to go about this task is to note something never taken to be noteworthy: The fact that nonoriginalism is named and conceived in terms of originalism is not, I believe, just coincidence. Rather, while grounded in political conflict, they are bound together in their mutual opposition because their opposition is generated by a particular set of metatheoretical premises about the nature of language, interpretation, and objectivity. Those premises have to do with what I call the positivist and interpretive theories of constitutional textuality. Dissolving the impasse of their mutual opposition requires an attack on the set of metatheoretical premises that generates their opposition in the first place. Consequently, I want to argue, there is no zero-sum theoretical situation here: A successful critique of originalism does not require that one adopt nonoriginalism. Instead, a critique of the *fundamental* premises of originalism undercuts nonoriginalism as well and forces a redefinition of the conventional dichotomy. This occurs, I believe, because it is not the case that the positivist theory underlies originalism and the interpretive theory underlies nonoriginalism; rather, my claim is that the positivist theory underlies both originalism and nonoriginalism, and application of the interpretive theory can take us *past* the current debate.[2]

In order to follow what may be a fairly abstract argument, recall my earlier, preliminary description of constitutional interpretation. To restate the obvious, "constitutional interpretation" means interpretation of the

---

[1] For the sake of clarity, at this point let me note once again that I use "Framers' intent" and "original understanding" to mean the same thing: the interpretive norms of the writers and ratifiers. Later in this chapter I will examine the distinction originalists like Robert Bork have come to draw between the intentions of the authors of the document and the public understanding of the language the authors used.

[2] My sense of transcending the originalism–nonoriginalism dichotomy may be analogous to Stanley Fish's move from reader-response theory to the concept of interpretive communities in *Is There a Text in This Class?* (Cambridge, MA: Harvard University Press, 1980). That is how Fish purported to escape a dialectic of objectivity and subjectivity. In some ways, Fish's evolution in that book, while concerned with literary analysis, recapitulates the objectivity problem in law. He went from a text-centered to a reader-centered interpretation (i.e., from formalism to legal realism) until he came up with his idea of interpretive communities.

Constitution, which implies that the constitutional text governs the range of possible interpretations in order to constrain the interpreters. The constitutional text thus provides the language of interpretation and constrains the range and substance of interpretation. For this reason, to be a constitutionalist of the American variety, therefore, is necessarily to be a textualist in the broad sense that one ascribes authority to a particular written text.

Yet how does one guarantee that constitutional interpretation occurs in the terms and within the terms of the constitutional text? The characteristic and controversial move of originalism is the translation of this claim into the principle, generally definitive of originalism in its particular forms, that the original understanding of the constitutional text always trumps any contrary understanding of that text in succeeding generations. In the words of Jefferson Powell:

> The central tenet of originalism as it is often understood is the existence of a clear demarcation between the original meaning of a constitutional provision and its subsequent interpretation. The originalist, we are told, is the interpreter who knows the difference and acknowledges it by according authority to the founders rather than to their successors.[3]

At its simplest, originalism holds that a constitutional provision means what it meant to the generation that wrote and ratified it, and not what it might mean differently to any subsequent generation. That is, should there arise a distinction between the original meaning and a current meaning of a particular constitutional provision, the original meaning is the authoritative, legally binding meaning. Originalism is a regulative theory of constitutional interpretation whose purpose is to provide such a guarantee; should there arise a distinction between the original meaning and a current meaning of a particular constitutional provision, the original meaning is the authoritative, legally binding meaning. Originalists themselves differ as to evidence of original meaning. For some, original meaning is grounded in the intentions of the Framers – the authors – of the Constitution, the position I have called hard originalism; for others, original meaning is grounded in the understanding of the ratifiers – the first readers – of the Constitution, the position I have called soft originalism. Both versions, however, subscribe to the more general principle that in constitutional interpretation the normative context of interpretation is that of those who wrote and ratified the language in question rather than that of any later interpreters. That is, originalism argues that the necessary check on our understanding of the text of the Constitution is the original understanding of the text of the Constitution, a standard

---

[3] H. Jefferson Powell, "Rules for Originalists," 73 *Virginia Law Review* 659, 676 (1987). Also see Raoul Berger, "Originalist Theories of Constitutional Interpretation," 73 *Cornell Law Review* 350, 350–1 (1988), and Richard Saphire, "Enough about Originalism," 15 *Northern Kentucky Law Review* 513, 516 (1988).

conventionally conceived as Framers' intent. In this way originalism points to binding capacity as its very essence, and that is why there is such strength in its appeal.

The originalist, then, translates the claim that in constitutional interpretation we should be bound by the text of the Constitution into the claim that the original understanding of the constitutional text always trumps any contrary understanding of that text in succeeding generations. How, then, is the concept of Framers' intent supposed to function in originalist theory? "Originalists," write Daniel Farber and Suzanna Sherry, "are committed to the view that original intent is not only relevant but authoritative, that we are in some sense obligated to follow the intent of the framers."[4] In and of itself, the claim that in constitutional interpretation we should be bound by the intent of the Framers is an unobjectionable statement of the idea of binding the future at the very core of the concept of a constitution. By writing and ratifying a constitution, the Framers clearly intended to establish a polity constituted and structured by a determinate set of procedural and substantive principles. The Constitution thus represents – that is, constitutes – the intent of the writers and ratifiers that subsequent generations live within and in accordance with a particular political structure. From one point of view, we are dealing with a tautology: If the Constitution constitutes the intent of the Framers, then the claim that in constitutional interpretation we should be bound by the intent of the Framers amounts to the claim that in constitutional interpretation we should be bound by the text of the Constitution. This is an assertion of the exclusively authoritative status of those principles constitutionalized by the writers and ratifiers.

The question, however, is, whose interpretation of that determinate set of principles by which the writers and ratifiers intended us to live is to count as authoritative? The characteristic and controversial move of originalism, as we have seen, is its translation of the claim that in constitutional interpretation we should be bound by the intent of the Framers into the proposition, generally definitive of originalism in all of its specific forms, that the original understanding of the constitutional text always trumps any contrary understanding of that text in succeeding generations. The reason this translation is controversial is that, to its proponents, originalism is synonymous with constitutionalism itself, such that to reject originalism is to reject constitutionalism. Originalists arrive at that position through a path of reasoning very much like this: Binding capacity is central to constitutionalism; originalism is central to the possibility of binding capacity; to reject originalism is to reject the possibility of binding capacity; to reject the possibility of binding capacity is to reject constitutionalism; and, consequently, to reject originalism is to reject constitutionalism.

---

[4] Daniel A. Farber and Suzanna Sherry, *A History of the American Constitution* (St. Paul, MN: West Publishing Company, 1990), 374.

The key step in this reasoning is point 2, the claim that originalism is central to the possibility of binding capacity. The written, textual character of the Constitution is asserted to be the central precondition of the document's binding capacity, and the belief in the binding capacity of a written constitution, the ability of a text to control the future, is an essential component not just of the American judicial tradition, but of the American political tradition as a whole. From the originalist perspective, however, any interpretive approach to the Constitution that is not originalist necessarily lands an interpreter in the land of the living Constitution, a land where there are no limits on government because the text means anything to anyone. Nonoriginalist constitutional interpretation, from this perspective, is either overtly unprincipled, in that it does not care to provide justification for a given reading of the text, or else is unprincipled in effect because the search for justificatory interpretive principles outside the text can result ultimately in nothing beyond the personal values of the interpreter.

What originalism does, in other words, is to equate nonoriginalism – that is, an understanding of the constitutional text that is not the original understanding – with noninterpretivism, the theory that interpreters may legitimately invoke extraconstitutional norms in adjudication, and originalism with interpretivism, the theory that interpreters may legitimately invoke only constitutional norms.[5] The premise of these equivalencies is the proposition that there cannot be several possible, equally legitimate understandings of the constitutional text. Unless we talk about the Constitution as originally understood, we are not talking about the Constitution at all. In order to see what underlies such claims, recall the distinction I have drawn between our now familiar fundamental propositions:

P_1: What binds the future is the constitutional text.

P_2: What binds the future is the original understanding of the constitutional text.

Again, originalism denies the possibility of such a distinction, while I do not. My argument, which I call the interpretive approach, holds that P_2 is a narrower claim than P_1 in that we can deny P_2 and yet still affirm P_1. Due to its positivist premises, on the other hand, originalism denies the possibility of distinguishing between P_1 and P_2: The proposition that what binds the future is the constitutional text and the proposition that what binds the future is the original understanding of the constitutional text are *identical*, such that the

---

[5] Strange as it might seem at first glance, some noninterpretivists seem in fact to be tacit originalists. How can that be? If one rejects the view that the Framers' intention binds us but accepts the claim that being bound by the Constitution is necessarily equivalent to being bound by the Framers' intent, then there is no other position to occupy but noninterpretivism. See Chapter 3.

denial of the latter necessarily amounts to a denial of the former. In denying this possibility, originalism is able to construct the following syllogism:

Major premise: At the core of the concept of a written constitution is its capacity to bind the future.

Minor premise: Binding the future means making the original under-standing of the constitutional text (i.e., a regulative set of norms for application to the reading of the text) authoritative.

Conclusion: Therefore, the concept of a written constitution requires making the original understanding of the constitutional text authoritative.

Corollary: To deny the authoritativeness of the original under-standing of the constitutional text is to deny the authoritativeness of a written constitution.

What differences are in play here? I have suggested that P_2 is a narrower claim than P_1 in that we can deny P_2 and yet still affirm P_1. Originalism, in contrast, sees P_1 and P_2 as identical, such that the denial of P_2 necessarily amounts to a denial of P_1. In other words, to deny the authoritativeness of the original understanding of the constitutional text is to deny the authoritativeness of the Constitution per se. To be bound by the Constitution is logically equivalent to being bound by the original understanding of the constitutional text; and, of necessity, not to be bound by the original understanding of the constitutional text is not to be bound by the Constitution at all. What is the basis of this difference? Originalism, I will suggest later, denies the semantic autonomy of the constitutional text: Fearful of what it considers the potential semantic anarchy of the text, originalism goes to the other extreme and denies its semantic autonomy. The core of originalist theory is the idea of interpretive justification by reference to the original understanding.

The originalist concept of Framers' intent, consequently, ceases to be ana-lytically equivalent to the Constitution itself and becomes instead an extrinsic check on how we read the constitutional text. To determine, for example, whether states have the power to criminalize abortion or sodomy, one ap-peals to one's understanding of the Constitution. What originalists seek to do is to clinch an argument over the proper understanding of the Constitution by appealing to what they call Framers' intent. This latter move is an attempt to justify an understanding of the text by appeal to norms that in some way transcend the text and that, as I will explore later, do not count as one more understanding of the text. For originalism, therefore, the real Constitution is not the written text itself, but rather the original understanding of the written text. Surprisingly, in view of their rhetoric, originalists thus do look beyond the four corners of the document. Referring to the natural-rights jurisprudence of the Framers that presumed a necessary connection between morals and law, Hadley Arkes, for example, argues that

> we cannot apply the Constitution, in the practical cases that arise every day, unless we can move, so to speak, "beyond the Constitution." We will persistently find a need to appeal to those moral understandings lying behind the text; the understandings that were never written down in the Constitution, but which must be grasped again if we are to preserve – and perfect – the character of a constitutional government.[6]

There is a delicious irony here. Consider this charge by Gary McDowell:

> In the name of interpreting the Constitution, the new theorists attack the very essence of constitutionalism – language. By undermining the binding force of language – the bond of society, as Locke saw it – the new theorists seek to supplant original intention with contemporary academic pretensions.[7]

Without committing myself to the defense of all those McDowell considers "new theorists," I would argue that originalism cannot accept the distinction between P_1 (the claim that what binds the future is the constitutional text) and P_2 (the claim that what binds the future is the original understanding of the constitutional text) because it is originalism itself that distrusts "the very essence of constitutionalism – language." My claim, again, is that the text, as opposed to a particular understanding of the text, is authoritative, whereas originalism argues that to consider the text authoritative can mean nothing other than that one particular understanding is authoritative.[8] It is therefore the originalist position rather than my own that assumes that the written constitution per se is indeterminate and thus meaningless. I am suggesting, by contrast, that the real Constitution is the text itself, independently of the original understanding of it, which presupposes my claim that P_1 and P_2 are separate propositions.

The key issue here is the idea of an understanding of the text as distinct from the text itself. Is this a fair conceptualization of originalism? Consider several descriptions of the theory from contemporary adherents as well as

---

[6] Hadley Arkes, *Beyond the Constitution* (Princeton, NJ: Princeton University Press, 1990), 17. Specifically, he writes at 19, "the various clauses of the Constitution and the Bill of Rights can be established, in their meaning, only by attaching them to the properties of a moral argument. And when we do that, we find ourselves tracing those clauses back to the structure of moral understanding that must lie behind the text of the Constitution." A positivist like Bork would reject this natural-rights philosophy, but he in effect still employs a concept of an unwritten Constitution insofar as he makes the actual historical decision, as opposed to the philosophy, of the Framers normative.

[7] Gary McDowell, "Introduction" to Gary L. McDowell, ed., *Politics and the Constitution: The Nature and Extent of Interpretation* (Washington, DC: National Legal Center for the Public Interest and The American Studies Center, 1990), x–xi.

[8] We necessarily "see" the text through an act of interpretation, but we maintain the regulative concept of the text independent of a given interpretation. Originalism implicitly privileges its own interpretation of the text as the text itself rather than as one particular interpretation among others. There is a certain Kantian (and Kuhnian) ring to all of this.

opponents. "For the originalist," according to Perry, "to enforce the Constitution is to enforce it *as originally understood* (by the ratifiers, or the framers and ratifiers)."⁹ Levy writes that "the term 'original intent' (or 'original intention') stands for an old idea that the Court should interpret the Constitution according to the understanding of it by its Framers."¹⁰ This focus on original understanding is also called the "historical approach." Consider this description by Stephen Munzer and James Nickel:

> The historical approach to constitutional interpretation regards the words and intent of the authors of the Constitution as the sole source of constitutional law. Under this approach, the Constitution is to be interpreted in the same manner as any other historical text. One looks to the intent of the authors and to the textual language as understood at the time the document was drafted. One may also rely on prior interpretations provided they comport with the words and intent of the framers.¹¹

The central claim of this approach, as Bork puts it, is that "there is a historical Constitution that was understood by those who enacted it to have a meaning of its own. That intended meaning has an existence independent of anything judges may say. It is that meaning that judges *ought* to utter."¹² And this meaning, Thomas Cooley argued over a century ago, does not change: "The meaning of the constitution is fixed when it is adopted, and it is not different at any subsequent time when a court has occasion to pass on it."¹³ That meaning, according to originalism, is what the Framers understood the constitutional text to mean at the time of its writing and ratification.

We must be very careful here, however, for while I am distinguishing between the principles the writers and ratifiers constitutionalized and their particular understanding of those principles, arguing that originalism translates the former into the latter, important originalists take great pains to avoid any charge of depending on subjectivist and psychological arguments. Bork is perhaps the most prominent of these originalists:

> What does it mean to say that a judge is bound by law? It means that he is bound by the only thing that can be called law, *the principles of the text*, whether Constitution or statute, *as generally understood at the enactment*.¹⁴

---

⁹ Perry, *Morality, Politics, and Law* (New York: Oxford University Press, 1988), 132 (emphasis in the original). Perry's use of the term "beliefs" to refer to what the Framers constitutionalized, cited in the text attached to footnote 12 above, suggests that what they established as authoritative was a set of *understandings*.

¹⁰ Leonard Levy, *Original Intent and the Framers' Constitution* (New York: Macmillan Publishing Company, 1988), x.

¹¹ Stephen R. Munzer and James W. Nickel, "Does the Constitution Mean What It Always Meant?" 77 *Columbia Law Review* 1029, 1030 (1977).

¹² Bork, *The Tempting of America: The Political Seduction of the Law* (New York: Simon & Schuster, 1990), 176.

¹³ Thomas Cooley, *A Treatise on Constitutional Limitations* (Boston: Little, Brown and Company, 1868), 55.

¹⁴ Bork, *The Tempting of America*, 5 (emphasis added).

The phrases I have emphasized in this passage do appear to bear out my point that, for originalism, the writers and ratifiers constitutionalized not the principles of the text per se, but rather those principles as qualified by the way they were generally understood at their enactment. Consider, however, this much lengthier statement that Bork offers later in his book:

What is the meaning of a rule that judges should not change? It is the meaning understood at the time of the law's enactment. Though I have written of the understanding of the ratifiers of the Constitution, since they enacted it and made it law, that is actually a shorthand formulation, because what the ratifiers understood themselves to be enacting must be taken to be what the public of that time would have understood the words to mean. It is important to be clear about this. The search is not for a subjective intention. . . . As Professor Henry Monaghan of Columbia has said, what counts is what the public understood. Law is a public act. Secret reservations or intentions count for nothing. All that counts is how that words used in the Constitution would have been understood at the time. The original understanding is thus manifested in the words used and in secondary materials, such as debates at the conventions, public discussion, newspaper articles, dictionaries in use at the time, and the like.[15]

Does this denial of dependence on subjective intention undercut my distinction between constitutional principles and the Framers' understanding of those principles?

The answer, I would suggest, is no, for Bork simply denies that originalism requires any information about individuals' private, subjective intentions or expectations about the Constitution. This is very clear in an earlier popular article by Bork:

The objection that we can never know what the Framers would have done about specific modern situations is entirely beside the point. The originalist attempts to discern the principles the Framers enacted, the values they sought to protect.[16]

Christopher Wolfe, too, argues that "the intent of the Constitution is to be found in the general principles it lays down and not in the specific examples that the framers had in mind as they wrote the provision."[17] Yet for both

---

[15] Ibid., 144. His reference is to Henry Monaghan, "Stare Decisis and Constitutional Adjudication," 88 *Columbia Law Review* 723, 725–7 (1988).

[16] Robert Bork, "Original Intent and the Constitution," *Humanities*, Vol. 7, No. 1 (February 1986), 26.

[17] Wolfe, *The Rise of Modern Judicial Review* (New York: Basic Books, 1986), 57. An unsophisticated originalism, and thus not a fair representative of the theory, would suggest that we have to decide cases the way the Framers would if they were alive today. Perry defends the integrity of the theory against this and related charges:

The most prominent misconceptions of how originalism requires a judge to decide a case are these: (1) decide it the way the ratifiers (or, if you prefer, the framers and ratifiers) wanted or would have wanted such a case to be decided; (2) decide it the way the ratifiers expected or would have expected such a case to be decided; (3) decide it the way the ratifiers resolved or would have resolved such an issue in their day; and (4) decide it the way the ratifiers

Bork and Wolfe the key to constitutional interpretation remains, if not the specific examples that the writers had in mind, the general principles that the writers had in mind. My emphasis is the phrase, "that the framers had in mind." What matters, in other words, is the public understanding of the text, the way the average person would understand the language of the Constitution. This public understanding is the central element of the originalism that Wolfe defends:

> To summarize the *Federalist* on constitutional interpretation briefly: the normal method of construing the Constitution is to start with the natural and obvious sense of the provisions, derivable from the popular usage of the words. If the words are dubious, the meaning can be sought in context, with an eye to the implications of the words used and of the document as a whole.[18]

However, note that the phrase "the natural and obvious sense of the provisions, derivable from the popular usage of the words" is contextually neutral – that is, it does not necessarily determine a specific social-historical context for "the popular usage of the words." I would not object to the passage as it stands. But the distinguishing mark of originalism is that it defines the social-historical context for the popular usage of the words as the

would have resolved such an issue in our day, were they still living. Originalism requires a judge to do none of these things.

Morality, Politics, and Law, 125 (footnotes omitted). Wolfe writes that "the people of the United States ratified a constitution that contained general principles, the full implications of which may not always have been apparent to them." Wolfe, *The Rise of Modern Judicial Review*, 58. A sophisticated originalism, like Bork's, would say simply that we have to take the original understanding of a constitutional principle and make our own application of it to the contemporary issue. This gets around the problem of subjective intentions and expectations but, for my purposes here, it reaffirms the idea that the regulative norm is the original understanding of a constitutional principle rather than the constitutional principle itself. See also Richard Posner, *Law and Literature* (Cambridge, MA: Harvard University Press, 1990), 229.

[18] Wolfe, *The Rise of Modern Judicial Review*, 24. Compare his characterization of constitutional interpretation in his succeeding book:

Interpretation began by looking at the words of the document in their popular usage and interpreting them in light of their context. That context included the other words of the provision at issue and extended to the much broader context of the document as a whole, especially its structure and subject matter.

The intent of provisions was commonly ascertainable from the terms and structure of the document; that is, intent could be grasped by an analysis of the document itself. The document was assumed to be, not a mere grab bag of disparate provisions, but a coherent whole, with objects or purposes that could be inferred and in light of which it ought to be read. Extrinsic sources of intent ... were subordinate but admissible evidence as long as they were employed with considerable caution.

Judicial Activism: Bulwark of Freedom or Precarious Security? (Pacific Grove, CA: Brooks/Cole, 1991), 11 (footnote omitted).

late 1780s.[19] Originalists, that is, always look to the people of 1787,[20] the premise that underlies and unites all of the various forms of the theory.

How, then, do originalists seek to employ the concept of original intent as an external check? Christopher Wolfe, for example, writes that originalism assumes "that the Constitution had an ascertainable meaning given to it by its authors and that meaning was the end or object of constitutional interpretation – it was authoritative."[21] Yet this reads as if the Constitution were an independent, empty shell into which the Framers poured – more important, *had* to pour – meaning; without the guidance of original understanding, the document remains an indeterminate text. What, then, is at issue here? The issue is the difference between what we can call "semantic anarchy" and "semantic autonomy." Originalism, I suggest, presumes the concept of semantic anarchy, according to which cutting a text free from the author's own intentions opens it up to as many meanings as there are reader-interpreters. Given this premise, the conclusion logically follows that the normative status of the original understanding is necessary if the Constitution is to have any binding capacity. For originalism, therefore, we have the choice of having either one meaning – that of the Framers' understanding – or a potentially infinite number of meanings.[22]

The ground of this premise is the positivist theory of constitutional textuality that is at the heart of originalism and that results in the alternatives that the Constitution either means what the writers and ratifiers thought it meant or means whatever anyone wants. The positivist theory of constitutional textuality is what one can call the "four corners" idea of the constitutional text, an idea not limited to originalists but also evident in some nonoriginalist writings. What might be the best guide to these contending positions is a 1980 article by Paul Brest entitled "The Misconceived Quest for the Original Understanding." As in the definition cited earlier, Brest explains originalism as "the familiar approach to constitutional adjudication that accords binding authority to the text of the Constitution or the intentions of the adopters."[23] Central in all of these explanations is the contrast between a public and a private conception of constitutional textuality. For the textualist, the constitutional text is public language in that its meaning

---

[19] The usual problem raised with respect to originalism is the fact that the meaning of words can change over time. The originalist response is very simple: What is normative is the meaning of the words as commonly understood at the time of the ratification of the Constitution.

[20] Or, of course, to the particular time a given amendment was written and ratified.

[21] Wolfe, *Judicial Activism*, 12 (footnote omitted).

[22] Interestingly, originalism in effect validates the legal realism it opposes: Its claim to be necessary makes sense only if one assumes that interpretation in and of itself is shot through with subjectivity.

[23] Brest, "The Misconceived Quest for the Original Understanding," 60 *Boston University Law Review* 204, 204 (1980) (footnote omitted).

is established socially:

> That an interpreter must read a text in the light of its social as well as linguistic context does not destroy the boundary between textualism and intentionalism. Just as the textualist is not concerned with the adopters' idiosyncratic use of language, she is not concerned with their subjective purposes. Rather, she seeks to discern the purposes that a member of the adopters' society would understand the provision to encompass.[24]

Textual meaning on this conception is tied to generally accepted language usage among members of the society at the time the text is written. For the intentionalist, on the other hand, the constitutional text is essentially a private language in that it is nothing but a representation of the mental states of writers and ratifiers:

> By contrast to the textualist, the intentionalist interprets a provision by ascertaining the intentions of those who adopted it. The text of the provision is often a useful guide to the adopters' intentions, but the text does not enjoy a favored status over other sources.[25]

For the intentionalist, then, the true meaning of the Constitution is not the constitutional text but rather an historically fixed and ascertainable set of mental states that stand, so to speak, behind the constitutional text. "The referent of a text understood as (simply) the linguistic embodiment of past normative judgments," Michael Perry has written, "is, in a sense, 'behind' the text. One must look behind the text to the original meaning if one is to understand the text."[26]

The positivism of this four-corners idea of constitutional textuality lies in the idea that those four corners contain and embody a message from – values constitutionalized by – the authors of the document. A positivist theory of

---

[24] Ibid., 208 (footnote omitted). Referring to Blackstone's rules of legal interpretation, Christopher Wolfe points to what he says "must be kept in view throughout the process of interpretation: the intention of the lawgiver that is being sought is the intention as expressed in the words of the law, not some intention that exists outside of or despite the words of the law." Wolfe, *The Rise of Modern Judicial Review*, 18–19. Chief Justice John Marshall himself, according to Wolfe, must be considered principally a textualist:

> There are two fundamentally different ways of examining the "intention" of the framers. One is to observe the "great objects" of the Constitution as they are contained within the document itself; the other is to examine extrinsic sources of the framers' intent. While Marshall resorted to each of these on given occasions, he placed considerably more emphasis on the former than on the latter.

Wolfe, *The Rise of Modern Judicial Review*, 48. Textualism, therefore, focuses on the language of a constitutional provision as the primary evidence of constitutional norms.

[25] Brest, "The Misconceived Quest for the Original Understanding," 209 (footnote omitted).

[26] Michael J. Perry, "The Authority of Text, Tradition, and Reason: A Theory of Constitutional 'Interpretation,'" 58 *Southern California Law Review* 551, 559 (1985).

textuality is an essentially reductionist theory that distinguishes between a text and its creators and ascribes meaning to the latter. It is helpful here to refer to literary theory: A literary text "must be regarded as the expression of the psychology of an individual, which in its turn is the expression of the *milieu* and the period in which the individual lived, and of the race to which he belonged."[27] In more analytical terms, a positivist theory of textuality reads a text

almost exclusively in relation to its factual causes or genesis: the author's life, his recorded intentions in writing, his immediate social and cultural environment, his sources. To use a common distinction, it was an extrinsic rather than an intrinsic approach to texts. It was not interested in the features of the literary text itself except from a philological and historical viewpoint.[28]

Against this literary-theory background, originalism is clearly a positivist theory of textuality, therefore, in that it treats a text not as an entity with meaning in and of itself, but rather as merely the expression of a meaning that stands behind it in the intentions and mental states of its authors. Larry Simon presents a succinct overview of this positivism of originalism:

All originalist theories rest at least implicitly on three claims. First, there existed as a matter of psychological and historical reality a collective state of mind (however defined) of the real group of people who participated in the drafting and/or adoption of the original Constitution and each of its amendments, and this state of mind determines the meanings that these people as a group intended various constitutional provisions to have. Second, judges and scholars today can, by historical research, come to reasonably reliable and certain understandings about this state of mind as it relates to a substantial number of important provisions in the Constitution. Third, the meanings supplied by research into this state of mind are authoritative – if not descriptively (because the courts do not in fact give the Constitution these meanings) then normatively (that is, the document ought to be given these meanings).[29]

What, then, is the *real* constitutional text – the document itself or the intentions, defined as the mental states, of the Framers standing behind it? If the real constitutional text is the document itself, then all understandings and interpretations of that text are relevant and none is privileged. If the real constitutional text is the intentions of the Framers standing behind

---

[27] Ann Jefferson and David Robey, eds., *Modern Literary Theory*, 2nd ed. (Totowa, NJ: Barnes & Noble Books, 1986), 9.

[28] Ibid. Positivism, Jefferson writes in her own contribution to this volume, was "largely based on the genetic approach; critics, or rather scholars, concentrated their energies on uncovering the sources and genesis of particular works, and the role of biography, history and history of ideas in these genetic studies obviously reduced the importance of literature itself in literary scholarship" (26).

[29] Larry Simon, "The Authority of the Constitution and Its Meaning: A Preface to a Theory of Constitutional Interpretation," 58 *Southern California Law Review* 603, 636 (1985) (footnotes omitted).

it and speaking to future generations, however, then one understanding is privileged and thereby always trumps any competing understanding.

On the positivist theory of textuality, the Constitution necessarily is the latter, with the consequence that understanding the Constitution is essentially a matter of discovery rather than interpretation. That is, because the meaning of the constitutional text is essentially subjective, in the sense that the text is at bottom a representation of the opinions or intentions of those people who created it, the Constitution, consequently, has no meaning of its own – its meaning lies behind the words of the text in the historical intentions of those who wrote the text. For this reason, there is always and necessarily an unwritten constitution – that is, something standing behind the written text. The positivist theory of textuality thus necessarily generates the ghost it constantly seeks to exorcise: the notion of an unwritten Constitution.

Given this premise of semantic anarchy that derives from the positivist theory of textuality, then, the conclusion logically follows that the normative status of the Framers' understanding is necessary if the Constitution is to have any binding capacity. But in that case an interesting question arises. The ratifiers of the Constitution were readers, as opposed to authors, of the constitutional text. But we today are readers of the constitutional text as well. Why is the ratifiers' understanding better than ours? If originalists say that the ratifiers' understanding is better than ours because they were contemporaries of the authors, then they imply that the further away we get from 1787 the more our understanding of the meaning of the Constitution fades. Bork, for example, claims that "particular respect is due to precedents set by courts within a few decades of a provision's ratification since the judges of that time presumably had a superior knowledge of the original meaning of the Constitution."[30] Look at the implication of this: The further away in time we get from the Constitution, the less sure of its meaning we can be. Yet that implication infects our understanding of the ratifiers' understanding as well as our understanding of the Constitution itself, so we have the same problem. An author may well be the best judge of what he meant or intended to say (my apologies to Freud), but he is not necessarily a better judge of what he actually said than anyone else: He becomes a reader of his own text. Indeed, that is why it is so difficult to read one's own text at a critical distance; one often reads the text in terms of what one meant to say rather than for what one actually said. If, on the other hand, originalism privileged the writers' understanding of the Constitution because they were the authors of the text, then its case would be stronger. The key assumption here, of course, is that an author has privileged access to the meaning of his text. Originalism presumes that an author does have such access, while I maintain that an author does not. While I would grant that an author has privileged access to what he wanted to write and thought he was saying, once he has written his text he

---

[30] Bork, *The Tempting of America*, 157.

becomes another reader of it and has no privileged access to what the text itself says, whatever he had intended for it to say.[31]

But what is really at stake in all this talk about "privileged access" and the author's versus the reader's understandings of a text? The theoretical issue, beyond the political ramifications of the originalism debate, is, in a word, objectivity. When we talk about objectivity in constitutional interpretation, what do we mean? It certainly has something to do with the well-known political claim that judges should interpret the law and not make law, a proposition that at once expresses an important truth of American political culture and yet obscures the complexity of that truth.[32] The crux of the problem of objectivity is that an objective interpretation of a text – where "text" is understood as a meaningful document or activity – tells us about the object itself; a subjective interpretation tells us about the subject. Consider, for example, an emotivist theory of ethics such as that proposed by Thomas Hobbes:

> But whatsoever is the object of any man's appetite or desire, that is it, which he for his part calleth *good*: and the object of his hate and aversion, *evil*; and of his contempt, *vile* and *inconsiderable*. For these words of good, evil, and contemptible, are ever used with relation to the person that useth them: there being nothing simply and absolutely so; nor any common rule of good and evil, to be taken from the nature of the objects themselves.[33]

When, therefore, our proverbial man-in-the-street Smith says "murder is evil" and "love is good," Hobbes's view is that such statements are actually reports about Smith. To say "murder is evil" is to say nothing more than "murder displeases me," and, conversely, to say "love is good" is to say nothing more than "love pleases me." Each statement is in actuality not about the purported object of the statement, but rather about the condition of the subject – the speaker – of the statement. Were there for Hobbes such a thing as objectivity, on the other hand, such statements would truly be descriptions of murder or love.

With regard to constitutional interpretation, then, "objective" means that an interpretation says something about the Constitution, whereas "subjective" means that an interpretation says something about the interpreter. That is the operative distinction drawn by two law-review articles on the problem of objectivity published in the early 1980s. In "Objectivity and Interpretation," the more widely cited and reprinted of the two, Owen Fiss writes:

---

[31] Similarly, in this book, I have in mind certain ideas that I believe I can express best in the language you are reading, but you, for your part, can read only my words, not my mind. Your response is necessarily to what I have said rather than to what I have wanted or intended to say, and we could argue about either.

[32] Objectivity was the focus of the argument between Justices Chase and Iredell in *Calder v. Bull*. See Chapter 3.

[33] Thomas Hobbes, *Leviathan*, Michael Oakeshott, ed. (New York: Collier Books, 1962), 41.

Objectivity in the law connotes standards. It implies that an interpretation can be measured against a set of norms that transcend the particular vantage point of the person offering the interpretation. Objectivity implies that the interpretation can be judged by something other than one's own notions of correctness. It imparts a notion of impersonality.[34]

The concept of objectivity, in other words, carries with it the notion of distinctness from the personal values of the interpreter. Likewise, in "Objectivity in Constitutional Law," Robert Bennett writes:

"Objective" is often used to mean contextually correct or authoritatively established, as when a multiple choice examination is described as an "objective" test because each question has only one "correct" answer. In this strong sense, objective sources for decisions would be ones that some authoritative standard identifies as yielding contextually correct decisions.[35]

On the conventional understanding of objective tests, the correct answer depends upon the particular personality of neither the test taker nor the test grader. Thus, as opposed to the alleged subjectivity of essay examinations, the square roots of 9 are $+3$ and -3, whoever the student and the teacher are.

Objectivity in this sense is politically important in the American scheme of government, because objectivity is what is at stake when one talks about a government of laws rather than of men. Judges, Bennett says, "understand that, in their role as judges, certain 'personal' bases of decisions are foreclosed."[36] Robert Bork writes:

In law, the moment of temptation is the moment of choice, when a judge realizes that in the case before him his strongly held view of justice, his political and moral imperative, is not embodied in a statute or in any provision of the Constitution. He must then choose between his version of justice and abiding by the American form of government.[37]

What Bork emphasizes as the American form of government is the principle of democratic accountability, essentially the idea behind what Larry Simon calls the "sovereign public" worldview.[38] The problem for objectivity, Simon suggests, is different from but related to the problem of judicial review in a democratic polity:

[34] Owen Fiss, "Objectivity and Interpretation," 34 *Stanford Law Review* 739, 744 (1982). See Paul Brest's criticism of Fiss, "Interpretation and Interest," in the same issue, 34 *Stanford Law Review* 765 (1982).
[35] Robert Bennett, "Objectivity in Constitutional Law," 132 *University of Pennsylvania Law Review* 445, 447 (1984).
[36] Ibid., 476.
[37] Bork, *The Tempting of America*, 1.
[38] Larry Simon, "The Authority of the Constitution and Its Meaning: A Preface to a Theory of Constitutional Interpretation," 58 *Southern California Law Review* 603, 604ff. (1985).

Two related concerns are central in the historical debate about constitutional interpretation; however, they are different in ways we would do well to acknowledge more consistently. The first is a concern about the extent to which the Supreme Court's constitutional judgment is or can be "objective." The second is a concern about the legitimacy of the institution of constitutional law, that is, of the Supreme Court declaring laws and other governmental action illegal under the authority of the Constitution.[39]

Given the countermajoritarian character of judicial review, some normative standard of objectivity in constitutional interpretation becomes the only available basis for holding accountable electorally unaccountable judges. The idea of a standard is central to the concept of objectivity. "Whether and to what extent constitutional judgment is or can be objective (or constrained)," Simon writes, "depends on the kinds of norms or value sources that judges do or can look to in deciding whether challenged actions are unconstitutional, and on what the process of 'looking to' those sources amounts to."[40] And for originalism, as we shall see in more detail, "original intent" is the generic, collective concept for "the kinds of norms or value sources that judges do or can look to in deciding whether challenged actions are unconstitutional." That is, original intent functions as the normative standard of objectivity.

For the moment, however, note Simon's phrase about whether constitutional interpretation can be "objective (or constrained)." The apparent interchangeability of "objective" and "constrained" is significant. Both Fiss and Bennett reason as follows: In constitutional interpretation – and in legal interpretation generally – objectivity is grounded in impersonality; absolute impersonality is impossible; therefore, absolute objectivity is impossible. In view of this reasoning, both Fiss and Bennett qualify their initial concept of objectivity by replacing it, in essence, with the concept of "constraint." They both seem to want to save the concept of objectivity by weakening it in that their standard is not "Is this right?" but rather "Could someone else come up with the same answer I did?" For Fiss, let me cite the full passage from which I drew the previous quotation on impersonality:

Objectivity in the law connotes standards. It implies that an interpretation can be measured against a set of norms that transcend the particular vantage point of the person offering the interpretation. Objectivity implies that the interpretation can be judged by something other than one's own notions of correctness. It imparts a notion of impersonality. *The idea of an objective interpretation does not require that the interpretation be wholly determined by some source external to the judge, but only that it be constrained.* To explain the source of constraint in the law, it is necessary to introduce two further concepts: One is the idea of disciplining rules, which constrain the interpreter and constitute the standards by which the correctness of the interpretation

[39] Ibid., 604.
[40] Ibid., 606.

is to be judged; the other is the idea of an interpretive community, which recognizes these rules as authoritative.[41]

The suggestion here is that despite the impossibility of a purely impersonal interpretation – after all, though some might still wish to claim that God speaks through his prophets, we can no longer say "the Law" speaks through the judges – we still may reasonably speak of objectivity in interpretation as long as there are constraints on the method and content of an interpretation. Fiss's constraints, we may simply note at this point without comment, are the disciplining rules that both define and are defined by the legal profession conceived as an interpretive community. "Bounded objectivity," as opposed to some concept of absolute objectivity, Fiss thus argues, "is the only kind of objectivity to which the law – or any interpretive activity – ever aspires and the only one about which we care."[42]

Bennett, too, qualifies the concept of objectivity in a very similar manner. The full passage from which I cited his basic definition earlier is this:

> "Objective" is often used to mean contextually correct or authoritatively established, as when a multiple choice examination is described as an "objective" test because each question has only one "correct" answer. In this strong sense, objective sources for decisions would be ones that some authoritative standard identifies as yielding contextually correct decisions. I will refer to judicial objectivity in this sense as judicial reliance on authoritative sources for decision. A second and weaker sense of "objective" refers to the use of sources for decision external to the decider's own (or "subjective") standards or values, without necessarily insisting that those external sources be authoritative. It is in this sense that I will use the term "objective."[43]

Bennett here proffers a strong concept of objectivity as that which produces and guarantees "right" answers, but he then relabels it "authoritative" and applies the term "objective" merely to standards beyond those of the interpreter that constrain him in the act of interpretation.[44] What Bennett wants to do is to make the case that while authoritativeness can guarantee objectivity, it is possible to have objectivity without authoritativeness:

> If judges feel themselves obliged to turn to some objective sources of values in preference to others, then the scope of their choice is constrained, but not necessarily through identification of an authoritative basis for decision. The puzzle of judicial objectivity is whether any such obligation can be identified and how its appeal might be distinguished from the obligation owed authority.[45]

---

41 Fiss, "Objectivity and Interpretation," 744 (emphasis added).
42 Ibid., 745 (footnote omitted).
43 Bennett, "Objectivity in Constitutional Law," 447.
44 Cf. Fiss: "Objectivity speaks to the constraining force of the rules and whether the act of judging is constrained; correctness speaks to the content of the rules and whether the process of adjudication and the meaning produced by that process are fully in accord with that content." Fiss, "Objectivity and Interpretation," 749.
45 Bennett, "Objectivity in Constitutional Law," 452.

The reason he wishes to focus on constraint rather than authoritativeness as the ground of objectivity is that he identifies the latter with the originalism he seeks to attack. The burden of his article is to argue that if that which is authoritative produces right answers, and if the X claimed to be authoritative (e.g., the doctrine of original intent) can be shown not to produce "right" answers, then X is not authoritative.

Bennett wants, then, to maintain that objectivity is possible without the specifically originalist concept of authoritative original intent. The fundamental constraint to which he appeals, beyond the requirement of public justification in the judicial opinion, is that "judges seem to view their task as projecting into the future what the work of their predecessors has delivered to them."[46] Broadly, he writes:

> The legitimacy or objectivity of a decision has to do more with its development from a preexisting tradition and natural growth from an institutional soil than with its approval by authority. This conception of objectivity explains the kind of constraint on arbitrary judicial power that is, in fact, generally accepted by judges; it produces real constraint on judicial choice while allowing growth in the law, and, in any event, it is the only form of check on judicial interpretation of broad constitutional language we can realistically hope to achieve.[47]

This is a reasonable and important claim, but Bennett's detachment of objectivity from authoritativeness is problematic. The problem with his distinction between authoritativeness and objectivity is that he merely shifts rather than solves the original problem of objectivity. Authoritative sources for adjudication may be objective in the strong sense of the term as he defines it, but objectivity in the weak sense of the term leaves the problem of how (according to what norms) we are to choose our sources of constraint. Bennett is not unaware of this problem:

> If the range of "objective" sources from which a court could choose is unlimited and there are no rules or devices of preference among the available choices (or definition of the judicial role that directs the judge to some of those sources rather than others), then the distinction between the chooser's values and the values chosen collapses. Under these assumptions, objectivity without authoritativeness would be impossible.[48]

By pointing to various institutional and professional norms of judging, Bennett falls back on what Fiss called "disciplining rules" and the "interpretive community." We must be careful here, however. I am constrained if

---

[46] Ibid., 480.

[47] Ibid., 475. In "Objectivity in Constitutional Law," 491ff., Bennett claims to make an argument different from that of Ronald Dworkin's metaphor of the chain novel. See Ronald Dworkin, "Law as Interpretation," 60 *Texas Law Review* 527 (1982), to which Bennett refers, and, more recently, *Law's Empire* (Cambridge, MA: Belknap Press of Harvard University Press, 1986), 228–38.

[48] Bennett, "Objectivity in Constitutional Law," 452.

I say, for example, that whatever my own personal judgment of a given issue might be, X is what a theory like that of John Rawls requires and I must follow that theory.[49] Yet we would not consider Rawls to be authoritative: Relying on Rawls may well constrain my own judgment, but the point is to rely on the Constitution to do so. Without accepting uncritically the claim that "the Law speaks through the judge," the concept of objectivity has to do with the validity of the statement, "This is what the Constitution requires."

When the originalist concept of Framers' intent ceases to be analytically equivalent to the Constitution itself, and becomes instead an extrinsic check on how we read the constitutional text, it is supposed to function as the guarantee of objectivity in interpretation. Objectivity involves the notion that the Constitution has its own meaning independently of what particular readers may from time to time say it is. Although Robert Bork says so much that is right that it is easy to miss so much that is wrong, this is right:

> there is a historical Constitution that was understood by those who enacted it to have a meaning of its own. That intended meaning has an existence independent of anything judges may say. It is that meaning the judges *ought* to utter. If law is more than naked power, it is *that* meaning the Justices had a moral duty to pronounce.[50]

To say that the Constitution is objective is to say that it is more than and not reducible to what the judges say it is, and to say that the Constitution is authoritative is to say that it is the Constitution that serves as our standard of constraint.

This is where originalism stakes its claim to a monopoly on objectivity. The clearest picture of originalism and the problem of objectivity can be found in the work of Robert Bork. The fundamental premise of all adjudication in a democratic polity, he states, is that "judges must consider themselves bound by law that is independent of their own views of the desirable."[51] More specifically, the ground – the necessary condition – of objectivity in constitutional interpretation is the Constitution itself. All else is the subjectivity of personal values:

> The hard fact is, however, that there are not guidelines outside the Constitution that can control a judge once he abandons the lawyer's task of interpretation. There may be a natural law, but we are not agreed upon what it is, and there is no such law that gives definite answers to a judge trying to decide a case.
>
> There may be a conventional morality in our society, but on most issues there are likely to be several moralities. They are often regionally defined, which is one reason for federalism. The judge has no way of choosing among differing moralities or competing moralities except in accordance with his own morality.

49 John Rawls, *A Theory of Justice* (Cambridge, MA: The Belknap Press of Harvard University Press, 1971).

50 Bork, *The Tempting of America*, 176.

51 Ibid., 5.

There may be immanent and unrealized ideals of democracy, but the Constitution does not prescribe a wholly democratic government. It is difficult to see what warrant a judge has for demanding more democracy than either the Constitution requires or the people want.

The truth is that the judge who looks outside the Constitution always looks inside himself and nowhere else.[52]

Bork argues significantly more, however, than that the ground of objectivity in constitutional interpretation is the Constitution itself. He maintains that the ground of objectivity in constitutional interpretation is the Constitution itself *understood in a particular way*: in terms of original intent or original understanding.[53] "What does it mean," he asks, "to say that a judge is bound by law? It means that he is bound by the only thing that can be called law, *the principles of the text*, whether Constitution or statute, *as generally understood at the enactment*."[54] On this argument, the nature of law is objectivity; the only possible ground of objectivity is original intent; therefore, the nature of law requires originalism. Original intent is taken by the advocates of originalism to be the normative standard for objective adjudication. Originalism claims to be concerned with the exercise of electorally unaccountable political power. The check on that power is the requirement of objectivity (the law rather than the judge), and the manifestation of the intent of the writers and ratifiers in their original understanding of the text is said to be that check. Originalism argues that to reject original intent or original understanding is to reject, deliberately or not, any possibility of objectivity.

Bork, however, has made a significant shift in his book, from the apparently subjective notion of original *intent* to the apparently more objective notion of original understanding.[55] In the mid-1980s, Bork argued that "only by limiting themselves to the historic intentions underlying each clause of the Constitution can judges avoid becoming legislators, avoid enforcing their own moral predilections, and ensure that the Constitution is law."[56] His focus here is on what we normally call the intentions of the Framers. By the time of the appearance of *The Tempting of America* in 1990, however, he writes, as we saw earlier, that originalists "do not seek the subjective intent

[52] Robert Bork, "The Struggle Over the Role of the Court," *National Review*, September 17, 1982, 1138. Similarly, in *The Tempting of America* Bork writes at 6 that "today's constitutional cognoscenti... would have judges remake the historic Constitution from such materials as natural law, conventional morality, prophetic vision, the understanding of an ideal democracy, or what have you."

[53] These are not the same thing. See the later discussion.

[54] Bork, *The Tempting of America*, 5 (emphasis added).

[55] At this point I would ask the reader to put aside my foregoing generic identification of these two notions and remain aware of a distinction between Framers' intent and original understanding.

[56] Robert Bork, Speech to the University of San Diego Law School, November 18, 1985, in Paul G. Cassell, ed., *The Great Debate: Interpreting Our Written Constitution* (Washington, DC: The Federalist Society, 1986), 52.

of the Framers but rather the objective meaning that constitutional language had when it was adopted."[57] In detail, he writes:

Though I have written of the understanding of the ratifiers of the Constitution, since they enacted it and made it law, that is actually a shorthand formulation, because what the ratifiers understood themselves to be enacting must be taken to be what the public of that time would have understood the words to mean. It is important to be clear about this. The search is not for a subjective intention. If someone found a letter from George Washington to Martha telling her that what he meant by the power to lay taxes was not what other people meant, that would not change our reading of the Constitution. Nor would the subjective intentions of all the members of a ratifying convention alter anything.... As Professor Henry Monaghan of Columbia has said, what counts is what the public understood. Law is a public act. Secret reservations or intentions count for nothing. All that counts is how the words used in the Constitution would have been understood at the time. The original understanding is thus manifested in the words used and in secondary materials, such as debates at the conventions, public discussion, newspaper articles, dictionaries in use at the time, and the like.[58]

The standard of objectivity, in other words, is no longer original intent – that is, the intentions of the authors – but rather the original understanding – that is, what the words of the document meant to the public, the readers of the document, in 1787 and 1788.

This is a conceptual and not merely a terminological change on Bork's part, for it marks what we can call a shift from hard originalism to soft originalism: It is an attempt to avoid the intractable difficulties of authorial intention in the case of the Constitution by moving to a purportedly new and coherent position. By the terms "hard" and "soft" originalism I mean something different from what Paul Brest calls "strict" and "moderate" originalism. Brest's terms have to do with how much attention we pay to, or how strictly we obey, the intentions of the Framers and the text of the Constitution.[59] Hard originalism and soft originalism, by contrast, have to do with how we understand the ground of objectivity: For the former, original *intent* is the key; for the latter, original *understanding*. This distinction is central to what we can call the epistemology of constitutional discourse, to which we now turn.

---

[57] Bork, *The Tempting of America*, 218.

[58] Ibid., 144 (footnote omitted).

[59] See Brest, "The Misconceived Quest for the Original Understanding." Brest, to recall, considers textualism to be a form of originalism, whereas my concern is to try to articulate a concept of textualism whereby originalism is one (putative) form of textualism. One irony of originalism is that while it considers deconstructionism, with its critique of objectivity, to be an enemy, they both seem to share the view that a text in and of itself is indeterminate. The metatheoretical difference between them is that originalism believes one can and must privilege original intent, while deconstructionism believes that nothing can be privileged.

6

The Epistemology of Constitutional Discourse (I)

The goal of originalism, we noted at the outset of this discussion, is to uphold the fundamental and widely acknowledged premise of American constitutionalism: The purpose of a written constitution is to bind the future. Recall the words of Sanford Levinson we noted previously:

Constitutions, of the written variety especially, are usefully viewed as a means of freezing time by controlling the future through the "hardness" of language encoded in a monumental document, which is then left for later interpreters to decipher. The purpose of such control is to preserve the particular vision held by constitutional founders and to prevent its overthrow by future generations.[1]

How do we "freeze time" or bind the future? We do this by establishing "the particular vision held by constitutional founders" as normative – that is, as the ground of objectivity – in constitutional interpretation. For hard originalism, the ground of objectivity is authorial intention. In *Validity in Interpretation* E. D. Hirsch, Jr., defends the concept of "authorial intention" against the theory of semantic autonomy, which maintains that textual meaning is independent of authorial intention, and Hirsch's position when transposed to the context of constitutional interpretation is precisely what I mean by the concept of hard originalism.

According to Hirsch, "once the author had been ruthlessly banished as the determiner of his text's meaning, it very gradually appeared that no adequate principle existed for judging the validity of interpretation."[2] There can be, in other words, no objectivity in interpretation absent the concept of authorial meaning, for all that is left is as many "meanings" as there are reader-interpreters. In his words:

Thus, when critics deliberately banished the original author, they themselves usurped his place, and this led unerringly to some of our present-day theoretical confusions.

[1] Sanford Levinson, "Law as Literature," 60 *Texas Law Review* 373, 376 (1982).
[2] E. D. Hirsch, Jr., *Validity in Interpretation* (New Haven, CT: Yale University Press, 1967), 93.

Where before there had been but one author, there now arose a multiplicity of them, each carrying as much authority as the next. To banish the original author as the determiner of meaning was to reject the only compelling normative principle that could lend validity to an interpretation. On the other hand, it might be the case that there does not really exist a viable normative ideal that governs the interpretation of texts. This would follow if any of the various arguments brought against the author were to hold. For if the meaning of a text is not the author's, then no interpretation can possibly correspond to *the* meaning of the text, since the text can have no determinate or determinable meaning.[3]

This corresponds exactly to the originalist argument that absent some norm of framers' or ratifiers' intent to establish an original understanding as normative, there will be as many legitimate interpretations of the Constitution as there are interpreters. If our wish is to use a text to control the future, the concept of authorial intention is indispensable, for it is the only barrier to the normativity of our own subjective values. As Hirsch writes, "when we construe another's meaning we are not free agents. So long as the meaning of his utterance is our object, we are completely subservient to his will, because the meaning of his utterance is the meaning he wills to convey."[4] Only some standard of objectivity enables an interpreter to subordinate his reading of a text to some external check, and it is only the concept of authorial intention, pace Hirsch, that can ground a standard of objectivity.

Appropriate attention to the details of Hirsch's rich, complex, and sophisticated argument would transcend the limits of the present discussion.[5] For our purposes here, suffice it to note that meaning, he says, "is that which is represented by a text; *it is what the author meant* by his use of a particular sign sequence; it is what the signs represent."[6] Without the concept of authorial intention, therefore, a text cannot have a determinate meaning, and thus we cannot speak of any possible standard of objective interpretation. Within the context of constitutional interpretation, two aspects of this are important for us here. First, the concept of original intent – that is, authorial intention – in hard originalism is both empirically and theoretically problematic. The empirical difficulty is that of discovering what particular historical individuals may have intended with the writing and ratification of

---

[3] Ibid., 5–6.
[4] Ibid., 142.
[5] David Couzens Hoy, for example, writes: "In contrast with the principles of the American New Criticism, Hirsch strives to guarantee the objectivity of interpretation by reviving the notion of the author's intention. Gadamer's and Heidegger's apparent historicism – their insistence on the historical conditions of knowledge and thought – would be undercut by this attempt at breaking out of the hermeneutical circle and anchoring the chain of interpretation in the bedrock of the author's intention and the one right interpretation following from it." *The Critical Circle* (Berkeley: University of California Press, 1978), 5. The hermeneutical point, however, is that Hirsch's gambit is impossible.
[6] Hirsch, *Validity in Interpretation*, 8 (emphasis added).

the Constitution. This is the subjective-intention problem that Bork, as we saw earlier, now seeks to avoid. The theoretical difficulties include those of determining whose intentions count (Framers? Ratifiers? The public?), what counts as an intention, and how we construct a collective intention out of a collection of individual intentions. Both empirical and theoretical difficulties with the concept of authorial intention in the constitutional context have received detailed exposition by Brest and Dworkin, among others,[7] and no

---

[7] See Paul Brest, "The Misconceived Quest for the Original Understanding," 60 *Boston University Law Review* 204 (1980), and Ronald Dworkin, "The Forum of Principle," in *A Matter of Principle* (Cambridge, MA: Harvard University Press, 1985), 33–71. Perhaps no better analysis of the difficulties inherent in the subjective-intention form of originalism, which I have called hard originalism, can be found in the dissenting opinion of Justice Scalia in the creationism case of *Edwards v. Aguillard*, 482 U.S. 578, at 636–8 (1987). Though lengthy, they bear repeating here:

For while it is possible to discern the objective "purpose" of a statute (i.e., the public good at which its provisions appear to be directed), or even the formal motivation for a statute where that is explicitly set forth (as it was, to no avail, here), discerning the subjective motivation of those enacting the statute is, to be honest, almost always an impossible task. The number of possible motivations, to begin with, is not binary, or indeed even finite. In the present case, for example, a particular legislator need not have voted for the Act either because he wanted to foster religion or because he wanted to improve education. He may have thought the bill would provide jobs for his district, or may have wanted to make amends with a faction of his party he had alienated on another vote, or he may have been a close friend of the bill's sponsor, or he may have been repaying a favor he owed the Majority Leader, or he may have hoped the Governor would appreciate his vote and make a fundraising appearance for him, or he may have been pressured to vote for a bill he disliked by a wealthy contributor or by a flood of constituent mail, or he may have been seeking favorable publicity, or he may have been reluctant to hurt the feelings of a loyal staff member who worked on the bill, or he may have been settling an old score with a legislator who opposed the bill, or he may have been mad at his wife who opposed the bill, or he may have been intoxicated and utterly unmotivated when the vote was called, or he may have accidentally voted "yes" instead of "no," or, of course, he may have had (and very likely did have) a combination of some of the above and many other motivations. To look for the sole purpose of even a single legislator is probably to look for something that does not exist.

Putting that problem aside, however, where ought we to look for the individual legislator's purpose? We cannot of course assume that every member present (if, as is unlikely, we know who or even how many they were) agreed with the motivation expressed in a particular legislator's preenactment floor or committee statement. Quite obviously, "what motivates one legislator to make a speech about a statute is not necessarily what motivates scores of others to enact it." *United States v. O'Brien*, 391 U.S. 367, 384 (1968). Can we assume, then, that they all agree with the motivation expressed in the staff-prepared committee reports they might have read – even though we are unwilling to assume that they agreed with the motivation expressed in the very statute that they voted for? Should we consider postenactment floor statements? Or postenactment testimony from legislators, obtained expressly for the lawsuit? Should we consider media reports on the realities of the legislative bargaining? All of these sources, of course, are eminently manipulable. Legislative histories can be contrived and sanitized, favorable media coverage orchestrated, and postenactment recollections conveniently distorted. Perhaps most valuable of all would be more objective indications – for example,

hard originalist has addressed them beyond making the claim that we must do the best we can with the materials we have. The second principal point to draw from Hirsch is an implicit assessment of Bork's new position. We can understand Bork's tacit move from the original intent of hard originalism to the original understanding of soft originalism only as an attempt to avoid and evade without discussion these difficulties with the former. He argues most recently, as we saw earlier, that law is a public act, that the search for the original understanding is not a search for subjective intentions, and that the original understanding is the only ground of interpretive objectivity. But from the standpoint of the hard originalism we can attribute to Hirsch, however, Bork's shift from original intent to original understanding destroys the very ground of the objectivity that Bork wants to uphold. Consider this argument by Hirsch:

> The myth of the public consensus has been decisive in gaining wide acceptance for the doctrine that the author's intention is irrelevant to what the text says. That myth permits the confident belief that the "saying" of the text is a public fact firmly governed by public norms. But if this public meaning exists, why is it that we, who are the public, disagree? Is there one group of us that constitutes the true public, while the rest are heretics and outsiders? By what standard is it judged that a correct insight into public norms is lacking in all those readers who are (except for the text at hand) competent readers of texts? The idea of a public meaning sponsored not by the author's intention but by a public consensus is based upon a fundamental error of observation and logic. It is an empirical fact that the consensus does not exist, and it is a logical error to erect a stable normative concept (i.e., *the* public meaning) out of an unstable descriptive one.[8]

Hirsch's critique of the stability and coherence of a concept of public consensus applies directly to Bork's concept of the public whose original understanding he wants to hold up as normative. Soft originalism, given

evidence regarding the individual legislators' religious affiliations. And if that, why not evidence regarding the fervor or tepidity of their beliefs?

Having achieved, through these simple means, an assessment of what individual legislators intended, we must still confront the question (yet to be addressed in any of our cases) how many of them must have the invalidating intent. If a state senate approves a bill by vote of 26 to 25, and only one of the 26 intended solely to advance religion, is the law unconstitutional? What if 13 of the 26 had that intent? What if 3 of the 26 had the impermissible intent, but 3 of the 25 voting against the bill were motivated by religious hostility or were simply attempting to "balance" the votes of their impermissibly motivated colleagues? Or is it possible that the intent of the bill's sponsor is alone enough to invalidate it – on a theory, perhaps, that even though everyone else's intent was pure, what they produced was the fruit of a forbidden tree?

Because there are no good answers to these questions, this Court has recognized from Chief Justice Marshall, see *Fletcher v. Peck*, 6 Cranch 87, 130 (1810), to Chief Justice Warren, *United States v. O'Brien*, supra, at 383–384, that determining the subjective intent of legislators is a perilous enterprise.

[8] Hirsch, *Validity in Interpretation*, 13.

Hirsch's argument, is no originalism at all. Indeed, we can ask whether Bork's distinction between the subjectivity of original intent and the objectivity of the original public understanding collapses. If we seek to avoid the problems endemic to determining the subjective intentions of the Framers and ratifiers of the Constitution, we merely shift from the authoritativeness of their intentions to the authoritativeness of the public understanding. Yet even if we can successfully identify the public whose understanding is at issue, what do we mean by a "public understanding"? It can be only the summed result of what each individual in the relevant collectivity intends by the particular language of the document. If this is the case, then we would seem to come back to individuals with their own subjective intentions.

Bork, however, is not alone here. If, using my terminology, he attempts to move to soft originalism from the hard originalism of the right, it is apparent that Michael Perry, in his most recent work in this area, attempts to move to soft originalism from the nonoriginalism of the left.[9] Perry's attempt, I suggest, does not succeed either, for what both Bork and Perry have in common is that neither has taken the interpretive turn and thus both maintain the same traditional concept of objectivity. Perry wants to argue that "the debate about the legitimacy of particular conceptions of constitutional interpretation – originalist, nonoriginalist, and nonoriginalist-textualist – is now largely spent."[10] That is so, he claims, because we are all originalists now. This is in fact not a significant move on Perry's part, because the nonoriginalism of his earlier work was always based on the premise of the theoretical validity of originalism. As he titled an appendix to "The Authority of Text, Tradition, and Reason: A Theory of Constitutional 'Interpretation'" in 1985, originalism is a real option.[11] However, it is nonoriginalism, he argued then, that "has more descriptive adequacy and normative appeal than the originalist conception."[12] Similarly, in *Morality, Politics, and Law* in 1988, Perry argued that "originalism's weaknesses, in my view, are not intrinsic, but comparative: Originalism lacks the

---

[9] For an analysis of the intellectual journey of Michael Perry, see Richard B. Saphire, "Originalism and the Importance of Constitutional Aspirations," 24 *Hastings Constitutional Law Quarterly* 599 (1997).

[10] Michael Perry, "The Legitimacy of Particular Conceptions of Constitutional Interpretation," 77 *Virginia Law Review* 669, 673 (1991).

[11] 58 *Southern California Law Review* 551, 597–602 (1985).

[12] Ibid., 556. By nonoriginalism Perry evidently has continued to mean what he initially called noninterpretivism. See his *The Constitution, the Courts, and Human Rights* (New Haven, CT: Yale University Press, 1982), 10–11. Originalists commonly conflate the interpretivism–noninterpretivism dichotomy with the originalist–nonoriginalist dichotomy, a move I argue is possible only on originalist premises and thus not necessary. See Chapter 3. That Perry likewise conflates the terms is indicative, despite his initial opposition to originalism, of his originalist assumptions.

strengths of the nonoriginalist theory of judicial role I elaborate and defend in [Chapter 6]."[13]

We are, however, now sophisticated originalists, as Bork defines the theory in *The Tempting of America*. Perry writes that "[t]he version of originalism embraced by Bork – 'objective meaning' originalism as distinct from 'subjective intentions' originalism – is not the only version, but is the most sophisticated."[14] The crux of the matter, what identifies Perry with Bork, is this:

> What is authoritative, for sophisticated originalism, is the principle (or principles) the ratifiers understood themselves to be establishing. (More precisely, what is authoritative is the principle that the enfranchised public understood, or would have understood, the ratifiers to be establishing.)[15]

Note carefully what Perry is arguing here. At the "constitutional moment" in American history, the relevant actors established as authoritative for and binding on themselves and subsequent generations not, on one side, the private and subjective intentions of the Framers of the Constitution, or, on the other side, the public text of the Constitution, but rather the "public understanding" of the text of the Constitution. Like Bork, Perry is attempting to map out a middle position here: The public understanding is conceived to be more public than private intentions and less public than the text itself. The question is whether the concept of public understanding holds up, for otherwise Perry's sophisticated originalism collapses back into unsophisticated originalism with all its vulnerabilities.[16]

I do not think the concept holds up. Consider the important discussion on pages 690–1 of Perry's article. He writes:

> One justification for judicial review presupposes and implicitly appeals to the fact that "the Constitution," in each and all of its various parts, is an intentional political

---

[13] Michael Perry, *Morality, Politics, and Law* (New York: Oxford University Press, 1988), 131. For a convincing assessment of Perry's work here, see David Couzens Hoy, "A Hermeneutical Critique of the Originalism/Nonoriginalism Distinction," 15 *Northern Kentucky Law Review* 479 (1988).

[14] Perry, "Legitimacy," 77 *Virginia Law Review* 669, 677 (1991) (footnote omitted).

[15] Ibid., 682.

[16] For an argument about the hermeneutical assumptions behind this version of originalism, see Frederick Mark Gedicks, "Conservatives, Liberals, Romantics: The Persistent Quest for Certainty in Constitutional Interpretation," 50 *Vanderbilt Law Review* 613 (1997). Both Bork and Perry, Gedicks writes at 615, stand "squarely in the tradition of Romantic hermeneutics, which sought to overcome the uncertainty and imprecision of textual interpretation by developing a 'science of interpretation' as epistemologically reliable as the methods of the natural sciences." Drawing on Hans-Georg Gadamer's argument that "the presuppositions of the Romantic quest for epistemological certainty in interpretation are inconsistent with how human beings understand texts" (ibid.), Gedicks argues at 616 that "[neither (nor any)] version of originalism is a useful way to investigate questions about the meaning of the Constitution."

act of a certain sort: an act intended to establish not merely particular configurations of words, but particular political-moral principles (policies, states of affairs, etc.), namely, the principles the particular configurations of words were understood to communicate.[17]

This statement as to the character of the Constitution as an intentional act is true, but it collapses back into what Perry calls "subjective originalism." The question is our access to those principles, and we find that it is only through "particular configurations of words" that we gain access to the political-moral principles of the document. Why? Perry continues:

The fundamental reason any part of the Constitution – any provision of the constitutional text – was ratified is that the ratifiers wanted to establish, and thought that in ratifying the provision they were establishing, a particular principle or principles: the principle(s) they understood the provision to mean or to communicate either directly, by naming the principle, or indirectly, by referring to it without naming it. Crediting that justification – assuming that "the Constitution" is wholly an intentional, political act of the indicated sort – it seems unlikely that there is a plausible justification for a conception of constitutional interpretation that countenances a judge enforcing principles that those responsible for the Constitution did not intend to establish, even indirectly. Although one can credit a different justification for judicial review, one that does not presuppose that "the Constitution" is wholly an intentional political act of the indicated sort, it is difficult to imagine what that different justification might be.[18]

Again, this claim is true, but what the people of the 1780s ratified was the language of the provision. Perry, not having made the interpretive turn, continues trying to reach beyond the language of the text to the principles of the text. Yes, the ratifiers thought that the language they adopted reflected the principles they sought to adopt better than different language they could have used but did not. Yes, the particular language of the Constitution is authoritative because it expresses the particular principles that were intended to be authoritative. Nevertheless, it is the language that has primary authoritativeness, because no matter how authoritative the principles may be, it is only *in the language of the text* that we have access to them. And as soon as one insists upon qualifying that language in terms of how it was understood by the public, we are back to the question of what individuals intended by agreeing to that language.

Finally, Perry makes this important argument in the next paragraph:

In the absence of that different justification, and assuming that a particular constitutional provision is deemed authoritative for purposes of constitutional adjudication, it is difficult to discern any justification for a judge construing the provision to mean *anything other than what it was originally understood to mean, other than what it was*

---

[17] Perry, "Legitimacy," 690.
[18] Ibid., 690.

ratified to establish. After all, if the provision is not deemed authoritative, why is the judge enforcing, and therefore interpreting, it? What Steven Smith has asked of statutes we can ask of constitutional provisions:

> If the statute is understood not as the expression of a collective decision by the established political authority but rather as a kind of thing-in-itself, a free-floating text, then why is its right to command any greater than that of, say, the political treatise or the science fiction novel?[19]

Try as he will, Perry cannot let go of intentionalism. Saying that the constitutional text was intended to be authoritative is *not* the same thing as saying that a particular understanding of it is authoritative, and yet that is precisely Perry's, and all originalists', position. He believes that the Smith citation clinches his argument against the claim that the text per se is authoritative, but the alternatives Smith poses are not mutually exclusive. It is entirely consistent to say that the Constitution is "the expression of a collective decision by the established political authority" and to say that the text, above and beyond any particular understanding of it, is authoritative. Again, Perry may want to hold on to the commonsense claim that the principles of the text are primary and the language is secondary, but he cannot avoid the fact that it is language that expresses the principles and it is language that is authoritative.

In response to such an argument, Perry offers this criticism:

> Yes, the words were enacted. But as I pointed out at the beginning of this Article, in the absence of a widely shared understanding of the words – especially, in the presence of competing understandings of the words – there arises the question of *whose* understanding of the words, the meaning of the words *to* whom, is authoritative. I have presented an argument for answering that the original understanding/meaning is authoritative. Those who do not like that answer must present an argument for answering that some nonoriginal understanding/meaning is authoritative. Saying that "the words were enacted, the original understanding was not" does not constitute such an argument; it does not tell us why we should privilege some present meaning (for example) over the original meaning. . . . Adapted to the context of constitutional (not statutory) adjudication, the point is that, in general, the ratifiers (on behalf of their polity) establish principles, not their own views about how those principles should be applied.[20]

Yes, the ratifiers establish principles and not their own views as to how they should be applied. But, again, in order to establish principles they have to establish language as authoritative – language that presumably expresses their understanding of their principles, but language that is public in a way that their understanding of their principles remains, ultimately, private. This is not to privilege some present meaning over the original meaning (and

---

[19] Ibid., 690 (one footnote omitted). A second footnote references the Smith citation as "Law without Mind," 88 *Michigan Law Review* 194, 112 (1989).

[20] Perry, "Legitimacy," 692 (footnote omitted).

Perry fudges "meaning" and "understanding" here), nor is it to privilege the original meaning over the present meaning. It is, rather, to privilege the language of the text over any particular understanding of that language, and thus to generate the kind of moral and political debate that Perry has always claimed to desire.[21]

Finally, while Perry argues that we should all be originalists now, he argues also that we should all be nonoriginalists, too. Just as he defined noninterpretivism in *The Constitution, the Courts, and Human Rights*, he *initially* defines nonoriginalism now as the view that "a judge may enforce not only principles communicated directly or indirectly by the constitutional text; a judge may also enforce some political-moral principles not communicated, even indirectly, by the constitutional text (as originally understood or otherwise)."[22] What he does now, however, is draw on his revised definition of nonoriginalism in *Morality, Politics, and Law*. To the nonoriginalist, he wrote there, "the meaning of the text is not singular. *One* meaning of the constitutional text, to the nonoriginalist, is the original meaning. To the nonoriginalist, however, that is not the only meaning of the text." Continuing, he said that "the text also has an aspirational meaning – it signifies the "basic, constitutive aspirations or principles or ideals of the American political community and tradition."[23] Now, instead of calling this view nonoriginalist, Perry argues that while originalism holds that a judge must enforce a constitutional provision according to its original meaning, that original meaning may be complex, in that it can have both specific aspects and general aspects.

Discussing the problem of equal protection and sex discrimination, for example, he states that "originalism authorizes a judge to enforce, in the name of the equal protection clause, not only the (relatively) specific principle that no state may discriminate on the basis of race, but also the (relatively) general principle that no state may discriminate on the basis of irrational prejudice."[24] While not many originalists would accept this interpretation of the equal protection clause, it is Perry's present argument that "originalism entails nonoriginalism: The originalist approach to constitutional interpretation necessarily eventuates in nonoriginal meanings."[25] This is difficult to accept. The central premise in Perry's argument is his reliance on the

---

[21] "The approach at issue here," he writes in a footnote, " – which can be, and in this Article is, elaborated *entirely without reference to authorial intentions* – leaves room for precisely the kind of community-constitutive rhetoric rightly prized by [James Boyd] White." "Legitimacy," note 43. My argument is that (1) the concept of public understanding collapses into some theory of authorial intentions, and (2) it is only the concept of the authoritative text rather than that of the authoritative understanding that can leave room for what Perry calls "community-constitutive rhetoric."

[22] Perry, "Legitimacy," 687.

[23] Perry, *Morality, Politics, and Law*, 132, 133.

[24] Perry, "Legitimacy," 696 (footnote omitted).

[25] Ibid., 698 (footnote omitted).

authoritativeness of the original understanding, distinct from that of the text itself, but the authoritativeness of the original understanding delegitimates the development of law that he wants. Consider the language he uses to express his point:

By specifying the principle to prohibit sex-based discrimination, the judge adds to the meaning of the principle, giving the principle (further) meaning that theretofore it did not have. After the specification the principle has, in that sense, a fuller meaning.[26]

Such talk of "adding" to the (original) meaning of the principle, of giving it "meaning that theretofore it did not have," or saying that "the present meaning of the clause is different from the original meaning,"[27] is all nonoriginalist in the sense that Perry wants to condemn in the earlier part of the article and Bork and other originalists would reject. There is a difference between "adding to" and rendering the implicit explicit, but Perry appears not to see its significance. The latter is originalist in the sense that he wants to defend, but he talks the language of the former, which is unalterably nonoriginalist.

Perry's argument, then, is now that

originalism entails nonoriginalism, that although we should all be originalists, we must all be nonoriginalists, too: The originalist approach to constitutional interpretation necessarily eventuates in nonoriginal meanings; over time an originalist approach to the interpretation of a constitutional provision yields a provision whose present meaning is different from – in particular, is fuller than – its original meaning, whose present meaning goes beyond the original meaning.[28]

Yet as soon as we make the distinction, to which Perry holds fast, between a present meaning different from an authoritative original meaning, we are necessarily back to the conventional originalism–nonoriginalism distinction that Perry wants to overcome. If the distinction between hard and soft – that is, unsophisticated and sophisticated – originalism stands, then Perry as well as Bork is caught between the problematic theoretical and empirical difficulties endemic to hard originalism and a Hirsch-style critique of soft originalism. Hard, or unsophisticated, originalism promises a rigorous ground for interpretive objectivity, but the theoretical and empirical difficulties vitiate that promise. Soft, or sophisticated, originalism avoids those difficulties of determining original intent, but the concept of original understanding, if it does not dissolve into a version of original intent and thus take us back to the problems of hard originalism, cannot deliver the rigorous ground for interpretive objectivity that all advocates of originalism demand. Viewed from the standpoint of Hirsch's position, soft originalism

[26] Ibid., 697.
[27] Ibid., 697.
[28] Ibid., 702.

is an incomplete interpretive turn, and Hirsch's entire argument is devoted to rejecting the interpretive turn. Perry grants the premise that the original meaning is normative, but that premise undermines his later claim that we must be nonoriginalists as well as originalists. The only way to get beyond the originalism–nonoriginalism debate, as Perry wants to do, is to make the interpretive turn, which he will not or cannot do.

What, then, does it mean to ask whether or not one has taken the interpretive turn?[29] According to originalism, which has not, the ground of objectivity in constitutional interpretation is original intent, conceived as a norm that stands outside of and hence controls the interpretive act. The positivism of originalism is literary – meaning is grounded in the biography and psychology of the author – and legal – conventionalism – but especially epistemological: the "givenness" of texts and meaning – that is, not theory dependent, not interpreted. As such, originalism is epistemologically positivist because it is essentially foundationalist: It seeks, as I just noted, a given noninterpreted norm that stands outside of and hence controls the interpretive act. On taking the interpretive turn, however, we understand the ground of objectivity as a norm that stands *inside* the interpretive act. The interpretive turn, in other words, is an antifoundationalist position that locates the ground of objectivity as internal rather than external to interpretation.[30] Moreover, despite my talk of Bork or Perry not taking the interpretive turn, my argument is that such a move is not merely an option to be chosen or not. Rather, the positivist theory of textuality generates contradictions that can be overcome – *aufgehoben*, in Hegel's terms – only by their reconceptualization in the interpretive paradigm. The interpretive turn bears a similarity to the notion of a paradigm in Thomas Kuhn's *The Structure of Scientific Revolutions*[31] in that original intent is internal to an interpretive framework in just the way nature is internal to a scientific paradigm. Original intent itself, on this view, is not discovered, but rather is constructed by interpretation, and thus cannot be the ground of objectivity in the sense in which originalism understands it.

To grasp this point, consider the underlying question of objectivity in a statement by Christopher Wolfe as well as in one by Bork that we noted

---

[29] I use this term somewhat differently from Michael Moore's description of it as "a general philosophical position proclaiming the senselessness and/or irrelevancy of metaphysics to the practice of some discipline, because that discipline's proper method has supposedly been discovered to be interpretation." Moore, "The Interpretive Turn in Modern Theory: A Turn for the Worse?" 41 *Stanford Law Review* 871, 873, n. 5 (1989).

[30] Antifoundationalism, in contrast to the positivist foundationalism of originalism, is one of two central features of the interpretive turn. The second is the notion of the constitutive character of the Constitution, in contrast to the merely regulative character possible under the originalist approach. For this latter feature, see Chapter 9.

[31] Thomas S. Kuhn, *The Structure of Scientific Revolutions*, 2nd. ed. enl. (Chicago: University of Chicago Press, 1970).

earlier. After describing what he considers traditional judicial review, Wolfe makes this claim about the modern view of interpretation:

Perhaps the best analogy one might offer is the following. An actor is said to "interpret" a particular character in a play. This might mean that his aim is to play his part so that it conforms as closely as possible to the intent of the author of the play. (That intent can, of course, be more or less clear.) It might also mean, however, that the actor has freedom, within the bounds of what is conceivably consistent with the play, to play the role in a variety of different ways, and that he is not necessarily bound by the author's intent. The quality of the actor's "interpretation" of a role, in this sense, could be said to turn much more on his "creativity" than on his conformity to the intention of the playwright. This broad (and, I suspect, modern) conception of an actor's job of "interpreting" a role seems to be the sense in which modern constitutional "interpretation" should be understood.[32]

How does one establish intent independently of the play in order to check a given interpretation of the play? If we look to intent to fix the meaning of a text, we necessarily look to other texts – taking texts in the broad sense of the term – each of whose meanings must be fixed by another intent, which then reproduces the same problem once again.[33] This is what happens when we separate intent from text. Shouldn't we just argue over the meaning of the text, rather than try to short-circuit the task of persuasion by an appeal to authority? Indeed, what makes a play great – about to speak across generations – is its openness to interpretations beyond the author's. Consider the same issue in Bork:

Interpreting the Constitution's general language according to our best understanding of the original intent of the Framers is the only way in which the Constitution

---

[32] Christopher Wolfe, *The Rise of Modern Judicial Review* (New York: Basic Books, 1986), 327–8. Compare Chief Justice Rehnquist:

Judicial interpretation thus involves the determination of what particular sets of words mean, and in that sense may be thought to be a subspecies of interpretation along with literary criticism and other kinds of interpretation of words. But the poet, the dramatist, the director, the reader are all free in a way to import their own meaning to words in a way that judges are not.

William H. Rehnquist, "The Nature of Judicial Interpretation, in Gary McDowell, ed., *Politics and the Constitution: The Nature and Extent of Interpretation* (Washington, DC: National Legal Center for the Public Interest and The American Studies Center, 1990), 6. But how are the poet and others "free" to bring their own meaning to words? They may explore various interpretations of a text without needing to fix on just one, but a judge too may explore various interpretations of a text. Both, however, when asked to fix on the single interpretation that in their best judgment is most accurate, true, and so on, would presumably feel constrained to commit to the "right answer" in their view.

[33] Stanley Fish refers to "the distinction, assumed by many historians, between a *text* as something that requires interpretation and a *document* as something that wears its meaning on its face and therefore can be used to stabilize the meaning of a text. My argument, of course, is that there is no such thing as a document in that sense." "Fish v. Fiss," 36 *Stanford Law Review* 1325, 1326, n. 5 (1984). That, succinctly, is the whole meaning of the interpretive turn.

can be law in the sense just discussed [providing constraint and limitations on judicial discretion]. No other method of constitutional adjudication can accomplish that.[34]

What this seems to say is that our interpretive guideline must be our best understanding of the Framers' understanding of the constitution. If the Framers' understanding of the Constitution checks our best understanding of it, then what checks our best understanding of the Framers' understanding of the Constitution? Originalism argues that the check on our understanding of the constitutional text is the Framers' understanding of that text. But our evidence of the Framers' understanding is other texts – what checks our understanding of *them*? Consequently, the Framers' understanding of the Constitution cannot check our understanding of the Constitution in the way originalism maintains, because we necessarily employ *our* understanding of the Framers' understanding of the Constitution. *We* decide what the original understanding was in order to use it to govern what we decide the Constitution means.

As it understands its own theory of textuality, therefore, originalism relies on the notion of discovery rather than interpretation. This is the positivist theory of constitutional textuality: Meaning is extrinsic to the actual text and located in historical, psychological, biographical, and other such considerations. Edwin Meese maintains, for example, that

[w]e know that those who framed the Constitution chose their words carefully. They debated at great length the most minute points. The language they chose meant something. They proposed, they substituted, they edited, and they carefully revised. Their words were studied with equal care by state ratifying conventions. This is not to suggest that there was unanimity among the framers and ratifiers on all points. . . . But the point is, the meaning of the Constitution can be known."[35]

This is the positivist point – the notion of the given.[36] Using the term "plain-fact" theory of law rather than "positivism" but meaning essentially the same thing, Ronald Dworkin offers a simplified but helpful statement of the positivist concept of the given:

The law is only a matter of what legal institutions, like legislatures and city councils and courts, have decided in the past. If some body of that sort has decided that workmen can recover compensation for injuries by fellow workmen, then that is the law. If it has decided the other way, then that is the law. So questions of law

---

[34] Robert Bork, *The Tempting of America: The Political Seduction of the Law* (New York: Simon & Schuster, 1990), 26.

[35] Edwin Meese, Speech before the Washington, DC, chapter of the Federalist Society Lawyers Division, November 15, 1985, reprinted in Paul G. Cassell, ed.,*The Great Debate: Interpreting Our Written Constitution* (Washington, DC: The Federalist Society, 1986), 34.

[36] Certainly the Constitution is "given," or else nothing would be at issue here. But the central question has to do with precisely what is given – facts or commands, as on the originalist theory of constitutional textuality, or a discourse or way of life, as on the interpretive theory of constitutional textuality?

can always be answered by looking in the books where the records of institutional decisions are kept.[37]

What "the law" is on any particular matter, according to this view, is nothing more than a purely factual question about decisions made by those social institutions authorized to make law for a given community. For the originalist, therefore, the meaning of the Constitution is nothing more than the purely factual question about decisions and arguments made by the Philadelphia convention and the ratification debates and state conventions, and such meaning is ascertained through discovery.

What concept of interpretation originalism does have seems to be one actually of application. Robert Bork, for example, says that all we need is a premise:

all an intentionalist requires is that the text, structure, and history of the Constitution provide him not with a conclusion but with a premise. That premise states a core value that the framers intended to protect. The intentionalist judge must then supply the minor premise in order to protect the constitutional freedom in circumstances the framers could not foresee.[38]

"Interpretation," on this view, consists of applying that premise to the specific case at hand, but the assumption remains that the premise derives from discovery.[39] The interpretation lies in the application rather than in the initial identification of the premise. As Meese argues, "Our approach understands the significance of a written document and seeks to discern the particular and general principles it expresses. It recognizes that there may be debate at times over the application of these principles. But it does not mean these principles cannot be identified."[40] There can be debate over the application of principles, but apparently not over their identity and, by implication here, the meaning of the principles themselves, for the identity and meaning are simply a matter of historical record. Note Meese's use of "interpret" as he describes what originalists consider the proper mode of adjudication:

Where there is a demonstrable consensus among the framers and ratifiers as to a principle stated or implied by the Constitution, it should be followed. Where there is

---

37 Dworkin, *Law's Empire* (Cambridge, MA: Harvard University Press, 1986), 7.
38 Robert Bork, Speech Before the University of San Diego Law School, November 18, 1985, reprinted in Cassell, *The Great Debate*, 46.
39 As Gregory Bassham states, originalists argue "that the fundamental value choices for purposes of constitutional adjudication have already been made by the framers. Judges need rarely if ever *make* significant constitutional value choices; they need only *discover* them. Their proper role, in brief, is that of dispassionate constitutional historian, not moral philosopher." *Original Intent and the Constitution* (Lanham, MD: Rowman & Littlefield Publishers, 1992), 77–8.
40 Meese, Speech before the Washington, DC, chapter of the Federalist Society Lawyers Division, reprinted in Cassell, *The Great Debate*, 36.

ambiguity as to the precise meaning or reach of a constitutional provision, it should be interpreted and applied in a manner so as to at least not contradict the text of the Constitution itself.[41]

On the positivist theory of constitutional textuality, therefore, interpretation occurs only when the discovered wording or meaning of a text is unclear, ambiguous, and so on – that is, "clear" versus "unclear" is a matter of qualitative difference or distinction in kind.

On the interpretive theory of constitutional textuality, by contrast, such a distinction between clear and unclear is a matter of degree, for on this theory meaning is always constructed rather than discovered, and the distinction between discovery and interpretation is a false one. There is no unmediated meaning, for interpretation necessarily occurs in every case of textual meaning. As Hans-Georg Gadamer argues, "Interpretation is not an occasional additional act subsequent to understanding, but rather understanding is always an interpretation, and hence interpretation is the explicit form of understanding."[42] From this point of view, any conception of the intention of the Framers is the product of interpretation rather than an object to be discovered. "There is," Dworkin writes, "no stubborn fact of the matter – no 'real' intention fixed in history independent of our opinions about proper legal or constitutional practice – against which the conceptions we construct can be tested for accuracy."[43] It is not the case that an intention of the Framers is available, which the interpretive theorist ignores, but rather that the allegedly discoverable intention of the Framers is the result

---

[41] Ibid.

[42] Hans-Georg Gadamer, *Truth and Method* (New York: The Seabury Press, 1975), 274. As Eagleton says, "For Gadamer, the meaning of a literary work is never exhausted by the intentions of its author; as the work passes from one cultural or history context to another, new meanings may be culled from it which were perhaps never anticipated by its author or contemporary audience.... All interpretation is situational, shaped and constrained by the historically relative criteria of a particular culture; there is no possibility of knowing the literary text 'as it is'." Terry Eagleton, *Literary Theory: An Introduction*, 2nd ed. (Minneapolis: University of Minnesota Press, 1996), 71. The interpretive theory of constitutional textuality affirms, as the originalist theory denies, the proposition that one cannot contrast the Constitution "as it is" with the Constitution "as it is interpreted" because the former is necessarily and always a version or species of the latter. "For Gadamer," Frederick Mark Gedicks maintains in "Conservatives, Liberals, Romantics," at 634, "what the constitutional text meant to the Framers and their contemporaries, and what it means to us in the light of contemporary notions of morality and justice, are simply different dimensions of the same question." In agreement with Stanley Fish and others, Eagleton argues that "nothing, in literature or the world at large, is 'given' or 'determinate', if by that is meant 'non-interpreted'." *Literary Theory*, 86. See, e.g., Stanley Fish, *Is There a Text in This Class?* (Cambridge, MA: Harvard University Press, 1980). Consequently, to return to Gedicks at 634, "Gadamer's argument that cognitive and normative interpretation cannot be separated is not trivial. It attacks the foundation of all originalist methodology, be it progressive or conservative, ultimately calling into question whether 'originalism' is phenomenologically possible."

[43] Ronald Dworkin, *A Matter of Principle* (Cambridge, MA: Harvard University Press, 1985), 39–40.

of interpretive construction that forgets the interpretive ground on which it stands.[44]

The point, generally speaking, is that adjudication involves judgment; it is a species of practical reasoning. To render a decision objectively, one would say, "In my judgment, this is the best decision; this is what the law requires in the case at hand." The attempted stronger claim for objectivity would be to say, as a formalist might, "The text requires this decision in the case at hand," thus claiming that the text – not the judge – decides the case. Yet this formulation, deliberately or not, hides the real framework of the claim. That framework is this: "In my best reading of the text, this is what the text requires in the case at hand." In other words, the point is that we cannot escape the "in my best judgment/reading" that, whether explicit or not, underpins any and all decisions.

Now, one way to look at this fact is to say that all adjudication is essentially subjective – it all and always is grounded in "my judgment." An alternative way to conceive it, however, is to see that this implication of subjectivity reflects a search for a chimerical standard of objectivity.[45] Certainly

---

[44] Dworkin himself sometimes slips in holding this position. Arguing the point in *Law's Empire* that creative interpretation is constructive rather than conversational, in the speaker's-meaning sense, he makes this claim on 51–2:

> Interpretation of works of art and social practices, I shall argue, is indeed essentially concerned with purpose not cause. But the purposes in play are not (fundamentally) those of some author but of the interpreter. Roughly, constructive interpretation is a matter of imposing purpose on an object or practice in order to make of it the best possible example of the form or genre to which it is taken to belong.

Dworkin's claim here seems to suggest an opposition between the purposes of some author and those of an interpreter, but his actual point is that what counts as the purposes of some author derives from those of an interpreter. There is no opposition in principle, because the former hinges upon the latter.

[45] This is the sense of Dworkin's discussion of metaphysical baggage in moral reasoning. In the course of a methodological discussion in Chapter 2 of *Law's Empire*, Dworkin writes: "We use the language of objectivity, not to give our ordinary moral or interpretive claims a bizarre metaphysical base, but to *repeat* them, perhaps in a more precise way, to emphasize or qualify their *content*.... We also use the language of objectivity to distinguish between claims meant to hold only for persons with particular beliefs or connections or needs or interests (perhaps only for the speaker) and those meant to hold impersonally for everyone." Dworkin, *Law's Empire*, 81. Moore, for example, argues this:

> One who shares the Framers' moral realism will not interpret the Bill of Rights according to "Framers' intent," "original understanding," or the "evolving standards of decency that mark the progress of a maturing society." Rather, he will develop a theory about what punishments are cruel, when speech is truly free, and what other rights persons possess, and interpret the Constitution in light of that theory.

Moore, "The Interpretive Turn," 41 *Stanford Law Review* 871, 883 (1989). Dworkin would agree with Moore's argument, but he would deny that we need the metaphysics of moral realism that Moore sees as essential to such a theory. The interpretive turn rejects foundationalism, whether the natural – i.e., the given as prior to and independent of human agency – foundationalism of Moore or the conventional – i.e., the given as the product of human agency – foundationalism of Bork.

a concept of objectivity that requires us to step outside our own skin is impossible to achieve, but we can reasonably conclude that we must therefore be trying to use a faulty concept of objectivity – and thus we need a concept of objectivity appropriate to adjudication and practical reasoning generally – rather than that objectivity is impossible.[46] The argument of the interpretive turn is that the ground of objectivity is internal to the act of interpretation; that, moreover, any such ground, like original intent in originalism, that purports to stand outside the act of interpretation in fact is itself the product of an act of interpretation itself. For example, although I suggested earlier certain problems with Bennett's analysis, his conclusion in "Objectivity in Constitutional Law" bears traces of the interpretive turn:

> Originalists appeal to the authority of those who enacted the Constitution, non-originalists to some moral or political ideal. What they have in common is an appeal to constraint on judicial choice that can be abstracted from the judicial process of decision by adjudication and then reimposed to govern particular decisions. The real constraint on judicial choice, however, is produced by engaging in the process of decision, rather than by governance from outside.[47]

In Hirsch, authorial intent controls potential interpretations; in Wolfe's theater analogy, the same; in constitutional theory – originalism – original intent or original understanding controls potential interpretations. The key premise is that establishing the author's or playwright's or Framers' intent is *not* just one more interpretation, but rather categorically different.

The interpretive turn, by contrast, argues that establishing intent *is* just one more interpretation. The traditional preinterpretive-turn assumption is that interpretation is literally anarchic – that is, an-archic, without a rule – and thus requires a rule imposed from without. That rule is said to be authorial intention. Now we can say that the author either does or does not have privileged access to the meaning of his text. If the latter, then the author is one reader among others – everyone plays equally on the same level field, as it were. In this case the author's point of view carries no a priori presumption of normativity. If, on the other hand, the author does have privileged access to the meaning of his text, there is still a problem for the advocate of preinterpretive objectivity. *We* have to establish what and who counts as the author's point of view. We seek the author's intent as an objective check on our interpretation of the author's text, but it is *our interpretation* of the author's text (or the text consisting of related historical data) that establishes the objective check we call the author's intent.[48]

---

[46] This, in theoretical reasoning, is the situation in which Kant found himself: If the conventional concept of objectivity condemned us to skepticism, then there must be something wrong with the conventional concept of objectivity.

[47] Robert Bennett, "Objectivity in Constitutional Law," 132 *University of Pennsylvania Law Review* 445, 496 (1984).

[48] In essence, I would suggest, we construct the author from the text, not, as the positivist paradigm would have it, the text from the author. What is meant by "author" in the latter

The philosophy of language underlying originalism separates text and intent in order to give priority to intent, because by its premises we cannot speak meaningfully about a text in the absence of intent. The originalist claim is that to assume that the constitutional text is authoritative necessarily implies the authoritativeness of original intent. Yet where originalism dissolves text into intent, the interpretive turn in essence dissolves intent into text: The text itself is a structure of intent on the latter view. Perry and Bork both want to argue that not just a text was adopted as authoritative, but a particular understanding of that text as well. Indeed, their argument is that one cannot adopt a text as authoritative without adopting a particular understanding of that text as well.[49] From the standpoint of the interpretive turn, this is better than saying that particular authorial intentions were adopted as authoritative, but it nevertheless continues to deny the semantic autonomy of the text. Given the interpretive turn, however, Bennett rightly claims that "we can comfortably assume that the constitutional text is authoritative without concluding that the authoritativeness of original intent is necessarily implied. If original intent is to be authoritative, it must establish this claim on its own."[50]

In other words, hard originalism claims that the authors' intent, and soft originalism claims that the ratifiers' understanding, is an external, objective check on constitutional interpretation. However, my argument here is not that the traditional concept of objectivity underlies originalism, while the interpretive-turn concept of objectivity underlies nonoriginalism. Rather, my claim is that the interpretive turn gets us past the debate between originalism and nonoriginalism. The effect of the interpretive turn, that is, is to say that the contrast is not between (1) our understanding of the Constitution

clause? An independent, objective, normative standard guiding interpretation. However, when we do the historical-psychological work to discover the author, we are engaged once again in an interpretive enterprise.

[49] Once again, Perry, who has always maintained the validity of originalism yet defended the comparative superiority of nonoriginalism, goes back to a Borkian sophisticated originalism that nonetheless collapses into an unsophisticated originalism, all because he holds on to the traditional concepts of language, interpretation, and objectivity. He has, in other words, not taken the interpretive turn. Perry originally (!) saw both originalism and nonoriginalism as viable theoretical options, and he just argued that the latter was better in comparative terms. Now he wants to collapse the distinction between the two, but he has not gotten past the distinction between interpretivism–noninterpretivism and originalism–nonoriginalism. He continues to run them together, which, if they were the same, would indeed validate his claim that the debate is shot. But if they are not the same, and there is a significant distinction, as I maintain, he cannot discount the originalism–nonoriginalism debate. The interpretivism–noninterpretivism debate *is* shot, but the latter argument is alive and well. Despairing of constitutional theory, Perry wants to retreat to a theory of judicial role (a theory that is perhaps more modest than the prophetic function he advocated in his earlier work) to guide constitutional interpretation, yet it is a theory of constitutional interpretation that underlies the reading of the document that guides one's choice of a theory of judicial role.

[50] Bennett, "Objectivity in Constitutional Law," 460.

and (2) the Framers' understanding of the Constitution, but rather is between (1) our understanding of the Constitution and (2) our understanding of the Framers' understanding of the Constitution. That is, the original intent or original understanding of the Constitution cannot serve as an objective check on our understanding of the Constitution *in the way that originalism presumes*, because what we take to be the original intent or original understanding of the Constitution is always and necessarily *our* understanding of what we determine to be the original intent or original understanding of the Constitution. And, as such, it would appear that our understanding of the Constitution always and necessarily involves our understanding of the original intent or original understanding of the Constitution, *and vice versa*, such that the interpretive turn undercuts the originalism–nonoriginalism dichotomy.

What is at stake here, in other words, is not just the viability of originalism, but that of nonoriginalism as well, for the same critique of extrinsic standards that dissolves the former position likewise dissolves the latter. That is, we distinguish, as we saw earlier, between the original understanding and contemporary understanding, and privilege either the former (originalism) or the latter (nonoriginalism). Yet the key point is that in both cases we search for the right normative standard governing interpretation, because both equally presume that interpretation in and of itself is essentially ungoverned. As Powell has noted:

There are, on the one hand, those who implicitly or explicitly wish to recast American constitutional discourse into what they see as the freer and richer context of general moral debate. On the other hand, there are those who regard the text as the container for an encoded message, and the constitutionalist as a cryptographer equipped with the proper key, whether it be the "framers' intent" or the gospel of economic efficiency. Yet others, by far the largest group, do not so much undercut the text as they ignore it. For them the question of "the Constitution's" meaning is simply an inquiry into the possible implications of Supreme Court decisions.[51]

Where originalists argue that the Framers' position is normative, nonoriginalists similarly argue that some other position – evolving moral standards, John Rawls' theory of justice, and so on – is normative. Both do so on the assumption that language in and of itself is anarchic and ungoverned, without a normative standard beyond it. I call this a "positivist" conception of language and textuality, because it is grounded in a Hobbesian atomistic view of language as a linguistic war of all against all in the absence of a standard of meaning.

The Constitution on this view thereby becomes not the binding force we take it to be, but the representation and embodiment of the truly binding standard beyond it. The positivist view of language and interpretation

---

[51] Powell, "Parchment Matters," 71 *Iowa Law Review* 1427, 1428 (1986).

underlies both originalism and nonoriginalism, and it always generates an "unwritten Constitution," a normative standard that is what is really authoritative and binding.[52] Paradoxically, the chief concern of those who advocate originalism is regularly stated to be an affirmation of the objective meaning of the Constitution independent of what particular interpreters might argue at particular times, and yet their own theory of textuality undermines the possibility of such an affirmation.[53] The analytical question is, what counts as an objective meaning of the Constitution? At the very least, "objective" would seem to mean that the meaning of the Constitution is independent of what any particular commentator might say it is. That is, it is not the case that the Constitution is just what the judges say it is. This, however, does not address the further question – does the text itself have a meaning of its own? Originalism denies this possibility in that it claims that the meaning of the Constitution lies behind the document in the intentions of the people who wrote it and ratified it. The originalist argument would be that the text in and of itself has no structured meaning, a claim that rests on what literary theorist Terry Eagleton calls

the classical "contractual" view of language, according to which language is just a sort of instrument essentially isolated individuals use to exchange their pre-linguistic experiences. This was really a "market" view of language, closely associated with the historical growth of bourgeois individualism: meaning belonged to me like my commodity, and language was just a set of tokens which like money allowed me to exchange my meaning-commodity with another individual who was also a private proprietor of meaning.[54]

The operative phrase here is "private proprietor of meaning," for on this Hobbesian view of language, words and meaning are ontologically private competitors in a linguistic war of all against all until one private proprietor of meaning becomes linguistically as well as politically sovereign. The result is that the only possible objective meaning – objective in the sense of independent of the personal values of contemporary readers – is that of the Framers, that is, the writers and ratifiers of the constitutional provision in question. The implication seems to be that meaning is always somebody's meaning, with the result that meaning will be nothing more than a given reader's understanding if it is not grounded immutably in the original understanding.

---

[52] As Daniel Farber writes in the context of discussing the idea of the "dead hand of the past," originalism "seeks in some sense to bestow ultimate constitutional authority to some ghost in the dead hand, rather than to the dead hand itself. Rather than focusing on the tangible legal structure that the Framers bequeathed, originalism seeks to invest authority in the departed creators of that structure, as if their minds still animated their creation." "The Dead Hand of the Architect," 19 *Harvard Journal of Law & Public Policy* 245, 249 (1996).

[53] Though related, the issue of the objectivity of the Constitution is distinct from that of the objectivity of judicial decision making.

[54] Eagleton, *Literary Theory*, 115.

The mirror metaphor Meese employs in one of his speeches is thus more significant than he might realize. "The Constitution," he argues, "is not a legislative code bound to the time in which it was written. Neither, however, is it a mirror that simply reflects the thoughts and ideas of those who stand before it."[55] This claim is fair enough, but the import of Meese's originalism is that the Constitution becomes "a mirror that simply reflects the thoughts and ideas of those" who stand *behind* it. What is significant either way is not who or what is reflected, but the idea of the mirror itself – viz., the idea that the constitutional text has no structure or substance of its own.

What clearer example of a disbelief in the binding capacity of language is there than Meese's talk of the danger of putting new meaning into old words? The paradox of originalism is its insistence on the central importance of the writtenness of the Constitution at the same time that it empties that writtenness of meaning (i.e., that it insists on the binding capacity of a written constitution at the same time that it empties that writtenness of meaning):

It is our belief that only "the sense in which the Constitution was accepted and ratified by the nation," and only the sense in which laws were drafted and passed provide a solid foundation for adjudication. Any other standard suffers the defect of pouring new meaning into old words, thus creating new powers and new rights totally at odds with the logic of our Constitution and its commitment to the rule of law.[56]

The assumption here is clearly that there is a distinction between meaning and words or language. As Michael Perry notes in discussing the originalism of Henry Monaghan,

Monaghan conceives of the constitutional text as the verbal or linguistic embodiment of the political morality the ratifiers understood the text to embody. Monaghan's conception of the constitutional text entails a conception of constitutional interpretation: to interpret the constitutional text is to search for the political-moral judgments understood by the ratifiers to be embodied in the text.[57]

---

[55] Meese, Speech before the Washington, DC, chapter of the Federalist Society Lawyers Division, reprinted in Cassell, *The Great Debate*, 33.

[56] Edwin Meese, Speech Before the American Bar Association, July 9, 1985, reprinted in Cassell, *The Great Debate*, 10.

[57] Michael J. Perry, "The Authority of Text, Tradition, and Reason: A Theory of Constitutional 'Interpretation,'" 58 *Southern California Law Review* 551, 555 (1985), referring to Henry Monaghan, "Our Perfect Constitution," 56 *New York University Law Review* 353, 383 (1981). Perry's own view, by contrast, is very close to the participatory notion sketched here as central to the interpretive theory of constitutional textuality:

The referent of the constitutional text, as an originalist like Monaghan conceives it, is "behind": one must look behind the text to the original understanding if one is to comprehend the text. The referent of the constitutional text conceived as the symbolization of the fundamental, constitutive aspirations of the political tradition, however, is not behind, but "in front of." The polity must respond to the incessant prophetic call of the text, must recall and heed the aspirations symbolized by the text, and thus must create and give (always-provisional, always-reformable) meaning to the text, as well as take meaning from it.

That is the essential positivism of the originalist theory of constitutional textuality. If indeed meaning is extrinsic to the text, then to deny the Framers' intentions as the meaning of the Constitution is to deny that the Constitution has any meaning at all. This argument is similar to a private-language argument, such that the meaning of the document can be nothing other than a system of signs for what went on in the heads of those who wrote it. As in phenomenological literary criticism, to use an example from the literary theorist Eagleton, "The text itself is reduced to a pure embodiment of the author's consciousness: all of its stylistic and semantic aspects are grasped as organic parts of a complex totality, of which the unifying essence is the author's mind."[58] On this view of language, a text is nothing but an expression of its inner meaning, and meaning, as Eagleton explains this theory, "is something which pre-dates language: language is no more than a secondary activity which gives names to meanings I somehow already possess."[59] It is for that rather abstract reason that the positivist theory of textuality argues that if meaning cannot be frozen in language by anchoring it in historically discoverable acts and intentions, then the constitutional text can have no binding and limiting power whatsoever. Paradoxically, therefore, the positivist theory of textuality underlying originalism's historicism is actually ahistorical, because it freezes language and meaning in the time and circumstances in which they originated, whereas the interpretive theory of textuality is actually the truly historical approach to constitutional interpretation, because it recognizes the basic social character and historicity of language.[60]

---

[58] Eagleton, *Literary Theory*, 59.

[59] Ibid., 60.

[60] For an interesting argument along these lines, see Barry Friedman and Scott B. Smith, "The Sedimentary Constitution," 147 *University of Pennsylvania Law Review* 1 (1998). There they write at 5–6:

> This Article challenges common thinking about the use of history in constitutional interpretation. It seeks to replace the apparent choice between anachronistic originalism or nonhistorical living constitutionalism with an approach that takes all of our constitutional history into account. This Article makes a simple claim: history is essential to interpretation of the Constitution, but the relevant history is not just that of the Founding, it is that of all American constitutional history. Only by taking all of that history into account is it possible to arrive at an understanding of today's constitutional commitments.

> In effect, the role of history depends upon one's assumptions as to the coherence of the Constitution itself and the significance of constitutional amendments, about which a huge literature has arisen on the mechanism of the amendment process. Briefly, if the Constitution, despite the reality of its origin as the result of numerous compromises, is not a coherent, principled text, and if amendments are no more than particularistic and random addenda, then we indeed could read the text without concern for the totality of its historical development. We would simply attend to the historical context of each phrase or provision in question. On the other hand, if the Constitution is to be understood as a coherent, principled text, then at least some amendments (most prominently, the Fourteenth – as the justices in the *Slaughterhouse* majority feared) would have to be seen as having altered – amended – the

The interpretive theory of constitutional textuality has a higher regard for that binding capacity than does the positivist theory. The interpretive theory of constitutional textuality is that the Constitution must be understood not as an object but as a social practice, an ongoing and participative interpretive activity – "Constitution," in other words, is a gerund rather than a noun. The interpretive theory can explain the text's binding capacity because such a theory undercuts the positivist dichotomy of the descriptive–empirical versus the prescriptive–normative in that it claims that the Constitution's meaning is reducible neither to the Framers' understanding nor to every person's meaning. There is no unwritten Constitution, for meaning is not extrinsic to the text, as in positivism; rather, meaning is intrinsic to the text. The speaker's-meaning theory of textuality is, as we have seen, essentially positivist in that it sees the text as a representation of meaning distinct from and standing behind it and command-oriented. Its binding capacity relies ultimately on the reader's – the object of the command – willingness to obey as a passive object of the speakers' commands, for the originalist argument is that where there is no command there is no obedience, and where there is no obedience there is no controlling the future. The interpretive theory of textuality, by contrast, is essentially textual (in that the text *is* the meaning) and participatory. Its binding capacity relies ultimately on the reader's willingness to participate as an active subject in the activity of constituting meaning. In the process of advocating their theory, originalists themselves, in just this sense, participate as active subjects in the activity of constituting meaning. They just don't know that they are doing that.

The binding capacity of the constitutional text – on the explanation of which originalism stakes its claim to exclusive legitimacy – is explicable by the interpretive claim that a written document has a public meaning, "public" in the sense that language is richer and broader than the particular subjective thoughts its author(s) may have had in mind. The positivist theory of textuality employed by originalism denies this public or social character of language, but that character is the essential point:

The hallmark of the "linguistic revolution" of the twentieth century, from Saussure and Wittgenstein to contemporary literary theory, is the recognition that meaning is not simply something "expressed" or "reflected" in language: it is actually *produced*

nature of that coherent, principled text. In that case, we could not now read the Constitution in terms of the Founding, but rather would necessarily have to read it through the lens of the Fourteenth Amendment. This is the sense in which Friedman and Smith argue that "the relevant history is not just that of the Founding, it is that of all American constitutional history." Bruce Ackerman's notion of transformative amendments – "the culminating expression of a generation's critique of the status quo – a critique that finally gains the considered support of a mobilized majority of the American people" – in *We the People I: Foundations* (Cambridge, MA: Belknap Press of Harvard University Press, 1991), at 92, might well come to mind, but, as I have noted already, his concern is more with the mechanisms of constitutional change than with my theme here.

by it. It is not as though we have meanings, or experiences, which we then proceed to cloak with words; we can only have the meanings and experiences in the first place because we have a language to have them in. What this suggests, moreover, is that our experience as individuals is social to its roots; for there can be no such thing as a private language, and to imagine a language is to imagine a whole form of social life.[61]

Language, in other words, is essentially a social activity, and social activity is essentially textual. An example of this public or social sense of language is a comment by Gadamer on what we do when we read a text:

When we try to understand a text, we do not try to recapture the author's attitude of mind but, if this is the terminology we are to use, we try to recapture the perspective within which he has formed his views. But this means simply that we try to accept the objective validity of what he is saying. If we want to understand, we shall try to make his arguments even more cogent. This happens even in conversation, so how much truer is it of the understanding of what is written down that we are moving in a dimension of meaning that is intelligible in itself and as such offers no reason for going back to the subjectivity of the author. It is the task of hermeneutics to clarify this miracle of understanding, which is not a mysterious communion of souls, but a sharing of a common meaning.[62]

Though only one of several voices in contemporary literary theory, Gadamer here, with his claim that "we are moving in a dimension of meaning that is intelligible in itself and as such offers no reason for going back to the subjectivity of the author," illustrates the *public* character of textuality. This public character involves a seemingly innocent phrase introduced at the outset of this essay, the distinction between a society "living under" the constitutional text and a society "living in" that text. The interpretive theory of constitutional textuality can explain the binding capacity of the constitutional text because it offers the conception of a society living in that text.

---

[61] Eagleton, *Literary Theory*, 60. One particular school of modern literary theory that emphasizes the public and constructed character of meaning is so-called reception theory, which focuses upon the reader's role in constituting a text. Eagleton's summary of reception theory at 76 is suggestive in the matter of Constitutional textuality:

The reader makes implicit connections, fills in gaps, draws inferences and tests out hunches; and to do this means drawing on a tacit knowledge of the world in general and of literary conventions in particular. The text itself is really no more than a series of "cues" to the reader, invitations to construct a piece of language into meaning. In the terminology of reception theory, the reader "concretizes" the literary work, which is in itself no more than a chain of organized black marks on a page. Without this continuous active participation on the reader's part, there would be no literary work at all.

Note how this reads, and how familiar it sounds, if we substitute "judge" for "reader" and Constitution for "text" and "literary work" – e.g., "the judge 'concretizes' the Constitution."

[62] Gadamer, *Truth and Method*, 259–60. For a discussion of Gadamer focusing directly on constitutional issues, see Gregory Leyh, "Toward a Constitutional Hermeneutics," 32 *American Journal of Political Science* 369 (1988).

As opposed to the premise of semantic anarchy, then, that a text means nothing (or anything) independently of the author's intended meaning, here we employ the concept of semantic autonomy to indicate that a text has a determinate, structured range of meanings – not one meaning but not an infinite number of meanings either – independently of authorial intention. Distinguishing between speaking and writing, Paul Ricoeur states that "writing renders the text autonomous with respect to the intention of the author. What the text signifies no longer coincides with what the author meant; henceforth, textual meaning and psychological meaning have different destinies."[63] In spoken discourse, he says, "the subjective intention of the speaking subject and the meaning of the discourse overlap each other in such a way that it is the same thing to understand what the speaker means and what his discourse means."[64] However, here is the key point:

With written discourse, the author's intention and the meaning of the text cease to coincide. This dissociation of the verbal meaning of the text and mental intention is what is really at stake in the inscription of discourse. Not that we can conceive of a text without an author; the tie between the speaker and the discourse is not abolished, but distended and complicated. . . . But the text's career escapes the finite horizon lived by its author. What the text says now matters more than what the author meant to say, and every exegesis unfolds its procedures within the circumference of a meaning that has broken its moorings to the psychology of its author.[65]

This idea of the determinate meaning of the text despite its independence of the author is what originalism appears unable to grasp. It is this conclusion that escapes originalism:

The text is a limited field of possible constructions. The logic of validation allows us to move between the two limits of dogmatism and skepticism. It is always possible to argue for or against an interpretation, to confront interpretations, to arbitrate between them, and to seek for an agreement, even if this agreement remains beyond our reach.[66]

---

[63] Paul Ricoeur, *Hermeneutics and Human Sciences* (Cambridge: Cambridge University Press, 1981), 139.

[64] Ibid., 200.

[65] Ibid., 201.

[66] Ibid., 213. For more insight into the general philosophical movement represented by Ricoeur, see also the argument of David Couzens Hoy:

> The idea that there is a sharp distinction between original meaning and present meaning arises, I believe, from believing that there is also a distinction between understanding the meaning of a text, and applying that meaning in a present context. This distinction between understanding and application was standard in an older hermeneutical tradition – one that grew out of a concern principally with Biblical interpretation, but that was influenced by more Cartesian assumptions about knowledge, mind, and language. A major move by twentieth-century hermeneutical philosophers like Heidegger and Gadamer (as well as by Anglo-American philosophers influenced by the later Wittgenstein or by Quine) was to challenge the conception of meaning presupposed by this distinction.

"A Hermeneutical Critique of the Originalism/Nonoriginalism Distinction," 491.

In order to escape skepticism, I suggest, originalism embraces dogmatism. Framers' intent becomes not the content of constitutional interpretation, but rather the extrinsic check on constitutional interpretation.

Going beyond originalism and nonoriginalism, then, means rejecting the atomistic conception of language, and thus the unwritten Constitution it generates, in favor of a holistic conception of language as social discourse. What is normative on this latter conception is neither the originalist nor the nonoriginalist standard, but the discourse of constitutional interpretation itself. Both originalism and nonoriginalism seek and appeal to a normative standard outside of interpretive debate, but there is no such position to which either side can appeal. There is no authority to appeal to in the normal sense of discovering the answer somewhere; because there is no a priori normative standard, all we have is our own persuasive powers. An example of what I mean by this would be the competing narratives we observe in a criminal trial. The jury never sees the actual events at issue. All they have as a basis for their judgment is their assessment of the persuasiveness of the prosecution's and defense's accounts of those events. The jury cannot compare each account to "what actually happened" and grade each account for accuracy. Instead, all the jury can do is to determine which account is more persuasive in terms of the seamlessness of the narrative and the way each incorporates the evidence. There is no external standard available.[67]

On an accurate understanding, therefore, all we have is the open sea of constitutional discourse; there is no port we can put into.[68] That is the meaning of the interpretive turn, the meaning of living textually in the American polity. Dissolving the originalism–nonoriginalism debate results in a leveling of the playing field – that is, neither side can claim exclusive normativity. Does this mean that no one is ever right? Yes and no. On the one hand, both sides can claim to be right in a regulative sense of the term: My act of arguing that I am right and you are wrong (e.g., I say that chocolate is good) makes a claim on you as a rational person to see and accept my position, and it makes a demand on me to attempt to persuade you of the rightness of my point of view. If I say that our disagreement is just a matter of opinion (e.g., I say simply that I like chocolate), then I make no claim on you as a rational person, and my only recourse is to exercise power to make you submit to my position. On the other hand, neither side can claim to be right in the substantive sense of the term: There is and can be no demonstration;

---

[67] Similarly, the authoritativeness of my own argument is subject to the same criterion I maintain is the basis for the authoritativeness of a suggested interpretation of the Constitution: its persuasiveness.

[68] As Michael Moore writes: "those who pretend to be suspending their own critical judgments by deferring to the past have not, in fact, suspended their individual reason at all. Rather, our critical judgments coincide with the judgments implicit in our tradition, so that when we 'defer' to the past we are in reality promoting our own political conclusions." "The Dead Hand of Constitutional Tradition," 19 *Harvard Journal of Law & Public Policy* 263, 272–3 (1996).

there can be nothing more and nothing less than persuasion. Instead, therefore, of asking what constitutional provision X suggests that the Framers or an evolving moral consensus might mean, the postinterpretive-turn question asks what the Framers or an evolving moral consensus suggests that constitutional provision X might mean.

Dissolving the impasse between originalism and nonoriginalism thus means legitimating difference and disagreement. Constitutionalism presumes difference: Why bother with the task of binding anyone to a particular political order if he can never stray from that order? Yet originalism seems to view difference and disagreement as a betrayal rather than an affirmation of constitutionalism. How does originalism explain differences of opinion and outright mistakes in constitutional interpretation? Recall that Bork argues that "judges must consider themselves bound by law that is independent of their own views of the desirable. They must not make or apply any policy not fairly to be found in the Constitution or a statute."[69] Only the method of original intent, he says, "can give us law that is something other than, and superior to, the judge's will."[70] In that light, consider the fascinating comment by Justice Anthony Kennedy in the flag-burning case of *Texas v. Johnson* (1989). That case, to recall it briefly, concerned the constitutionality of a Texas statute that criminalized the desecration of a venerated object. Gregory Lee Johnson was convicted under this statute of desecrating an American flag by burning it as a means of political protest at the Republican National Convention in Dallas in 1984. In a majority opinion written by Justice William Brennan, the Court overturned Johnson's conviction and struck down the statute. Aside from its controversial contribution to freedom-of-expression doctrine under the First Amendment, the case is of interpretive interest because of Justice Kennedy's revealing remarks about his own reactions to the issues involved. Concurring in the result, Kennedy writes of the great personal difficulty he has in reaching his decision:

The hard fact is that sometimes we must make decisions we do not like. We make them because they are right, right in the sense that the law and the Constitution, as we see them, compel the result. And so great is our commitment to the process that, except in the rare case, we do not pause to express distaste for the result, perhaps for fear of undermining a valued principle that dictates the decision. This is one of those rare cases.[71]

Here we have a clear instance of the binding capacity of the Constitution so centrally important to originalism. Justice Kennedy clearly finds himself caught between the pull of his personal political views and the pull of his oath to uphold the Constitution according to his own best reading of it.

---

[69] Bork, *The Tempting of America*, 5.
[70] Ibid., 26.
[71] *Texas v. Johnson*, 491 U.S. 397, 420–1 (1989).

Taking his words at face value, we can see clearly that he subordinated his own independent views of the desirable to the superior command of the Constitution – just as Bork requires of a judge and considers only originalism capable of making possible.

The problem is, however, that Bork argues that the Court – hence, Kennedy – reached the wrong conclusion in the case.[72] It follows either that Kennedy did not reason from originalist premises, but still felt himself under some interpretive constraint other than that of originalism, or that originalist premises admit the possibility of incorrect conclusions. Now, to be fair, we must note that Bork does grant that "two judges equally devoted to the original purpose may disagree about the reach or application of the principle at stake and so arrive at different results."[73] Wolfe makes the same point more fully:

It is essential to avoid the impression that interpretation is a simple process that is capable of banishing controversy, because such a view would necessarily create expectations that could not be met. Because a constitution contains broad principles that must be applied to concrete issues, and because there will always be difficult cases in which the application is not clear, reasonable people will inevitably differ on important questions of interpretation.[74]

In a way, this is the whole point of my argument: Reasonable people will indeed inevitably differ on important questions of constitutional interpretation. Yet in almost all major interpretive controversies that come to mind, especially in the privacy area, originalists appear to deny that someone differing from them is indeed interpreting the Constitution. The possibility of two distinct but legitimate interpretations of the Constitution dissolves into the claim that *I* am interpreting the Constitution and *you* are interpreting some extraconstitutional norm that you are attempting to graft onto the Constitution.

Thus, consider Wolfe's central thesis: "If the traditional understanding of constitutional interpretation and judicial review was rooted in fidelity to the Constitution, its original intention as derived from a fair reading of the document, then the modern approach is characterized by its tendency to seek freedom from the Constitution and that intention."[75] Bork, too, writes that "the ratifiers' original understanding of what the Constitution means is no longer of controlling, or perhaps of any, importance."[76] What originalism does, as I have argued elsewhere and shall not rehearse here,[77] is

---

[72] Bork, *The Tempting of America*, 127–8.

[73] Ibid., 163.

[74] Wolfe, *The Rise of Modern Judicial Review*, 38.

[75] Ibid., 205.

[76] Bork, *The Tempting of America*, 6.

[77] Dennis J. Goldford, "Reply to Wolfe and Morgan," in "Polity Forum: On Constitutional Interpretation," *Polity* (Winter 1990), 296–9. I argued, controversially, that nonoriginalism

to equate nonoriginalism – that is, an understanding of the constitutional text that is not the Framers' understanding – with noninterpretivism, the theory that interpreters may legitimately invoke extraconstitutional norms in adjudication, and interpretivism, the theory that interpreters may legitimately invoke only constitutional norms, with originalism.[78] The premise of these equivalencies is the proposition that there cannot be several possible, equally legitimate understandings of the constitutional text. Unless we talk about the Constitution as originally understood, we are not talking about the Constitution at all. Thus, for originalism, P_1 equals P_2: To be bound by the Constitution is logically equivalent to being bound by the original understanding of the constitutional text; and, of necessity, not to be bound by the original understanding of the constitutional text is not to be bound by the Constitution at all.

For originalism, therefore, the real Constitution is not the written text itself, but rather the Framers' understanding of the written text. I am suggesting, by contrast, that the real Constitution is the text itself, above and beyond the Framers' understanding of it. "The most important evidence of original intent," Levy argues in this vein, "is the text of the Constitution itself, which must prevail whenever it surely embodies a broader principle than can be found in the minds or purposes of its Framers."[79] Later in his book he puts this more directly: "The Framers formulated principles and they expressed purposes. Those principles and purposes, both explicit and implied, were meant to endure, not their Framers' understanding of them."[80] I agree with these statements, which presuppose my claim that P_1 and P_2 are separate propositions. Recall, however, that I acknowledged at the outset that originalism cannot accept this distinction. But why not? Consider this charge by McDowell:

In the name of interpreting the Constitution, the new theorists attack the very essence of constitutionalism – language. By undermining the binding force of language – the

is not noninterpretivism but rather another form of interpretivism – a view that originalism's premises do not allow it to accept. To say that even nonoriginalists are interpretivists is to say that we are all textualists. Does that mean that even an intentionalist is a textualist? Yes – intentionalism reflects a view of how to read a text. Even someone wanting, as I would not, to read the Constitution as shorthand for Rawls, for example, is faced with the task of persuading us that such a reading is possible. A true noninterpretivist would cut out the middle step and just cite Rawls. In other words, there is a categorical difference between taking *A Theory of Justice* (Cambridge, MA: The Belknap Press of Harvard University Press, 1971) as authoritative in our polity and reading our authoritative Constitution in terms of *A Theory of Justice*.

[78] See Chapter 3.

[79] Levy, *Original Intent and the Framers' Constitution* (New York: Macmillan Publishing Company, 1988), xi.

[80] Ibid., 350.

bond of society, as Locke saw it – the new theorists seek to supplant original intention with contemporary academic pretensions.[81]

I would argue that originalism cannot accept the distinction between (P_1) the claim that what binds the future is the constitutional text and (P_2) the claim that what binds the future is the Framers' understanding of the constitutional text, because it is originalism itself that distrusts "the very essence of constitutionalism – language." My claim, again, is that the text, as opposed to a particular understanding of the text, is authoritative, whereas originalism argues that to consider the text authoritative can mean nothing other than that one particular understanding is authoritative.[82] It is therefore the originalist position rather than my own that assumes that the written constitution per se is indeterminate and thus meaningless. Take, for example, the Eighth Amendment's prohibition of "cruel and unusual punishment." I myself believe, contrary to Justice William Brennan and probably in accord with most originalists, that this prohibition does not include the death penalty, but that is secondary to the broader theoretical issue. The logic of originalism is such that if the prohibition of cruel and unusual punishment is not understood in strict accordance with the ratifiers' understanding of the provision, then that provision is substantively not in the Eighth Amendment. That is, absent the original understanding, the prohibition of "cruel and unusual punishment" becomes an indeterminate phrase that means nothing and everything. Doesn't this put the originalists uncomfortably close to the deconstructionists they vigorously oppose? In this sense, originalists in effect agree with the deconstructionists they oppose so vociferously that a text in and of itself, uncontrolled by some regulative intent, is indeterminate.

This is the sense in which I maintained earlier that the originalist concept of Framers' intent ceases to be analytically equivalent to the Constitution itself and becomes instead an extrinsic check on how we read the constitutional text. An originalist would deny that an insistence on using the language in the sense in which the Framers used it is going beyond or behind the text of the Constitution, but, clearly, if she admits that her opponents can read the text as Justice Brennan sought to do, in terms of twentieth-century American English, then she implicitly argues that the language requires the control and constraint imposed by the norm of Framers' intent. That suggests that Framers' intent is not necessarily and exclusively attached to the language of the text – and it is her presupposition of the emptiness of the language that

---

[81] McDowell, "Introduction," *Politics and the Constitution*, x–xi.

[82] We necessarily "see" the text through an act of interpretation, but we maintain the regulative concept of the text independent of a given interpretation. Originalism implicitly privileges its own interpretation of the text as the text itself rather than as one particular interpretation among others.

impels her to insist on the control imposed by Framers' intent. If Framers' intent were in fact the only way to understand the text itself, then what is the originalist worried about? No one could make any sense of the document in terms other than Framers' intent. That the originalist worries about constraint on interpreting the language of the text, conversely, suggests an implicit admission that the language can indeed make sense independently of Framers' intent.

That claim, however, is the thesis of semantic autonomy, and it is the necessary condition of the possibility and legitimacy of constitutional discourse and debate. I have suggested that if the Constitution constitutes the intent of the Framers, then the claim that in constitutional interpretation we should be bound by the intent of the Framers amounts to the claim that in constitutional interpretation we should be bound by the Constitution. This is an assertion of the exclusively authoritative status of those principles constitutionalized by the Framers. My argument, however, has been that the central interpretive issue is phrased better as one of understanding rather than as one of intent. The originalist concept of Framers' intent, in other words, ceases to be analytically equivalent to the Constitution itself and becomes instead an extrinsic check on how we read the constitutional text. The characteristic and controversial move of originalism, as I have defined it and tried to provide evidence, is its translation of the claim that in constitutional interpretation what binds the future is the constitutional text into the claim, generally definitive of originalism in all of its specific forms, that what binds the future is the Framers' understanding of the constitutional text. Originalism denies the possibility of my distinction between these two claims, arguing that they are one and the same and thus stand or fall together. In so doing, originalism attempts to clinch disputes over the proper understanding of the Constitution by appealing to what they call original intent, a concept that functions as an appeal to norms that in some way transcend the text and thus do not count as one more understanding of the text. Originalism, in other words, presumes the semantic anarchy of the constitutional text and the consequent necessity of a norm of original intent to regulate constitutional interpretation. My argument has been, however, that originalism, surprisingly, is engaged in a fruitless attempt to discover interpretive standards beyond textuality, but textuality is all we have. As Michael Moore has written:

The only noncontroversial thing that constitutes the Constitution is the written document itself. We can mark this noncontroversial nature of the written document by making its written text the only object of our interpretive efforts. Everything else should have to fight for legitimacy in that tournament of theories called constitutional interpretation.[83]

---

[83] Michael Moore, "Do We Have an Unwritten Constitution?" 63 *Southern California Law Review* 107, 121–2 (1989).

The concept of Framers' intent central to originalism is not an extrainterpretive standard that governs theories of constitutional interpretation; it is itself one more theory of constitutional interpretation. As such, it is not the norm of interpretive legitimacy, but rather one more contender in the struggle over interpretation in which persuasion is the only arbiter. Outside of its own boundaries, originalism cannot take seriously Wolfe's claim that "reasonable people will inevitably differ on important questions of interpretation."[84] I wish to do so. Yet does this not undermine the binding character of the Constitution? It is this key question that I will address in Chapter 8. Before doing so, however, it is important to turn first to an examination of the explicit epistemological and literary-theory arguments of a recent strong and sophisticated defense of originalism.

[84] Wolfe, *The Rise of Modern Judicial Review*, 38.

7

The Epistemology of Constitutional Discourse (II)

In two imposing works entitled *Constitutional Interpretation*[1] and *Constitutional Construction*,[2] Keith Whittington has offered one of the most sophisticated accounts of constitutional interpretation in the recent literature of constitutional theory. The former volume, in particular, addresses the question of whether that form of constitutionalism centered on a written text dictates the originalist approach to interpretation as a, if not *the*, necessary condition of its possibility. Originalism, of course, is the theory that we should understand constitutional provisions in the terms in which they were understood by those who wrote and ratified those provisions. In Whittington's words:

The critical originalist directive is that the Constitution should be interpreted according to the understandings made public at the time of the drafting and ratification. The primary source of those understandings is the text of the Constitution itself, including both its wording and structure. The text is supplemented by a variety of secondary sources of information, however. Historical sources are to be used to elucidate the understanding of the terms involved and to indicate the principles that were supposed to be embodied in them. The guiding principle is that the judge should be seeking to make plain the "meaning understood at the time of the law's enactment."[3]

---

[1] *Constitutional Interpretation: Textual Meaning, Original Intent, and Judicial Review* (Lawrence: University Press of Kansas, 1999).

[2] *Constitutional Construction: Divided Powers and Constitutional Meaning* (Cambridge, MA: Harvard University Press, 1999).

[3] Whittington, *Constitutional Interpretation*, 35, citing Robert Bork, *The Tempting of America: The Political Seduction of the law* (New York: Simon & Schuster, 1990), 144. According to James Gardner, "any fair description of originalism would include the following six premises."

First, the Constitution embodies the authoritative choices that the people of the United States have made about the ways in which their society and government are to be structured. Second, these authoritative choices were made at the time of the framing and ratification of the Constitution and its amendments. Third, the choices so made were intended to be, and are permanent, [sic] until altered by the people themselves through the constitutional process

Does constitutionalism indeed require originalism? Whittington's answer, simply and resoundingly, is: yes.

The virtue of Whittington's approach to this question is that he recognizes that we cannot ground adherence to the intentions of the Framers on the claim that the Framers intended that we do so. In his words:

> Methods of interpretation require justification, and those justifications are distinct from the method itself. The interpretation of the Constitution is a matter of constitutional law and, primarily, of judicial practice. An interpretive method provides guidance for that practice. The justification for adopting any particular interpretive method depends on external reasons of normative political theory. As a consequence, originalism cannot be justified by reference to intent of the founders or by a purely historical argument. Originalism, like other methods of interpretation, must be justified by reference to our best understanding of the constitutional project.[4]

Originalism in fact rests, as Whittington notes perceptively, on both a normative political theory and a literary theory:[5] "Originalism is justified not

---

of amendment. Fourth, the content of these choices, and consequently the meaning of the Constitution, is [sic] largely determinate and generally knowable through examination of the constitutional text and by appropriate historical research into the intentions of the Constitution's framers.... Fifth, the role of judges in constitutional cases is simply and exclusively to discover and give effect to the meaning of the Constitution as embodied in the constitutional text and the original intentions of the founders. Sixth, any judicial decision that deviates from the original meaning of the Constitution, at least in the absence of a constitutional amendment authorizing such a deviation, is an illegitimate substitution of the value judgments of the court for those of the people.

"The Positivist Foundations of Originalism: An Account and Critique," 71 *Boston University Law Review* 1, 6–7 (1991) (footnotes omitted).

4 Whittington, *Constitutional Interpretation*, 3. At 49 he writes: "Originalism is a strategy for interpreting the constitutional text, a strategy that recommends recurring to the framers in order to define its meaning. The justification for originalism is a separate step requiring a different form of argumentation [from the framers' interpretive intentions]. To this extent, choosing an originalist interpretive strategy is not a 'neutral' or nonpolitical activity. The choice of an interpretive method does indeed require justification external to the practice itself."

5 The heart of *Constitutional Interpretation* is Chapter Four, "A Defense of Originalism and the Written Constitution," in which Whittington takes what he calls an "internal perspective" and presents the literary theory he deems conclusive, and Chapter Five, "Popular Sovereignty and Originalism," in which he takes what he calls an "external perspective" and presents the political theory he deems equally if not actually more conclusive in originalism's favor. As he writes at 181:

> Grounding originalism in the nature of a written text and a theory of popular sovereignty supplies an independent basis for it, regardless of the interpretive intentions of the founders. Originalism is the appropriate method of interpretation because it provides stability in the law in the sense that it enforces the will of the law and because it provides an avenue for the expression of popular sovereignty.

only because it was implicated in the choice of this kind of constitution, a written text. It is also justified because it is implicated in the very possibility of constitutional choice."[6] The written nature of the Constitution and the theory of popular sovereignty, Whittington argues, together establish that (written) constitutionalism indeed requires originalism.[7]

The claim that originalism rests on both a literary theory and a political theory raises, however, a question as to the relation between the two theories. On the one hand, it may well be that the political theory justifying originalism presupposes that originalism is indeed a plausible interpretive approach, in which case the political theory would necessarily depend upon a literary theory that can establish that very plausibility. On the other hand, while Whittington offers a theory of popular sovereignty as our best understanding of American constitutionalism and as dictating an originalist jurisprudence, he also suggests that originalism is required independently of political theory on literary-theory grounds alone. It is this latter suggestion that is the focus of my attention in this chapter. Specifically, I shall examine critically two distinct though related theoretical claims that Whittington uses in order to argue that constitutionalism requires originalism. First, he claims that we must draw a fundamental, bright-line distinction between constitutional interpretation, conceived as an act of discovery, and constitutional construction, conceived as an act of creation. Second, he claims that we must reject as flawed any notion that a text can be autonomous, that is, considered independently of its author's intentions. Both of these claims are elements of literary positivism, a foundationalist theory that emphasizes what it takes to be the facticity of the given, and Whittington advances them to oppose theories of indeterminacy, which he recognizes as fatal to the possibility of constraint at the heart of constitutionalism. I will argue that, in fact, originalism and theories of indeterminacy are mirror images of each other, and that it is only a theory of textual autonomy and a concomitant reconsideration of the

---

[6] Whittington, *Constitutional Interpretation*, 111. At 47 he states that "an originalist interpretive approach is somehow required by the very fact that the United States has a written constitution. The rejection of originalism in favor of some other approach would represent a fundamental usurpation by the judiciary of powers not granted to it under the Constitution and a perversion of the constitutional enterprise."

[7] Whittington also argues, at 14, that "the debate over interpretive method has been built on a debate over the legitimacy of judicial review." The question is, however, what he means by "built on." I would argue that these are independent, though related, issues. The "Who"? and the "How?" are distinct questions – unless only the courts are authorized to engage in constitutional interpretation. Yet surely that answer is no, for the very question of the legitimacy of judicial review is premised on the authority of Congress and the president, at the very least, to make constitutional judgments of their own. As Whittington says at 36, originalism "gives the presumption to the current majority's legislative action. As equal branches of government themselves charged with obeying the Constitution, the nonjudicial branches cannot be presumed to violate the Constitution as a regular practice."

discovery–creation distinction that can provide the constraint Whittington and other originalists desire.[8]

Put most succinctly, Whittington's overarching claim is that taking interpretation seriously "requires that we adopt an originalist approach to interpretation."[9] The reason, he says, is this:

> Originalism best fulfills the requirements of constitutional interpretation. It is not the only method available for interpreting the Constitution; there are other ways to interpret. But the adoption of a method should presumably be guided by the purposes of interpretation. Some methods are better than others at producing faithful interpretations of the constitutional text.[10]

Why does originalism best fulfill the requirements of constitutional interpretation? It does so, Whittington maintains, because we (1) have chosen as an act of popular sovereignty (2) to live under a written constitution:

> I intend to demonstrate that originalism is the method most consistent with the judicial effort to interpret the written constitutional text and that an originalist jurisprudence facilitates the realization of a political system grounded on popular sovereignty. Other methods are consistent with efforts to interpret the written Constitution, but they are flawed. Ultimately, adherence to originalist guidelines provides the most direct and consistent route to a correct interpretive practice.[11]

A problem, however, appears to arise immediately from this statement. Whittington wants to argue that there are interpretive methods other than originalism that are legitimate ways to interpret a written constitution. "The originalist approach," he writes later, "is not the only possible conception of the significance of a written text.... In addition to the originalist understanding, the nature of the constitutional text can be conceived of as a fixed referent

---

[8] One should not understand the case I wish to make against originalism as pointing to a preference for nonoriginalism, at least as that theory is commonly understood. It is precisely the assumption that we are locked into a zero-sum choice between originalism and nonoriginalism that I attempt to challenge. What I shall attempt to do in this chapter is to focus on the issue of the autonomy of the text.

[9] Whittington, *Constitutional Interpretation*, 4.

[10] Ibid., 3. The raises the classical problem of method, however: We need access to the text independently of the interpretive method in order to say that the method is "faithful" or "accurate." The "methodism" approach implies that we can look at the text, determine its meaning, and then look at the meaning produced by the method and judge it to be faithful and accurate (or unfaithful and inaccurate). However, why then would we need the method in the first place if we can – and must – determine the meaning of the text in order to assess the accuracy of the reading produced by the method? There is a circularity here: We presumably need a method to determine the meaning of a text, and yet we determine the meaning of the text in order to evaluate the method. The classic statement of this problem is found in Hans-Georg Gadamer, *Truth and Method* (New York: Seabury Press, 1975). Whittington addresses Gadamer in his book but dismisses him, in my view, much too quickly.

[11] Whittington, *Constitutional Interpretation*, 3.

for political debate, a promissory note, or as essentially indeterminate."[12] Yet Whittington has already suggested that taking interpretation seriously necessitates originalism, saying elsewhere in no uncertain terms that "originalism is required by the nature of a written constitution."[13] The ambiguity here is whether Whittington wants to claim that, given the writtenness of the Constitution, originalism is an option or a necessity. If the former, then he is arguing that the literary theory stands not on its own but instead is dictated by an independent political theory. If the latter, then he is arguing that the literary theory itself stands on its own and dictates originalism, independent of any additional justification furnished by political theory, and he would have to say that other methods are *not* consistent with efforts to interpret the written Constitution. However Whittington would reconcile this apparent inconsistency, I shall focus here on his literary-theory claim that originalism is required by the very nature of a written constitution.

The literary theory Whittington advances is, simply, a positivist theory of textuality conjoined with both an epistemological positivism and a legal positivism. Reflected in his understanding of the Constitution as "a means of communicating between the founders and the government,"[14] a positivist theory of textuality involves the idea that the four corners of a text contain and embody a message from the authors of that text. Such a theory of textuality is an essentially reductionist theory that distinguishes between a text and its creators and anchors meaning in the latter. In positivist terms, a literary text "must be regarded as the expression of the psychology of an individual, which in turn is the expression of the *milieu* and the period in which the individual lived and of the race to which he belonged."[15] More precisely, a positivist theory of textuality reads a text

almost exclusively in relation to its factual causes or genesis: the author's life, his recorded intentions in writing, his immediate social and cultural environment, his sources. To use a common distinction, it was an extrinsic rather than an intrinsic approach to texts. It was not interested in the features of the literary text itself except from a philological and historical viewpoint.[16]

A positivist theory of textuality, in other words, rejects the idea of the autonomy of a text in favor of the idea of anchoring a text in the personality,

---

[12] Ibid., 61–2.
[13] Ibid., 15.
[14] Ibid., 64.
[15] Ann Jefferson and David Robey, eds., *Modern Literary Theory*, 2nd ed. (Totowa, NJ: Barnes & Noble Books, 1986), 9.
[16] Ibid., 9. Positivism, Jefferson writes in her own contribution to this volume, was "largely based on the genetic approach; critics, or rather scholars, concentrated their energies on uncovering the sources and genesis of particular works, and the role of biography, history and history of ideas in these genetic studies obviously reduced the importance of literature itself in literary scholarship" (26).

milieu, and intentions of its author. Against this literary-theory background, originalism invokes a positivist theory of textuality, therefore, in that it treats a text not as an entity with meaning in and of itself, but rather as merely the expression of a meaning that stands behind it in the intentions and mental states of its authors. Whittington, we will see, attempts – unsuccessfully, I will argue – to reject this idea of meaning standing behind a text, but he likewise rejects the idea of the autonomy of the text.

The sharp distinction Whittington draws between constitutional interpretation and constitutional construction exhibits the essential epistemological and legal positivism of originalism. By "epistemological positivism" I mean the emphasis upon the facticity – the brute givenness – of constitutional meaning, and by "legal positivism" I refer to the familiar theory that includes the notion of the inevitable existence of gaps in the law. Consider Whittington's statement of the distinction between interpretation and construction:

As the name suggests, constitutional interpretation is a fairly familiar process of discovering the meaning of the constitutional text. The results of this process are recognizable as constitutional law capable of being expounded and applied by the courts. Though still concerned with the meaning of the text, constitutional construction cannot claim merely to discover a preexisting, if deeply hidden, meaning within the founding document. It employs the "imaginative vision" of politics rather than the "discerning wit" of judicial judgment. Construction is essentially creative, though the foundations for the ultimate structure are taken as given. The text is not discarded but brought into being.[17]

The contrast here between interpretation and construction is that between discovery and creation. Characteristic of interpretation is the idea of discovery, of uncovering a preexisting meaning already there in the text, whereas construction is a creation of meaning that is, in some sense, *not* already there in the text. Interpretation, therefore,

represents a search for meaning already in the text. Interpretation is discovery. Although the process of discovery may be complex and require good judgment by the interpreter, it nonetheless results in something that has plausibly been found in the original text. Interpretation is not essentially creative, for though new formulas are developed and promulgated, these new texts are sustained only by their direct link to the original. If that connection becomes too tenuous, they can no longer be maintained as interpretations of the original.[18]

We see here the essential facticity of meaning, the notion of the given that characterizes the various forms of positivism generally. Interpretation is thus the process by which we unlock the textual safe and find the meaning hidden inside.

---

[17] Whittington, *Constitutional Interpretation*, 5.
[18] Ibid., 6.

Construction, on the other hand, differs from what this and similar metaphors suggest. Whittington writes:

> The case of constitutional construction is quite different. Constitutional interpretation is essentially legalistic, but constitutional construction is essentially political. Its precondition is that parts of the constitutional text have no discoverable meaning.... Regardless of the extent of judicial interpretation of certain aspects of the Constitution, there will remain an impenetrable sphere of meaning that cannot be simply discovered.[19]

There are, in other words, "legal gaps in the Constitution,"[20] and this is simply the legal positivism we find in such writers as Benjamin Cardozo and H. L. A. Hart. Compare Whittington's idea, presented earlier, that construction employs the "imaginative vision" of politics with Cardozo's theme here:

> If you ask how [the judge in the process of adjudication] is to know when one interest outweighs another, I can only answer that he must get his knowledge just as the legislator gets it, from experience and study and reflection; in brief, from life itself. Here, indeed, is the point of contact between the legislator's work and his. The choice of methods, the appraisement of values, must in the end be guided by like considerations for the one as for the other. Each indeed is legislating within the limits of his competence. No doubt the limits for the judge are narrower. He legislates only between gaps. He fills the open spaces in the law.[21]

Construction is essentially political, as Whittington puts it, because the judge is engaged in legislating to fill in the "open spaces in the law," but legislating, as Cardozo puts it, only between gaps. Constitutional construction is legitimate, according to Whittington, because while it is essentially creative, in that it extends rather than finds the meaning of the text, it nevertheless extends the core meaning of the text rather than creates one de novo. However, Whittington is ambiguous about the essential creativity of constitutional construction: "Constitutional interpretation discovers meaning, and constitutional construction develops it in relation to the existing text, but constitutional creation invents wholly new meaning."[22] He has stated that construction is essentially creative, but here he distinguishes creation from construction as a separate concept. In this latter sense, the only legitimate form of constitutional creation lies within the amendment process rather than in the courts.[23] Yet whether Whittington identifies constitutional

---

[19] Ibid., 7.

[20] Ibid.

[21] Benjamin Cardozo, *The Nature of the Legal Process* (New Haven, CT: Yale University Press, 1921), 113. Also see H. L. A. Hart's discussion of the open texture of the law in *The Concept of Law*, 2nd ed. (Oxford: Oxford University Press, 1994), 128ff.

[22] Whittington, *Constitutional Interpretation*, 11.

[23] When dealing with hard cases, Whittington rejects the claim, found in Cardozo and Hart, that the judge acts, and properly so, as a legislator, creating de novo: "Legal interpretation,"

construction with or distinguishes it from constitutional creation, his central claim is that there is a core nucleus of meaning embedded in a text.[24] And that core nucleus, the focus of his literary-theory argument, is the author's intentions.

The first step in Whittington's literary-theory focus on authorial intentions is his emphasis on the written character of the Constitution as the key to the possibility of constraint that he takes, plausibly, to be the promise of constitutionalism in general. Whittington and I are in agreement that the purpose of the Constitution is to bind the future,[25] and we also agree on the fundamental importance of the writtenness of the Constitution. Where we disagree is on the proposition that originalism is the necessary implication of this writtenness and the necessary condition of the possibility of the Constitution's binding character. Whittington begins with the claim that there are three principal arguments that support and, indeed, compel the proposition that constitutionalism requires originalism:

The first of these arguments draws upon the revolutionary break from Great Britain and the perceived need to fix the inherited fundamental principles of government in a clear and permanent text. The second contends that a stable textual reference is necessary in order to make the Constitution law in the sense of being judicially enforceable. The third argument draws more generally from the nature of writing

he writes at 42, "includes not only the explication of the core meaning of the law but also subsidiary rules for extending that meaning. Such interpretive guidelines are *not the product of judicial additions to the law* or internally included in the law itself but are constitutive of the judicial function" (emphasis added). The positivist distinction between making law and interpreting law is central here:

According to the originalists, the legislature is charged with making law, but the judiciary is supposed to be limited to applying preexisting law. Grounded in the textual separation of the "judicial power" from the "legislative powers," this originalist argument would exclude the more explicit modern use of extraconstitutional sources to create principles to guide the nation. It would also exclude any interpretive strategy that does not seek to understand the purpose and intent of the actual lawmakers. Deviating from the intent of the Constitution would be tantamount to creating a new fundamental law from the bench, thereby exceeding the judicial role by creating constitutional law instead of merely elaborating and applying it.

Whittington, *Constitutional Interpretation*, 40.

[24] This therefore clearly is a rejection of a hermeneutical conception of interpretation such as Gadamer's: "Interpretation is not an occasional additional act subsequent to understanding, but rather understanding is always an interpretation, and hence interpretation is the explicit form of understanding." Gadamer, *Truth and Method*, 274. Whittington's focus on discovery is his way of contending that first one understands and only then, afterward, interprets.

[25] In Whittington's words (*Constitutional Interpretation*, 203): "Judicial review and constitutionalism necessarily imply that current majorities will be constrained by standards fixed outside their own deliberation. The real issue revolves around what those standards will be and who will determine them. Those problems are universal to American constitutional theory."

and law, claiming that all writing and especially legal writing carries the intent of the author.[26]

His first argument here is that the only way to fix principle against the transience of the moment is to embed it in a written constitution meant to stand above politics: "In order to prevent government actions, which may have significant and lasting consequences, from being taken in pursuit of momentary interests, a written constitution, properly construed, serves as a reminder and a barrier, constraining politics within a relatively narrow range of deliberately chosen rights, powers, and institutions."[27] This, I grant, is a perfectly reasonable and important argument. He continues:

In order to realize the fundamental law as a judicially enforceable instrument to restrain the legislature, the unwritten principles behind government had to be fixed in writing. As a fixed and written text, the supreme law of the Constitution can be self-consciously considered and properly ratified and can have the specificity to provide judicial instruction.[28]

However, Whittington's key move is to derive from this argument – that the only way to fix principle against the transience of the moment is to embed it in a written constitution meant to stand above politics – the more controversial argument that the only way a written text can fix principle is through originalist interpretation. He writes: "Fixing constitutional principles in a written text against the transient shifts in the public mood or social condition becomes tantamount to an originalist jurisprudence."[29] The standard

---

[26] Ibid., 50.

[27] Ibid., 53.

[28] Ibid., 54.

[29] Ibid., 53. Later in his text, at 60, he writes: "The written document was intended to reduce uncertainty and create stability, something tangible to which the judiciary could refer in recalling the legislature to basic principles." Whittington continues to emphasize the importance of the writtenness of the Constitution, with which I agree. However, his argument is that that very writtenness of the Constitution implies and necessitates originalism, on the premise that the text can have no binding power without the anchor of original intent. My own argument, contrary to the views of both originalists and the indeterminacy theorists whom Whittington is concerned to refute, is that a text can indeed bind independently of any notion of original intent. Nevertheless, he writes:

The implications of introducing the device of a written constitution into the British tradition of constitutionalism require an originalist approach to interpreting the document. Thus, the form of constitutionalism developed in the United States uniquely authorizes originalism. Other forms of constitutionalism are possible, as the British case indicates.... But the structure of a written constitution suggests as complementary features the practice of judicial review and the interpretive method of originalism. The distinctiveness of written texts can be located in their relative specificity of principle, their capacity to act as legal instruments, and their invocation of an originalist intent. In each instance, such characteristics require the adoption of originalist methods of interpretation.

Ibid., 215–16.

originalist argument follows from that proposition: To accept the importance of fixing constitutional principles in a written text requires originalism; consequently, to reject originalism is to render impossible the fixing of constitutional principles in a written text.

The key concept in Whittington's second argument here is the idea of a fixed text, for "The constitutional constraint on the people's agents," he says, "can emerge from the text as intended... only if the text has the fixed meaning it is uniquely capable of carrying."[30] He grounds this argument on three subarguments, if you will:

The first contention needed to build this argument is that only a fixed text can provide judicial instruction and therefore be judicially enforceable against legislative encroachment. The judicial requirement of a fixed text not only authorizes judicial review but also limits it within the context of determinate meaning.[31]

The second aspect of accepting a written constitution as law is that only a fixed text can be adequately ratified, that is, legislated into fundamental law.[32]

The third part of the argument for the text as law derives from the two premises thus established and posits that the written Constitution, ratified by the sovereign people in convention, is the fundamental law, authorizing and limiting government action and thereby establishing judicial review of legislative behavior. The people can constrain their governmental agents only by fixing their will in an unchanging text.[33]

Left unexplained, however, is the very notion of a fixed text. What is a fixed text? Let us suppose that a legislature passes a law – or that we enact a constitutional amendment – that states that judges should decide criminal-procedure cases according to the norm of "conduct that shocks the conscience," to be defined in terms of "evolving standards of decency." Would Whittington consider such a law or amendment to be a fixed text? On the one hand, the enacted provision does fix a norm for use in adjudication; on the other hand, variability is built into that norm.[34] "In interpreting the written law," Whittington writes, "the judiciary may not strike out on its own and articulate new principles but must act in good faith to carry out the will of those who created the law, whether for good or ill."[35] This is true enough, but we lack an explicit argument that "conduct that shocks the conscience" or "evolving standards of decency" is not a principle. To the extent that this example parallels Ronald Dworkin's distinction between concepts

---

[30] Ibid., 56.
[31] Ibid., 54.
[32] Ibid., 55.
[33] Ibid., 56.
[34] Perhaps a rough analogy would be the notion of the market price one finds on the menu for certain types of seafood in better restaurants. The menu does not fix a particular price, but it is reasonable to say that it does fix the criterion of price.
[35] Whittington, *Constitutional Interpretation*, 57.

and conceptions,[36] Whittington rejects any notion of varying conceptions of fixed concepts as inconsistent with the idea of a fixed text.[37]

Whittington thus links his second argument – that a stable or fixed text is necessary to make the Constitution judicially enforceable law – to his third argument: The meaning of a text is grounded in the intent of the author. It is authorial intent, in other words, that fixes and stabilizes a text. In Whittington's words: "The final argument for the claim that a written constitution requires an originalist interpretation is that writing, especially legal writing, is a means of transmitting intent."[38] More precisely, he contends that originalists

stand on theoretical arguments that hold that all texts, and especially legal texts, carry a knowable, authoritative meaning corresponding to the original intent of the writer. Unlike other approaches, an originalist interpretive method accounts for significant features of our particular constitutional tradition: the existence of a written constitution and a judiciary committed to interpreting that text. Only an originalist judiciary is consistent with the constitutional project that we claim to be pursuing.[39]

Leaving the question of the ratifiers' understanding to his chapter on popular sovereignty, and thus neglecting the important question as to the normative importance of that understanding as distinct from the Framers' intentions, Whittington clearly ties his case to the viability of the literary theory of authorial intent as the ground of textual meaning. To his credit, he recognizes the significance to the originalist project of theories of indeterminacy:

Recent theory has challenged the idea that the reader is a passive participant in the process of written communication. Instead of assuming that the writer's intentions are clearly displayed in the text, we must face the possibility that writing may be essentially indeterminate. In terms of the preceding argument, the radical indeterminacy kicks out from under originalism the suppositions that principles can be fixed by writing, that texts can provide relatively clear instructions upon which to base judicial action, and that texts communicate the intent of their writers. If these legs are removed, the originalist case necessarily collapses.[40]

Whittington provides capsule accounts of structuralism, poststructuralism and deconstructionism, reader-response theory, and hermeneutics. These theories all

question the prominence of the writer, replacing him with the constitutive force of the reader who is now empowered to imbue the lifeless text with meaning. Having written the Constitution, the founders have sent it into the world on its own. Its

---

[36] See Ronald Dworkin, *Taking Rights Seriously* (Cambridge, MA: Harvard University Press, 1978), 131–49.

[37] See Whittington, *Constitutional Interpretation*, 182–7.

[38] Ibid., 59.

[39] Ibid., 61.

[40] Ibid., 68.

text necessarily transcends the context within which it was created and enters into a flux of new contexts, which equally determine the meaning of the document. In attempting to fix their will in writing, the founders in fact lost control over their product, and if this alienated text is to have any meaning at all, it must be supplied by its consumers.[41]

As surprising as it may seem, however, originalism and theories of indeterminacy share a common premise: Authorial intent is the necessary condition of the possibility of fixing textual meaning. Theories of indeterminacy quite logically argue for and affirm the impossibility of fixed meaning once they dethrone the privileged position of the author; originalism logically argues for – and fears the impossibility of – fixed meaning once it dethrones the privileged position of the author. Originalism and theories of indeterminacy are locked in an embrace with each other, bound by their shared premise of the importance of authorial intent.

Significantly, however, we encounter in a key section of the passage just cited the beginning of Whittington's attack on the idea of the autonomy of the text. That section focuses on the issue of texts and contexts: "Having written the Constitution, the founders have sent it into the world on its own. Its text necessarily transcends the context within which it was created and enters into a flux of new contexts, which equally determine the meaning of the document." The context of this statement itself suggests that Whittington intends it to constitute a critical rejection of a point of view, but he is not sufficiently careful about avoiding a contradictory position. On the one hand, his statement calls to mind the famous words of Justice Oliver Wendell Holmes: "When we are dealing with words that also are a constituent act, like the Constitution of the United States, we must realize that they have called into life a being the development of which could not have been foreseen completely by the most gifted of its begetters."[42] No one, surely, could doubt that the founders did indeed send the Constitution into the world on its own in the hope that it would transcend the context of its creation. Whittington does acknowledge this in another passage later in his book:

A historical, legal text such as the Constitution will undoubtedly extend to new situations over time, whether because entirely new fact situations arise or because political change has brought certain aspects of the text into greater prominence. Each additional application may well extend our inventory of knowledge of the text, allowing us to perceive new difficulties or implications that were previously hidden and to expand our inventory of particularized meanings encompassed by the general terms of the textual language. But consistent interpretation will not produce contradictory meanings, for example. Each generation must read the Constitution

[41] Ibid., 76.
[42] *Missouri v. Holland*, 252 U.S. 416, 433 (1920).

for itself and its own concerns, but such situated readings do not produce new texts; rather, they fill in the text that has always existed.[43]

Nevertheless, while we ordinarily say that it is by virtue of principles that we can transcend a particular context, Whittington contends that "the Constitution is more than a statement of principles; rather, it is a historical compromise reflecting numerous interests, principled and otherwise."[44]

The danger here is twofold. First, as he attempts to reject interpreting the Constitution in terms of some independent moral code, Whittington might go to the other extreme and view the text as a whole as fundamentally unprincipled. In that regard, consider this passage:

Rather than being designed to represent the best ideals of justice of an evolving society, the document is fundamentally political and marked by specific historical, political, and institutional concerns, creating a framework for future political struggle, not a blueprint for an ideal society. For a text that is primarily to serve as a vehicle for ahistorical conceptions of justice, specific prohibitions against ex post facto laws, bills of attainder, the denial of habeas corpus, titles of nobility, the quartering of soldiers in private homes, or requirements for jury trials in cases involving over twenty dollars and the relinquishment of fugitive slaves to their owners seem misplaced. Such provisions suggest a document primarily concerned with settling particular, historically contingent political disputes. (Ibid., 84)

Whittington has to be careful here, for this line of argument risks precisely the implication that the Constitution is indeed trapped in a particular context in the past and irrelevant to the present. Is the Constitution implicitly, if not explicitly, a principled document? If it is a mélange of particular principled provisions and historically specific provisions, then as a whole it is not a principled document. On the other hand, surely there is a reason – a rationale, a principle – that explains and justifies why the founders considered it necessary to constitutionalize such historically specific provisions as Whittington has noted.

The second danger is that Whittington may become trapped in the very historicity of context on which he insists. "All writing and communication occurs [sic] within a context," he states, "which may help clarify the meaning of the words used in the text. . . . As contexts and conventions change, greater effort may be necessary to recover the original contexts in order fully to discover the intended meaning, but meaning ultimately remains as long as the text qua text survives."[45] There would seem to be a problem in a position that grounds constitutional interpretation in a norm – original

---

[43] Whittington, *Constitutional Interpretation*, 104–5. I would agree strongly with the argument he makes here, but my own view is that this argument does not commit us to originalism.
[44] Ibid., 84.
[45] Ibid., 60.

intentions – that is destined to become less and less determinate over time. Indeed, consider this lengthy but remarkable passage:

> The founders were not primarily concerned with our political disputes, or even with disputes that are closely analogous; they had their own problems with which to contend. In writing a constitution to endure over time, they did not set out to confine themselves to those immediate problems, but their conception of politics and constitutionalism was naturally defined by their own experiences and historical context. Both their text and, more important, their explanation of it were laid out within a particular historical situation. Interpreting their intentions will always require bridging the distance between their situation and our own. It is possible to span that distance. But as time passes and the problems to be resolved grow more distant, that path becomes more uncertain and the cracks in the initial material grow wider. In time, we find ourselves increasingly operating at the margins of constitutional meaning, where interpretation is less likely to provide clear answers. Judicial review should become less relevant to our political life over time, not more.[46]

This is an astounding statement, for it validates much of the dead-head objection to the Constitution and undermines Whittington's own argument for the importance (not just the legitimacy) of judicial review, leaving us at the hands of contemporary majorities. He denies that the past is absolutely inaccessible, but it is difficult to see that there is a significant practical difference in suggesting that the past becomes asymptotically inaccessible. The very history on which Whittington relies as the ground of constitutionalism, conceived as limitations or constraints on popular majorities, appears here to undermine the possibility of constitutionalism.

While Whittington argues that a text is embedded in a particular historical context in at least *some* sense, such that its original context becomes normative for understanding it, his central argument is that the fundamental element of a text's original context is the intention of the author(s) of that text.[47] As he puts his point succinctly, "a text cannot logically be separated

---

[46] Ibid., 210. I merely note the fact that the founders believed that certain political problems transcend particular historical periods. That is why they referred to Greek and Roman history so often.

[47] For an earlier intentionalist attack on the idea of the autonomy of the text, see Paul Campos, "That Obscure Object of Desire: Hermeneutics and the Autonomous Legal Text," 77 *Minnesota Law Review* 1065 (1993), with particular reference to the sources listed in footnote 72 at 1082. According to Campos:

> Strong intentionalism refutes the fallacy of the autonomous text, a fallacy that remains of crucial rhetorical importance to practically all theories of legal interpretation. If strong intentionalism is correct, then a text can only mean what its author intends it to mean, and it follows that interpreting a text simply consists in looking for that intention. Textual meaning and authorial intention are not separable concepts, and searching for one is by necessity synonymous with seeking the other.

> Ibid., 1091. The analysis and critique of Whittington's position I am about to offer would apply to the arguments Campos makes in this article.

from the intentions of the person who wrote it. 'Interpretation,' if it is to have any meaning at all, is the effort to discover the author's intentions embedded in the text."[48] Meaning is necessarily anchored in authorial intentions, and thus a text cannot stand autonomously:

> Each theory of indeterminacy assumes that the text can be logically separated from the context of its writing and from the intent of the author, that the text is somehow autonomous. This assumption is flawed. The written text is identical to the author's intent; there can be no logical separation between them and thus no space for an autonomous text capable of adopting new contexts. As is readily conceded by indeterminacy theorists, writing presupposes an intentional agent who can give it meaning. The text is not inherently meaningful but requires active intelligence to breathe life into barren marks. Indeterminacy theorists move from this assumption, however, to the claim that the absence of the writer gives the text autonomy, so that the reader must supply meaningful agency. This claim does not follow from the original assumption but represents a transformation of that assumption – imagining that the text as text continues to exist in the absence of the intentional agent who created it. In fact, textuality is meaningful only if the originating agent is not truly absent from the text. A "text" that is completely autonomous of its writer ceases to be a text after all; that is, it can no longer be interpreted as a meaningful sign.[49]

Here we find the core of the literary theory Whittington contends grounds and necessitates the connection between originalism and constitutionalism: the claim that a written text is identical to and thus cannot be autonomous of its author's intent. This claim requires careful attention.

The question that arises immediately is this: Given the claim that a written text is identical to and thus cannot be autonomous of its author's intent, is Whittington arguing that a writer can never *not* express his intended meaning? He certainly would not want to argue that all of my students have to be A students because they all intend to write A essays and examinations, but how can he escape such an implication? Whittington does grant that

> though our meaning is identical to our intentions, we may still fail to express what we wanted to say such that others can understand it. Such failures lead to the common fact that we sometimes change our text to make it "mean" what we originally wanted. Such experiences can be accommodated within this analysis in three ways. The first instance happens when we intend to use a given convention but fail to do so successfully. For example, a student required to translate a foreign-language test may be capable of conveying the gist of the passage and yet be incapable of correctly using the appropriate grammatical forms. While his text has expressed part of his intention it has not embodied it completely; he has failed to express his intent.[50]

---

[48] Whittington, *Constitutional Interpretation*, 99. At 95 he writes: "The text cannot exist independently of the intentional agent who has infused it with meaning."

[49] Ibid., 94.

[50] Ibid., 97–8.

Failure to express our meaning, of course, involves something more than grammatical difficulties, but Whittington does not elucidate this vital point. Precisely what does it mean to fail to express one's intent? That question runs into Whittington's next point: "The second instance of such rephrasings occurs when we restate our original text in order to clarify its meaning to the reader. In this case, we in fact did fully express our intent in the original utterance. We failed, however, to satisfy our goal, or motive, which was to communicate information to another."[51] He says either that this does not involve changing our intent or that the old text did not embody our intent, but how does he know this? What does "fail to communicate information to another" mean in contradistinction from "fail to express one's intent"? In both cases, however he would distinguish them when pressed, Whittington contends that original meaning remains unchanged. "The third instance," he notes, "transpires when the author genuinely changes meaning along with the rephrasing. Such rephrasings may better convey our current intentions, but they do not convey our original intent."[52]

To think more deeply about the relation between text and intention, consider at a general level my project in this chapter. I have read Whittington's book and have attempted to question certain aspects of the impressive set of arguments he makes in it. Now, suppose that Whittington were here to answer me. What would the structure of our discussion be? He might, and no doubt would, object that I have not adequately understood his arguments, but what is at issue in such an objection? I would distinguish between his arguments as he intended them – and it is these that he surely would object that I have misunderstood – and his arguments as he has expressed them in his book, that is, his text. Whittington might well claim that his arguments as he intended them are indeed fully expressed in his actual text, but it is certainly conceivable, if not easy to do, that I could show him that I indeed understood the text correctly. His response would be either that he now sees that he was wrong in what he argued or, more likely, that his text did not fully express his argument. But in that latter case he has now become a reader of his own text, just as I have been. He may occupy a privileged position in determining what he intended to argue, but he does not occupy a privileged position in determining what he actually, textually argued. My argument, in other words, is with Whittington's text, not directly with Whittington. He may decide that I have not understood his text accurately. However, he also might discover that my reading of his text is a legitimate reading and thus would learn that his intentions were not in fact successfully embedded in his text.

[51] Ibid., 98.
[52] Ibid. This point, though part of Whittington's proposed explanations of the common belief that at times we are "not saying what we mean," need not concern us further in this context.

This is similar to writing an essay question for my students. I think through the wording of the question very carefully in order to structure and limit the possible range of answers as narrowly as possible, for I don't want to send the student down any tangents or erroneous paths. Now suppose that a student comes to me and complains that he doesn't understand why he received a D, a grade I use to indicate that he gave some evidence of course material but just did not address the question as written. If there is no possible way the student can offer a reasonable reading of the question that would justify the apparently erroneous direction he took, then he suffers the consequences of the D. However, if the student can indeed explain how one could reasonably read the question in the way he did, then I will have failed to "lock all the doors" and keep him structured as I had intended, and I cannot penalize him for not reading the question as I had intended. Just as I tell students, "I can read only your essay, not your mind," so too can they tell me, "We can read only your essay question, not your mind." To be sure, students tend to be speaker's-meaning practitioners when they read an essay question and ask themselves, "What does he want here?" or "What is he looking for?" but I caution them about that tactic, telling them, "Read the question itself and provide the analysis it asks you to provide; don't try to read through the question to get into my mind." If the exam question is only a proxy for my own intentions, then the students can never object successfully to my evaluation of their essays, for they cannot employ the actual, textual question as a basis of appeal against my intentions. If, however, the exam question is a text with its own autonomy, then the students can do just that. The exam question thus is capable of being a normative standard for me, the author of the question, as well.

Now consider an example of the possibility of a disjunction between meaning and intention in Whittington's own text. The question is whether we find intentions *in* the text or in some sense *behind* the text. On the one hand, he writes: "The point of originalist theory, however, is that intentions are not hidden away in the mental world of the speaker but are in fact externalized in the text itself."[53] Given this externalization of intentions in language, he adds, "the text and authorial intentions are identical, leaving no space for the interpretation of an autonomous text."[54] Whittington is concerned, then, to argue that originalism does not appeal to anything extratextual: "Far from abandoning the text in favor of an external authority or from opening the door to a search for a preferred context within which to read the document, originalism seeks to make evident what is already contained within it."[55] In

---

[53] Ibid., 99.
[54] Ibid. The idea of "externalizing" intentions in language suggests the private-language theory typical of early-modern philosophy but discredited in the twentieth century by Wittgenstein and others.
[55] Ibid., 176.

more detail, he states:

An originalist interpretation of the text does not seek to locate the intentions lurking "behind the text," to reimagine and recapture its "origins," but pursues the intentions embedded in the text and conveyed through it. The misguided quest for origins treats the text itself as an empty object to be manipulated by whoever comes into contact with it, nothing more than a signal of another. In fact, the text is not simply a sign of others, but a sign from others, conveying meaning in itself and not merely pointing to something behind it.[56]

To be sure, such phrasing – "the intentions embedded in the text and conveyed through it" – suggests a distinction between intentions and text, with the former prior to and independent of the latter. And I would suggest also, with amplification later on, that it is originalism itself that "treats the text itself as an empty object to be manipulated by whoever comes into contact with it" in asserting its necessity as an interpretive norm. But for the moment, let us grant Whittington's claim that intentions are not to be located behind the text. On the evidence of the foregoing citations, that is what his text tells us.

On the other hand, however, consider what Whittington writes elsewhere in his analysis. First, early on he makes a standard originalist claim: "To give the words of the Constitution new meanings over time would deny both the value and risk of a system of written constitutions."[57] In support of this claim, though, he states: "The Constitution is composed of the underlying conceptions to which the words refer, not the textual language itself."[58] This statement suggests that the Constitution is not the actual words on the page ratified over time, but rather a set of underlying conceptions to which the words refer. "[I]t was not merely a set of words but a set of distinct ideas that was ratified by the people."[59] So it appears that meaning is prelinguistic, or at least initially distinct from language. Yet Whittington says shortly thereafter that "meaning is not something that exists behind language. To search for intent is not an attempt to avoid language in search of something hidden by it. Rather, meaning, or intention, is embedded in the language itself, is realized with the utterance."[60] If this apparent inconsistency is indeed real, then surely Whittington did not *intend* to create it, but he *wrote* it.

The key point here is that, as Whittington surely would not deny, there can be a difference between what we say or write and what we intended to say or write. A common example of this is the phrase "I could care less," which we often hear from young people. In most cases, someone using that phrase is saying precisely the opposite of what she intends to say and thinks she is

[56] Ibid., 102.
[57] Ibid., 58.
[58] Ibid.
[59] Ibid., 59.
[60] Ibid.

saying. She actually intends to say "I couldn't care less," and perhaps uses "I could care less" as verbal shorthand for "It's not as if I could care less." Nevertheless, what she says with "I could care less" is that she *does* care, even though she presumably intended to indicate that she does *not* care.[61] Thus, second, consider the phrasing Whittington employs in this passage:

The goal of originalism is not to reimagine the fleeting thoughts in the mind of some private individual at the time of the founding. It is rather to examine the articulated elaborations of textual meaning with which the Constitution was defended and upon which the ratifiers relied in reaching their judgment as to the desirability of the document. Given the availability of substantial historical material on *the intentions behind the text*, as well as a proper understanding of the nature of textual meaning itself, there can be little justification for adopting a general rule against the introduction of authorial intentions in the case of the Constitution or for accusing advocates of originalism of an effort to engage in the legal equivalent of mind reading.[62]

Despite claiming not to look behind the text for authorial intentions, Whittington in this passage talks literally of "historical material on the intentions behind the text." I would suggest that what he thus says is not what he intended to say, though there is no denying that he indeed says it, but it is difficult to see how his emphasis on the identity of intention and meaning could allow him to escape this problem.

In order to bolster his case that authorial intentions and meaning are identical, Whittington calls upon an essay by Quentin Skinner entitled "Motives, Intentions and the Interpretation of Texts."[63] Following Skinner, Whittington sets out three different senses of "meaning":

We can distinguish between three common forms of "meaning": literal meaning, reader's meaning, and speaker's meaning. Focus on the reader's meaning ("What does this mean to me?") is inconsistent with the interpretive enterprise itself. Literal meaning (the "plain meaning") can only be regarded as an interpretive halfway house to the discovery of the speaker's meaning ("What did the speaker mean by this?").[64]

Skinner indeed does focus on the idea of the speaker's meaning, saying: "For it seems that a knowledge of the writer's intentions in writing, in the sense

---

[61] Examples of this phenomenon are endless, but allow me to recount one more. During my dissertation year in Germany, as I slowly became more capable in the use of the German language, I happened one day to refer to a female friend as "Meine Freundin." Looking in the dictionary, one would find that "Freundin" is the feminine version of "Freund," the male gender of "friend." However, what I unknowingly and *unintentionally* was saying by the phrase "Meine Freundin" was not that she was a female friend but, mildly embarrassingly, my girlfriend. To refer to her as my female friend, I should have said "Eine Freundin von mir" – a (female) friend of mine. The point here is that my verbal text had a comprehensible public meaning that was not at all the object of my private intention.

[62] Whittington, *Constitutional Interpretation*, 162 (emphasis added).

[63] Quentin Skinner, "Motives, Intentions and the Interpretation of Texts," in James Tully, ed., *Meaning and Context* (Princeton, NJ: Princeton University Press, 1988), 68–78.

[64] Whittington, *Constitutional Interpretation*, 177.

I have sought to isolate, is not merely relevant to, but is actually *equivalent* to, a knowledge of the meaning₃ of what he writes."[65] However we might assess Skinner's claim independently of this discussion, however, it appears that Whittington neglects certain key statements Skinner makes that would weaken if not undercut the originalism he wishes to defend. First, Skinner opens up the possibility of unintended meaning:

> I have argued that we need to know what a writer may have meant by what he wrote, and need (equivalently) to know his intentions in writing, in order to interpret the meaning of his works. This must first be distinguished, however, from the much stronger claim which is often advanced to the effect that the recovery of these intentions, and the decoding of the "original meaning" intended by the writer himself, must form the whole of the interpreter's task. . . . I see no impropriety in speaking of a work's having a meaning for me which the writer could not have intended. Nor does my thesis conflict with this possibility. I have been concerned only with the converse point that whatever the writer is *doing in* writing what he writes must be relevant to interpretation, and thus with the claim that *amongst* the interpreter's tasks must be the recovery of the writer's intentions *in* writing what he writes.[66]

In Skinner's account here, some amount of space opens up between text and authorial intent: A text could indeed have some meaning that was no part of the author's intention. And Skinner goes further in this direction:

> This thesis must also be distinguished from the claim that if we are concerned with a writer's intentions in this way we must be prepared to accept any statements the writer himself may make about his own intentions as a final authority on the question of what he was doing in a particular work. It is true that any agent is obviously in a privileged position when characterizing his own intentions and actions. It follows that it must always be dangerous, and ought perhaps to be unusual, for a critic to override a writer's explicit statements on this point. I see no difficulty in principle, however, about reconciling the claim that we need to be able to characterize a writer's intentions in order to interpret the meaning of his works with the claim that it may sometimes be appropriate to discount his own statements about them. This is . . . only to make the (perhaps rather dramatic, but certainly conceivable) charge that the writer himself may have been self-deceiving about recognizing his intentions, or incompetent at stating them.[67]

I would agree – prescinding, at least, from questions of psychology Freudian or otherwise – that an author is in a privileged position regarding his own intentions, as Skinner notes here. Yet this passage suggests that Skinner would accept my contention that the author is not in a privileged position regarding the meaning of his own text, a privilege that follows from Whittington's argument. As in my earlier example of student essays, the text is evidence of the author's intentions, but we construct and determine the author's intentions

[65] Skinner, "Motives Intentions and the interpretation of texts," 75–6.
[66] Ibid., 76.
[67] Ibid., 76–7.

from the meaning of the text; we do not, in the ordinary course of reading and understanding, construct and determine the text from the author's intentions. This allows for the possibility of the author's being, in Skinner's words, "self-deceiving about recognizing his intentions, or incompetent at stating them."

Still, Whittington refers to what he calls the "ontological identity of text and authorial intent."[68] Yet if there were such an ontological identity, originalism, at least with respect to the literary theory underlying it, would be unnecessary and redundant, for it presumably would be impossible to read a text in any terms other than authorial intent. "Originalism," he states, "is merely the implication of being governed by a written text."[69] If that is the case, then Whittington simply cannot consistently contend that "although originalism is the appropriate mode of judicial interpretation of the Constitution, it is not the only possible method available."[70] The reason is that if originalism is only one of several possible interpretive methodologies for reading a text, then nothing in the text qua text would seem to require us to choose originalism[71] – but it is the text qua text that, Whittington contends, necessitates originalism. For him, to say that the text is authoritative is to say that the author's intentions are authoritative. If "author's intentions" is a concept synonymous with "text," then I agree with him.

However, Whittington, like most originalists, plays a double game with the relation between text and intentions. On the one hand, he sees intentions as embodied in the text, as not at all extratextual. My response would be that the intentions embodied in the text may or may not be the intentions of the writers themselves (as in the earlier example of my students' essays). My claim is that whether or not the text successfully and completely embodies the intentions of its authors, it is the text itself that is authoritative and not the authors' intentions. On the other hand, Whittington maintains the originalist argument that we check our interpretation of the text by reference to the original intentions of the privileged-position authors. For him, if the

---

[68] Whittington, *Constitutional Interpretation*, 96.

[69] Ibid., 203.

[70] Ibid., 164.

[71] At best, it would appear that Whittington would have to argue that it is the purpose of the constitutional text, as opposed to its textuality per se, that necessitates originalism. As he writes in *Constitutional Interpretation* at 218:

> To the extent that the courts are concerned with interpreting the law, they must adopt a jurisprudence of original intent, not because it is the only available method of interpretation, but because it is the best. Originalism is most capable of realizing the goals internal to the interpretive project itself and of actualizing the obligations of democratic constitutionalism. The abandonment of originalism risks the abandonment of those projects as well, and it ensures the corruption and inadequacy of our pursuit of them.

This contention floats throughout his argument, but my focus here is on his claims based upon textuality per se.

text is autonomous, it cannot bind, for only the anchor of original authorial intent can certify an interpretation of the text.

At the same time, Whittington is correct when he states: "Without an intentional agent behind the marks, the very concept of a text or of interpretation becomes nonsensical."[72] Yes, this is true, but the concept of "intentional agent" is what I would call regulative rather than ontological. When we read a text we necessarily posit an author with intentions who created the text; I posit Whittington speaking to me through his text, just as you posit me speaking to you through my text here.[73] We construct the author from the text, not the text from the author. Or, put differently, the question of realized intention is manifested in the space, if any, between the author and the author constructed from the text. (What is the argument from design but a construction of the author from his text?) Whittington's ontological concept goes too far:

A text cannot be taken as autonomous. At the very least, we cannot accept the idea that marks on a piece of paper constitute a meaningful text if we take the marks as being autonomous of an author. An author must always be implied, if he is not already known. In either case, whether the author is implied or actual, he comes with the text. He is included and inseparable from textual meaning. If this is so, then the claim that the original intentions of the author are extratextual rests on a confusion about the nature of a text. Of course, there may be difficulty in identifying who the author is, or more relevantly, what the authorial intent is; but originalism provides an answer as to where to look. The notion of the Constitution as a "public" document in [*sic*] which "we" are the authors leads back to originalism as well.... "[74]

To say that an author must always be implied if he is not already known is the way we identify a text as a meaningful text, as Whittington believes, but he means more by this idea than merely the regulative idea of an author. He is suggesting the notion of the author's privileged position vis-à-vis the text, based on the assumption that the text cannot be privileged or authoritative if the author is not privileged or authoritative. The author on this view is not one more reader of the text but rather the "owner" of the text. Nevertheless, the author is inseparable from textual meaning only in the sense that we understand a text to be a (meaningful) text in terms of there being an author. Whittington's various statements that there are various ways to interpret (read) the Constitution suggest that it can be read independently of its authors. Originalism cannot escape the charge that its notion of authorial

---

[72] Ibid., 94.
[73] This concept of positing explains why we can be surprised – pleasantly or unpleasantly – when we have occasion finally to see, hear, or meet an author whose work we have been reading. The surprise comes from the disjunction between the image we have posited and the real author in the flesh.
[74] Whittington, *Constitutional Interpretation*, 177.

intent is an extratextual norm employed to regulate the legitimate readings of the text from a privileged position.

And that, finally, is the core significance of originalism in Whittington's account of the theory that constitutional provisions should be understood in the sense in which they were understood by those who wrote and ratified them. The core of this theory is the contention that the author has a special, privileged access to the meaning of his text, access that always trumps any contrary interpretations by readers of his text. Originalism distinguishes itself as an interpretive method by differentiating and privileging the meaning intended by the author from all other possible meanings. What is at stake here is, again, evident in the juxtaposition of these two familiar propositions:

P_1:   What binds the future is the text of the Constitution.

P_2:   What binds the future is the original understanding – in Whittington's formulation, the authors' understanding – of the text of the Constitution.

The essential originalist argument is that P_1 and P_2 are identical, such that the rejection of P_2 entails the rejection of P_1. My own contention is that these two propositions are distinct rather than equivalent, so that we can affirm P_1 even as we reject P_2. I accept the premise that the purpose of the Constitution is to bind the future; that is, to provide a constraint on contemporary majorities. What I take issue with is the claim that this premise requires originalism. But why not affirm P_2? Does constitutionalism require originalism? There are three possible answers. First, yes, constitutionalism does require originalism. Second, constitutionalism allows for originalism as one option among others. Whittington seems to vacillate between these two possibilities.

The third answer, my own, is that constitutionalism is inconsistent with originalism in the sense that originalism cannot accomplish what its adherents ask of it as a literary theory. First, it maintains that what binds the future is the original understanding of the meaning of the text of the Constitution. But if the meaning of the text of the Constitution can be nothing other than the original understanding, then originalism is unnecessary and redundant. If originalism is necessary and not redundant, on the other hand, then the meaning of the text could legitimately differ from the original understanding, and thus we cannot, as Whittington wants to do, justify the authorial-intention core of originalism as the obvious and necessary implication of any meaningful text. Second, if originalism is an interpretive method necessary to govern the range of potential meanings of the text, necessary because texts need an external control on how we read them, then originalism is impossible in this sense because the controls – the historical documents by which we are to determine authorial intent – are texts themselves and thus likewise are in need of external control on how we read them as well.[75] Consequently, if originalism is necessary (texts need an external control), it is not possible (the controls themselves are texts, leading to an infinite regression); if originalism is possible (we can read the texts themselves without any external controls), it's not necessary (we thus can read the Constitution ourselves without any external controls). Even Whittington, pointing to difficulties with the following claim as he tries to draw back from the precipice overlooking "interpretation all the way down," says that "we must admit that we can only understand a text as we understand it; that is, there is no way to step outside our context in order to check its accuracy. Ultimately, Fish, Hans-Georg Gadamer, and the others are correct in claiming that there are only interpreted truths."[76]

As discordant as it may seem, the position for which I am arguing, of which only the tip is visible here, is expressed aptly in a famous formulation by Marx: "Men make their own history, but they do not make it just as they please; they do not make it under circumstances chosen by themselves, but under circumstances directly found, given and transmitted from the past."[77] Whereas originalists emphasize constraint exclusively, and at least some nonoriginalists emphasize freedom – the living Constitution – exclusively, I argue that we must attempt to articulate a coherent account of how living within the terms of a written constitution allows us to make our own history, yet not just as we please.[78] I accept the premise that the purpose of a constitution is to bind the future, but I take issue with the claim that this premise entails originalism and do so because the practice of interpretation does not occur as Whittington describes it.[79] Intention, so central to his

---

75 Whittington notes, but does not consider deeply enough, this important issue: "As noted by reader-response theorists, the historical evidence marshaled to support originalist interpretations of the Constitution requires just as much interpretation as the original text itself. The constitutional text is surrounded only by other texts, each of which requires interpretation and thus the reader's active participation in order to make it meaningful." Whittington, *Constitutional Interpretation*, 75 (footnote omitted). See Chapter 7.

76 Ibid., 92.

77 Karl Marx, "The Eighteenth Brumaire of Louis Bonaparte," excerpted in Robert C. Tucker, ed., *The Marx-Engels Reader*, 2nd ed. (New York: W. W. Norton & Company, 1978), 595.

78 Friedman and Smith hint at this idea when they write: "Each generation's constitutionalism is an act of both fidelity and creation. The Constitution that is passed on by each generation is the product of both that generation's fidelity to past commitments and its application of those commitments to new problems." "The Sedimentary Constitution," 147 *University of Pennsylvania Law Review* 1, 7 (1998). This is the sense in which, somewhat similarly to my own approach, they argue that we need "to replace the apparent choice between anachronistic originalism or non-historical living constitutionalism [i.e., nonoriginalism] with an approach that takes all of our constitutional history into account." Ibid., 5.

79 I thus am not arguing against originalism from the outside, counterposing some alternative mode of interpretation such as nonoriginalism and justifying it on some other set of grounds.

account of interpretation generally and originalism specifically, is a slippery and complex concept. In the latter stages of his analysis Whittington lays out what he considers the significance of intention:

> It is this necessary relationship between textual meaning and authorial intent that distinguishes the use of historical material from the use of other extratextual material and gives rise to three primary implications. First, originalism cannot properly be understood as drawing from a grab bag of external information in order to divert textual meaning in a particular direction. Rather, originalism draws upon sources of information that are in a sense required by the constitutional text itself. . . . Second, originalism cannot properly be understood to deal with the "secret and unwritten" intentions of the founders. To the extent that the text is accepted, the intentions expressed in that text are accepted as well. . . . Finally, originalism should not be concerned with the motivations and purposes of the text. Like other pieces of information, evidence of founding motivations is relevant to textual meaning only to the extent that it sheds light on the intentions embodied in the text. Evidence of motivations is just a tool for reaching textual intentions, not direct evidence of those intentions themselves.[80]

When he writes that "to the extent that the text is accepted, the intentions expressed in that text are accepted as well," I would agree with that statement without reservation. The problem, however, is that, as I have tried to show, intention functions in Whittington's account both as something embedded in a text and as a – logically external – check on that text. It functions here, in other words, both as the meaning of a text and as a check on the meaning of a text.

I would argue, by contrast, that one can maintain "meaning" as a fixed, regulative concept – that is, that which holds us to the proposition that there is an objective content to the text – while saying that it is our understanding (of that meaning) that changes over time. The key is that our understanding must always be tied to the constitutional text as opposed to some other written or unwritten text. Metaphorically speaking, I say against originalists that we play baseball, but that there is a huge number of possible games – not just one and one game only – that are all equally baseball; I say against nonoriginalists that we are committed to play baseball and not football or basketball. Whittington believes that autonomy equals indeterminacy. If indeterminacy means something beyond the author's intent, then this is true by definition, and it is what Whittington shares with the postmodernists. But I argue that beyond the author's intent is not indeterminacy but autonomy, and contrary to both originalism and postmodernism, I contend that

---

Rather, I argue against originalism from the inside, accepting its concept of a constitution as binding but maintaining that its notion of interpretation is inadequate to its concept of a constitution. I am making, therefore, a philosophical rather than a historical or even political argument.

[80] Whittington, *Constitutional Interpretation*, 179.

semantic autonomy is not equivalent to semantic anarchy. When a shipyard builds a ship and launches it into the world, however the ship is built – and the way it is built could well structure where it can go in the world – the shipyard does not and cannot control that ship as it makes its way in the world. The same holds for language: We do not control our language once we have launched it into the world. Originalists implicitly accept that claim in their asserted need to control the meaning of that language as it makes its way in the world. Justice Story had it right: "Nothing but the text itself was adopted by the people."[81] It is the practice of constitutional interpretation that is privileged and authoritative, rather than the Constitution itself, because the Constitution is realized in the practice and discourse of interpretation. The "Constitution itself," considered outside of and apart from the practice of interpretation, is a regulative abstraction, because it is only within the practice of constitutional interpretation that we come to a determinate – and corrigible – understanding of the meaning of the text of the Constitution. What binds us is the founders' intention that we live within the polity constituted by the Constitution and negotiate our differences in an ongoing manner within that structure.

In the end, Whittington makes a point about his argument that I would apply to the enterprise of constitutional interpretation generally:

> In developing possible implications of a written constitution, we would be well advised to go back to the founders, not in search of authorities but in search of other people who have thought about this particular issue. Unlike us, the founders were immediately faced with the question of whether or not to have a written constitution and thus may be expected to have considered the matter in depth. Thus, if we recur to the founders for arguments on this issue, we must bear in mind that those arguments have weight because of their content, not their source.[82]

However, in footnote 9, at the end of this passage, Whittington takes back his argument here, whereas I would not: "This is in contrast to interpreting the text of the Constitution itself, when the words of the founders carry weight because of who they are (the authors), not because their ideas were necessarily good."[83] So, evidently Whittington argues that we need an independent substantive argument to justify why we should obey the founders because of who they were (the authors) rather than because of what they said. I think he betrays his own best insight here. Ultimately, it is always *we*, informed by the thoughts of the writers and ratifiers as well as by those of others we think relevant, who decide, in our own best judgment, what the Constitution means. As Whittington writes: "We expect judges and lawyers,

---

[81] Joseph Story, *Commentaries on the Constitution of the United States* (Boston: Hilliard, Gray and Company, 1833), Vol. 1, 389.
[82] Whittington, *Constitutional Interpretation*, 49.
[83] Ibid., 236, endnote 9.

when acting in their official capacities, to adhere to their best understandings of the requirements of this Constitution."[84] That, ultimately, is all we have. So, does constitutionalism require originalism? No: If we need originalism, it is not a possible interpretive strategy; and if it is a possible interpretive strategy, then we do not need it.

[84] Ibid., 110–11.

8

The Ontology of Constitutional Discourse (I)

Against the background of the extensive and highly political debates over interpretivism and noninterpretivism, or originalism and nonoriginalism, in American constitutional theory in recent years, H. Jefferson Powell published an interesting article in 1986 that draws attention to the constitutional text in an effort to establish that, in his words, "parchment matters."[1] The participants in those debates, he claims, have tended to dissolve the actual constitutional text into various nontextual discourses:

> There are, on the one hand, those who implicitly or explicitly wish to recast American constitutional discourse into what they see as the freer and richer context of general moral debate. On the other hand, there are those who regard the text as the container for an encoded message, and the constitutionalist as a cryptographer equipped with the proper key, whether it be the "framers' intent" or the gospel of economic efficiency. Yet others, by far the largest group, do not so much undercut the text as they ignore it. For them the question of "the Constitution's" meaning is simply an inquiry into the possible implications of Supreme Court decisions.[2]

The first group, clearly, includes those, mostly liberals, who would dissolve constitutional interpretation into general moral theory. The second group, mostly conservatives, includes those who are originalists or advocates of the law-and-economics school. The third group, descended from the legal realists, include those who dissolve constitutional interpretation into the policy preferences of individual justices. Powell, by contrast, argues for the necessity of maintaining a clear and steady focus on the actual text of the Constitution as a historical document. The written, textual character of the Constitution,

---

[1] H. Jefferson Powell, "Parchment Matters: A Meditation on the Constitution as Text," 71 *Iowa Law Review* 1427 (1986).
[2] Ibid., 1428.

he holds, has been central to the American legal system in particular and American society in general:

> No matter how remote from the apparent meaning of the historical document a "constitutional" decision may seem to others, the judges who announce it invariably do so in the name of words penned in 1787, 1789, 1868, and so on. No matter how important the role of extratextual beliefs about justice, efficiency, or human nature in their thinking, those who argue for "constitutional" protection for freedom of contract or gay rights invariably do so by referring, however generally, to the historical document.[3]

As an actual historical document, Powell suggests, the Constitution has played and continues to play three "vital roles," to use his term, in American society: a definitional role, a conserving role, and a revolutionary role. At the root of the idea of the vital roles the Constitution plays in American society is the widely acknowledged and accepted proposition that the purpose, the very nature, of a constitution – especially a written constitution – is its capacity to bind the future. Through its definitional role, the Constitution as an actual historical document serves to ensure that all American political debate, indirectly if not directly, leads back to questions as to the meaning of the constitutional text. It is through that connection that we know that our political debate is American political debate rather than British or Russian political debate. Through its conserving role, the Constitution as an actual historical document serves to ensure that all American political debate leads back to that particular set of general and specific principles with which the Framers constituted the American polity. And finally, through its revolutionary role, the Constitution as an actual historical document serves to ensure that all American political debate leads back to a particular set of normative principles against which any current institutions or practices may be evaluated and possibly found wanting.

In all of these roles – definitional, conserving, revolutionary – the Constitution, as I have emphasized throughout this discussion, binds the future.

---

[3] Ibid., 1427. Compare Michael Perry, "The Authority of Text, Tradition, and Reason: A Theory of Constitutional 'Interpretation,'" 58 *Southern California Law Review* 551, 552 (1985):

> It is axiomatic in American political-legal culture that the text of the Constitution ought to play a justificatory role in – be authoritative for – constitutional decision making. There is, however, no axiomatic or canonical conception of the constitutional text. What is the constitutional "text"? Ought we to understand or conceive of the "text" as: (a) the verbal or linguistic embodiment of the political morality constitutionalized by the ratifiers; (b) particular marks on a page; (c) a symbol of some sort? And, in the same vein, what does it mean to "interpret" the text?

> For an excellent discussion of the question of the constitutional text, somewhat related to the concerns of this book, see Sanford Levinson, "'The Constitution' in American Civil Religion," 1979 *The Supreme Court Reporter*, 123, and *Constitutional Faith* (Princeton, NJ: Princeton University Press, 1988), Chapter 1.

American constitutionalism, I have argued, rests on the fundamental premise that the purpose of a constitution, especially a written one, is to bind future generations to the vision of its founders. The written, textual character of the Constitution is, on this view, the central precondition of its capacity to ensure that American society continues to develop in accordance with the vision of the Founders. The interesting theoretical question, though, is how a constitution can and does control the future. How, in Powell's words, does parchment matter? More broadly, how do texts structure and constrain human activity? How can we satisfactorily explain the binding capacity of the Constitution, a phenomenon taken for granted in the literature but not adequately explored? The first step in answering such questions is to recognize that to speak of the Constitution's capacity to bind the future presupposes more broadly the capacity of language and texts to structure and constrain human action. As Will Harris notes, however, the existence of this broader capacity is not at all obvious and clear:

American constitutional interpretation takes for granted the elemental preposterousness of its subject, namely the presumption that a political world can be constructed and controlled with words. . . . The words narrate the polity into existence and, as its working principles unfold, the polity becomes a kind of large-scale text in its own right. Moreover, a polity that is sustained by words in turn gives those words political meaning.[4]

"The American political arrangement," he continues, "was brought into existence, and it purports to continue to define itself, by a written text. Its ultimate source of an image or order is the capacity of language to regularize thought and action."[5] But what does "the capacity of language to regularize thought and action" mean? What are the preconditions of preserving a founding vision against attempts by succeeding generations to alter it? To suggest in this way that a political world can be constructed and controlled with words points to an important intersection between the social sciences' traditional interest in explaining the structure and dynamics of social phenomena and the humanities' traditional interest in language and texts. That intersection is the grounding of human texts in human activity and the structuring of human activity by human texts. In the present reflections on the text of the Constitution, I shall call the relation between the text of the Constitution and the society "living under" or "living in" that text constitutional textuality. In these terms, an explanation of the binding capacity of the Constitution involves a theory of constitutional textuality, because such

---

4 William F. Harris II, "Bonding Word and Polity: The Logic of American Constitutionalism," 76 *American Political Science Review* 34, 34 (1982). See also his rather densely written larger work, *The Interpretable Constitution* (Baltimore: Johns Hopkins University Press, 1993), which touches upon some of my themes here as it heads in a different direction.
5 Harris, "Bonding Word and Polity," 36.

binding capacity consists of a particular relation between the Constitution and American society.

Nevertheless, the positivist theory of constitutional textuality that originalism presupposes cannot explain the binding capacity of the Constitution on which originalism stakes its claim to validity. Specifically, my thesis is this: I accept the claim that a constitution is supposed to bind the future, but I argue that the constitutive character of the Constitution is the key to its binding capacity and that originalism cannot account for the binding capacity of the Constitution because its positivist metatheory cannot account for the constitutive character of the Constitution. If the binding capacity of the Constitution is to be explained satisfactorily, the Constitution must be conceived in Kantian fashion as constitutive of the forms of ordinary political and legal experience rather than as merely one particular element – even if a regulative element – of ordinary political and legal experience, and that it is an interpretive theory of constitutional textuality rather than originalism's positivist theory that can provide such an account.

The interpretive theory of constitutional textuality, however, must not be taken to be synonymous with nonoriginalism or noninterpretivism, for both originalism and nonoriginalism, interpretivism and noninterpretivism, are grounded in the positivist theory of constitutional textuality. Thus the interpretive theory of constitutional textuality is not one side of the conventional dichotomy, but rather is an alternative to the theory that grounds the conventional dichotomy. With that proviso in mind, this is the argument I shall sketch: If the binding capacity of the constitutional text is to be explained, the constitutional text must be conceived, analogously to Kant's concept of the synthetic a priori, as *in* ordinary political and legal experience – that is, constitutive of ordinary political and legal experience – yet not *of* ordinary political and legal experience, and it is the interpretive theory of constitutional textuality rather than originalism's positivist theory of constitutional textuality that can provide such an account.[6] The crucial difference between these two theories of constitutional textuality is that the interpretive theory conceives the Constitution as, in a manner to be explained later, an inherently public text and social practice, whereas originalism's positivist theory conceives the Constitution as an inherently private text and object. The paradox of originalism is that the positivist theory of constitutional textuality it employs is not adequate to its emphasis on the binding capacity of

---

[6] There are two points about this distinction that I wish to emphasize. First, one can argue that either these theories of constitutional textuality are real and distinct alternatives, or they are not real and distinct alternatives because the positivist theory, upon analysis, dissolves into the interpretive theory. Second, while I suggest here the more limited claim that the positivist theory of constitutional textuality simply explains the binding capacity of the constitutional text less well than does the interpretive theory, one could argue the stronger claim that the positivist theory cannot explain that binding capacity at all. In each case, my position is the latter.

a constitution. The purpose of a constitution may well be to get everything down on paper, in language, in order to bind and limit future generations, but the presupposition of originalism's focus on the Framers' intentions is a marked lack of trust in the capacity of language to bind. Indeed, while originalism sees binding character and democratic character as consistent, they are in fact, on originalist premises, contradictory. The interpretive approach enables us to resolve the paradox in the broader concept of constitutive character, which is in the end the true political character of constitutional discourse.

Let us begin by recalling that originalism conceives itself to be the necessary and sufficient condition of constitutionalism. The basic premise of constitutionalism, as we have noted repeatedly, is the idea that the purpose of a constitution is to bind the future. In propositional form, we have seen that this is that basic premise:

P_1: What binds the future is the constitutional text.

The distinctive claim of originalism, however, we have expressed propositionally in this form:

P_2: What binds the future is the original understanding of the constitutional text.

While everyone would subscribe to P_1, the distinctive move that originalism makes, as my central theme has maintained, is to identify P_1 with P_2: To say that what binds the future is the constitutional text is necessarily to say that what binds the future is the original understanding of the constitutional text, such that to deny that what binds the future is the original understanding of the constitutional text is necessarily to deny that what binds the future is the constitutional text. Given its positivist theory of textuality, originalism denies the possibility of such a distinction, whereas the interpretive theory does not. The latter argues that P_2 is a narrower claim than P_1 in that we can deny P_2 and yet still affirm P_1. What is at work here is a nonpositivist theory of language according to which language is essentially social and public rather than individual and private. Language, in other words, is an essentially social activity, and social activity is essentially textual in the sense that it is an ongoing system of meaning. Society and text, as I will explain, are mutually constitutive. By contrast, originalism sees the proposition that what binds the future is the constitutional text and the proposition that what binds the future is the original understanding of the constitutional text as *identical*, such that the denial of the latter necessarily amounts to a denial of the former. In other words, to deny the authoritativeness of the original understanding of the constitutional text is to deny the authoritativeness of the Constitution per se. Why? Originalism, at bottom, denies the constitutive character of the Constitution.

What, then, is the constitutive character of the Constitution? Its truth is grounded in what I suggest is the central feature of the American polity: We are a society constituted, which is to say ordered, in terms of a fundamental text. The Constitution is a written document, but it is a written document with social reality. This is what we mean when we say, with deceptive simplicity and redundancy, that the Constitution *constitutes*. The Constitution has a social reality in that it is not simply a legal document, as are so many written constitutions around the world that may or may not be in force. Rather, its social reality lies in the fact that through it we actually define who we are as a people not just in a symbolic sense but, more significantly, in a substantive sense. Hanna Pitkin captures this fundamental dimension of the American Constitution in her discussion of what she sees as two uses of the term "constitution":

> The first of these uses is "constitution" in the sense of composition or fundamental make-up, the "constituent parts" of something and how they are put together, its characteristic frame or nature.... With respect to a community, this use of "constitution" suggests a characteristic way of life, the national character of a people, their ethos or fundamental nature as a people, a product of their particular history and social conditions. In this sense, our constitution is less something we *have* than something we *are*.[7]

From this point of view, one that in many respects is classically Aristotelian, a constitution is the form of a society; that is, it is what orders social life, and thus every society identifiable as a society necessarily has a constitution. While constitutions may be written or unwritten, it follows from this postulate that a society without a constitution is no society at all; the only state of affairs without a constitution is a condition of anarchy. The written nature of the American Constitution has contributed to the development of a legalistic, and thus more narrow, notion of constitutionalism centered on courts, but constitutional theory is an intellectual domain whose concern with general issues in constitutionalism identifies it as more a species of social and political theory than of conventional constitutional law. While the latter tends to focus on doctrinal matters from a court-centered perspective, constitutional theory subsumes constitutional law within the broader intellectual framework of constitutionalism conceived as the general concern with that basic question of politics, the problem of order.

Against this background, the social reality of the Constitution is grounded in the phenomenon captured by what Pitkin sees in the second use of the term:

> its function as a verbal noun pointing to the action or activity of constituting – that is, of founding, framing, shaping something anew. In this sense, our constitution is

---

[7] Hanna Fenichel Pitkin, "The Idea of a Constitution," 37 *Journal of Legal Education* 167, 167 (1987).

neither something we have nor something we are so much as something we *do* – or at any rate *can* do.[8]

"Constitution" is a noun, that is, only insofar as it is a gerund. Michael Perry, in his analogy between religious communities and political communities, describes this same phenomenon to which Pitkin points us. At some length, here is his conception:

> The notions of community, tradition, and foundational text figure prominently both in my understanding of sacred texts and their interpretation and in my conception of the constitutional text and its interpretation. Consider the connections, in the American experience, among (1) the American political community, or polity, (2) the American political tradition of which the polity is the living embodiment, and (3) the constitutional text. [B]y community I mean, roughly, a group of persons united principally by their self-identification as the present bearers of, participants in, a tradition. By tradition I mean a particular historical narrative, in which the central motif is an aspiration to a particular form of life, to certain projects, goals, ideals, and the central discourse is "an historically extended, socially embodied argument" about how that form of life is to be cultivated and revised. By foundational text I mean that text that, in the community and tradition in question, is seen to charter, to mandate, the form of life to which the community and tradition aspire, and thus the text that, for the community and tradition, symbolizes that mandate.[9]

The social reality of the Constitution lies in the fact that we are a people who constitute ourselves as a people in and through the terms of a fundamental text.[10] The relationship is reciprocal: The American people constitute the text as the text constitutes the American people. As Pitkin suggests, "one might even want to argue that our constitution is more something we do than something we make: we (re) shape it all the time through our collective activity. Our constitution is (what is relatively stable in) our activity; a stranger learns its principles by watching our conduct."[11] In other words, as both Pitkin and Perry affirm, we Americans are a people who live textually.

Yet how is it possible to live textually? The crux of the interpretive theory of constitutional textuality is the proposition that language is inherently

---

[8] Ibid., 168.

[9] Perry, "The Authority of Text, Tradition, and Reason," 563–4 (footnote omitted).

[10] In *We the People I: Foundations* (Cambridge, MA: Belknap Press of Harvard University Press, 1991), Bruce Ackerman states that "our constitutional narrative constitutes us as a people" in that "the narrative we tell ourselves about our Constitution's roots is a deeply significant act of collective self-definition; its continual re-telling plays a critical role in the ongoing construction of national identity" (36). The Constitution, in other words, "is more than an idea. It is an evolving historical practice, constituted by generations of Americans as they mobilized, argued, resolved their ongoing disputes over the nation's identity and destiny" (34). I believe we can accept this claim without thereby necessarily committing ourselves to Ackerman's theory of constitutional change.

[11] Ibid., 168.

social and public. Language in human experience is not just something "in the head" in contradistinction to "the world," but rather helps constitute the social world. Stressing this constitutive character of language, the interpretive theory conceives the Constitution as a discourse, or social practice. Now, ordinarily, when one hears the word "discourse," one thinks of speech or talk in contradistinction to the action or behavior one associates with a social practice. Saying to someone, "I am beating you," is certainly different from actually beating him. But the term "discourse" also connotes a social practice – a "form of life," as Wittgenstein would say – in its essential linguisticality. It would be redundant, in this sense, to say that the Constitution is both a discourse and a social practice, because a social practice is essentially discursive and discourse is not just talk or in the head but action.[12] Consequently, the interpretive theory of the relation between the constitutional text and American society rejects the idea of a gap between text and world because text and world must be conceived to be mutually constitutive.[13]

The positivist theory of constitutional textuality, in contrast, has to deal with the problem of a gap between text and world because it conceives language as individual and private. If I may introduce a term from philosophy, we can say that this theory is essentially Cartesian in that it considers the individual and private to be logically prior to the social and public. Language is ultimately yours or mine rather than ours. The interpretive theory is post-Cartesian (and yet also Aristotelian) in that it argues just the reverse: It considers the social and public to be logically prior to the individual and

---

[12] "[Law] is the constitution of a world by the distribution of authority within it; it establishes the terms on which its actors may talk in conflict or cooperation among themselves. The law establishes roles and relations and voices, positions from which and audiences to which one may speak, and it gives us as speakers the materials and methods of a discourse. It is a way of creating a rhetorical community over time. It is this discourse, working in the social context of its own creation, this language in the fullest sense of the term, that *is* the law. It makes us members of a common world." James Boyd White, *When Words Lose Their Meaning* (Chicago: University of Chicago Press, 1984), 266 (footnote omitted).

[13] This point of view, of course, overlaps with themes one finds in Critical Legal Studies. Robert Gordon, for example, writes that legal discourses "are among the discourses that help us to make sense of the world, that fabricate what we interpret as its reality. They construct roles for us like 'Owner' and 'Employee,' and tell us how to behave in the roles. (The person cast as 'Employee' is subordinate. Why? It just is that way, part of the role.) They wall us off from one another by constituting us as separate individuals given rights to protect our isolation, but then prescribe formal channels (such as contracts, partnerships, corporations) through which we can reconnect. They split up the world into categories that filter our experience – sorting out the harms we must accept as the hand of fate, or as our own fault, from the outrageous injustices we may resist as wrongfully forced upon us." "Law and Ideology," 3 *Tikkun*, 15 (1988). While I endorse this focus on the constitutive character of discourse, I am not certain at present as to how far I wish to follow the Critical Legal Studies program.

private, and thus sees language as ultimately ours rather than yours or mine.[14] It is for this reason that the interpretive theory of constitutional textuality conceives the Constitution as a discourse or social practice: The Constitution is not merely a document, on this view, but a form of life, an all-encompassing institution; it is not merely regulative, but constitutive. It is not just another important object within our experience, but instead constitutes the formal structure of our social experience as Americans. To claim that the Constitution is a discourse or social practice is therefore to assert both the grounding of human texts in human activity and the structuring of human activity by human texts. Consequently, when the interpretive theory of constitutional textuality refers to the Constitution as social discourse, it is claiming that we do not so much live under the Constitution, which is how the positivist theory must portray American society, as within the Constitution. Constitutional interpretation thus is not the province of courts or experts alone, but instead becomes an activity central to American citizenship generally.[15]

As introduced in Chapter 5, the positivist theory of constitutional textuality I locate at the heart of originalism consists, to begin with, of the idea that the text contains and embodies a message from the authors of the document

---

[14] In the broadest philosophical terms, the interpretive approach denies that there is something objective that stands outside interpretation and to which we have direct – that is, neutral, nonhistorical – access. According to Richard Bernstein, objectivism "is a substantive orientation that believes that in the final analysis there is a realm of basic, uninterpreted, hard facts that serves as the foundation for all empirical knowledge. The appeal to these 'facts' presumably legitimizes empirical claims about the world. 'Objectivism' – a doctrine which in its primitive or sophisticated forms is shared by many mainstream social scientists – turns out to coincide with the 'myth of the given' which has been so devastatingly criticized by contemporary philosophers." *The Restructuring of Social and Political Theory* (Philadelphia: University of Pennsylvania Press, 1978), 111–12 (footnote omitted). The positivist view asserts, to the contrary, that there is objectivity in the sense of a given standing outside any interpretation. Regarding language, the Constitution, and originalism, the positivist theory of textuality points to an objectivity standing outside language when it takes the intentions of the Framers as norms standing outside interpretation and thus regulative of the constitutional text and its interpretation. The interpretive theory, on the other hand, argues that outside a particular language there is only more language. In its broadest social sense, language on this view does not represent; it constitutes. At the same time, the denial of objectivism is not, the interpretive approach argues, a denial of objectivity. According to Bernstein: "If by 'objectivity' we mean that in any domain of human inquiry – whether physical phenomena, or an existing political system, or even the interpretation of a text – there are intersubjective standards of rationality or norms of inquiry by which we attempt to distinguish personal bias, superstition, or false beliefs from objective claims, then adherence to such an ideal of objectivity governs any systematic inquiry." *The Restructuring of Social and Political Theory*, 111. The interpretive theory argues that objectivity is socially constituted.

[15] For an interesting account of this idea see Paul Brest, "Constitutional Citizenship," 34 *Cleveland State Law Review* 175 (1986), as well as Sotirios Barber, *On What the Constitution Means* (Baltimore: Johns Hopkins University Press, 1984).

awaiting discovery by future readers of the text.[16] This theory of textuality is an essentially reductionist position that distinguishes between a text and its creators and ascribes meaning to the latter.

Against this literary-theory background, originalism is clearly a positivist theory of textuality in that it conceives language as private; it treats a text not as an entity with intrinsic public meaning, but rather as merely the expression of an extrinsic private meaning that stands behind it in the intentions and mental states of its authors or in the understanding of its initial readers.[17] The real Constitution is therefore not the public, written text itself, but rather the private intentions, defined as the mental states or the contemporaneous language use of the writers and ratifiers standing behind it and speaking to future generations. As such, the meaning of the Constitution is essentially subjective: Because the written text is at bottom a representation of the opinions or intentions of those people who created it, it consequently has no meaning of its own. Its meaning lies behind the words of the text in the historical intentions of those who wrote the text and the understanding of those who ratified the text. For this reason, whether one is an interpretivist or a noninterpretivist, an originalist or a nonoriginalist, there is always and necessarily an unwritten constitution – that is, something standing behind the written text. The positivist theory of textuality thus necessarily generates the ghost it constantly seeks to exorcise, the notion of an unwritten constitution.

Thus, while originalism's chief concern is to uphold the binding capacity of the Constitution by establishing the objective meaning of the Constitution independent of what particular interpreters might argue at particular times, its positivist theory of textuality undermines the possibility of objective meaning. The key to these claims, however, is a coherent account of the relation between the constitutional text and American society. To indicate what I think is problematic about theorizing this relation, consider a statement by Louis Fisher in his book *Constitutional Dialogues* that unself-consciously suggests a particular concept of constitutional textuality. Fisher does a fine job of showing that constitutional interpretation is indeed an activity of not just the judiciary, but the other branches of the federal government as well as state governments and citizens generally. "Constitutional law," he writes, "is a process that operates both inside and outside the judicial arena, challenging the judgment and conscience of all three political branches at the national level, the state governments, and the public at large."[18] The comment I find suggestive, however, is this: "Constitutions draw their life from forces outside the law: from ideas, customs, society, and the constant

---

[16] See Chapter 5, p. 165–7.
[17] See the quotation from Larry Simon, "The Authority of the Constitution and Its Meaning," on p. 166, footnote 29.
[18] Louis Fisher, *Constitutional Dialogues* (Princeton, NJ: Princeton University Press, 1988), 8.

dialogue among political institutions."[19] What is significant here is the spatial language – "outside" – which evokes a sense of the Constitution as a discrete object – specifically, a document – within our experience and separable from other independent aspects of our experience. What is the significance of the claim that "ideas, customs, society, and the constant dialogue among political institutions" are "forces outside the law" and thus outside the Constitution? It is to claim that the Constitution in and of itself is inert and lifeless, until and unless it receives its life and reality from the various forces outside the law. The problematic aspect of the relation between the constitutional text and American society is explaining how something that is lifeless until made real by forces outside the law can bind, structure, and constrain those very forces.

Fisher's unself-conscious counterposing of constitutions and forces outside the law such as "ideas, customs, society, and the constant dialogue among political institutions" in fact generally reproduces a fifty-year-old argument by Karl Llewellyn that is relevant to the concept of constitutional textuality. One of the leading lights of the legal-realist movement in the United States, Llewellyn sought to change our understanding of law from a system of rules to a system of behavior. In "The Constitution as an Institution,"[20] Llewellyn drew Fisher's distinction between the Constitution and forces outside the law in terms of, respectively, the Document and the living or unwritten Constitution. He argued that what he called "orthodox constitutional theory" reified the constitutional text by considering the Document itself as the Constitution. The implication of this orthodox theory, according to Llewellyn, is that to understand the operation of the American constitutional system, all we have to do is to read the text of the Constitution, and this he, echoed by contemporary political scientists, considered a ridiculous claim.[21] It fails to take account of important ongoing aspects of the American constitutional system that developed historically. Most succinctly, Llewellyn held that "the working Constitution is in good part utterly extra-Documentary (the privilege of Senatorial filibuster; the powers of the Conference Committee; the President's power of removal; the Supreme Court's power of review; the party system; the campaign fund)."[22]

Llewellyn's main concern in attacking the orthodox theory was to "dethrone the words," as he put it; he drew a sharp distinction between the text of the Constitution and what he considered to be the reality of the Constitution. The real, working American Constitution, he argued, is "in essence

---

[19] Ibid., 11.
[20] 34 *Columbia Law Review* 1 (1934).
[21] In view of Llewellyn's own language in his article, "ridiculous" is not too strong a word to use.
[22] Llewellyn, "The Constitution as an Institution," 15.

not a document, but a living institution built (historically, genetically) in [the] first instance *around* a particular Document."²³ The Constitution, that is, is not the words of the text, but the empirical practice of the American system. In "Constitutionalism: An Analytic Framework," Thomas Grey makes clear that in much constitutional discussion, the term text is highly ambiguous, sometimes meaning the written constitutional document, sometimes understanding the Constitution as a set of norms both written and unwritten. The distinction between writtenness and unwrittenness is what is important:

constitutional norms differ in the source of their authority. Some derive their force from enactment; these are what have traditionally been called the "written" constitutional norms. Of the remaining ("unwritten") constitutional norms, some derive their authority from acceptance in the relevant community ("customary" or "traditional" constitutional norms), while others are founded on the claim that they express moral or political truth ("natural law" norms).²⁴

By Grey's account, written constitutional norms have their source in enactment, while unwritten constitutional norms have their sources elsewhere, and thus one ascertains the content of each set of norms differently:

What have been called written constitutions (or written constitutional norms) are those that derive their status from the fact of their enactment by some authorized body, according to some established procedure. The content of an enacted constitutional norm is derived by interpretation of the enactment itself – the text of the enacted document, as well as what can be learned from other evidence of the meaning intended by those who enacted it. Unwritten constitutional norms have other sources of authority than enactment, and their contents must be elucidated by techniques other than interpretation.²⁵

This contrast between written and unwritten constitutional norms is significant, for in much constitutional discussion there is assumed to be a hard and fast distinction between the text and the non-text, a distinction that gives rise to the spatial metaphor of norms that are internal to the text and those that are external to the text. That is precisely what sets up Llewellyn's argument. In making such an argument, Llewellyn himself reached back to the eighteenth-century British view of a constitution that the Americans of the 1780s rejected. According to Charles McIlwain, "the traditional notion of constitutionalism before the late eighteenth century was of a set of principles embodied in the institutions of a nation and neither external to these nor in existence prior to them."²⁶ This concept of constitutionalism implies that

²³ Ibid., 3.
²⁴ Thomas Grey, "Constitutionalism: An Analytic Framework," in J. Roland Pennock and John W. Chapman, eds., *Constitutionalism* (Nomos XX) (New York: New York University Press, 1979), 191.
²⁵ Ibid., 202.
²⁶ Charles H. McIlwain, *Constitutionalism: Ancient and Modern*, rev. ed. (Ithaca, NY: Cornell University Press, 1947), 12.

a society without a constitution is no society at all, and that any ongoing society must by definition have a constitution. It is not the American idea of fundamental law; according to Gordon Wood:

> Most eighteenth-century writers, from Bolingbroke in 1733 to Charles Inglis, the American Tory, in 1776 (in almost identical terms) could not conceive of the constitution as anything anterior and superior to government and ordinary law, but rather regarded it as the government and ordinary law itself, as *"that assemblage of laws, customs and institutions which form the general system; according to which the several powers of the state are distributed, and their respective rights are secured to the different members of the community."*[27]

On this understanding, a constitution is simply what we call the political system. There is no distinction between fundamental law and statutory law: Every act of Parliament is in a sense part of the constitution, and all law is thus constitutional.

The American position, by contrast, is that a constitution is not coextensive with government and ordinary law, but rather is anterior and superior to government and ordinary law. A constitution, on the American view, embodies a system of principles anterior and superior to ordinary government in order to secure persons in their rights against governmental power. Thomas Paine put this point most deliberately:

> A constitution is a thing *antecedent* to a government, and a government is only the creature of a constitution. The constitution of a country is not the act of its government, but of the people constituting a government.
>
> It is the body of elements to which you can refer and quote article by article, and which contains the principles on which the government shall be established, the manner in which it shall be organized, the powers it shall have, ... and, in fine, everything that relates to the complete organization of a civil government and the principles on which it shall act and by which it shall be bound.[28]

Using an apt analogy, Paine illustrated the essential, normative binding power of a constitution:

> A constitution, therefore, is to a government what the laws made afterward by that government are to a court of judicature. The court of judicature does not make the laws, neither can it alter them; it only acts in conformity to the laws made, and the government is in like manner governed by the Constitution."[29]

---

[27] Gordon S. Wood, *The Creation of the American Republic, 1776–1787* (New York: W. W. Norton & Company, 1969), 260–1, citing Inglis. As the *Oxford English Dictionary* puts it, a constitution is "The system or body of fundamental principles according to which a nation, a state, or body politic is constituted and governed."

[28] Thomas Paine, *The Rights of Man*, excerpted in Kenneth Dolbeare, *American Political Thought* (Monterey, CA: Duxbury Press, 1981), 57.

[29] Ibid.

There is a contrast, then, in McIlwain's words, "between the new conception of the conscious formulation by a people of its fundamental law, the new definition of 'constitution'; and the older traditional view in which the word was applied only to the substantive principles to be deduced from a nation's actual institutions and their development."[30] Using more modern terminology, we can say that on the former, American conception a constitution is normative and prescriptive, while on the latter, British conception a constitution is empirical and descriptive.

But, as should be evident, it was in essence the normative and prescriptive American conception of a written constitution that Llewellyn rejected as being neither empirical nor descriptive. Despite the presence of the written text, he wrote, "I am not arguing that the United States *ought* to have the sort of constitution loosely designated as 'unwritten.' I am arguing that they *have* such a Constitution, and that nobody can stop their having such a Constitution."[31] The unwritten Constitution is the test for the reality of the written Constitution, he argued, and not, as the orthodox theory would have it, the other way around: "Wherever there are today established practices 'under' or 'in accordance with' the Document, *it is only the practice which can legitimatize the words as being still part of our going Constitution. It is not the words which legitimatize the practice.*"[32] It is in this sense that Llewellyn presaged Fisher's distinction between constitutions and the forces outside the law that endow constitutions with life and reality. Both are at bottom talking about the relation between text and world that I call constitutional textuality, and both distinguish between text and world in such a way that they ground the text in human activity while they appear to deny – explicitly in Llewellyn's case and, if I am not doing him a disservice, implicitly in Fisher's case – that the text is capable of structuring human activity. Put differently, it appears that Llewellyn, and perhaps Fisher, asserts that the world constitutes the text while denying that the text constitutes the world. The interpretive theory of constitutional textuality would hold, I believe, both sides of this coin: The world constitutes the text insofar as the text constitutes the world.[33]

Yet I would suggest that Llewellyn's concept of institutions in his article points in the direction of the interpretive theory of constitutional textuality. To be sure, he seems to reaffirm the positivist theory when he states that "it is institutions which test whether there is still force in the Words, and how much force, and what that force is. It is institutions which validate the

---

[30] McIlwain, *Constitutionalism: Ancient and Modern*, 2–3.
[31] Llewellyn, "The Constitution as an Institution," 2, note 5.
[32] Ibid., 12.
[33] I hypothesize that the positivist theory of constitutional textuality is a reductionism that might be characterized as holding *either* side of this coin alone. Legal realism argues that the world constitutes the text, whereas what Llewellyn called the orthodox theory argues that the text constitutes the world. The interpretive theory thus would differ from the positivist theory in that it supersedes rather than takes one leg of the dichotomy.

Words, not the Words which validate the institutions."[34] But in a longer passage, Llewellyn offers a nuanced and suggestive definition of institutions:

An institution is in first instance a set of ways of living and doing. It is not, *in* [the] *first instance*, a matter of words or rules. The existence of an institution lies first of all and last of all in the fact that people do behave in certain patterns *a, b* and *c,* and do not behave in other conceivable patterns *d* to *w.* And the probability that an institution will continue coincides with whatever probability there is that people will continue so to behave. Every living constitution is an institution; it *lives* only so far as that is true. And the difference between a "written" and an "unwritten" constitution lies only in the fact that the shape of action in the former case is *somewhat* influenced by the presence of a particular document, and of particular attitudes toward it, and particular ways of dealing with its language.[35]

What is important here is Llewellyn's characterization of the Constitution as an institution, which in talking of "a set of ways of living and doing" he defines as a form of life. The Constitution, in other words, is a social practice, and when Llewellyn points to certain determinate patterns of behavior he is talking of a structured social practice. It "involves ways of behavior deeply set and settled in the make-up of these people – and it involves not patterns of doing (or of inhibition) merely, but also accompanying patterns of thinking and of emotion."[36] Characterizing the Constitution in this way as an institution, and thus as a structured social practice, is a step toward the perspective of the interpretive theory of constitutional textuality.

Nevertheless, Llewellyn's account here remains grounded to a great degree on the positivist theory of constitutional textuality because it maintains the gap between text and world. Llewellyn appears to bridge the gap because he redefines "Constitution": If Constitution were the text – what he calls the Document – he still would have to explain how it relates to the society structured by it, but by conceiving Constitution as the unwritten constitution – the ongoing, living institution, the structured social practice – he relegates the text to a shadow existence. At first counterposing the document and actual social practice, Llewellyn dissolves the reality of the document into actual social practice. And yet an element of the document does hang on in his account:

Neither, as has been indicated, would I deny the shaping influence of the Document – which is to say, of men's ways and attitudes with reference to the Document – upon the going Constitution. The argument is that there is only one way of knowing whether, and how far, any portion of the Document is still alive; and that is to watch what men are doing and how men feel, in the connection.[37]

---

34 Llewellyn, "The Constitution as an Institution," 17.
35 Ibid., 17–18 (footnote omitted).
36 Ibid., 18.
37 Ibid., 14–15 (footnote omitted).

Here the document does appear to have an effect on actual social practice, but then that effect dissolves again. The fundamental dichotomy that runs through Llewellyn's discussion – and through legal realism generally – is that between the Constitution conceived as normative, as a set of rules and words, and the Constitution conceived as empirical, as actual social practice. In his effort to deny what he takes to be the orthodox theory's adoption of the former conception exclusively, Llewellyn affirms the latter conception exclusively. The interpretive theory of constitutional textuality affirms both conceptions – or, put differently, it undercuts the dichotomy. It argues that the Constitution is indeed actual social practice, but that actual social practice is itself rule-governed behavior because it occurs in terms of individuals' understanding of both the norms they are following and their activity of following norms. What Llewellyn calls the Document – what I call the text – structures the actual social practice he considers the Constitution because people engaged in actual social practice understand themselves, at least indirectly, as standing in some relation to the constitutional text. American citizens, implicitly when not explicitly, are all ongoing interpreters of the Constitution. By conceiving the Constitution as a discourse that *constitutes* the forms of actual social practice, the interpretive theory of constitutional textuality attempts to avoid the empirical–normative split that places the Constitution in the normative realm.

We can see the intellectual descendants of Llewellyn and a similar disregard of the essentially constitutive nature of the Constitution, and of law generally, in contemporary methodological conventions in the field of judicial behavior. Lawrence Baum's concern in his *American Courts: Process and Policy*[38] is with "Understanding Courts as Institutions," as he entitles the first section of his first chapter, and the question of how properly to understand an institution is the major metatheoretical issue here. Specifically, that issue is the nature of the theoretical significance that Baum ascribes to what he himself states as the central fact about courts: "The courts work within a legal framework. In other words, the decisions of judges and juries involve the application of legal rules to the facts of specific cases."[39] Similarly, what theoretical effect does the following fact Baum cites about courts have on our choice of an adequate analytical approach to law and written constitutions? The training of lawyers and judges, he states,

emphasizes the duty of adherence to the law. People who become judges have been taught that they should withstand external pressures in order to follow legal rules,

---

[38] Lawrence Baum, *American Courts: Process and Policy* (Boston: Houghton Mifflin Company, 1986). The undergraduates at whom Baum aims this book more than likely presume the legal perspective he describes, and thus he might overemphasize the personal perspective in order to achieve some compensatory balance. Nevertheless, because the personal perspective dominates the judicial-politics paradigm, we may legitimately focus on it here as an analytical foil.

[39] Baum, *American Courts*, 9.

and to a considerable degree judges do follow what they see as the dictates of the law, even in the face of outside influence.⁴⁰

The question is, what is involved in our taking seriously what Baum calls here "the duty of adherence to the law" and "the dictates of the law"? Baum's work is interesting here because it represents the conventional wisdom of the behavioral approach to law in the judicial-politics field, an approach that cannot account for the constitutive – and thus binding – character of law and the Constitution.

Baum lays out three principal approaches to understanding courts as institutions, modes of analysis he calls the "legal perspective," the "personal perspective," and the "environmental perspective." According to the legal perspective on court processes,

> the behavior of decision makers can be explained almost entirely by the law. According to this perspective, judges are given and accept the duty to follow legal rules; therefore, they do so. Under the direction of judges, jurors also make their decisions by applying the appropriate legal rules. Thus it follows that if we wish to explain court decisions we need only refer to the applicable provisions of the law.⁴¹

From this point of view, according to Baum, court decisions are motivated by a simple commitment to the law, whereby, as Supreme Court Justice Owen Roberts once stated, "The judicial branch of the government has only one duty, – to lay the article of the Constitution which is involved beside the statute which is challenged and to decide whether the latter squares with the former."⁴² Such "mechanical" jurisprudence,⁴³ if it truly ever has existed in practice, creates for Baum "...the difficulty of explaining some kinds of behavior by judges and juries in legal terms. Why, for example, do the members of a panel of appellate judges, each applying the same body of law to the same case, disagree as to the appropriate decision?"⁴⁴ The need to

---

⁴⁰ Ibid., 14.

⁴¹ Ibid., 9. Elsewhere, though, Baum does state that while the Court may not be entirely different from other political institutions, it is, as a court of law, not entirely like them either: "As a political body, the Supreme Court is similar to other government institutions, such as Congress and the administrative agencies. Yet it would be a mistake to view the Court as identical to those other, nonjudicial policymakers. The Court's behavior and its position in the political system are affected in fundamental ways by the fact that it is a *court*." Lawrence Baum, *The Supreme Court* (Washington, DC: CQ Press, 1981), 2.

⁴² Cited in Philip Bobbitt, *Constitutional Fate* (New York: Oxford University Press, 1982), 29.

⁴³ Cf. Roscoe Pound, "Mechanical Jurisprudence," *Columbia Law Review*, Vol. 8, 1908, 605ff.

⁴⁴ Baum, *American Courts*, 10. This raises the problem of the nature of disagreement in law, in the attempted explanation of which Dworkin distinguishes between theoretical and empirical disagreement in order to assert the reality of the former. *Law's Empire*, he states at 11, "is about theoretical disagreement in law. It aims to understand what kind of disagreement this is and then to construct and defend a particular theory about the proper grounds of law." Though not unrelated to our concerns here, this issue is beyond the scope of the present discussion. It is worth noting, however, that if Baum's account of judicial decision making

explain such disagreement empirically in view of the alleged impersonality of the legal perspective gives rise to Baum's second approach to law and written constitutions, the personal perspective.

From this point of view, court decisions are motivated not by a simple commitment to the law, but rather by the judge's own values, self-interest, and personality:

> In its strongest form, the legal perspective assumes that court decision makers are motivated only by a commitment to the law. In contrast, what might be called the personal perspective allows for a broader range of motivations that can influence behavior. Judges, for instance, may act on the basis of their own values, self-interest, or personality characteristics. Thus the processes of the courts and the outcomes of their cases can be seen in terms of the motivations of the people who produce them.[45]

The key factor from this perspective is not the law, but rather the individual judge's policy preferences. If the terms "objective" and "subjective" refer to sources of decision-making criteria external and internal to the judge,[46] then what Baum calls the legal perspective is an objectivist approach that sees court decisions as motivated by a simple commitment to the law, whereas what he calls the personal perspective is a subjectivist approach that sees court decisions as motivated by the judge's own values, self-interest, or personality characteristics. In these terms, the answer to his question as to why "appellate judges, each applying the same body of law to the same case, disagree as to the appropriate decision" is his claim (in reference to the Supreme Court) that

> differences in the responses of justices to the same case are primarily a product of their preferences about the policy issues in the case. External pressures and the law may move the whole Court in one direction or the other, but disagreements among the justices result chiefly from their views about policy.[47]

Baum clearly considers this perspective appropriate and fruitful, but he does want to avoid turning the study of courts and law into merely a branch of

---

is to be complete, it would have to account as well for agreement in law and generally for what disposes judges to follow the dictates of the law when, on his view, they could and often do choose not to do so.

[45] Baum, *American Courts*, 11–12.

[46] "Whether and to what extent constitutional judgment is or can be objective (or constrained) depends on the kinds of norms or value sources that judges do or can look to in deciding whether challenged actions are unconstitutional, and on what the process of 'looking to' those sources amounts to. Whether the Supreme Court is behaving legitimately when it exercises the authority of the Constitution, by contrast, depends on what the authority of the Constitution is." Larry Simon, "The Authority of the Constitution and Its Meaning: A Preface to a Theory of Constitutional Interpretation," 58 *Southern California Law Review* 603, 606 (1985).

[47] Baum, *American Courts*, 272.

psychology. Consequently, he sets forth a third approach to the subject, what he calls the "environmental perspective." This approach, he says, "views courts in relation to the government and society of which they are a part. In other words, it looks to the various ways in which courts are shaped by external forces."[48] Such external forces include, according to Baum, the pattern of social values and attitudes and the distribution of economic and political power, but he adds that such forces confront the relative autonomy that courts enjoy due to such factors as life terms, norms restricting direct lobbying of judges and juries, and legal training.

The metatheoretical issue in all of this is in Baum's concept of the dictates of the law. External forces may well be what he calls the "pattern of social values and attitudes" and the distribution of economic and political power, and they may well interact with the institutional autonomy of the courts, and judges certainly do have personal values and policy preferences – but where in all of this is some theory of law? One cannot ask an author to write a different book from the one he actually provides us, but the whole issue of courts here seems to beg the question of what law as a system of rules is – that is, what is the significance of that for understanding the behavior of courts? Conversely, what understanding of law as a system of rules is presupposed by a given perspective on the behavior of courts? Consider again Baum's overview of the personal perspective, which he appears to regard as at least first among equals:

> By recognizing these sorts of personal motivations, we can understand courts as institutions with their own dynamics. It is useful to think of the set of people who participate in a particular court as an organization or a work group. All the participants bring to the work group their own motivations, and the processes of the court and the outcomes of its cases emerge from the interaction of these motivations.[49]

We surely would want to argue that courts are institutions with their own dynamics, but note that in Baum's description any such dynamics seem metatheoretically reducible to the interaction of individual motivations.[50] There appears to be no obviously independent structural context, beyond the external forces Baum mentions, that explicitly, specifically, and meaningfully includes the law or a written constitution themselves. The courts do indeed operate within a legal framework, a framework that provides and mandates certain procedural guidelines that Baum appears to treat as a kind of internal functional equivalent to the external forces. Yet such guidelines are an immensely important element of what one means by the concept of a legal framework. As we saw Baum state earlier, central to a legal framework

---

[48] Ibid., 13.
[49] Ibid., 13 (footnote omitted).
[50] See the later discussion of institutionalism.

is the duty of adherence to the dictates of the law. Yet what is the theoretical significance of his distinction among three sets of criteria in adjudication: (1) "the dictates of the law," (2) "external pressures" or "outside influence," and (3) a judge's "own values, self-interest, or personality characteristics"? What meaning has Baum's approach left for the notion of "the dictates of the law," and how do the dictates of the law relate to the other two sets of adjudicatory criteria? Baum himself does not tell us and, in fact, does not take the dictates of the law seriously.

The reason he does not take the law itself seriously is that, in his own words, "two important conditions make adherence to the law an inadequate explanation of judicial behavior. First, there is the considerable discretion that the law often leaves to court decision makers."[51] That discretion, Baum asserts briefly, stems from a deliberate legislative intent to leave certain matters up to judges and juries, and more commonly from unintended ambiguities in the law. The more important factor in the inadequacy of legal explanation, however,

has to do with the participants' motivations, which do not derive from the law alone. Undoubtedly, most judges strongly believe that they should follow the law in deciding cases and supervising court proceedings. But judges also hold attitudes about desirable public policy, feel emotional needs (such as the wish for self-esteem), and perceive external pressures to handle cases in certain ways. All these factors create motivations that affect the judges' behavior, either consciously or unconsciously. And the same is true of jurors.[52]

Given a claim such as this, however, it is difficult to see how Baum can take seriously his claim that "the law does remain central to the operation of the judiciary. Most courts are pervaded by a legal atmosphere in which people speak and think in terms of legal principles."[53] As a result, beyond a couple of descriptive or behavioral references, Baum offers no analysis, or any indication of the significance, of the claim that people operate in terms of legal principles.

The question, then, is, what does it mean to say that people operate in terms of legal principles? What does it mean to explain behavior, especially political behavior, in terms of legal principles? To place this issue in

---

[51] Ibid., 10.

[52] Ibid.

[53] Ibid., 11. Contrast his claim elsewhere, however, that "the Supreme Court makes decisions within the framework of the law. The policy choices that the Court faces are framed as matters of legal interpretation. In this respect the Court's task differs from that of Congress and of some administrative agencies, and the legal context in which the justices work provides a constraint from which legislators are free." Baum, *The Supreme Court*, 2. The analytical task, then, is to retain and explain the distinctive nature of decision making "within the framework of the law," of framing policy choices "as matters of legal interpretation," and of the "constraint" of the legal context while providing a coherent account of the political nature of the Court. Somehow, though, this task tends to get lost in judicial-politics accounts.

a broader context, it is helpful to understand an analysis like Baum's in terms of two general approaches that political science has traditionally taken to constitutional-legal practice. The first approach, one that is in scholarly terms rather outdated, is what we can call the "objectivist" or "formalist" theory of constitutional-legal practice. On this view, we understand government and politics in terms of – that is, by reducing them to – constitutional-legal practice. A standard example of this formalist approach is the study of the presidency in terms of that institution's formal structure, powers, and responsibilities. The classic work of this sort is perhaps Edwin Corwin's *The President: Office and Powers*,[54] according to which one understands the politics of the presidency in terms of its legal and constitutional development since 1787. To understand by analogy, imagine the relation between the official rulebook of baseball and an actual baseball game. Strange as it may seem, to say that we understand government and politics in terms of constitutional-legal practice is like saying that we can understand and appreciate baseball merely by reading the rulebook without ever bothering to watch an actual game. With regard to the issue of constraints on the political power and discretion of judges, there is on this view nothing at all personal in judicial decision making; instead, judges are empty vessels, so to speak, through which the Constitution is poured. When a judge renders a decision, it is not the judge but rather the Constitution that is talking.

In reaction to what many people took to be the naive character of this mode of analysis, there developed a second approach, legal realism and sociological jurisprudence, which we can call the "subjectivist theory" of constitutional-legal practice. The contemporary field of judicial behavior in mainstream social science and, indeed, the putatively more radical orientation of the Critical Legal Studies movement are the metatheoretical descendants of legal realism and sociological jurisprudence. On this view, we understand constitutional-legal practice in terms of – that is, by reducing them to – government and politics. The reason for this is the metatheory of contemporary social science. With the turn toward the behavioral approach in political science by the end of the 1950s, the objectivist, constitutional-legal approach came to be seen as purely normative and prescriptive analysis, unnecessary and even deleterious to a properly empirical description and explanation of political behavior. As Joseph Bessette and Jeffrey Tulis characterize this development, "political scientists were turning their attention away from formal rules and procedures to focus instead on actual political behavior, which, it was argued, was little influenced by laws and constitutions."[55] Using the baseball analogy again, we can say that on this approach, we just

---

54 Fourth ed. (New York: New York University Press, 1957), originally published in 1940.
55 "The Constitution, Politics, and the Presidency," in Joseph M. Bessette and Jeffrey Tulis, eds., *The Presidency in the Constitutional Order* (Baton Rouge: Louisiana State University Press, 1981), 4.

watch what those people standing or running around out in the stadium are doing; we do not need or look at the rulebook at all. With regard to the issue of constraints on the political power and discretion of judges, on this view judges speak through constitutional-legal practice in the sense that constitutional-legal practice consists of empty vessels through which the personal or class values and preferences of judges are poured. Consequently, one must attend to the origin and structure of such values and preferences. As one writer on legal theory states this, the emphasis of legal realism is

on the need to explore the sociological background of legal rules; it explains valid law within a given community as being a prediction of what the courts will probably decide in particular cases; and it postulates the need to investigate the actual way in which the various forms of judicial and administrative process function and insists that this must not be limited to a mere study of the paper rules that ostensibly bind and guide judges and officials.[56]

When a judge renders a decision, then, her legal terminology should not obscure the fact that it is she and not the Constitution that is talking.[57] Much of social science takes this approach, radically or otherwise, to constitutional-legal practice: The fields we call "legal process," "judicial behavior," or "judicial politics" tend to look at courts as political bodies not significantly different in kind from political bodies like legislatures. In other words, not only is the constitutional-legal framework essentially irrelevant to an understanding of the political behavior of presidents, governors, legislators, and so on, but, one may say without too much exaggeration, it is irrelevant also to an understanding of courts and the legal system.

As should be obvious, both of these theories about constitutional-legal practice, the objectivist and the subjectivist, are extremely reductionist approaches that collapse one side of the assumed dichotomy of law and politics into the other. Perhaps due to the earlier sway of the objectivist approach, the scholarly emphasis has been markedly on the subjectivist side for some time. In the proper attempt to reject the claim that rules analysis is sufficient, however, that emphasis led to the improper attempt to reject the claim that rules analysis is necessary. In general form, the metatheoretical problem is the familiar one of the role of ideas and norms in human affairs; more specifically, it is the issue of the explanatory role of rules in understanding both political phenomena generally and constitutional-legal phenomena in particular. Legal realists, and their contemporary social-science descendants, "tend to minimize the normative or prescriptive element in law. Law appears to the realist as a body of facts rather than a system of rules, a going institution rather than a set of norms. What judges, attorneys, police and prison officials

[56] Dennis Lloyd, *The Idea of Law* (Harmondsworth, England: Penguin Books, 1970), 217.
[57] Indeed, pursuing this approach more radically leads to the thought that law is a branch of psychology, a step taken by the Scandinavian realist Karl Olivecrona. See Lloyd, *The Idea of Law*, 26.

actually do about law cases – essentially this, to the legal realists, appears to be the law itself."[58] The methodological individualism of legal-process behavioralism appears to reduce law to simply the private policy preferences of Hobbesian or Lockeian individuals, and this is to misunderstand the character of law and legal systems. As Sotirios Barber has argued, "American legal realism was part of a broader intellectual persuasion that sought to deny the reality of general ideas, as opposed to what were called 'empirical facts,' and ends or purposes, as opposed to ultimately subconscious 'behavioral determinants' of events most people call 'actions.'"[59] Social scientists tend to reduce ideas, norms, and institutions to the behavior of atomistically conceived individuals, with the consequence that an allegedly empirical metatheoretical approach in fact is simply conceptually incapable of describing and explaining constitutional-legal practice empirically. Without the idea of a rule, which involves more than "the ideas of orders, obedience, habits, and threats," as H. L. A. Hart wrote in 1961, "we cannot hope to elucidate even the most elementary forms of law."[60] As any American who has observed a cricket match without understanding the rules of cricket can attest, we can talk about what people are doing in a physical sense yet nevertheless not really understand the meaning or point of what they are doing.

The general theoretical point I would make is that absorbing or dissolving law into judicial process or policy studies, as the field seems to do, is analogous to reducing chess to the behavior of the individual pieces in such a way that one misses the constitutive character of what we mean by chess as a rule-governed game. Dennis Lloyd sets out this theoretical point very nicely as follows:

Certainly the law, in no derogatory sense, does resemble a kind of game. The characteristic of a game is a self-contained system of rules which provide a framework of reference and meaning for certain types of contest which can be fought out to a result within that framework. Any such game employs a number of general concepts, or notions, which are conventional in the sense that their meaning and function are arbitrarily defined by the rules of the game, but which can operate perfectly meaningfully within their particular linguistic framework. The pawn or the knight in chess is not just the name of a particularly shaped piece of wood standing on a chequered board, but is a general concept whose meaning is given by a study of the rules of chess. Does a pawn "exist" in a sense other than an actual piece of wood of a certain shape? Or is it a mere fiction in the mind of a chess-player? Surely it can be said that the confusion here is to apply the language of existence to something to which it is not readily applicable. A pawn does not exist in the sense of being a tangible entity, but it is a meaningful concept which functions intelligibly within the context of a game of chess. . . . We know that chess is a game and that the pieces only operate

---

[58] Edgar Bodenheimer, *Jurisprudence: The Philosophy and Method of the Law* (Cambridge, MA: Harvard University Press, 1962), 116 (footnote omitted).

[59] Barber, *On What the Constitution Means*, 15.

[60] H. L. A. Hart, *The Concept of Law* (Oxford: Oxford University Press, 1961), 78.

within that game. This does not imply, however, that the concepts of chess are therefore meaningless superfluities, so that chess can be reduced to no more than people sitting opposite each other and moving the pieces about in particular patterns. For the meaning and purpose of these activities is contained in the system of rules. Chess can no more be reduced to human behavior and psychological reactions than can a legal system. The one, like the other, is a normative system within whose framework, linguistic though it may be, human behaviour is rendered intelligible.[61]

We can understand a chess game whose moves are printed in the newspaper without having to learn, however interesting they may be, the psychology, sociology, biography, and so on of the players. What we have to understand, whether the phenomenon under investigation is chess or constitutional-legal practice, is the system of rules that defines and structures the game or practice for the actual participants, and the equally central point is that the defining and structuring of the practice for the actual participants is *not* reducible to the psychology, sociology, biography, and so on of those individuals. In that sense, I think that law can and must be understood in an accurate and very interesting way as empirical and normative – to use questionably valid social-science commonplaces – at one and the same time. Law must be seen to have an ontologically public rather than private character; it must be seen to have a social reality irreducible to the sum total of individual preferences. To say that law is or is reducible to psychology means that law is ontologically private, whereas to conceive law as a game means that law is ontologically public. In other words, law is constitutive.

Paradoxically, perhaps, the way we see law as public is to understand the phenomenon of constitutional-legal practice from the internal point of view of its participants as well as the external point of view of detached observers.[62] As Hart described this distinction:

When a social group has certain rules of conduct, this fact affords an opportunity for many closely related yet different kinds of assertion; for it is possible to be concerned with the rules, either merely as an observer who does not himself accept them, or as a member of the group which accepts and uses them as guides to conduct. We may call these respectively the "external" and the "internal points of view."[63]

---

[61] Lloyd, *The Idea of Law*, 286–7 (footnote omitted).

[62] The paradox lies in the fact that the public character of constitutional-legal practice is comprehensible only from the internal point of view, whereas the private character of law is the direct implication of the external point of view.

[63] Hart, *The Concept of Law*, 86. Dworkin likewise claims that law is an argumentative practice and thus can be grasped accurately only if one accords the necessary attention to its internal dimension: "Of course, law is a social phenomenon. But its complexity, function, and consequence all depend on one special feature of its structure. Legal practice, unlike many other social phenomena, is *argumentative*. Every actor in the practice understands that what it permits or requires depends on the truth of certain propositions that are given sense only by and within the practice; the practice consists in large part in deploying and arguing about these propositions." Dworkin, *Law's Empire*, 13. Despite areas of agreement between them,

Behavioral approaches such as Baum's want to have a purely external account of legal or judicial behavior in the sense of describing it from our – the observers' – standpoint, rather than taking into account the internal side of what courts believe themselves to be doing. While we need not eliminate the external account in favor of the internal account, as realism rightly argues, we need not go to the other extreme, as realism seems to do, of rejecting or eliminating the internal account in favor of the external account. In the latter case, according to Hart,

> an observer is content merely to record the regularities of observable behavior in which conformity with the rules partly consists and those further regularities, in the form of the hostile reaction, reproofs, or punishments, with which deviations from the rules are met. After a time the external observer may, on the basis of the regularities observed, correlate deviation with hostile reaction, and be able to predict with a fair measure of success, and to assess the chances that a deviation from the group's normal behaviour will meet with hostile reaction or punishment.[64]

If, however, such an observer, Hart continues, "does not give any account of the manner in which members of the group who accept the rules view their own regular behaviour, his description of their life cannot be in terms of rules at all, and so not in the terms of the rule-dependent notions of obligation or duty. Instead, it will be in terms of observable regularities of conduct, predictions, probabilities, and signs."[65] Why does it matter whether an observer can account for behavior in terms of rules? It matters because the external observer simply will not understand the social phenomena he wishes to study:

> What the external point of view, which limits itself to the observable regularities of behaviour, cannot reproduce is the way in which the rules function as rules in the lives of those who normally are the majority of society. These are the officials, lawyers, or private persons who use them, in one situation after another, as guides to the conduct of social life, as the basis for claims, demands, admissions, criticism, or punishment, viz., in all the familiar transactions of life according to rules. For them the violation of a rule is not merely a basis for the prediction that a hostile reaction will follow but a *reason* for hostility.[66]

The external point of view taken by behavioral social science purportedly in the service of doing empirical justice to social phenomena, in other words, turns out to be incapable of rendering a truly empirical account of those phenomena.

however, we must remain aware that Dworkin's major jurisprudential concern has been to attack the position of legal positivism that Hart has articulated and defended so skillfully.

[64] Hart, *The Concept of Law*, 87.
[65] Ibid., 87.
[66] Ibid., 88.

If we are to account successfully for the social synthetic a priori – that is, the constitutive – character of constitutional-legal practice, we have to employ a metatheoretically fundamental concept of social practice of the sort that James March and Johan Olsen touched upon in their discussion in 1984 of what they called the "new institutionalism."[67] Recall Baum's description of the personal perspective on law and the courts:

Judges, for instance, may act on the basis of their own values, self-interest, or personality characteristics. Thus the processes of the courts and the outcomes of their cases can be seen in terms of the motivations of the people who produce them.

This focus on individuals has proved very useful in the study of the Supreme Court's decision making, with scholars typically viewing the Court's decisions primarily as reflections of one motivational factor, the justices' policy preferences. Divisions on the Court can be explained by differences in values, and the Court's collective position results from the sum of the nine justices' views on policy.[68]

This perspective on law and the courts, an essentially behavioral approach to such phenomena, would appear to be precisely the kind of methodology that March and Olsen describe here:

[S]ubstantial elements of modern theoretical work in political science assume that political phenomena are best understood as the aggregate consequences of behavior comprehensible at the individual or group level.

Such theories depend on two presumptions. The first presumption is that a political system consists of a number (often a large number) of elementary actors.... The second presumption is that collective behavior is best understood as stemming from the (possibly intricate) interweaving of behavior understandable at a lower level of aggregation. Discovering, or deducing, the collective consequences may be difficult, even impossible; but the central faith is that outcomes at the collective level depend only on the intricacies of the interactions among the individual actors, that concepts suggesting autonomous behavior at the aggregate level are certainly superfluous and probably deleterious.[69]

Their claim that "Outcomes at the system level are thought to be determined by the interactions of individuals acting consistently in terms of the axioms of individual behavior, whatever they may be"[70] is precisely the claim we see in Baum's statement that "the processes of the courts and the outcomes of

---

[67] James G. March and Johan Olsen, "The New Institutionalism: Organizational Factors in Political Life," *American Political Science Review*, Vol. 78, No. 3 (September 1984), 734–49. "This new institutionalism can be presented and discussed as an epistemological perspective of profound importance to understanding social science" they say at 738, though their own concern in the article is not this broad. For interesting directions in the area of law and courts, see Cornell W. Clayton and Howard Gillman, eds., *Supreme Court Decision-Making: New Institutionalist Approaches* (Chicago: University of Chicago Press, 1999).
[68] Baum, *American Courts*, 11–12.
[69] March and Olsen, "The New Institutionalism," 735–6.
[70] Ibid., 736.

their cases can be seen in terms of the motivations of the people who produce them."

The new institutionalism, by contrast, emphasizes the embeddedness of political phenomena in institutions – that is, social practices – conceived as preexisting structures of rules, norms, expectations, and the like that define and constrain individual choice. The concept of structure is fundamental, as March and Olsen explain:

> By a political structure we mean a collection of institutions, rules of behavior, norms, roles, physical arrangements, buildings, and archives that are relatively invariant in the face of turnover of individuals and relatively resilient to the idiosyncratic preferences and expectations of individuals. In contrast to theories that assume action is choice based on individual values and expectations, theories of political structure assume action is the fulfillment of duties and obligations. The difference is important. In a choice metaphor, we assume that political actors consult personal preferences and subjective expectations, then select actions that are as consistent as possible with those preferences and expectations. In a duty metaphor, we assume that political actors associate certain actions with certain situations by rules of appropriateness. What is appropriate for a particular person in a particular situation is defined by the political and social system and transmitted through socialization.[71]

The polis, so to speak, once more becomes logically prior to the atomistic individual. On such a view, one must understand constitutional-legal practice not epiphenomenally as reducible to or translatable into the preferences of isolated, rationally calculating independent decision makers, but rather as having its own social reality and integrity.[72] Having such reality and integrity, constitutional-legal practice structures the field of political phenomena and, most important, thus can be understood to have the capacity to constrain – that is, *not* to determine, but rather to define, legitimate, and limit – political behavior.[73] Only from this perspective can we ascribe real and proper significance to Baum's claim "that . . . to a considerable degree

---

[71] Ibid., 741.

[72] The "market" is a similar phenomenon that exemplifies the reality of social forms, in that we talk of the market as a real entity that structures behavior. March and Olsen in "The New Institutionalism" continue to affirm the autonomy – what I would call the constitutive character – of institutions: "Without denying the importance of both the social context of politics and the motives of individual actors, the new institutionalism insists on a more autonomous role for political institutions. . . . [Such institutions] are arenas for contending social forces, but they are also collections of standard operating procedures and structures that define and defend interests. They are political actors in their own right" (738).

[73] Recall in this context Thomas J. Anton's analysis in "Pluralism and Local Politics," *Administrative Science Quarterly*, Vol. 7, No. 4 (March 1963), 425–57, of the difference between the structural approach of sociology and the atomistic approach of political science – what Anton calls "pluralism" in this article – to the question of power. The latter employs "a view of society (or community, or any other social unit) as an aggregation of different individuals motivated by self-interest, predominantly rational (in the sense that they are conscious of

judges do follow what they see as the dictates of the law, even in the face of outside influence."[74]

To speak of the embeddedness of political phenomena in institutions conceived as preexisting structures of rules, norms, and expectations that define and constrain individual choice is, however, to point to the thesis that constitutional discourse is not just linguistic, but ontological. It is to the theoretical underpinnings of this idea of the constitutive character of the Constitution that we now turn.

their interests and active in seeking their fulfillment), and free from any permanent relationships with anyone or anything else" (447). More broadly,

Sociologists are interested in analyzing communities as systems of action; pluralists see communities as nothing more than aggregations of individuals whose behavior, far from being systematic in any way, is more or less randomly determined. The sociologist understands power as one aspect of all human action and closely related to other aspects; the pluralist thinks of power as a substance, separate from other substances, and therefore capable of being weighed and measured. The basic unit of analysis for the sociologist is the role, composed of repeated actions of persons in the system; the basic unit of analysis for the pluralist is the actor-individual, whose actions are seen as basically unique and nonrepetitive. (447–8)

Conceived in "pluralist" terms as an atomistic individual "whose actions are seen as basically unique and nonrepetitive," a judge in the exercise of his powers quite logically raises the question of how one can control his discretion.

[74] Baum, *American Courts*, 14.

9

The Ontology of Constitutional Discourse (II)

The interpretive analysis of constitutional-legal practice is an attempt to take seriously the idea of rule-governed behavior in a way that, as the previous chapter argued, the objectivist and subjectivist theories do not. It does so by reaffirming the internal approach necessary for an adequate understanding of the constitutive character of constitutional-legal practice. On this interpretive analysis, we understand constitutional-legal practice in terms of government and politics, and we understand government and politics in terms of constitutional-legal practice. Consider how one would assess a standard legal-realist claim from the interpretive point of view:

> Law is defined not as a set of logical propositions but in terms of official action. Law is what courts (or other officials) do, not what they say. Until a court has passed on certain facts, some realists argued, there is no law on the subject yet in existence, for the opinion of lawyers is only a guess as to what the courts will decide. Since law is defined in terms of official action (and not of the rules which should guide action), it follows that any force that will influence a judge in reaching a decision (whether corruption, indigestion, or partiality for the other sex) is a fit subject for jurisprudence. Much scorn is poured on the classical jurists for being deceived by what the courts said they were doing instead of examining what they actually did.[1]

Notice the fundamental distinction, the dichotomy, that runs through this passage – that between law conceived as a set of logical propositions or as what courts say and law conceived as official action or as what courts do. This is the dichotomy that the interpretive framework attempts to undercut: Law is indeed official action or what courts do but, as the internal point of view instructs us, official action or what courts do occurs in terms of the participants' rule-governed behavior, their own understanding of the norms

[1] G. W. Paton, *A Text-book of Jurisprudence*, 4th ed. (Oxford: Oxford University Press, 1972), 23–4.

they are following. Using the baseball analogy, this approach makes the commonsensical claim that we can truly understand a baseball game only if we both know the rules and watch an actual game. With regard to the issue of constraints on the political power and discretion of judges, this view claims that while judges certainly have their own preferences and values, constitutional-legal practice structures and limits those personal preferences and values because constitutional-legal practice provides a kind of language or computer program through which – and only through which – judges are able to speak.[2]

Epistemologically, all of this is an attack on methodological atomism as a viable basis upon which to understand law. The new emphasis on the public character of law suggests that law is indeed a social synthetic–a priori, and is thus anti-Cartesian if we define Cartesianism to be, among other things, the logical priority of the private over the public.[3] Think of Hobbes's system for a moment: Law is the command of the sovereign, underlying which are norms that are those of the individual to whom everyone else defers. Norms, in this Hobbesian – that is, epistemologically Cartesian – view are still private and individual rather than public and social. The only things real are private, individual, atomistic interests that conflict with each other and require adjustment by law conceived as the agency of dispute resolution. A more accurate understanding of the social synthetic–a priori character of law, in contrast, is to recognize that as members of a society we are engaged in an activity – a game, as it were – bigger than any individual, with its own integrity. The whole idea of a game is that it is not reducible to the preferences of an individual or the set of preferences of a collection of individuals, and yet at the same time it is not a metaphysical entity. This

---

[2] See John Brigham, *Constitutional Language: An Interpretation of Judicial Decision* (Westport, CT: Greenwood Press, 1978), for an account of this notion of language. According to Brigham, "an activity such as law creates a unique sphere in which a variety of meaningful activities are carried on. We understand these activities, i.e., we have some idea of what constitutes the legal 'form of life,' when we become familiar with the conventions that comprise the activity of interpreting the Constitution. The grammatical structures evident in the Constitution indicate the kinds of interpretations that are possible with regard to the words and concepts in the Constitution" (59).

[3] At the root of what H. Jefferson Powell ascribes to the Framers as their original interpretive theory is the notion of the essentially public character of language. See Powell, "The Original Understanding of Original Intent," 98 *Harvard Law Review* 885, 895–6 (1985): "The late eighteenth century common lawyer conceived an instrument's 'intent' – and therefore its meaning – not as what the drafters meant by their words but rather as what judges employing the 'artificial reason and judgment of law' understood 'the reasonable and legal meaning' of those words to be" (ibid). Thus, Powell states that "Madison's interpretive theory rested primarily on the distinction he drew between the public meaning or intent of a state paper, a law, or a constitution, and the personal opinions of the individuals who had written or adopted it. The distinction was implicit in the common law's treatment of the concept of 'intent,' but Madison made it explicit and thereby illuminated its implications and underlying rationale." Ibid., 935.

compares, of course, to the parallel undercutting of the normative–empirical dichotomy. "No doubt," the legal realist maintains, "the rules were one of several factors influencing court decisions, but to know these was only a beginning, for these only represented what courts *say*, and what really matters is not words but actions, not what the court *says*, but what it *does*."[4] One must be careful about assuming the clarity and validity of this purported dichotomy: What the court actually does may well diverge from what it nominally says, but what the court actually does is structured by its sense of rules and the language of the law. The distinction, in other words, is between the court's stating the norms it is actually following and stating the norms it believes itself to be following – not between following norms and not following norms.

Consequently, by accepting the social reality of constitutional-legal forms, the interpretive approach reasserts the essentially public character of constitutional-legal practice and thus takes the Constitution seriously. It conceives our constitutional-legal system as a social synthetic–a priori, to borrow a Kantian term, with an ontological reality of its own that is at once normative and empirical or, preferably and more accurately, constitutive. As such, constitutional-legal practice in the broadest, unified sense must be conceived macroscopically as a social activity with its own structural logic capable of constraining the behavior of individuals making their own decisions within its framework. It is this character and capacity of law that the behavioral paradigm dissolves, leaving us no way to understand and talk about the constitutive character of the Constitution. And without a way to understand the constitutive character of the Constitution, we have no way to understand the binding character of the Constitution.

When the interpretive theory of the relation between the constitutional text and American society rejects the idea of a gap between text and world on the grounds that text and world must be conceived to be mutually constitutive, it situates itself within the general paradigm of interpretive social science counterposed to the paradigm of behavioral social science.[5] The latter, Charles Taylor wrote in his well-known 1971 article entitled "Interpretation and the Sciences of Man,"

allow[s] for an intersubjective social reality which is made up of brute data, identifiable acts and structures, certain institutions, procedures, actions. It allows for beliefs, affective reactions, evaluations as the psychological properties of individuals. And it allows for correlations for example, between these two orders or reality: that

---

[4] Dennis Lloyd, *The Idea of Law* (Harmondsworth, England: Penguin Books, 1970), 214–15.

[5] Let me tempt the philosophically inclined reader with the claim that the idea that text and world must be conceived as mutually constitutive is grounded on the essentially Kantian concept of the structure of experience. In many ways, the contrast between the behavioral and interpretive paradigms replicates the contrast between Hume and Kant – not to mention, with an eye on the notion of interpretive communities, Hegel.

certain beliefs go along with certain acts, certain values with certain institutions, and so forth.[6]

The central idea here in the behavioral paradigm, a species of positivism, is that of two distinct orders of reality and their interrelation: the objective, brute-fact order of social and natural reality, and the subjective order of human feelings, beliefs, values, and so on. The interrelation of these two orders is that the objective world of social reality is in principle independent of the subjective order of human beliefs. In Taylor's words,

> there are certain beliefs, affective reactions, evaluations which individuals make or have about or in relation to social reality. These beliefs or reactions can have an effect on this reality; and the fact that such a belief is held is a fact of objective social reality. But the social reality which is the object of these attitudes, beliefs, reactions can only be made up of brute data.[7]

Most important to the issue of constitutional textuality, language, according to the behavioral (i.e., positivist) view in this passage, can represent objective social reality but is not itself part of objective social reality except as a function of the individual. Consider, for example, the application of French subtitles to a film such as *My Dinner with Andre*. Such subtitles superimposed on the film at the bottom of the screen remain wholly external to the substance of the film itself. That is, the French is not part of the internal, objective reality of the film.

By contrast, consider the English dialogue of *My Dinner with Andre*. Here the language itself is indeed internal to the objective reality of the film, for it constitutes the substance of the film itself. The interpretive paradigm declares "the artificiality of the distinction between social reality and the language of description of that social reality. The language is constitutive of the reality, is essential to its being the kind of reality it is."[8] Language – and thus the constitutional text – in other words, does not stand outside social reality but rather is constitutive of social reality. Separating language, as subjective, from social reality, as objective, implies the independence of both of each other and limits the reality of constitutional text to nothing more than what Llewellyn considered a "document." By contrast, according to Taylor, "We have to admit that intersubjective social reality has to be partly defined in terms of meanings; that meanings as subjective are not just in causal interaction with a social reality made up of brute data, but that as intersubjective they are

---

[6] Charles Taylor, "Interpretation and the Sciences of Man," originally published in *The Review of Metaphysics*, Vol. 25, No. 1 (September 1971), reprinted in *Interpretive Social Science: A Reader*, Paul Rabinow and William M. Sullivan, eds., (Berkeley: University of California Press, 1979), 42. I cite the latter source here.

[7] Ibid., 42.

[8] Ibid., 45.

constitutive of this reality."[9] The reason for this is the essential textuality of social reality, well put by Richard Bernstein:

> Human action cannot be properly identified, described, or understood unless we take account of the intentional descriptions, the meanings that such actions have for the agents involved, the ways in which they interpret their own actions and the actions of others. These intentional descriptions, meanings, and interpretations are not merely subjective states of mind which can be correlated with external behavior; they are constitutive of the activities and practices of our social and political lives.[10]

This is precisely the sense in which I earlier ascribed to the interpretive theory of constitutional textuality the argument that as the Constitution functions in American society it is not a mere document, but rather an actual social practice that is itself a system of rule-governed behavior because it occurs in terms of individuals' understanding of both the norms they are following and their activity of following norms. There is an ontological character to the Constitution that there is not to, say, *Gone With the Wind* or the various adventures of Harry Potter. We *live* in the world constituted by the Constitution: *This* is the sense in which the Constitution is a living – and thus binding – document, whereas we enter into the *Gone With the Wind* world or Harry Potter's world only imaginatively. As such a living text, the Constitution is already a structure of constraint. The constitutional text, I noted, structures actual social practice because people engaged in actual social practice understand themselves, at least indirectly, as standing in some relation to the constitutional text, and this self-understanding is nothing other than what Bernstein describes as "the intentional descriptions, the meanings that such actions have for the agents involved, the ways in which they interpret their own actions and the actions of others."

For the interpretive theory of constitutional textuality, therefore, language is not individual and private, inherently subjective counterposed to an objective, brute-data reality; rather, language is social and public in that it is constitutive of social reality. The way this constitutive character of language operates is illustrated nicely, as Taylor himself pointed out in his article, by John Searle's concepts of constitutive rules and institutional facts. What particularly exemplifies the constitutive character of language relevant to the idea of constitutional textuality is the distinction Searle draws, at some

---

[9] Ibid., 50. Cf. Richard Bernstein: "Human beings are *self-interpreting* beings, and this fact is of central importance for understanding social and political life. The beliefs that human beings have about themselves and others are not simply subjective states in their minds; they are – to use a Kantian expression – *constitutive* of the actions, practices, and institutions that make up social and political life." Richard J. Bernstein, *The Restructuring of Social and Political Theory* (Philadelphia: University of Pennsylvania Press, 1978), 61.

[10] Ibid., 229–30.

length here, between constitutive and regulative rules:

> As a start, we might say that regulative rules regulate antecedently or indepen-
> dently existing forms of behavior; for example, many rules of etiquette regulate
> inter-personal relationships which exist independently of the rules. But constitutive
> rules do not merely regulate, they create or define new forms of behavior. The rules
> of football or chess, for example, do not merely regulate playing football or chess,
> but as it were they create the very possibility of playing such games. The activities
> of playing football or chess are constituted by action in accordance with (at least a
> large subset of) the appropriate rules. Regulative rules regulate a pre-existing activity,
> an activity whose existence is logically independent of the rules. Constitutive rules
> constitute (and also regulate) an activity the existence of which is logically dependent
> on the rules.[11]

The concept of a regulative rule, as Searle explains it here, is consistent
with the positivist theory of textuality because the rule itself has no inherent
connection with the activity it regulates. As Searle says, interpersonal relations exist independently of rules of etiquette; similarly, a treaty purports to
regulate relations between already existing nations that already engage in
behavior that predates the treaty.

   The Constitution, however, is not a treaty among preexisting states – at
least, that is what we learned from the outcome of the Civil War. It is the
self-constitution of the people of the United States, and thus is constitutive
rather than merely regulative. Gordon Wood illustrates this when he writes
that "when the Americans began conceiving of their written constitution as
something more than a Magna Carta, indeed, as a set of fundamental principles circumscribing all parts of the government, representatives included,
the constitution's imaginary characterization as a charter or reciprocal agreement between rulers and people lost its meaning."[12] The notion of a charter
here as a reciprocal agreement presupposes the preexistence of rulers and
ruled, the presupposition rejected by American constitutionalism, and thus
conceives a constitution as regulative. The particular American version of
constitutionalism that Wood describes is, by contrast, constitutive in what
we can see to be Searle's sense of the term:

> There was, however, another contractual analogy that ran through the Whig mind of
> the eighteenth century. This was the idea of the social compact, the conception John
> Locke had developed in his *Second Treatise on Civil Government*, not a governmental
> contract between magistrates and people, rulers and ruled, but an agreement among
> isolated individuals in a state of nature to combine in a society – a social compact
> which by its very character was anterior to the formation of government.[13]

---

[11] John Searle, *Speech Acts* (Cambridge: Cambridge University Press, 1969), 33–4.

[12] Gordon S. Wood, *The Creation of the American Republic, 1776–1787* (New York: W. W.
Norton & Company, 1969), 282.

[13] Ibid., 283. Thomas Paine's comparison of a constitution to the structure of a language is, in
view of my concern with language and textuality, quite apt: "The American constitutions

Although the fact that the Constitution is superior to government and ordinary law might strongly suggest that it is solely a regulative rule, the very anteriority of the Constitution manifests its constitutive function. The Constitution is anterior and superior to government and ordinary law because it is the self-constitution of a people who establish government and ordinary law for their particular ends and purposes.[14]

That constitutive function, as Searle put it in the passage just cited, is to "create or define new forms of behavior." Comprising its most essential achievements, the Constitution sets up a national government and prescribes its relation to the states (Articles I–III), sets out relations among the states themselves (Article IV), sets up the procedure whereby the people act in their sovereign capacity (Articles V and VII), and sets up the relation between the national government and individuals (Bill of Rights) and between the states and individuals (Fourteenth Amendment). These institutions, relations, and procedures did not predate and exist logically independent of the Constitution, but instead were constituted by and are "logically dependent on" the Constitution.[15] The constitutive character of the Constitution is thus definitional in that the Constitution as fundamental law ultimately defines us as a people who participate in constitutional discourse. In the words of Jefferson Powell:

The most fundamental role the Constitution-as-historical-document plays in American constitutional discourse is that of definition.... As a matter of empirical fact, what links discussions in the United States of national authority and local autonomy, the rationality of legislation and the fairness of police procedures, the treatment of women and minorities, and the power of government to shape or suppress opinion, is their common reference to this particular document. Take away that reference and this incredibly diverse culture of moral and political discussion lacks both a common denominator and a historical context. That aging document, and the history of our wrestling with it, give shape and coherence to the multitude of arguments over power and its exercise that make up a fundamental level of our common life.[16]

were to liberty, what a grammar is to language: they define its parts of speech and practically construct them into syntax." *The Rights of Man* (4th ed.), 93, cited in the Oxford English Dictionary's definition of "constitution."

14 In the words of Richard Saphire, "we refer to the Constitution, and to the Declaration of Independence and the Constitution's preamble as well, because of what we believe they say about our identity as a people, a people who have always viewed ourselves as committed to a vision of what life in an organized society can and should be." "Is the Constitution Working?" 12 *University of Dayton Law Review* 351, 356 (1986).

15 This implies, of course, that "state" as used in the Constitution differs from "state" as used in the Articles of Confederation, just as "strike" functions differently in bowling, baseball, and labor relations.

16 H. Jefferson Powell, "Parchment Matters: A Meditation on the Constitution as Text," 71 *Iowa Law Review* 1427, 1428–9 (1986). Richard Saphire writes that "the Constitution is not so much a place we look to for answers as it is a place we turn to as a forum for civilized discourse and debate. We turn to the Constitution – and often to the courts – because

Politics has to do with the common concerns of a society, and the fact that so often in the United States political matters become translated into constitutional issues indicates the constitutive character of the American Constitution. It is this definitional aspect of the Constitution that Llewellyn appeared to miss in the contrast he drew between the living constitution and the Document, for, we can say, he viewed the written text as a purely regulative rule that as such has no essential connection with the social reality it purports to regulate. "Where the rule is purely regulative," Searle writes, "behavior which is in accordance with the rule could be given the same description or specification... whether or not the rule existed, provided the description or specification makes no explicit reference to the rule."[17] Consequently, Llewellyn quite logically, given his premises, urged that we attend to behavior rather than rules or words.

We recall, however, that Llewellyn spoke of the Constitution as an institution, an ongoing social practice or way of life. Searle's argument is that an institution is a system of not merely regulative rules but, at bottom, constitutive rules. Institutional facts are facts or phenomena that presuppose the existence of the institution that constitutes them. Though extended, Searle's discussion is illuminating:

> Let us imagine a group of highly trained observers describing an American football game in statements only of brute facts. What could they say by way of description? Well, within certain areas a good deal could be said, and using statistical techniques certain "laws" could even be formulated. For example, we can imagine that after a time our observers would discover the law of periodic clustering: at statistically regular intervals organisms in like colored shirts cluster together in roughly circular fashion (the huddle). Furthermore, at equally regular intervals, circular clustering is followed by the phenomenon of linear interpenetration. Such laws would be statistical in character, and none the worse for that. But no matter how much data of this sort we imagine our observers to collect and no matter how many inductive generalizations we imagine them to make from the data, they still have not described American football. What is missing from their description? What is missing are all those concepts which are backed by constitutive rules, concepts such as touchdown, offside, game, points, first down, time out, etc., and consequently what is missing are all the true statements one can make about a football game using those concepts. The missing statements are precisely what describes the phenomenon on the field *as a game of football*. The other descriptions, the description of the brute facts, can be explained in terms of the institutional facts. But the institutional facts can only be explained in terms of the constitutive rules which underlie them.[18]

---

it provides a *structure* for carrying on this debate." "Is the Constitution Working?", 357. Conceiving the Constitution as a place to look for answers is the positivism in originalism, whereas the conception of a structure of discourse is the point of the interpretive theory under discussion here.

[17] Searle, *Speech Acts*, 35.

[18] Ibid., 52. This is very Kantian, of course: The regularities one uncovers follow from the rules, whereas an empiricist would argue that the rules follow from the regularities. Cf. H. L. A.

When applied to the Constitution, what this extended example suggests is that by virtue of the constitutive character of the constitutional text, the social phenomena of social reality we call American society are, at some ultimate level of social analysis, "institutional facts" defined and structured by the Constitution as an institution. Institutional facts, Searle writes,

> are indeed facts; but their existence, unlike the existence of brute facts, presupposes the existence of certain human institutions. It is only given the institution of marriage that certain forms of behavior constitute Mr. Smith's marrying Miss Jones. Similarly, it is only given the institution of baseball that certain movements by certain men constitute the Dodgers' beating the Giants 3 to 2 in eleven innings.[19]

Likewise, many societies employ concepts such as "citizen" and "president," but the argument here is that just as many games involve a ball but differ in what that means in each game, concepts like citizen and president are institutionally – that is, constitutionally – defined in each society.[20]

Once again, however, this constitutive character of the Constitution presupposes the constitutive, and thus public and social, character of language. Perhaps the most difficult aspect of this conception is its difference from the psychological individualism of behavioral political science. As Taylor argues,

> what we are dealing with here is not subjective meaning which can fit into the categorical grid of behavioral political science, but rather intersubjective meanings. It is

---

Hart's contrast between the internal and external perspectives on understanding law in *The Concept of Law* (Oxford: Oxford University Press, 1961), 87–8. In this regard, consider also Herman Belz's conceptualization of constitutionalism:

> Constitutionalism shapes political life in a variety of ways. Constitutional principles can become matters of commitment and belief possessing intrinsic value that motivate political action.... *When citizens and governing officials internalize constitutional values, acting out of fidelity to law rather than expediency, constitutionalism gives direction to political life.* Constitutionalism has a configurative effect also in providing the forms, rhetoric, and symbols by which politics is carried on.

> Herman Belz, *A Living Constitution or Fundamental Law? American Constitutionalism in Historical Perspective* (Lanham, MD: Rowman & Littlefield Publishers, 1998, emphasis added), 154. Despite writing in an overt tone of regulative function, Belz implicitly suggests, in the italicized portion of the quotation, the constitutive character of the Constitution.

[19] Searle, *Speech Acts*, 51.

[20] Edwin Hargrove and Michael Nelson, for example, write that "The Constitution is the presidency's genetic code. Because of it the presidency is, by nature, a single-person office, chosen for a fixed term by a uniquely national constituency, sharing virtually all the powers of the federal government with an equally distinct and independent Congress. The constitutional presidency contains, as does an individual's configuration of DNA molecules, some ingredients whose meaning has been clear and unchanging from the moment of conception.... The Constitution also contains sentences and phrases that are the legal equivalent of genetically rooted baldness: their meaning, though determined at the very start, could be discovered only later.... Finally, there are those attributes whose meaning can be found only in the vagaries of individual choice and environmental circumstances." *Presidents, Politics, and Policy* (New York: Alfred A. Knopf, 1984), 12.

not just that the people in our society all or most have a given set of ideas in their heads and subscribe to a given set of goals. The meanings and norms implicit in these practices are not just in the minds of the actors but are out there in the practices themselves, practices which cannot be conceived as a set of individual actions, but which are essentially modes of social relation, of mutual action.[21]

Whereas the positivist theory of textuality reduces language and meaning to the subjective meaning that individuals carry around in their heads, the interpretive theory conceives language and meaning as, in Taylor's terms, intersubjective meaning. Intersubjective meaning in this sense is "material," as a Marxist might put the point; it constitutes the individual, whereas on the positivist approach the individual constitutes meaning. What this concept of intersubjective – that is, constitutive – meaning does is to allow us to speak of the objectivity of a social practice, independent of the sum total of subjective opinions held by participants in the practice.

This objectivity, for example, is central to an interpretive theory of law like Ronald Dworkin's. The interpretation of a social practice like law, Dworkin maintains, is creative rather than conversational or scientific in that it aims "to interpret something created by people as an entity distinct from them, rather than what people say, as in conversational interpretation, or events not created by people, as in scientific interpretation."[22] If the term "objectivity" refers to what is not created by people, and if the term "subjectivity" refers to what is created by people but has no independent existence of its own, then constitutional practice is a social phenomenon at once subjective and objective. It partakes of subjectivity because it is created and constituted by the activities of human beings, in contradistinction to the objectivity of natural phenomena; and it partakes of objectivity because it is distinct from and transcends the activities and intentions of any given set of individuals. In Dworkin's words:

Social practices are composed, of course, of individual acts.... But a social practice creates and assumes a crucial distinction between interpreting the acts and thoughts of participants one by one, in that way, and interpreting the practice itself, that is, interpreting what they do collectively. It assumes that distinction because the claims and arguments participants make, licensed and encouraged by the practice, are about what *it* means, not what they mean.[23]

A social practice like law, in other words, has a meaning or point of its own that is independent of what any particular interpreters might understand

---

[21] Taylor, "Interpretation and the Sciences of Man," 48. The difference between the behavioral concept of ideology and one based on this approach is striking.

[22] Ronald N. Dworkin, *Law's Empire* (Cambridge, MA: Harvard University Press, 1986), 50.

[23] Ibid., 63.

it to be at any given time.[24] This is not to suggest that interpreters cannot know the point of the social practice, but rather that the point of the social practice, as objective in the sense just defined, is not reducible to the opinions or understanding of particular interpreters. Only on such a basis is the Constitution always in principle distinct from whatever anyone ever says about it, thus allowing it to be invoked as a critical standard against current practices that are alleged to be unconstitutional. Only on such a basis, in other words, can one support Powell's claim that

only the text can claim the dignity of being "the Constitution." Extratextual pronouncements, whether written by scholars or Presidents, issued by congressional committees, or even declared by the United States Supreme Court, are at most about "the Constitution."[25]

The point about this is the so-called revolutionary role of the text. It is the idea that because the Constitution is always in principle distinct from whatever anyone ever says about it, it can be invoked as a critical standard against current practices that are alleged to be unconstitutional. Without this objectivity, the Constitution does not have the transcendent character necessary for a capacity to bind.

Such objectivity, however, is grounded in the constitutive character of the Constitution, which requires our ability to conceive ourselves as living within the text. To refer to the conception of a society living within the constitutional text is to conceive the constitutional text as a social practice, and Dworkin's account of an interpretive practice in Chapter 2 of *Law's Empire*, while not necessarily definitive, provides an illustration of this conception. The essential factor in the intelligibility of the idea of the constitutional text as a social practice is Dworkin's proposition that an interpretive practice has a point. To enable us to grasp that proposition, he provides an example in this extended paragraph:

Imagine the following history of an invented community. Its members follow a set of rules, which they call "rules of courtesy," on a certain range of social occasions. They say, "Courtesy requires that peasants take off their hats to nobility," for example, and they urge and accept other propositions of that sort. For a time this practice has the character of taboo: the rules are just there and are neither questioned nor varied. But then, perhaps slowly, all this changes. Everyone develops a complex "interpretive" attitude toward the rules of courtesy, an attitude that has two components. The first is the assumption that the practice of courtesy does not simply exist but has value, that it serves some interest or purpose or enforces some principle – in short, that it has some point – that can be stated independently of just describing the rules that make up the practice. The second is the further assumption that the requirements of

---

24 Think of the notion of the "market" in the world of business and economics. Analysts and commentators regularly and uncontroversially talk about what the market thinks and does on any given day.

25 Powell, "Parchment Matters," 71 *Iowa Law Review* 1427, 1433 (1986).

courtesy – the behavior it calls for or the judgments it warrants – are not necessarily or exclusively what they have always been taken to be but are instead sensitive to its point, so that the strict rules must be understood or applied or extended or modified or qualified or limited by that point. Once this interpretive attitude takes hold, the institution of courtesy ceases to be mechanical; it is no longer unstudied deference to a runic order. People now try to impose meaning on the institution – to see it in its best light – and then to restructure it in the light of that meaning.[26]

There are in this passage three principal elements, however abstractly conceived, in the interpretive character of a social practice. The first element, actually comprising what Dworkin considers a "preinterpretive" stage of analysis, is an identifiable body of rules or norms – here, the rules of courtesy – that people agree constitutes the practice. At this stage, the practice, the body of rules, simply exists – it just is, so to speak, in the sense of brute facticity. It would not be inaccurate to suggest that, in Dworkin's terms, this preinterpretive stage is as far as originalism's positivist theory of textuality goes. Constitutional norms simply exist within the text, to be taken or left.

The interpretive theory of textuality, however, goes further, and in doing so provides an explanation of the problem with which we began, the simultaneously empirical and normative character of the Constitution. The specifically interpretive attitude develops, according to Dworkin, with the second element here: People begin to see the practice as not just existing, but as existing for a reason. It is no longer the case for the participants in the practice that the body of rules just is, but rather that they understand the body of rules as something that serves a purpose or has a point. By saying that an interpretive practice has a point, however, we are ascribing to such a practice its own internal normative structure. That is, because the practice is said to have meaning, it includes as an essential component of its empirical existence an ongoing judgmental and justificatory activity. The brutely existing practice defines the point, but the point "turns around," as it were, and defines the practice and what it requires. As Dworkin writes:

this assumed point acquires critical power, and people begin to demand, under the title of courtesy, forms of deference previously unknown or to spurn or refuse forms previously honored, with no sense of rebellion, claiming that true respect is better served by what they do than by what others did. Interpretation folds back into the practice, altering its shape, and the new shape encourages further reinterpretation, so the practice changes dramatically, though each step in the progress is interpretive of what the last achieved.[27]

This critical component, the "folding in" of the point, is the third element of the interpretive process. The practice henceforth consists of a complex

---

[26] Dworkin, *Law's Empire*, 47.
[27] Ibid., 48.

activity: People who participate in the practice do so in terms of their interpretation of what the practice requires participants in such activities to do in order to be true to the point of the practice. As a result, argumentation and debate become inherent elements of the practice, because the practice takes on an objectivity vis-à-vis the participants whose very activity creates the practice. In this important sense, what is "given" by the Framers is not an object, but a social text – the social practice of an ongoing constitutional convention. With this objectivity, the constitutional text is thus constitutive in the way the rules of a game are constitutive of the game itself.

Precisely because it recognizes the sociality and historicity of language, the interpretive theory of constitutional textuality I have attempted to sketch here has a higher regard for the binding capacity of language than does the positivist theory. The latter conceives the text as a representation of meaning distinct from and standing behind it and is command-oriented.[28] It denies the public, social, historical character of language. The positivist idea of binding capacity relies ultimately on the interpreter's willingness to obey, as a passive object of the speakers' commands, for the originalist argument is that where there is no command, there is no obedience, and where there is no obedience there is no controlling the future. On the positivist theory of textuality that grounds originalism, consequently, we do not constitute ourselves through the forms of the Constitution; rather, the Framers – not the Constitution – constitute us. At best, from the originalist perspective, the Constitution binds by imposing, controlling, and subordinating, all in Searle's regulative sense. The interpretive theory of textuality, by contrast, is essentially textual (in that the text is the meaning) and participatory. Its idea of binding capacity relies ultimately on the reader's willingness to participate as an active subject in the activity of constituting meaning; we are actively self-constituting as political subjects and objects simultaneously. From the interpretive perspective, the Constitution binds constitutively and thereby more fully and effectively; it binds insofar as it is constitutive rather than merely regulative.

"The Constitution," Walter Berns writes, "derives its binding authority – binding on the governed and the government alike – only from the fact that it is an act of the people in their constituting capacity."[29] The only way to make the text binding is through an ongoing, not a past, act of constituting, and yet the positivism of originalism's theory of constitutional textuality requires that there can be only past, never ongoing, acts of constituting. It is not

---

[28] Here is where the regulative–constitutive distinction affects the issue of binding capacity. If the Constitution is purely regulative, á la Searle, then it governs behavior logically independent of it, from the outside – it is an imposition on self-contained activity. If the Constitution is constitutive, then the regulatory structure is built into the system of behavior constituted by the text.

[29] Walter Berns, *Taking the Constitution Seriously* (New York: Simon & Schuster, 1987), 236–7.

the case that the originalist is concerned with the intentions of the Framers and the interpretive theorist is not; rather, the disagreement is over whether those intentions are that we take orders from the Framers or participate in a social practice, the ongoing constitutional convention, that they instituted. The ironic implication of originalism's theory of constitutional textuality is that the Constitution becomes decreasingly binding with the passage of each day, for the Constitution every day becomes further and further removed from that constitutive act when the "act of the people in their constituting capacity" is conceived in positivist terms. The binding capacity of the Constitution presupposes its intelligibility. That is, if the Constitution is to be capable of binding the future, it must be capable of being understood by the future. Inversely, if it is not capable of being understood by the future, it will not be capable of binding the future. Originalism, which tells us that we are to understand and abide by the original understanding of the Constitution rather than the Constitution itself, suggests that those in the founding generation had a better understanding of the Constitution than we do, because they were present at the creation. If that is the case, then we have a decreasing understanding of the Constitution merely with the passage of time, and that means that the Constitution's binding capacity must decrease over time.

Originalism simultaneously affirms and denies the democratic and binding authority of the Constitution, because it simultaneously affirms and denies the binding capacity of language. That is, originalism claims to be the only theory by which the Constitution democratically binds the future, but the theory's distinction between the constitutional text and the original intention or understanding actually undermines the democratic and binding character of the text. We must infer from originalism's focus on the original understanding that, despite its emphasis on the constitutional text, what binds us is not the language of the text but rather the people who wrote and ratified the language of the text. The paradox here is that if originalism truly believed in the binding capacity of language that it affirms, it would lose its raison d'être. That is, originalism can claim to be a necessary guide to constitutional interpretation only because it denies the binding capacity of language that it purports to affirm. Oddly enough, as the originalist Walter Berns insists on the central importance of the writtenness of the Constitution by citing Thomas Paine's statement that "an unwritten constitution is not a constitution at all," his insistence empties that writtenness of content at the very same time. The focus on the authoritativeness of the written text in originalism constantly dissolves that text into an unwritten metatext standing behind it.

I consider the Constitution to *constitute* the American polity – that is, to structure and order the polity in terms of a set of principles. The underlying assumption is that the Constitution is intelligible as a principled document despite the compromises that went into it. People on both sides of the originalism debate accept this view. I agree with Levinson and Berns that the purpose of a constitution is to bind the future. But where originalists see originalism as the necessary condition or premise of constitutionalism, I argue that originalism is inconsistent with or even undermines constitutionalism in the sense of binding capacity and democracy. Originalism insists on the capacity of language to bind, as the foundation of constitutionalism, yet originalism considers itself necessary because of (what it does not see as) a disbelief in the binding capacity of language. Textuality is the key.

The real binding force of the Constitution, the central characteristic of constitutionalism, according to originalism, is its constitutive character. Because of its ability to explain the ongoing, constitutive character of the constitutional text it is the interpretive theory of constitutional textuality, rather than the positivist theory on which originalism rests, that can explain the binding capacity of the Constitution. Constitutions, unlike treaties, bind insofar as they constitute, and originalism, in view of its theory of interpretation (anarchic and in need of an external regulator), cannot explain how constitutions constitute. The difference here is between the positivist position of treating the constitutional text as an object and the interpretive position of treating the constitutional text as an activity or a social practice. It is not the case that the positivist is concerned with the intentions of the Framers, whereas the interpretive theorist is not; rather, the disagreement is over whether those intentions are that we take orders from the Framers or participate in a social practice, the ongoing constitutional convention, that they instituted. The ironic implication of originalism's theory of constitutional textuality is that the Constitution becomes decreasingly binding with the passage of each day, for the Constitution every day becomes further and further removed from that constitutive act when the "act of the people in their constituting capacity" is conceived in positivist terms. Because of its ability to explain the ongoing, synthetic–a priori character of the constitutional text, it is the interpretive theory of constitutional textuality, rather than the former, grounded in the positivist theory of constitutional textuality that originalism employs, that can explain the binding capacity of the constitutional text.

Only an interpretive theory of constitutional textuality allows for the possibility of the Constitution's having a meaning or point of its own, the key precondition of the binding capacity of the constitutional text. When we conceive constitutional practice as constitutive, in the sense suggested earlier, we can understand the written Constitution as the structure of the way of life that grounds it. On the interpretive approach, we live in the constitutional text, whereas on originalism's positivist approach, the constitutional text consists of a set of standards under which we live but that is essentially imposed, in an Austinian sense, from outside our experience. The "deep structure" of the Constitution, therefore, is not an abstract, unwritten set of moral and political principles, nor is it a discrete set of over-and-done-with historical events, but rather the ongoing, concrete, historical practice

of constitutional discourse. At the same time, its built-in critical component enables constitutional practice to avoid having to accept tradition and
precedent uncritically.

As incongruous as it may appear, this interpretive perspective on what I
call the deep structure of the Constitution might be considered a constitutional version of the notion of the social construction of reality or even of
Marx's famous claim: "Men make their own history, but they do not make
it just as they please; they do not make it under circumstances chosen by
themselves, but under circumstances directly found, given and transmitted
from the past."[30] We are active creators, as nonoriginalists might suggest,
but we create only within the structured context of the past, as originalists
would insist. In other words, we create the structures within which we live.
"Create" and "structures" are the key terms. Similarly, from a different but
related perspective, Georgia Warnke makes a hermeneutic version of this
same argument: "The past acquires its meaning in light of present experiences and anticipations while the meaning of the present and anticipation
of the future are conditioned by the way in which the past has been understood."[31] It is only an interpretive theory of law and textuality, I suggest, that
embeds the ongoing critical, justificatory component in constitutional practice as a fundamental and essential element of that practice, thus allowing
for the constitutive character of the Constitution.

For a brief example of how the interpretive context of constitutional
discourse is constitutive, consider the first section of the Fourteenth
Amendment: "No State shall make or enforce any law which shall abridge
the privileges or immunities of citizens of the United States; nor shall any
State deprive any person of life, liberty, or property, without due process of
law; nor deny to any person within its jurisdiction the equal protection of the
laws." Understood analytically, this section states that every citizen of the
United States has, by virtue of that citizenship, a "package" of fundamental rights protected against state infringement. In view of the plenary police
power of the states to enact legislation to protect the health, safety, welfare,
and morals of their people, the problem for well over a century has been
that of how to determine what rights are included in that package, for they
limit that police power. The constitutive dimension of the interpretive context of the Fourteenth Amendment turns on the evisceration of the privileges
or immunities clause effected by the *Slaughterhouse Cases*.[32] As a matter of
conceptual clarity and coherence, discussion of the substantive rights that
comprise that package ought to occur in terms of the concept of "privileges

---

[30] Karl Marx, "The Eighteenth Brumaire," excerpted in Robert Tucker, ed., *The Marx-Engels
Reader*, 2nd ed. (New York: W. W. Norton & Company, 1978), 595.

[31] Georgia Warnke, *Gadamer: Hermeneutics, Tradition and Reason* (Cambridge: Polity Press,
1987), 38.

[32] 83 U.S. 36 (1873).

or immunities," but the consequence of *Slaughterhouse* was to shift that discourse of substantive rights, not always clearly and coherently, to the due process clause.

This shift to the due process clause constitutes the "grammar" or rules of meaning shared by members of the legal community and by citizens in general as we talk about rights protected by the federal Constitution against state infringement. Constitutional interpretation is structured, in that there are only certain ways of talking about particular issues, but it is not determined if by that we mean that there is a single right answer to constitutional questions. Such rules of meaning, as John Brigham has written, "indicate the kinds of interpretations that are possible with regard to the words and concepts in the Constitution."[33] To gain acceptance of their arguments as legitimate, participants in constitutional interpretation must speak the language of that practice, and this requirement structures and limits discretion:

> Since constitutional law is a language because it has a unique grammar, certain statements do not make sense in the context of constitutional law. This view of constitutional law as language suggests the "legal" constraints on judicial interpretation. Some things come to be understood as appropriate to say when the language of constitutional law is learned. The determination of what is appropriate in this sense need rely neither on logic nor on an appeal to the world. What is appropriate is to a great extent a function of the grammar of constitutional law.[34]

From the positivist perspective, constraint exists solely if there is only one appropriate answer to a constitutional problem; if there is more than one answer, then there is no answer and hence no constraint on judicial decision making. This, however, is a faulty concept of objectivity that sets a standard for itself that it must strive constantly to meet yet never will be able to meet. From the interpretive perspective, on the other hand, constraint involves the existence not of a single right answer but rather of a structured range of legitimate answers for the rightness of which one can only persuade, not demonstrate. As Brigham notes,

> we might say that any number of decisions are possible in a case before the Supreme Court, but the possibility of grounding a choice in an intelligible explanation limits the range of discussion. Only a finite number of concepts can be brought to bear, and they can only be used in a finite number of ways. By describing the constraints on the Justices in terms of the symbols available in the constitutional tradition, the student of the decision can focus on the intelligible options open to a Justice. The conventions in

---

[33] Brigham, *Constitutional Language*, 59.

[34] Ibid., 99. This is the reason Justice William O. Douglas made the famous if unfortunate statement in *Griswold v. Connecticut*, 381 U.S. 479 (1965), 384, that "specific guarantees in the Bill of Rights have penumbras, formed by emanations from those guarantees that help give them life and substance." The Court had given up the use of substantive due process reasoning, despite Justice Harlan's continued adherence to it in his concurring opinion, though Justice Black in dissent accused Justice Douglas of allowing its return.

the Constitution, as in language, reveal the possibilities that are available if a Justice wishes to make sense.[35]

It is just the intelligibility of a structured range of possible interpretations that explains the constitutive nature and internal constraints of constitutional discourse, but it is the interpretive theory of law rather than the positivist theory of law that can establish the intelligibility of this ontological character of constitutional interpretation.

By conceiving the constitutional text as constitutive, the interpretive approach asserts the social reality of constitutional forms and thus reasserts the essentially public character of constitutional practice. The interpretive theory, in other words, ascribes to the constitutional system a social synthetic–a priori character and thus takes the Constitution seriously as a fundamental analytical component of social theory. Grasped as a social practice with its own structural logic and social reality irreducible to the sum total of individual preferences, the constitutional system is, analytically, capable in principle of explaining the conditions of individuals making their own decisions within its framework and, politically, capable of directing and constraining the behavior of those individuals. The interpretive theory of law and textuality subsumes the conventional normative–empirical dichotomy in the broader concept of constitutiveness, reasserts the idea that the *polis* is logically prior to the individual, and thus reclaims the principle that the concept of a constitution or, more broadly, constitutional practice is, like Aristotle's concept of the polity, the central concept of social and political analysis.

This consideration, however, leads back to the question of the binding capacity of the Constitution. On the positivist speaker's-meaning theory of textuality that grounds originalism, we do not constitute ourselves through the forms of the Constitution; rather, the Framers constitute us. On an interpretive understanding of constitutional practice, we are actively self-constituting as political subjects and objects simultaneously. Constitutional politics is thus not just a discourse, but a way of life as well. The Framers instituted an ongoing constitutional convention; they set up a social practice, a living text, as it were. Contrary to the implications of originalism, living under the terms of the American written Constitution consists of participating in the ongoing constitutional convention that began – not ended – with the signing of the document in Philadelphia in September 1787. It is the ongoing and constitutive character of our national constitutional convention that grounds the text's binding power.

---

[35] Brigham, *Constitutional Language*, 60–1.

10

Conclusion

The Political Character of Constitutional Discourse

My general theoretical concern in this essay in constitutional theory has been with the nature of constitutionalism and constitutional interpretation. In the course of my discussion, I have proceeded from two premises axiomatic in the American political system. The first premise is that the purpose of a written constitution is to bind the future to the vision of its framers. The second premise is that the Constitution is a species of positive law that rests on democratic consent and forms the framework of our society, such that judges, government officials, and citizens alike must interpret the Constitution and not some abstract, extraconstitutional moral code. No one wishing to be taken seriously in American constitutional discourse can reject these fundamental premises.

The interpretive paradigm of originalism, perhaps more than any other, prides itself on its commitment to these premises. Nevertheless, the paradox of originalism, I have argued, is that the positivist theory of constitutional textuality originalism presupposes to explain American constitutionalism and constitutional interpretation cannot account for the combination of the binding character and democratic character of the Constitution on which originalism stakes its claim to theoretical and political validity. The purpose of a constitution may well be to get everything down on paper in order to bind and limit future generations, but originalism's focus on what it conceives as original intent – what here we have called the writers' and ratifiers' original understanding – in fact presupposes a marked lack of trust in the capacity of language to bind. To the extent that originalism can establish the democratic character of the Constitution, it undermines the binding character of the text; and to the extent that originalism can establish the binding character of the text, it undermines the democratic character of the Constitution. I have argued that if the combination of the binding and democratic character of the Constitution is to be explained satisfactorily, the Constitution must be conceived as constitutive, and that it is an interpretive theory of constitutional textuality rather than originalism's positivist theory that can provide such an account.

In the course of making this case, I have attempted to uncover the assumptions about language, texts, and meaning that are in play here. If one presumes that the meaning of a text is what the author understood himself to be saying in that text (hard originalism) or what the first readers of the text understood it to mean (soft originalism), then originalism is correct to say that there is effectively no determinate constitutional text in the absence of the writers' and ratifiers' interpretive context. Not to interpret the Constitution in terms of the writers' and ratifiers' understanding of what they were doing is, on such a view, not to interpret the Constitution at all. Thus, for originalism, to be bound by the Constitution is logically equivalent to being bound by the original understanding of the constitutional text; and, of necessity, not to be bound by the original understanding of the constitutional text is not to be bound by the Constitution at all. Given originalism's assumptions about language, texts, and meaning, therefore, the originalist is correct to say that nonoriginalism necessarily equals noninterpretivism, the presumptively illegitimate position that one may enforce norms beyond those found to be explicit or clearly implicit within the four corners of the constitutional text.

The logic that creates this equivalence, however, undermines the classically and legitimately political character of constitutional interpretation. This is a fundamentally important implication of originalism, for, at bottom, the entire originalism–nonoriginalism debate has to do with the political character of constitutional interpretation. In what sense might we properly characterize constitutional interpretation as political? Whereas public opinion, for example, conventionally holds that courts are not political bodies like legislatures and executives, political scientists routinely assert the political nature of courts specifically and constitutional-legal practice as a whole. Lawrence Baum, a leading student of judicial politics cited in earlier chapters, makes just such an assertion about the U.S. Supreme Court:

The Supreme Court is "political" in a variety of ways. Most of the people appointed to the Court have been active participants in politics, and appointments frequently are the subject of considerable political contention. Interest groups often help to bring cases to the Court. The justices' perceptions of public and congressional opinion affect the Court's decisions. Those decisions themselves often lead to major controversies in government and the nation at large, and the justices may be attacked by members of Congress and other political leaders who disagree with their policies.[1]

In Baum's description here, the Supreme Court clearly operates within a political environment consisting of all of the governmental and nongovernmental actors and processes typically regarded as composing the American

---

[1] Lawrence Baum, *The Supreme Court* (Washington, DC: CQ Press, 1981), 2.

political system, and it has a major role in making public policy. Nevertheless, saying that the Court operates in a political environment and plays a role in the policy-making process does not yet tell us what kind of political character it might have. One might say, for example, that the Court itself is not an inherently political body but that, nevertheless, its adjudicative activities regularly create political consequences. Alternatively, one might say that the Court is not a political body because the justices are appointed rather than elected – except that such a claim would create the counterintuitive implication that the Senate was not a political body before the Seventeenth Amendment came into effect. Yet again, one might say that the Court is indeed an inherently political body not just because its adjudicative activities have political consequences, but because adjudication itself involves interest articulation, conflict, negotiation, agenda setting, and all the other elements of the ordinary political process. The question still stands, therefore, as to the sense in which we might properly characterize constitutional interpretation as political, and an answer depends upon both our theory of constitutional interpretation and our use of the term "political."

To pose an answer, we need to recognize that, analytically, we employ the term "political" in at least two senses. Ordinarily, when we refer to the political branches of American national government, we have in mind Congress and the presidency rather than the courts, for we label political those branches that make public policy and are electorally accountable. When deciding a particular public-policy issue, for example, the most basic legitimate reasons a legislator can cite to justify her decision, as a legislator, are her constituents' wishes or her own values.[2] By contrast, when deciding a particular case, the legitimate reasons a Supreme Court justice can cite to justify his decision, as a justice, necessarily exclude public opinion and his own values. Those reasons, rather, boil down to the claim that the Constitution requires the particular decision. The justice, or any other judge, must in principle be able to say, "This is what the Constitution requires, whatever the contrary interests and demands of popular majorities or other political actors." In this sense of political, then, the legislator is a policymaker who represents a popular majority and is thus political; the justice, by contrast, is not a policymaker and, while he may be understood to represent the people in their sovereign capacity, he does not represent a popular majority and is not political. In the course of rendering a decision binding on the parties to the case, the justices, in short, issue a legal decree.

There is, however, an important but oft-overlooked second sense of "political" in terms of which we may properly characterize constitutional interpretation as political, a sense that is important because it illuminates

---

[2] This is highly simplified, of course. For a good account of the range of considerations a legislator takes into account, see John W. Kingdon, *Congressmen's Voting Decisions*, 2nd ed. (New York: Harper & Row, 1981).

the nature of constitutionalism and constitutional interpretation. This sense was captured in the interplay of abstract constitutional theory and concrete, practical politics with which we started. Speaking of the Supreme Court and judicial review in the first of his two 1985 speeches to which we have referred, former Attorney General Meese advanced a general claim about the political character of constitutional interpretation:

> The Court is what it was understood to be when the Constitution was framed – a political body. The judicial process is, at its most fundamental level, a political process. While not a partisan political process, it is political in the truest sense of that word. It is a process wherein public deliberations occur over what constitutes the common good under the terms of a written constitution.[3]

As the framework within which the American judicial process specifically, and the American political system generally, operates, constitutional interpretation is political in this sense because its articulation of the ends and powers of government in relation to individual liberty and autonomy is an articulation of the classical question of *res publica*, the public good. To be sure, at one level politics is indeed an interest-oriented struggle over who gets what, when, and how. Yet at a second, logically prior level, politics is a principled struggle over the rules that structure the society in which we live. It is logically prior to the first level because it sets the structure and boundaries within which interest-oriented politics in that former sense is conducted; it structures the lower-level struggle over who gets what, when, and how.

The Constitution is political, therefore, in that it is constitutive; it establishes the order that defines American society as a community with a common good. So conceived, constitutional interpretation is not an activity limited to courts, for the president and Congress always engage in constitutional interpretation when they assert their respective legislative and executive powers under the Constitution, and states always engage in constitutional interpretation when they assert their police powers under the Constitution. And, more broadly, citizens themselves engage in constitutional interpretation, although in much less formal and specialized terms, both when they decide whom to elect to federal or state office to carry out policies they implicitly assume to be constitutional and when they assert claims of constitutional rights against the federal or state governments. Whether one agrees or disagrees with the Bush administration's particular jurisprudential agenda, this conception of constitutional interpretation as "public deliberations over what constitutes the common good under the terms of a written constitution" is, I submit, fundamental to the American political tradition as a whole in that it structures our tradition of political practice and debate. The concept of structure is central: The Constitution does not license any and all forms of

---

[3] Paul G. Cassell, ed., *The Great Debate: Interpreting Our Written Constitution* (Washington, DC: The Federalist Society, 1986), 3.

public debate over the common good. Because the Constitution is a species of positive law grounded, at least theoretically, in democratic consent, judges, government officials, and citizens alike must interpret the Constitution, not some abstract moral code. And it is through interpreting the Constitution that we as a polity deliberate over what constitutes the common good.

To maintain that we may – indeed, must – properly characterize constitutional interpretation as political returns us to the Chase–Iredell debate noted in Chapter 3 and argues that, at bottom, we are all necessarily, inescapably Chaseians. At length, this is Chase's classic statement:

> I cannot subscribe to the omnipotence of a State Legislature, or that it is absolute and without control; although its authority should not be expressly restrained by the Constitution, or fundamental law, of the State. The people of the United States erected their Constitutions, or forms of government, to establish justice, to promote the general welfare, to secure the blessings of liberty, and to protect their persons and property from violence. The purposes for which men enter into society will determine the nature and terms of the social compact; and as they are the foundation of the legislative power, they will decide what are the proper objects of it: The nature, and ends of legislative power will limit the exercise of it. This fundamental principle flows from the very nature of our free Republican governments, that no man should be compelled to do what the laws do not require; nor to refrain from acts which the laws permit. There are acts which the Federal, or State, Legislature cannot do, without exceeding their authority. There are certain vital principles in our free Republican governments, which will determine and over-rule an apparent and flagrant abuse of legislative power; as to authorize manifest injustice by positive law; or to take away that security for personal liberty, or private property, for the protection whereof of the government was established. An ACT of the Legislature (for I cannot call it a law) contrary to the great first principles of the social compact, cannot be considered a rightful exercise of legislative authority. The obligation of a law in governments established on express compact, and on republican principles, must be determined by the nature of the power, on which it is founded.[4]

The central concept in this passage is not natural law, as I suggested contrary to conventional understanding in Chapter 3, but rather what Chase calls "the great first principles of the social compact." (The concept of a social compact, in fact, appears twice in this passage.) The Constitution institutionalizes these great first principles, and thus constitutional interpretation must be characterized as political because it is ultimately about these great first principles.

Yet in what way is constitutional interpretation ultimately about these great first principles, such that we are all necessarily and inescapably Chaseians? There are two fundamental reasons. First, consider the conventional distinction between statutory construction and constitutional interpretation. Statutory construction is "legal," rather than political, in the most

---

4 *Calder v. Bull*, 3 Dallas 386, 387–8 (1798).

technical sense of the term: It deals with the question of how a statute applies to a particular set of factual circumstances, yielding concrete results for the parties involved. The general premise of statutory construction is that the statute in question is valid, leaving only the question of how it applies in the case at hand. Constitutional interpretation, by contrast, is essentially political, in the broadest sense of the term, in that it deals with the question of whether government has the authority and power to enact the statute or to take the action under challenge. To address this question, to ask whether government has, under "the great first principles of the social compact," a particular power, is to ask a fundamentally political question. Even if Hamilton's notion that constitutional interpretation is a technical, legal matter to be decided by the courts won out over Jefferson's notion that it is rather a value-laden political matter to be decided by the legislature and the people themselves, Jefferson was correct to point to its essentially political nature.[5]

The second reason we are all Chaseians is that Iredell's argument against Chase is, at bottom, grounded in Chase's own position. Iredell, we saw in Chapter 3, talks about natural justice. If the national or a state legislature, he writes,

shall pass a law, within the general scope of their constitutional power, the court cannot pronounce it to be void, merely because it is, in their judgment, contrary to the principles of natural justice. The ideas of natural justice are regulated by no fixed standard; the ablest and the purest men have differed upon the subject; and all that the court could properly say, in such an event, would be, that the legislature (possessed of an equal right of opinion) had passed an act which, in the opinion of the judges, was inconsistent with the abstract principles of natural justice.[6]

This argument by Iredell, aside from the fact that Chase was talking about the principles of our own social compact rather than what Iredell here calls "the abstract principles of natural justice," is nothing other than itself an argument from the fundamental principles – the political theory – of our social compact. For Iredell to maintain that "all that the court could properly

---

[5] Unself-consciously, even *Black's Law Dictionary*, 6th ed. (St. Paul, MN: West Publishing Company 1990), affirms the essentially and classically political character of constitutions and constitutional law. A constitution, *Black's* states at 311, is "[t]he organic and fundamental law of a nation or state, which may be written or unwritten, establishing the character and conception of its government, laying the basic principles to which its internal life is to be conformed, organizing the government, and regulating, distributing, and limiting the functions of its different departments, and prescribing the extent and manner of the exercise of sovereign powers." And constitutional law, *Black's* continues at 311, is "[t]hat branch of the public law of a nation or state which treats of the organization, powers, and frame of government, the distribution of political and governmental authorities and functions, the fundamental principles which are to regulate the relations of government and citizen, and which prescribes generally the plan and method according to which the public affairs of the nation or state are to be administered." There is, I submit, nothing more political than this.

[6] *Calder v. Bull*, 3 Dallas 386, 398–9 (1798).

say ... would be, that the legislature (possessed of an equal right of opinion) had passed an act which, in the opinion of the judges, was inconsistent with the abstract principles of natural justice" is to make a claim in terms of the idea of separation of powers, a central element of the political theory of American government. Try as one will, there is, it appears, no escaping from political theory: Iredell is caught in the vice of having to use political theory to make an argument against Chase's use of political theory. There is no non-Chaseian argument for Iredell: Both appeal to the political theory of our social compact. So too, as originalism justifies its claim to exclusive interpretive legitimacy in terms of democracy, rule of law, separation of powers, and the like, it is doing nothing other than making an argument in terms of the fundamental principles – the political theory – of our social compact.

Against this background, it is not difficult to reconcile the claim that constitutional interpretation is essentially political in nature with the claim that in the course of rendering a decision binding on the parties to the case, a court issues a legal decree. Without doubt, what matters to parties obtaining a binding constitutional judgment is the legal decree itself. Yet what matters to everyone else in the American political system is the set of arguments that underlie that decree: I submit that those arguments, on both sides, are themselves essentially political, and that the Constitution is the site of struggle among competing political arguments about the basic principles of our social compact.

Perhaps nowhere in our constitutional discourse does that struggle appear more often and more controversially than in attempts to establish what rights against the states the due process clause of the Fourteenth Amendment protects. The incorporation debate, discussed in Chapter 1, arose in the process of attempts to determine the content of those liberties protected in terms of the due process clause. The formulation in *Palko v. Connecticut*[7] of the criteria by which we are to make that determination is especially revealing of the political character of constitutional interpretation. Justice Cardozo set out a framework of two distinct and potentially colliding criteria within which nearly all constitutional discourse about rights is conducted, a framework evident in such controversial issues today as abortion and homosexual rights. Cardozo's first criterion for what counts as rights protected by the due process clause is the famous notion of rights "implicit in the concept of ordered liberty,"[8] while the second criterion is the idea of "principle[s] of justice so rooted in the traditions and conscience of our people as to be ranked as fundamental."[9] These two criteria differ from one another in that they represent the distinction in political theory between the claim that rights

[7] 302 U.S. 319 (1937).
[8] Ibid., 325.
[9] Ibid., 325, citing *Snyder v. Massachusetts*, 291 U.S. 97, 105 (1934).

or liberties are grounded in reason, as in classical liberalism, and the claim that rights or liberties are grounded in tradition, as in classical conservatism.

These are unresolved and, most likely, irresolvable political positions over which people will continue to argue, and we find their conflict evident in the disagreement between the majority and minority positions in the abortion case of *Roe v. Wade* and the homosexual sodomy cases of *Bowers v. Hardwick* and *Lawrence v. Texas*. Briefly and somewhat simply, in *Roe* Justice Harry Blackmun, for the Court, justified a right to abortion essentially in terms of the criterion's being implicit in the concept of ordered liberty: "This right of privacy, whether it be founded in the Fourteenth Amendment's concept of personal liberty and restrictions upon state action, as we feel it is, or, as the District Court determined, in the Ninth Amendment's reservation of rights to the people, is broad enough to encompass a woman's decision[on] whether or not to terminate her pregnancy."[10] That is, Blackmun sought the ground of this right in reason, even if he failed to do so in sufficient detail. By contrast, Justice Rehnquist, in dissent, opposed the right to abortion quite clearly in terms of the criterion of tradition: "The fact that a majority of the States reflecting, after all, the majority sentiment in those States, have had restrictions on abortions for at least a century is a strong indication, it seems to me, that the asserted right to an abortion is not 'so rooted in the traditions and conscience of our people as to be ranked as fundamental,' Snyder v. Massachusetts, 291 U.S. 97, 105 (1934)."[11]

[10] 410 U.S. 113, 153 (1973).
[11] Ibid., at 174. The problem with *Roe v. Wade* is somewhat similar to the reaction to the recent Circuit Court opinion striking down the phrase "under God" in the Pledge of Allegiance: A fair reading of the opinion indicates that, whatever its debatable and politically unpopular conclusion, its reasoning was certainly not incoherent. As conservative columnist Ramesh Ponnuru wrote in the July 29, 2002, *National Review* about the Pledge case: "In the context of the church–state case law that the Supreme Court has built up over the last 55 years, their ruling was, at the very least, defensible.... What Goodwin and Reinhardt did was take orthodox liberal church–state jurisprudence to its logical conclusions." ("One Branch Among Three," *National Review*, Vol. LIV, No. 14, 31.) Ponnuru simply holds that that jurisprudence itself is faulty. So too with *Roe*: The problem with *Roe* is that Blackmun really did not make an argument other than to say that whatever the right to privacy may be, it is surely broad enough to encompass a woman's right to opt for an abortion under certain circumstances. In other words, one might consider *Roe* problematic because of the substance of its argument, but one might consider *Roe* more fundamentally problematic because it offers little or no argument at all, even though it derives from the jurisprudential tradition known as the right to privacy.

Apart from the moral question of abortion, it is well to remember the nature of the constitutional controversy. One aspect of the Constitution is that it draws a line between the domain of individual rights and the domain of majority rule, and the role of the Supreme Court is to police that line, determining what goes on which side. It is *not* the role of the Court, all agree, to move the line. Thus, the disagreement over *Roe* has to do with whether the Court took an issue like abortion, which previously had been considered to fall on the majority-rule side of the line, and determined that in fact, based upon an improved understanding, it falls on the individual-rights side of the line. Those who support *Roe* argue that the Court simply, if controversially, thought through the issue

Similarly, in *Bowers*, Justice Byron White justified rejecting Hardwick's constitutional claim for a right to engage in homosexual sodomy by saying, with reference to the *Palko* criteria, that "neither of these formulations would extend a fundamental right to homosexuals to engage in acts of consensual sodomy."[12] Though White mentioned the concept of ordered liberty, his statement that "[p]roscriptions against that conduct have ancient roots"[13] and his short survey of American legal history indicate that the real basis of his position was tradition. In dissent, Justice Blackmun relied fully on the right to privacy, citing *Thornburgh v. American College of Obstetricians & Gynecologists* to argue that "[o]ur cases long have recognized that the Constitution embodies a promise that a certain private sphere of individual liberty will be kept largely beyond the reach of government."[14] Here too, as in *Roe*, Blackmun appealed to reason over tradition.

Finally, in *Lawrence v. Texas* we find the same conflict between reason and tradition, with the majority taking the former approach to overrule *Bowers* and argue that state prohibitions on homosexual sodomy infringe the right to privacy. Though stating that, contrary to the *Bowers* contention, "there is no longstanding history in this country of laws directed at homosexual conduct as a distinct matter," Justice Anthony Kennedy, for the Court, wrote that the statutes in question violate the right to privacy because they "do seek to control a personal relationship that, whether or not entitled to formal recognition in the law, is within the liberty of persons to choose without being punished as criminals."[15] Taking the position based upon tradition,

---

and determined that the previous understanding placing it on the majority-rule side of the line was wrong, that abortion actually and accurately falls on the individual-rights side. Those who oppose *Roe* argue that the Court in fact illegitimately moved the line itself.

Abortion policy, therefore, is constituted not by what the Court said in *Roe*, but rather by the entire political-legal discourse generated by *Roe*. In other words, abortion policy is the balance (or tension) existing between the Court's decisions and the political branches of the federal and state governments in matters such as the state of abortion funding, the availability of abortion providers, and so on. The subsequent history of controversy over *Roe* indicates that the decision spawned a theoretical (and, of course, political) argument over the concept of privacy, the role of women in American society, and the nature of constitutional interpretation. Constitutional colloquy may be initiated by the Court, but it is conducted by the entire political system, and there is and can be no normative standard outside of that discourse. This is to say, in other words, that the Court is not the *sole* arbiter of constitutional meaning; the ultimate unit of analysis in constitutional interpretation is not the Court but the political and interpretive interplay among courts, legislatures, executives, and the public. As Linda Greenhouse writes in an article discussing the end of the 2002 term of the Supreme Court, referring to the affirmative-action and gay-rights decisions, "those rulings, like many Supreme Court decisions, are part of an ongoing constitutional conversation that involves the court, the various branches and levels of government, and the public." *New York Times* National Edition, July 1, 2003, A18.

[12] 478 U.S. 186, 192 (1986).
[13] Ibid., 193.
[14] Ibid., 203, citing *Thornburgh*, 476 U.S. 747, 772 (1986).
[15] *Lawrence v. Texas*, No. 02-102 (slip opinion), 16 and 17.

by contrast, Justice Antonin Scalia in dissent held that "Bowers' conclusion that homosexual sodomy is not a fundamental right 'deeply rooted in this Nation's history and tradition' is utterly unassailable."[16]

All of this is to reaffirm the contention set forth in the first part of the Introduction that, as the legal expression of essentially political conflict, controversies in American constitutional theory are the theoretical and principled expression of intensely partisan, practical concerns. The conflict in *Roe, Bowers,* and *Lawrence* over the content of the liberty protected against state infringement by the due process clause manifests the long-standing conflict in political theory between reason and tradition, theory and history, as the legitimate source of political norms.[17] The analysis this book has offered enables us to understand constitutional argument and disagreement not as error or heresy, something to be avoided and eliminated, but rather as naturally, essentially, and inescapably political. Alexander Bickel was right on target when he said that partisans on both sides of contested constitutional issues should be able legitimately to claim a common commitment to determining the meaning of the Constitution. The framers, he wrote,

knew, and this was perhaps their greatest wisdom, that in order to last and be stable and thus affect the behavior of posterity in any degree, a constitution must make it possible for future battles to be fought out by men who, on both sides of contested issues, can in good faith profess allegiance to the organic law and to the regime established by it. They were aware, in other words, of the function of the Constitution as the symbol of nationhood, meant to transcend and to endure beyond the fiercest political differences.[18]

---

[16] Ibid., 69.

[17] Similarly, conflicts over other constitutional provisions amount to a kind of applied political theory as well. Federalism cases, for example, turn on the basic political question as to the nature and structure of the union, just as separation-of-powers cases turn on the basic question as to the design and operation of the three branches of the federal government (e.g., *U.S. v. Lopez,* 514 U.S. 549 [1995]). In like manner, the religion clauses represent another site of struggle over conflicting political perspectives. As a matter of political theory, the free exercise clause has to do with the long-standing question as to the conflict between the authority of individual conscience and the authority of the state (e.g., *Employment Division v. Smith,* 494 U.S. 872 [1990]). The establishment clause, for its part, has to do with the equally long-standing question of whether it is the role of government to endorse and enforce a particular set of religious beliefs, as classical conservatism would maintain, or whether the proper role of government is to remain agnostic toward competing religious claims and thus refrain from endorsing and enforcing a particular set of religious beliefs, as classical liberalism would claim (e.g., *Lemon v. Kurtzman,* 403 U.S. 602 [1971], and *Lynch v. Donnelly,* 465 U.S. 668 [1984]). (Along those lines, *Roe, Bowers,* and *Lawrence* also turn on the question of whether government should endorse and enforce a particular set of moral beliefs or leave them to individuals to choose as they see fit.) Finally, cases under the equal protection clause turn ultimately on conflicts over the meanings of equality in American society (e.g., *Brown v. Board of Education,* 347 U.S. 483 [1954], and *Regents of the University of California v. Bakke,* 438 U.S. 265 [1978]).

[18] Alexander Bickel, *The Least Dangerous Branch* (New Haven, CT: Yale University Press, 1986), 105.

Nevertheless, the logic of originalism in fact undermines this political conception of constitutional interpretation. Insofar as it privileges not the constitutional text but rather, more narrowly, what we discover to be the original understanding of the constitutional text, originalism destroys the political character of constitutional interpretation, because the idea of a privileged standpoint is incompatible with the idea of the legitimacy of difference that is the crucial presupposition and raison d'être of politics and political argumentation. In other words, I affirm the notion of public deliberations "over what constitutes the common good under the terms of a written constitution," but I have contended that the foundationalist logic of originalism undermines the central condition of such deliberations, the legitimacy of difference, and thus the possibility of true argumentation over constitutional principle. In contrast, because the antifoundationalist premise of the interpretive paradigm can account successfully for the legitimacy of difference and thus the possibility of true argumentation over constitutional principle, it is the theory that enables us to understand the essentially political character of constitutional interpretation.

Originalism undermines the legitimacy of difference because it is a version of the positivist claim that what the law is on any particular matter is nothing more than the purely factual question about decisions made by those social institutions authorized to make law for a given community.[19] On this view, a question about the meaning of the (original) Constitution is nothing more than a purely factual question about either the eighteenth-century public understanding of the text and/or decisions and arguments made by the Philadelphia Convention and the ratification debates and state conventions. Constitutional interpretation, consequently, is a matter of discovering and appealing to the proper historical authority, whether the writers' understanding of their intentions or the ratifiers' understanding of their language. Because originalism's theory of constitutional meaning ultimately points behind and beyond the constitutional text to either historical intentions or "dictionaries," so to speak, it implies the denial of legitimate constitutional argumentation, because we are told not to interpret the Constitution but rather to listen to – obey – whatever or whoever stands behind it. The positivist theory that grounds originalism necessarily generates not the legitimacy of argument but the alternatives of conformity or rebellion. It ascribes to constitutional principles the character of brute facticity and leaves those who wish to follow such principles the one option of either accepting them or rejecting them. One can argue over the application of principle, but one cannot argue over the identification of principle; instead of

---

[19] "Originalism sought its anchor [for the rule of law] in the definiteness not just of a text but of a historical truth about that text: what particular persons intended by the words they used." Charles Fried, *Order and Law: Arguing the Reagan Revolution* (New York: Simon & Schuster, 1991), 61. "The originalist impulse is to turn interpretation into a factual inquiry about what particular people thought about the meaning of a particular text" (62).

"public deliberations" and debate, the constitutional situation is one of "love it or leave it." Consequently, under originalism, we can ask not whether the original understanding of the constitutional text was right, but only what that understanding was.

By contrast, as opposed to an appeal to authority that denies the political character of constitutional interpretation, accounting for genuine "public deliberations . . . over what constitutes the common good under the terms of a written constitution" requires a theory of constitutional interpretation that allows for the possibility of political argumentation. Such public deliberations under a written constitution involve two principal elements: the argumentative and the public. First, political argumentation is an essential trait of political practice, and for political argumentation to be possible, one must refuse to privilege one particular view to the exclusion of others and thus must accept the legitimacy of multiple argumentative positions. Politics, in other words, is not a matter of $2 + 2 = 4$ (in a base-10 system), but rather a matter of moral choice. One certainly may argue over applications of principle, but one must be able to argue over the meaning of principle itself.

Second, the public character of debate is likewise an essential trait of political practice in the sense that deliberations must be open to all citizens. If political deliberations are merely a matter of the historical investigation and discovery typical of the positivist theory of law, then they are not really public in the sense of being open to all citizens, for they instead become the province of historians and other such experts. On the interpretive approach, by contrast, we find room for the possibility of democratic public debate because the interpretive approach allows us to grasp the notion of a text's having a meaning of its own. With such a meaning, debate and argument are not only possible, but also constant, ongoing, and, above all, legitimate. We as readers of the Constitution face not the apparently factual question of what the writers and ratifiers meant by adopting the text, but rather the interpretive question of what the text itself means, a question open to all citizens. We seek the original understanding, consequently, not as an end in itself, but rather as a means of assisting our own attempt to reach an understanding of the Constitution. Our knowledge of the Framers, to put the matter differently, is part of our effort to understand the Constitution; the Constitution is not part of our effort to understand the Framers.

Moreover, when we conceive constitutional interpretation more accurately in this interpretive rather than positivist manner, we can understand the constitutive character of the Constitution. On the positivist theory of law that grounds originalism, we do not constitute ourselves through the forms of the Constitution; rather, the Framers so constitute us. In an interpretive understanding of constitutional interpretation, we are actively self-constituting as political subjects and objects simultaneously. A political conception of constitutional interpretation thus grasps interpretation not just as a discourse, but as a way of life as well. That is to say, a discourse in this sense is not merely linguistic, but ontological. As J. B. White writes about law generally, constitutional interpretation

is the constitution of a world by the distribution of authority within it; it establishes the terms on which its actors may talk in conflict or cooperation among themselves. The law establishes roles and relations and voices, positions from which and audiences to which one may speak, and it gives us as speakers the materials and methods of a discourse. It is a way of creating a rhetorical community over time. It is this discourse, working in the social context of its own creation, this language in the fullest sense of the term, that *is* the law. It makes us members of a common world.[20]

In the understanding of constitutional interpretation that lies at the root of originalism, by contrast, we are passively constituted as political objects only. From the standpoint of the positivist approach, constitutional interpretation consists of appeal to an authoritative set of standards in accordance with which we live but that is essentially imposed by the Framers as political superiors standing behind, above, and outside the ongoing political community and giving orders to that community as a political inferior. Vis-à-vis the Framers, this difference is that between our participating in a structured conversation and our taking dictation – that is, between actively engaging in a structured dialogue and passively hearing a monologue.

On the interpretive approach, those who wrote and ratified the Constitution count as the Framers only because and insofar as *we*, meaning each generation, agree among ourselves to ascribe that status to them. We are a people who constitute ourselves as a people who live within the terms of our Constitution, and it is only on such a basis that the Constitution enjoys a reality missing from many written constitutions around the world that remain mere pieces of paper. Originalism misses the self-constitution of the American people that establishes the Framers in an ongoing, transhistorical sense. What I have called interpretive constitutional theory – and not originalism – explains how we have Framers at all, and thus grounds the democratic character of our Constitution that originalism purports to uphold. As even Keith Whittington has recognized, "the decision to interpret the written Constitution and be bound by the intentions of the founders is a present one, made by living political actors. It is not a decision that is or could be imposed on the present generation by the past."[21]

It is important to reiterate the complementary side of the democratic character of the Constitution, its binding character. In and of itself, the claim that in constitutional interpretation we should be bound by the intent of the Framers is an unobjectionable statement of the idea of binding the future at the very core of the concept of a constitution. By writing and ratifying the

[20] James Boyd White, *When Words Lose Their Meaning* (Chicago: University of Chicago Press, 1984), 266.
[21] Keith Whittington, "It's Alive! The Persistence of the Constitution," 8–11, in *Symposium: The Constitution of the Living Dead: Binding the Present to the Past*, Vol. 11, No. 2 (2002), 10.

Constitution, the Framers clearly intended to establish a polity constituted and structured by a determinate set of procedural and substantive principles. The Constitution thus represents – that is, constitutes – the intent of the Framers that subsequent generations live within and in accordance with a particular political structure. We have seen, however, that the key question is, whose interpretation of that determinate set of principles by which the Framers intended us to live is to count as authoritative? The characteristic and controversial move of originalism, once again, is its translation of the claim that in constitutional interpretation we should be bound by the intent of the Framers to the proposition that the original understanding of the constitutional text always trumps any contrary understanding of that text in succeeding generations. This, I have argued, is an attempt to justify an understanding of the text by appeal to norms that in some way transcend the text and that thus do not count as one more understanding of the text.

The originalist contention is that to be bound by the Constitution is logically equivalent to being bound by the original understanding of the constitutional text; and, of necessity, not to be bound by the original understanding of the constitutional text is not to be bound by the Constitution at all. For originalism, therefore, the real Constitution is not the written text itself, but rather the original understanding of the written text. This positivist view of language always generates an "unwritten Constitution," a foundational normative standard that is what is truly authoritative and binding. Yet by equating nonoriginalism – an understanding of the constitutional text that is not the Framers' understanding – with noninterpretivism – the theory that interpreters may legitimately invoke extraconstitutional norms in adjudication – originalism eventuates in the proposition that there cannot be several possible, equally legitimate understandings of the one constitutional text. Against this position, to allow for the reality of the political character of constitutional interpretation means rejecting the atomistic and foundationalist conception of language, and thus the unwritten Constitution it generates, in favor of a holistic, nonfoundationalist conception of language as social discourse. That is the significance of the interpretive turn, the linguistic revolution of the twentieth century.

What is normative on this latter conception is not some extraconstitutional standard like original understanding or abstract moral theory, but rather the discourse of constitutional interpretation itself. Both originalism and nonoriginalism seek and appeal to a foundation, a normative standard outside of interpretive debate, but the interpretive claim is that there is no such position to which either side can appeal. All we have is our own persuasive powers. While especially originalism argues that we need a strong normative standard to prevent the Court from creating new rights unrelated to the text of the Constitution, there can be no such strong normative standard outside the discourse of constitutional interpretation. Rather, the discourse itself – the generation of arguments back and forth over particular constitutional issues, and assessments of the persuasiveness of those arguments – is its own normative standard. You and I, for example, might disagree about the existence of a right to privacy or, more immediately, about the account of the nature of constitutional interpretation I offer here. My point is that what manages, constrains, and (perhaps) resolves any such disagreement is not some external authority to which each of us might appeal,[22] but rather the course – the back-and-forth, the "dialectic" – and persuasiveness of our discussion of that disagreement itself. It is nonetheless true that constitutional interpretation is principled, with a normative bite, but it is so in the only way it can be – because we take it as our task, our political commitment, to explain what the *Constitution* means and not what we personally mean, not what we would like it to mean, not what a popular majority wants, and so forth. Our hope is that our fallible understanding of the meaning of the constitutional provisions continues to improve over time, even as we affirm that that meaning, absent textual changes, remains fixed and binding.[23]

It follows, then, that all we have is the open sea of constitutional discourse; there is no port we can put into. That is the meaning of the interpretive turn, the meaning of living textually in the American polity. Dissolving the originalism–nonoriginalism debate results in a leveling of the playing field – that is, neither side can claim exclusive legitimacy or deny it to the other. Does this mean that no one is ever right? Yes and no. On the one hand, both sides can claim to be right in a regulative sense of the term: My act of arguing that I am right and you are wrong (e.g., I say that chocolate is good) makes a claim on you as a rational person to see and accept my position, and it makes a demand on me to attempt to persuade you of the rightness of my point of view. If I say that our disagreement is just a matter of opinion (e.g., I say simply that I like chocolate), then I make no claim on you as a rational person, and my only recourse is to exercise power to make you submit to my position. On the other hand, neither side can claim to be right in the substantive sense of the term: There is and can be no demonstration; there can be nothing more and nothing less than persuasion.

Dissolving the impasse between originalism and nonoriginalism thus means legitimating difference and disagreement. We perhaps should say that the debate is not only not resolved, but not dissolved either. It is redefined.

---

[22] After all, contrary to our usual assumption, we do not find X persuasive because it is an authority; instead, more fundamentally, we consider X an authority because we find it persuasive.

[23] "Had those who drew and ratified the Due Process Clauses of the Fifth Amendment or the Fourteenth Amendment known the components of liberty in its manifold possibilities, they might have been more specific. They did not presume to have this insight. They knew times can blind us to certain truths and later generations can see that laws once thought necessary and proper in fact serve only to oppress. As the Constitution endures, persons in every generation can invoke its principles in their own search for greater freedom." Justice Kennedy, for the Court, *Lawrence v. Texas*, No. 02-102 (slip opinion), 36–7.

That is, the debate is still present, but it is not the debate as originalists understand it. It is a debate, occasioned by the requirement to interpret the text, among competing political principles, that is not a jurisprudence of results. It is, rather, a debate "over what constitutes the common good under the terms of a written constitution." Constitutional discourse is thus a form of metapolitics – that is, not politics as interest and policy, but politics as principle. As such, of course, there will be differences of opinion; of course, different justices will hold and advance different metapolitical positions.

Is it not the case, however, that the Constitution shuts off certain types of conversation and debate? I suggest that the Constitution does *not* shut off certain types of conversation and debate; rather, by its supermajority provisions, it ensures that some conversations and debates have to be much more serious, much more a matter of principle than interest, than others. As in the concept of deliberative democracy,[24] binding the future does not so much shut off certain avenues of conversation as it structures the conversation. Externally, the Constitution binds the future in that, for example, it establishes a political system that is neither a monarchy nor a simple majoritarian democracy. Internally, however, it still allows for – indeed, impels – multiple conversations about the meaning of the fundamental principles of our social compact. And while the Court's decrees decide matters for the parties to a case, even the most settled doctrine can in time come to be subject to change – witness the Court's federalism decisions over the past few years.[25] The point is, we cannot simply say, "X is forbidden": Implicitly if not explicitly, any such claim rests on argument and persuasion. What appears to be obvious is so simply because it enjoys an unquestioned consensus, but at some point questions can arise. Consequently, I am suggesting that all interpretations, however apparently fixed and settled, are necessarily provisional.

The consequence of this analysis is not an undermining of any first-order interpretive claims in constitutional theory – in the sense, for example, of proving that there is or is not such a thing as a right to privacy – but neither is it merely a plea to get our labels right. It is, rather, a deprivileging of conventional interpretive claims by originalism in order to account for the essentially political conception of constitutional interpretation. Specifically, if we wish to take seriously the idea of the "process wherein public deliberations occur over what constitutes the common good under the terms of a written constitution," we have to be committed to the conditions of the possibility of political argumentation. But because originalism undermines those conditions by ascribing to the Framers a privileged position in constitutional interpretation, it denies the classically political character of

---

[24] See, for example, Joseph M. Bessette, "Deliberative Democracy: The Majority Principle in Republican Government," in Robert A. Goldwin and William A. Schambra, eds., *How Democratic Is the Constitution?* (Washington, DC: AEI, 1980), 102–16.

[25] E.g., *U.S. v. Lopez*, 514 U.S. 549 (1995).

constitutional interpretation; it cannot take that character seriously. If the Framers are privileged, then there can be no political argumentation and thus no political conception of constitutional interpretation. Conversely, if there truly is to be political argumentation and thus a political conception of constitutional interpretation, then the Framers cannot be privileged.

It is by recognizing this that we really can understand the full significance of the claim with which we began, that constitutional interpretation is a fundamentally *political* practice because it is a "process wherein public deliberations occur over what constitutes the common good under the terms of a written constitution." Originalism is a theory of interpretation that privileges the not always well-known opinions of a not always well-defined set of historical actors about the meaning of general constitutional principles and provisions – their interpretation of constitutional matters, on this view, always trumps ours. By asserting such a claim, however, originalism undermines the characterization of constitutional interpretation as fundamentally political, for the idea of a privileged standpoint is inconsistent with the idea of multiple diverse, legitimate standpoints that is a crucial presupposition of political argumentation. Politics, as Sheldon Wolin has written, presumes the legitimacy of difference:

In its political aspect, a community is not held together by truth but by consensus. The range and nature of the consensus that a society arrives at exerts a strong and often determining influence upon the particular decisions made by a society, causing a modification in both means and ends different from what an "objective" or purely technical judgment might dictate. This gives to political judgments a character different from that of a "true" philosophical or theological proposition. In large measure, a political judgment is usually "judicial" in quality; that is, for the most part it involves a judgment concerning conflicting claims, all of which possess a certain validity. As Aristotle shrewdly pointed out, there is no problem of political judgment when one claim alone is admitted to be valid and enthroned above all the rest. The result of this condition, however, is that the political association is replaced by the state of siege. But once the political association is defined as a compound of many diverse parts, and once it is allowed that these "parts" will have different opinions, interests, and claims, the politicalness of the judgment will depend on a sensitivity to diversities. A political judgment, in other words, is "true" when it is public, not public when it accords to some standard external to politics.[26]

Originalism is unable to take this idea of political judgment and consensus seriously because, by making its particular concept of Framers' intent a "standard external to politics," it denies the fundamental condition of such a process, the idea of multiple diverse, legitimate argumentative standpoints.

---

[26] Sheldon Wolin, *Politics and Vision* (Boston: Little, Brown and Company, 1960), 62–3 (footnote omitted). Also see Lief Carter, *Contemporary Constitutional Lawmaking* (New York: Pergamon Press, 1985), 15–16.

An interpretive rather than positivist theory of constitutional interpretation makes it a fundamentally political practice, for it is only an interpretive theory of law that can ground the possibility of there being different interpretations to articulate and defend. Argumentation is an essential trait of political practice, and originalism's claim that there are in principle plain-fact answers to be discovered through historical investigation undermines the possibility of real argumentation over matters of principle and, hence, of a classically political conception of constitutional interpretation. For originalism, constitutional argument is like argument over whether, in a base-10 system, $2 + 2 = 4$. In other words, there is a right answer rather than a legitimate difference of opinion. For the interpretive understanding of constitutional interpretation, constitutional argument is like argument over whether one should be a liberal or a conservative. The former is not political; the latter is. As Wolin states, "The political act has to do with the reconciliation of a wide range of *valid* claims."[27] More broadly, White's description of law here applies to the political character of constitutional interpretation:

The law is best regarded not so much as a set of rules and doctrines or as a bureaucratic system or as an instrument for social control but as a culture, for the most part a culture of argument. It is a way of making a world with a life and a value of its own. The conversation that it creates is at once its method and its point, and its object is to give to the world it creates the kind of intelligibility that results from the simultaneous recognition of contrasting positions.[28]

The notion of a culture of argument, however, does not mean that courts have unbounded discretion to exercise their personal policy preferences. The significance of the Constitution is less that the text provides answers to arguments over the basic political, social, moral, economic, or religious issues and more that these arguments are conducted in terms of the text.[29] The debate over the impeachment of President Bill Clinton illustrates this. Originalists want to argue that the Framers are authoritative in constitutional interpretation. I argue that it is the activity of constitutional interpretation *itself*, which includes our conversation across generations, that is authoritative. In the former case, the Framers are presumed to stand outside the interpretive process as an external check on that process, whereas in the latter case, the Framers stand inside the interpretive process. What binds

[27] Wolin, *Politics and Vision*, 64 (emphasis added).

[28] White, *When Words Lose Their Meaning*, 267.

[29] Rogers Smith has written: "The appeal to constitutional texts serves both as a common set of terms and understandings that can bind together a diverse polity and as a reminder of the system's original principles and the elements that seem to have worked over time." "Twilight of the Living Dead?" in *Symposium: The Constitution of the Living Dead: Binding the Present to the Past*, Vol. 11, No. 2 (2002), 1–7, 4. Actually, there may be a common set of terms, but it is the absence of a common set of understandings that triggers constitutional controversy and makes the Constitution a site of political conflict.

the future is not the reason but the *reasoning*. That is, it is the activity of interpretation, taking place in terms of the (formal, not substantive) norm of original intent, that binds – not original intent as a norm standing *outside* the interpretive process. The search for authority or foundations outside of the activity of constitutional interpretation is, metaphorically, a search for training wheels on a bicycle. The nature of constitutional interpretation is that there are no training wheels. There is only the ongoing process of seeking balance, leaning sometimes to the right and sometimes to the left. There are no foundations outside the tradition of constitutional discourse. The tradition of constitutional discourse is ultimately about, in the words of Justice Samuel Chase, the fundamental principles of our social compact.

To say that constitutional interpretation involves the possibility of political argumentation, therefore, means that the Framers bequeathed succeeding generations an ongoing and participative argumentative discourse rather than merely the answer to an argumentative discourse in which they alone participated. Consider this nicely succinct statement of the structure of the originalist argument:

> In its simplest terms, that position may be stated as follows: "In constitutional adjudication, the duty of the court is to interpret the constitutional text. The proper mode of interpreting a legal text is to determine the intent of the drafter or drafters of that text and to apply that intent to the case before the court. Therefore, in constitutional cases the court should apply the intent of the framers."[30]

No one committed to the proposition that the purpose of the Constitution is to bind the future can reject this argument. The central and divisive question, however, is, what counts as "the intent of the framers"? Discussions of constitutional interpretation tend to confuse genus and species in this matter. Fidelity to original intent is the whole point of having a constitution, and if originalism is identical to original intent, then, of course, the very concept of a constitution requires originalism. Indeed, if originalism understands the intent of the Framers to comprise simply the Constitution itself, then originalism's claim that "in constitutional adjudication judges should be bound by the intent of the Framers" would amount to the important truism that "in constitutional adjudication judges should be bound by the Constitution." The central question, however, is where one locates the intent of the Framers – in the discourse established by the text or in a historically specific round of that discourse? Originalism as a theory of constitutional interpretation is one species of a commitment to original intent; it is not generically identical to that commitment. Contrary to the implications of originalism, the American practice of living under the terms of a written constitution is political because it consists of participating in the ongoing constitutional

---

[30] Earl Maltz, "The Failure of Attacks on Constitutional Originalism," 4 *Constitutional Commentary* 43, 46 (1987).

convention that began – not ended – with the signing and ratification of the document and its amendments. And it is precisely the ongoing nature of that political, constitutional convention that affords the Constitution its binding and democratic character. That dual character – the complex phenomenon that we in the United States attempt to live in and within the terms of a written text – is the central fact about the American Constitution, and it is only by transcending the premises of the originalism–nonoriginalism debate that we can explain that unique and fascinating fact.

Index